CAMBRIDGE LIBRARY COLLECTION

Books of enduring scholarly value

Technology

The focus of this series is engineering, broadly construed. It covers technological innovation from a range of periods and cultures, but centres on the technological achievements of the industrial era in the West, particularly in the nineteenth century, as understood by their contemporaries. Infrastructure is one major focus, covering the building of railways and canals, bridges and tunnels, land drainage, the laying of submarine cables, and the construction of docks and lighthouses. Other key topics include developments in industrial and manufacturing fields such as mining technology, the production of iron and steel, the use of steam power, and chemical processes such as photography and textile dyes.

History and Description of the Crystal Palace

In May 1851, the doors opened on the Great Exhibition, a celebration of British industry and international trade that spawned numerous imitations across the globe. The scale of the exhibition was immense and publishers responded quickly to the demand for catalogues, guidebooks and souvenir volumes. In a marketplace swamped with exhibition literature, Tallis' three-volume *History and Description of the Crystal Palace,* originally published in 1852 and reproduced here in the 1854 edition, quickly established itself as the definitive history for middle-class readers. Illustrated with high-quality steel-engraved plates of the most popular and eye-catching exhibits, Tallis' book provides a fascinating contemporary account of this cultural and commercial highlight of the Victorian age, and reveals the mind-set of a society at the peak of its imperial power. Volume 1 describes the preparations for the exhibition and focuses particularly on the 'foreign and colonial' departments and the decorative arts.

History and Description of the Crystal Palace

*And the Exhibition of
the World's Industry in 1851*

VOLUME 1

JOHN TALLIS
EDITED BY J.G. STRUTT

CAMBRIDGE
UNIVERSITY PRESS

CAMBRIDGE UNIVERSITY PRESS

Cambridge, New York, Melbourne, Madrid, Cape Town,
Singapore, São Paolo, Delhi, Tokyo, Mexico City

Published in the United States of America by Cambridge University Press, New York

www.cambridge.org
Information on this title: www.cambridge.org/9781108026703

This edition first published 1854
This digitally printed version 2011

ISBN 978-1-108-02670-3 Paperback

THE GREAT EXHIBITION

of the Industry of all Nations,

Opened by Her Majesty Queen Victoria.

MAY 1ST 1851

JOHN TALLIS & Cº.

LONDON & NEW YORK.

THE CRYSTAL PALACE

DESCRIBED AND ILLUSTRATED BY BEAUTIFUL ENGRAVINGS CHIEFLY FROM DAGUERREOTYPES BY BEARD. MAYALL. &c&c

JOHN TALLIS AND COMPANY. LONDON AND NEW YORK.

DEDICATED TO H.R.H. PRINCE ALBERT, K.G., ETC., ETC., ETC.

TALLIS'S

HISTORY AND DESCRIPTION

OF THE

CRYSTAL PALACE,

AND THE

Exhibition of the World's Industry in 1851;

ILLUSTRATED BY

BEAUTIFUL STEEL ENGRAVINGS,

FROM ORIGINAL DRAWINGS AND DAGUERREOTYPES,

BY BEARD, MAYALL, ETC., ETC.

PRINTED AND PUBLISHED BY JOHN TALLIS AND CO.,
LONDON AND NEW YORK.

CONTENTS.

VOL. I.

ILLUSTRATIONS.

VOL. I.

TALLIS'S HISTORY AND DESCRIPTION
OF
THE CRYSTAL PALACE.

INTRODUCTION.

THE fame of the Crystal Palace has gone forth to the utmost bounds of the civilized world. The extent of its aim, as an Exhibition of the natural productions, the arts, sciences, manufactures, and fine arts of all nations,—the ingenuity of its plan, the vastness of its departments, its exactness in particular, its beauty as a whole, its success in all the objects for which it was undertaken, the feelings of amity and benevolence it called forth, the enlargement of mind it gave rise to, the practical benefits necessarily springing out of the scientific contemplation of its contents, the unceasing source of delight it afforded to the thousands upon thousands who flocked, day after day, to behold its treasures, the brilliancy of its opening, the harmony of its close, the thankfulness and gratitude inspired in every reflective mind, during months of peaceful and rational enjoyment, undisturbed by any painful accident or jarring feelings,—all these are chronicled in such variety of form and language, as to defy the power of oblivion,—and we may safely pronounce that the House of Glass will exist in the annals of history, long after the vaunted pyramids of Egypt, of which the builders and the object are already alike unknown, shall have crumbled into dust.

In contributing yet another to the almost countless number of publications that have already appeared on this apparently inexhaustible subject, some statement of the grounds upon which the proprietors rest their hopes of success, in a field wherein they have to meet so many competitors, beforehand with them in the lists, may be reasonably expected. Those grounds, they flatter themselves, will be found, without any necessity of more laboured explanation on their part, in the superior excellence of the engravings, which they were unwilling to endanger by hurrying the execution of them; and in the taste and acumen of the descriptions, which emanate from an artist equally skilled in the use of the pen as the pencil, and whose productions in both those departments have frequently elicited the admiration of the public.

In order that the engravings should be faithful transcripts from the actual objects they profess to delineate, the proprietors have been at the expense of having all those objects taken on the spot by the Daguerreotype, with a patience and exactitude that would not pass over the smallest imperfection or deficiency, and whatever was not fortunate in the first instance was reproduced, till complete success was obtained. The labour of rendering upon steel *fac-similes* of these minute creations was immense, as will be readily believed upon inspection of them: the expense was of course proportionate; but this expense, great—it may almost be said enormous—as it has been, the proprietors have willingly taken upon themselves, in the full confidence that they shall ultimately be remunerated by the generosity of an enlightened Public, alike quick to discover excellence, and liberal in rewarding it; and which they flatter themselves will regard these exquisite gems of Art with feelings somewhat akin to those inspired by the skilfully pourtrayed features of a valued friend, delighting equally from the truth of the resemblance, and the pleasing remembrances they call forth.

With regard to the account of the rise and progress of the Crystal Palace itself, the ensuing pages will be found to present rather the lively and graphic description that might be given in the course of social converse, than the detailed statistical statements which, however desirable they might be, while it was yet in its infancy, and advancing step by step towards the maturity to which the public so anxiously looked, watching its growth through every step of its intermediate stages, would now, on a retrospective view, appear unnecessarily minute, and even tedious to general readers. From the same consideration the objects selected for representation are chiefly such as will always continue to gratify the lovers of beautiful forms and elegant designs; and of which the descriptions will be found permanently useful, in guiding the taste, and inciting to excellence in whatever branch of ingenuity or of the fine arts it may be sought.

"A thing of beauty is a joy for ever!"

says the poet; and we fully agree with one of our contemporaries, who, in happy illustration of the sentiment says, "We would have every thing in a house touched by the divining rod of the poet. An inkstand, instead of being a literal glass bottle, or a fine piece of or-molu, or bronze, significant of nothing but costliness, might be fashioned to represent a fountain, with a Muse inspiring its flow; our goblets might bubble over amongst hop-leaves, and stems of blossoms; our decanters be composed of transparent vines, clustering in wild confusion, or drooping over trellis-work, as we see them in the sunny south; our bell-ropes, that carry more messages than the electric wires, might be converted into hanging garlands; our water-jugs be made to flatter the palate with their look of coolness; snow creaming over the edges, and harts drinking at brooks, in the shadows down the sides: lively colours, tastefully toned and harmonized, might be scattered over our rooms, under a thousand pretences of necessity; and in every article of furniture the forms of a classical antiquity, which always possessed the charm of innate grace, delicacy, and refinement, might be successfully revived."

There is no doubt that the Crystal Palace has done much already, to further so desirable an end, and as every effort to perpetuate the remembrance of its contents must be regarded as conducing to the general advancement of taste, and the promotion of the beautiful, the proprietors trust that theirs will come in for its full share of the approbation which it will be their endeavour to deserve.

CHAPTER I.

The English have always been renowned for improving on the inventions of others. The facetious Joe Miller, the father of *impromptu* jest-books, informs us that a Frenchman, boasting of his nation being the primary introducers of frills, at the bosom and wrists of male fashionables, the Englishman replied, "We will not dispute with you the honour of inventing the frill, we only claim the merit of having added the shirt to it." Now it must be acknowledged, that the merit of the first idea of a Public Exhibition of the choicest productions of a country, in art and science, an Exhibition undertaken solely for the display of excellence, and for encouragement of every effort towards the attainment of it, without any immediate thought of profit to the originators, beyond their share in the general good that might accrue from it to society at large, is decidedly due to the French. Exhibitions of goods, merely considered as marketable commodities, assumed to be the best of their kind, were indeed common enough in all countries pretending to civilization, at the fairs which formed the annual meetings of our forefathers, with their relatives and friends; but exhibitions in which the perfecting of the articles exhibited should be the primary object, and the commerce to be afterwards derived from them merely secondary, have only taken place among us, during the latter half of the preceding century to the present time. And here we may claim priority over our neighbours, for it is now nearly a century ago since the Society of Arts, in London, first offered prizes for specimens of manufactures, in the various mechanical arts which are at once the evidence and the reward of a desire to increase the comforts and refinements of social existence. The Royal Academy, at the same time, took the loftier productions of the fine arts under its protection; organized exhibitions of paintings, sculptures, and engravings, and adjudged prizes among the exhibitors, according to the degrees of merit their productions were found to display.

Gradually these examples were followed by each of the metropolitan cities, and the principal manufacturing towns of the United Kingdom began, one after another, to promote annual or triennial exhibitions among the manufacturers and artizans of the articles most worthy of notice. Of all these local exhibitions, that of Birmingham, in the autumn of 1849, was the most comprehensive and important, so that it may be justly esteemed as a precursor of that wonder of the world which, less than two years after, was destined to "rise like an exhalation," and cast all its predecessors into the shade.

Still those preceding exhibitions had all been of a private and local character, receiving neither sanction nor assistance in any way from government, or public money, save in the solitary instance of the exhibition of manufactures relative to the decoration of the Houses of Parliament, which was instituted by the Fine Arts Commissioners. Whilst in France, on the contrary, the very first exhibition of industrial products took place in 1798, expressly as a national institution; it was followed by a second in 1801, a third in 1802, and a fourth in 1806. A lapse of thirteen years then occurred, filled up with the successes and defeats, and defeats and successes of warfare; the dethroning and re-throning of monarchs, and every other "change, chance, and circumstance" of that war, "which, were their subjects wise," as Cowper justly observes, "kings would not play at."

In 1819, however, the blessings of peace began to be felt in the tranquillity and security that ever are to be found in her train. The exhibitions of French industry were

c

then renewed, and systematically continued, and from that time the influence of them began to be decidedly felt throughout Europe.

Nevertheless it was not till the great success of the exhibition in Paris of 1844, awakened a general desire throughout the United Kingdom to give its industry the advantage of a similar appeal to the public, as to the actual position it might hold in the scale of excellence, that the idea was entertained of organizing an exhibition on a still more extended scale in London. It is a well-known fact, that almost all the great works and important institutions of this country are the offspring of the wishes and exertions of the people at large; nor ought we, in fact, to quarrel with, or comment upon the reluctance that government always betrays towards aiding or bringing forth any new undertaking, until its value be tested and proved by individuals, when to that very reluctance we no doubt owe much of our national spirit of independence, which will not be driven off the ground it has once taken up ; and for which we are indebted, not only for all our most valuable acquisitions at home, but also for a great proportion of the respect and confidence with which we are regarded abroad.

In 1848, his Royal Highness Prince Albert, had, with that courtesy, benevolence, and enlargement of mind which have so justly endeared him to the English nation, readily consented to lay before the government a proposal submitted to him, for the establishment of a self-supporting exhibition of British industry, to be controlled and protected by a royal commission; but not even his approval of the scheme, and conviction of its eligibility, could conquer the accustomed apathy of the parties whom he had to address ; and the great mass of the people who were most interested in the measure, were, perhaps, not sorry to find that if they really meant to carry it into execution, it must be by their own exertions alone. The Society of Arts had made an attempt, though an abortive one, in 1845, to establish an exhibition of national industry ; in 1847 they renewed it with more success; in 1848 with more still; insomuch that the council were encouraged to announce the intention of the society to hold annual exhibitions from that time, as the means of establishing a quinquennial exhibition of British industry, on an enlarged scale, to be held in 1851.

His Royal Highness Prince Albert was of course informed of these proceedings, from time to time ; and immediately after the closing of the session of 1849, he took the subject under his own personal superintendence. As President of the Society of Arts, he commissioned several of its members to proceed forthwith to the manufacturing districts, in order to ascertain the sentiments of the leading inhabitants : these commissioners visited sixty-five places, comprehending the most important cities and towns of the United Kingdom ; public meetings were held in them, local committees formed, amounting to three hundred and thirty in number, and nearly five thousand influential individuals registered their names as supporters of the proposed Exhibition. With so favourable a commencement, the Queen willingly granted her royal commission for its organization and protection, to her " most dearly-beloved consort," and to all " the right trusty, and right entirely well-beloved cousins and councillors," whose names are mentioned in the deed, in due succession, according to the dignity of their offices.

The next point to be settled was the site on which the edifice was to be reared. Divers places were proposed ; Battersea Park, Victoria Park, Wormwood Scrubs, Wandsworth, Primrose Hill, even the Isle of Dogs ; divers objections were raised to each. Government had offered the area of Somerset House for the purpose, or, if that situation were not deemed eligible, some other on the property of the Crown. Prince Albert pointed out the vacant space in Hyde Park, on the south side, parallel with, and between the Kensington drive and the ride famous for fashionable equestrians of both sexes, known by the somewhat inappropriate name of Rotten-row ; and the result proved that a more judicious choice could not have been made. The distance was sufficiently removed from the busiest parts of the capital, to prevent any interruption to its commerce, yet not so far as to be inconvenient, or cause unnecessary loss of time to the crowds of visitors that were to be expected. The approach to it, through the most attractive parts of the metropolis, and the noble park so inestimable to the people, predisposed the mind to agreeable anticipations; the allotted portion of ground comprised upwards of twenty-six acres, presenting a length of two thousand three hundred feet, and a breadth of five hundred, and here and there lofty elms extended their venerable branches, to be gradually enclosed within the Crystal Palace, of which they were destined to become one of the most interesting ornaments. There was also an additional advantage in this site; an advantage which Prince Albert, with the goodness of heart that in him reveals itself on all occasions of public benefit, pointed out as deserving of particular attention, and that was, that it "admitted of equal good access to high and low, rich and poor; and that those who went down in omnibuses, would have equal facilities of approach with those who went in their private carriages." What a contrast did this generous consideration afford to the selfish murmurings of a throng of idle loungers in the fashionable world, who loudly exclaimed against the hardship and injustice of being obliged to sport themselves and their steeds on one side of the Serpentine instead of the other !

The Royal Commission obtained, and the ground fixed upon, the next subject for consideration was the "Ways and Means;" in other words, how to provide the money, which forms the sinews of all great undertakings, in peace as well as war. The Messrs. Munday had, at a very early period of the discussion on the subject, proposed, with a degree of liberality and confidence, which, as the Royal Commissioners did them the justice to acknowledge, reflected the highest credit upon them, to deposit twenty thousand pounds as a sum for prizes; to advance whatever other sums might be necessary for preliminary expenses; to provide offices, to erect a suitable building, and to take upon themselves the whole risk of loss, on certain conditions, which conditions were equally declared by the Royal Commissioners, to be "strictly reasonable, and even favourable to the public."

Nevertheless, the wishes of the people so evidently turned towards considering the Exhibition entirely as a national and self-supporting institution, that it was judged expedient by the Royal Commissioners to set the contract of Messrs. Munday aside, on repaying them the sums they had advanced, with the interest accruing, and to organize an Executive Committee, with Lieutenant-Colonel D. Reid, R.E., at its head, as chairman, and to charge it with the duty of arranging the financial operations. Accordingly, the first step of the new commissioners was to appeal to all classes of the community, for subscriptions to carry out the object proposed: to point out to them that the scale on which the undertaking could be completed must depend entirely upon the amount of the sums received on its behalf; and to call upon them to make such liberal arrangements as would enable the Executive Committee to realize the plans proposed, in a manner worthy of the character and position of the country, and of the invitation it had sent forth to all nations, to compete with it in a spirit of generous and friendly emulation.

It will be easily imagined that in our land of commerce, and of all the enlarged ideas to which commerce gives rise, a land wherein, very lately, we have seen, at a meeting on a political question, subscriptions pouring forth at the astounding rate of a thousand pounds a minute, an appeal like this would be willingly responded to. Seventy-five thousand pounds were subscribed in the different manufacturing towns and seaports of the United Kingdom; of which sum nearly forty thousand were contributed by the city of

London alone.   A guarantee fund of two hundred and thirty thousand pounds was formed by a limited number of persons, including most of the commissioners and other friends of the undertaking, one of them opening the list with the munificent subscription of fifty thousand pounds ; and upon the security of this fund the Bank of England consented to make such advances of money as might be requisite from time to time.

Having now seen the "ways and means" provided for, we must proceed to lay the foundations of the palace itself with our readers, and request their accompanying us in the rapid survey of its rise and progress, which is all that our limits will allow for this portion of our remarks.

The Building Committee having announced its desire to receive plans and suggestions respecting the edifice, from individuals of any country whatsoever that might be willing to offer them, they were speedily furnished with designs from no fewer than two hundred and thirty-three contributors :—viz.—one hundred and twenty-eight from residents in London and its environs ; fifty-one from provincial towns in England ; six from Scotland ; three from Ireland ; twenty-seven from France ; three from Holland ; two from Belgium ; two from Switzerland ; one from Naples ; one from Rhine-Prussia ; one from Hamburgh ; and seven anonymous.   Of these plans the Building Committee reported, that a large proportion of them were remarkable for elaboration of thought and elegance of execution ; that every possible mode of accomplishing the object in view had been displayed by the respective contributors, regarding economy of structure and distribution, and uniting these qualities with various degrees of architectural symmetry : that our "illustrious Continental neighbours" had especially distinguished themselves " by compositions of the utmost taste and learning, worthy of enduring execution ; examples of what might be done in the architectural illustration of the subject, when viewed in its highest aspect ; and, at all events, exhibiting features of grandeur, arrangement, and grace, which had not failed to be duly appreciated.   Another class were praised for the "enthusiasm" with which, bearing in mind "the great occasion and object of the Exhibition," they had magnanimously "waived all considerations of expense," and indulged their imaginations, and employed the resources of their genius and learning, in the composition of arrangements presenting the utmost grandeur and beauty of architecture ; and reminding the architectural student of all the conditions of his art—" the Egyptian hypo-style, the Roman thermæ, or of the Arabic or Saracenic inventions."

But, as Sancho Panza has wisely observed, "fine words butter no parsnips."   Of all these elaborately-eulogised plans, not one was found alike fit, worthy, and possible for adoption ; whilst the "faint praise" given to the "practical character" of the English, as "remarkably illustrated in some very striking and simple methods, suited to the temporary purposes of the building, *due attention having been paid to the pecuniary means allotted to this part of the undertaking*," and the disproportionate number of foreigners to whom "the highest honorary distinction" was awarded, being in the proportion of fifteen to eighteen among them, whilst amongst the English it was only *three* out of one hundred and eighty-five, together called forth a burst of indignation from the public, as well as from the number of candidates, who thought their claims had not been fairly dealt with.   They complained that, whilst they had confined themselves strictly to the conditions specified, that only *suggestions* were to be given, that the plan or drawing was to be a mere outline-sketch upon a single sheet, and the written description or explanation of the plan to be comprised in a single sheet, their competitors had indulged in "elaborated designs, elegantly executed," many on a larger scale, and even with the advantage of colour.

The design for the edifice which the Building Committee submitted to the Commissioners, was no sooner made known to the public, than in the same manner another storm of disapprobation, plentifully intermixed with ridicule, broke upon their heads; and, truth to say, the *idea* was sufficiently open to objection. The realization of it would have brought forth a fabric four times the length of either Westminster Abbey, St. Paul's, or York Minster; in fact, two thousand two hundred feet long, and four hundred and fifty wide. The main building was to be sixty feet in height, the dome more than one hundred and fifty in height, and two hundred in diameter; making it eleven feet larger in diameter than that of St. Peter's at Rome, and forty-five more than that of St. Paul's; whilst fifteen million of bricks would have been used in the building, altogether! Little did the committee imagine at that moment, that the structure was finally destined to stand forth in all the combined advantages of lightness, strength, and security, without the aid of brick, stone, or mortar! their places more efficiently and more economically filled by wood, iron, and glass. Yet so it was; a self-taught genius waved the wand with which he had before effected wonders, and up rose

THE CRYSTAL PALACE.

It is scarcely necessary to say that this genius, this magician was Mr. Paxton, or, as he will be known to future generations, Sir Joseph Paxton; and truly his descendants may be justly proud of an honour which ought to be continued to them, as it was granted to him on the sole ground that can render honorary distinctions really honourable, namely, that of merit.

CHAPTER II.

THE PAXTON PLAN—CONTRACT WITH FOX AND HENDERSON—VAST EXTENT OF ARRANGEMENTS— RAPID ADVANCEMENT OF THE BUILDING—VISIT OF THE SOCIETY OF ARTS—ARRANGEMENT FOR THE DISTRIBUTION OF GOODS—COURTESY TO STRANGERS—PRINCE ALBERT'S SPEECH.

MR. PAXTON had long been known to the public as the superintendent of the Duke of Devonshire's horticultural departments, at Chatsworth and Chiswick, and for the improvements he had introduced into the buildings connected with them, particularly in the introduction of sheet glass for level roofs to conservatories. The idea was originally suggested to his mind by an attentive examination of the large umbrella-shaped leaf, and the longitudinal and transverse girders and supporters at the back of the gigantic and magnificent water-lily, known by the name of the *Victoria Regia*, imported into this country from South Africa, and which flowered for the first time in our clime, on the 9th of November, 1849, in a house expressly fitted up for it in the gardens at Chatsworth, where the water wherein it was placed was kept in motion by a small water-wheel, invented for the purpose by Mr. Paxton.

The account which Mr. Paxton gives of the considerations which first induced him to send in a design, the last in the field, to the Executive Committee, is admirable in its simplicity and truthfulness. It was not until one morning when he was present with his friend Mr. Ellis, at an early sitting in the House of Commons, that the idea presented itself to him, in consequence of a conversation that took place between them relative to the construction of the new House of Commons, in the course of which Mr. Paxton observed that he was afraid they would be committing another blunder in the building for the Industrial Exhibition, adding, that he had a notion concerning it in his own head, and that if his friend would accompany him to the Board of Trade,

D

he would ascertain whether it was too late to send in a design.   Upon inquiring of the Executive Committee whether they stood so far pledged to the plans already submitted to them, as to be precluded from receiving another, they replied certainly not; for though the specifications would be out in a fortnight, there was no reason why a clause should not be introduced allowing another design to come under consideration. "Then," said Mr. Paxton, "if you will introduce a clause to that effect, I will go home, and in nine days I will bring you my plans all complete."   This was on Friday the 11th of June, 1850.

He had, however, to go from London to the Menai Straits, to see the third tube of the Britannia Bridge placed, after which he returned to Derby, to attend to some business at the board-room; but his thoughts were fixed upon his design, and he sketched it on a large sheet of blotting-paper, whilst the conversation was going on all around him.   This precious embodiment of his first ideas on so momentous a subject was taken possession of by his wife, as he stated at a subsequent meeting, in excuse for not producing it; and the importance she annexed to its preservation, was a proof at once of her affectionate pride in her husband's talent, and of her judgment in appreciating the value of a proof of it, equally demonstrative of its readiness and precision. All that night he sat up to consider and correct it, and by the aid of his friend Mr. Barlow, he was enabled to finish all his plans by the Saturday following, and to start with them that day for London.   To the honour of Mr. Stephenson and Mr. Brunel, they no sooner were made acquainted with Mr. Paxton's plan, than they acknowledged its merit, though it interfered with their own previous views on the subject, particularly Mr. Brunel's, which had embraced the idea of the monster dome; but he had the generosity to help Mr. Paxton in his plan for covering in the tall trees which were so dear to the public, that their preservation was made a *sine qua non*, by taking their measurement himself the next morning, and communicating it to Mr. Paxton, saying to him with equal frankness and good feeling, "although I mean to try to win with my own plan, I will give you all the information I can."

This is the true spirit in which men of science and genius should meet each other, and we may hope that instances of it will every day become more and more frequent, under the influence of that enlargement of sympathy and sentiment, which the increased facility of intercourse among nations with each other is the surest means of promoting.

We have already said that it was on a Saturday that Mr. Paxton came up to town with his design, and encouraged by the gracious approbation he met with from Prince Albert, he went forthwith to Messrs. Fox and Henderson, to ask them if they would make a tender for the building on his plan, which they accordingly did, enabled to do so by wording it as "an improvement" on the design of the committee.   The contract was finally taken by these gentlemen for the sum of £79,800, and the materials after the close of the Exhibition; or for £150,000 if the building should be permanently retained.   This was subsequently proved to be the lowest practicable tender that was submitted to the Building Committee; and not the least admirable thing connected with it, was the wonderful quickness and exactitude with which the necessary estimates were formed.   It unfortunately happened that the next day was the first Sunday on which the delivery of letters was forbidden by the new postal arrangement.   Nevertheless, by the aid of the electric telegraph and railway parcels, the great iron masters and glass manufacturers of the north were summoned to come up to town on the Monday, to contribute their several estimates to the tender for the whole; and on the Monday,—

"Punctual as lovers to the moment sworn,"

they presented themselves at the office of Messrs. Fox and Henderson in Spring-gardens. Within one week from this meeting, the cost of every pound of iron, every inch of glass, and every pound of wood required for the building was calculated, and every detailed working drawing prepared.

"What was done in those few days?" says an able writer, in that excellent periodical, *Household Words*. "Two parties in London, relying on the accuracy and good faith of certain iron-masters, glass-workers in the provinces, and of one master-carpenter in London, bound themselves for a certain sum of money, and in the course of some four months, to cover eighteen acres of ground, with a building upwards of a third of a mile long (1851 feet—the exact date of the year,) and some four hundred and fifty feet broad. In order to do this, the glass-maker promised to supply in the required time, nine hundred thousand square feet of glass (weighing more than four hundred tons,) in separate panes, and these the largest that ever were made of sheet glass; each being forty-nine inches long. The iron-master passed his word in like manner, to cast in due time three thousand three hundred iron columns, varying from fourteen feet and-a-half to twenty feet in length; thirty-four *miles* of guttering tube, to join every individual column together, under the ground; two thousand two hundred and twenty-four girders; besides eleven hundred and twenty-eight bearers for supporting galleries. The carpenter undertook to get ready within the specified period two hundred and five *miles* of sash-bar; flooring for an area of thirty-three millions of cubic feet; besides enormous quantities of wooden walling, louvre work, and partition."

It was on the 30th of July, 1850, that possession of the ground was obtained; on the 26th of the following September the first pillar was fixed. What a multiplicity of arrangements had to be formed in that short intervening period; "Details of construction had to be settled, elaborate calculations as to the strength and proportion of the several constituent parts to be made, machinery for economising labour to be devised, contracts for the supply of materials to be entered into, and thousands of hands set actually to work."

From the first moment of its commencement the interest of the public in the progress of the building was intense. Every day crowds of pedestrians were to be seen bending their steps towards the great attraction; fortunate did those think themselves that could obtain a peep, through the interstices of the wood-work, at the piles of materials withinside; more fortunate still those who by special interest, or some well imagined plea of business, could gain a short admittance among the operatives themselves—and in fact, to the eye of benevolence, not the Crystal Palace in all its finished glories, presented a spectacle more interesting, than that offered in its progress, by the united labours of the industrious classes who were to bring it to perfection.

First, up went the boarding round the destined space—away went the green sward, untouched by the spade, yet soon cut up as if the artillery of an army had passed over it. Then rose the wooden walls; then columns; then girders spanned across, first at formal and naked distances, but rapidly thickening like a forest of masts; or rather, if we may be allowed the comparison, like huge webs woven by beings who from below looked only like insects, ingeniously crossing the interstices—then galleries spread around, and stair-cases sprang up to meet them—and so onward went the work of a fabric, of the magnitude of which an idea may be formed more intelligible than any that can be communicated by mere figures, when it is stated to be four times the size of St. Peter's at Rome, and six times that of St. Paul's in London.

The workmen seemed to find strength and energy in proportion to the vastness of the field in which they were employed: 18,392 panes of glass were fixed in the roof in one week, by eighty men; 108 panes, or 367 feet 6 inches of glazing being accomplished by one of the glaziers in a single day.

It had been agreed upon by the contractors, that the members of the Society of Arts and their friends should be admitted, to examine the building previous to its being given up on a day specified, as sufficiently complete, to the authorities.   The day appointed for this purpose was only the preceding one, so closely now was the time calculated upon: but certainly, whatever might have been the anticipations of the visitors, eight hundred in number, they found, immediately upon their entrance, those anticipations exceeded as far, in fact, as the interior of the edifice has ever been found to exceed in its beauty, and the harmony of its proportions, the expectations formed by its exterior. Even the most practised eyes, accustomed to the gigantic scale on which the mighty works of the present era are carried out, could recal nothing to compare it to; in fact, there was nothing comparable with it.   It was as the time-revealed skeleton of some enormous animal, the vastness of which could only be ascertained by its measurement with surrounding objects.

It would be difficult to describe the effect produced upon the minds of the spectators, when they found themselves withinside the structure, of which every point was still in progress.   All manner of operations seemed going on at once; sawing, planing, glazing, painting, hammering, boarding.   Here white vapours curled among the yet leafless branches of the imprisoned elms, from little steam-engines, each steadily fixed from day to day at its appointed duties.   There clouds of dust covered the too curious spectator, from circular-saws, busily employed in cutting to equal lengths, the Paxton gutters. Then again were machines kindly guiding those same gutters, first through a trough of paint, and then through an aperture provided with brushes, which pressing closely upon them, in their passage, turned them out of it on the other side, all trimly coated.   One vast apparatus was busying itself with the making of putty; another with manufacturing sash-bars—here were vast boilers to generate steam for the machinery—there pipes diverging east and west, to convey to the fountains, and various parts of the building, the three hundred thousand gallons of water supplied per diem, by the Chelsea Water-works Company, by contract, at fifty pounds per month.   Massive cranes were relieving ponderous waggons of their loads, and wheels and pulleys were everywhere in motion.

The din of voices and sounds amid the multitude of operatives, and the variety of operations may easily be imagined.   Well might the overseers of different parties of workmen be obliged to communicate with them through a speaking-trumpet.   Yet, amid all this seeming "confusion worse confounded," though in fact the perfection of well-organized regularity, Professor Cowper, with philosophic self-possession, delivered a lecture upon the construction of the building, and was surrounded, whilst delivering it, by an audience of the most distinguished and brilliant of both sexes, blended with the humbler, but potent classes, whose labours everywhere speaking for them, in the impos-ing spectacle around, proclaimed at once their industry, and their power, and that without them nothing great or beneficial could ever be achieved.

A portion of the western part of the building had been converted into a temporary saloon for the occasion, by being enclosed with sixteen large and splendid carpets, courteously lent for the occasion by Messrs. Jackson and Graham, and suspended from poles fastened to the girders: the space was entered by an opening of drapery at the east end, and within a platform was erected, whence the professor pointed out the scientific principles on which the building was constructed, and illustrated them by various diagrams and models, well calculated to allay the fears of the timid, and silence the doubts of the sceptical.   He then proceeded to various parts of the building to explain the use of the different machines, and was followed by a vast crowd, plunging through mud, scrambling over timber, balancing themselves on joists, and climbing up ladders, in despite of a heavy rain, all eager for information.

The arrangements for the reception and placing of the articles to be sent to the Exhibition necessarily required much calculation. The commissioners, anxious to treat their foreign contributors with all the courtesy and hospitality due to invited guests, resolved to appropriate to their use one-half of the exhibiting space of the whole building; being more than the entire ground which France occupied for her own Exhibition in 1844 and 1845. Over the admission of British articles, the Commissioners reserved to themselves full power of control; but the power of admitting foreign articles was confided absolutely to the authority of the country by which they might be sent: they were to be allowed to enter any of our ports free of examination or duties, and everything in the shape of gratuity or subscription, from any foreigner whatever, resident at home or abroad, was scrupulously discouraged and refused: in short, everything was done in harmony with the noble sentiments which Prince Albert had uttered at the splendid banquet given by the Lord Mayor of London, in honour of the projected Exhibition, to such of the chief magistrates of the various towns, cities and boroughs throughout the United Kingdom, as were enabled to avail themselves of his munificent invitation—sentiments which deserved to be written in letters of gold; and as they were not framed for that occasion only, but will apply equally to future ages, we will not deny ourselves the pleasure of laying a part of them before our readers:—

" I conceive it to be the duty of every educated person closely to watch and study the time in which he lives, and, as far as in him lies, to add his humble mite of individual exertion, to further the accomplishment of what he believes Providence to have ordained.

" Nobody, however, who has paid any attention to the particular features of our present era, will doubt for a moment that we are living at a period of most wonderful transition, which tends rapidly to accomplish that great end—to which indeed all history points—the realization of the unity of mankind: not a unity which breaks down the limits and levels the peculiar characteristics of the different nations of the earth, but rather a unity, the results and product of those very national varieties and antagonistic qualities.

" The distances which separated the different nations and parts of the globe, are gradually vanishing before the achievements of modern invention, and we can traverse them with incredible speed; the languages of all nations are known, and their acquirement placed within the reach of everbody; thought is communicated with the rapidity, and even by the power of lightning. On the other hand, the great principle of the division of labour, which may be called the moving power of civilization, is being extended to all branches of science, industry, and art. Whilst formerly the greatest mental energies strove at universal knowledge, and that knowledge was confined to few, now they are directed to specialities, and in these again even to the minutest points. Moreover, the knowledge now acquired becomes at once the property of the community at large: whilst, formerly, discovery was wrapt in secrecy, it results from the publicity of the present day, that no sooner is a discovery or invention made, than it is already improved upon and surpassed by competing efforts. The products of all quarters of the globe are placed at our disposal, and we have only to choose which is the best and cheapest for our purposes, and the powers of production are entrusted to the stimulus of competition and capital.

" Thus man is approaching a more complete fulfilment of that great and sacred mission which he has to perform in this world. His reason being created after the image of God, he has to use it to discover the laws by which the Almighty governs his creation, and, by making these laws his standard of action, to conquer nature to his use—himself a divine instrument. Science discovers these laws of power, motion, and transformation; industry applies them to the raw matter which the earth yields us in abundance, but which becomes valuable only by knowledge; art teaches us the immutable laws of beauty and symmetry, and gives to our productions forms in accordance with them. The Exhibition of 1851 is to give us a true test and a living picture of the point of development at which the whole of mankind has arrived in this great task, and a new starting-point, from which all nations will be able to direct their future exertions. I confidently hope that the first impression which the view of this vast collection will produce on the spectator, will be that of deep thankfulness to the Almighty, for the blessings which he has bestowed upon us already here below; and the second, the conviction that they can only be realized in proportion to the help which we are prepared to render to each other; therefore, only by peace, love, and ready assistance, not only between individuals, but between the nations of the earth. This being my conviction, I must be highly gratified to see here assembled the magistrates of all important towns of this realm, sinking all their local, and possibly political differences—the representatives of the different political opinions of this country, and the representatives of the different foreign nations—to-day representing only one interest."

E

CHAPTER III.

APPROACH OF THE TIME FIXED FOR OPENING THE EXHIBITION—FOREIGN COUNTRIES AND STATES
SENDING THEIR CONTRIBUTIONS.

THE first of May was the day originally fixed upon for throwing open the world's wonder to the world's gaze; and the Commissioners felt themselves pledged to the world at large, to observe the punctuality which is one of the proudest boasts of an Englishman; and one of the most important characteristics of British commerce, by which, in conjunction with integrity, that commerce stands highest in repute among nations.

The prisoned elms had, despite their strange captivity, already put forth the tender green, with which they are foremost among the denizens of the woods, to greet the sweet though changeful April; the little birds began to chirrup about the glittering roof, and made sundry efforts, often successful, to penetrate into the interior, through the openings left for air, and to hop once more among the leafy boughs, familiar to them as their homes. Everything announced that spring was rapidly advancing—that May-day was, in fact, close at hand: but how much yet remained to be done, ere she was to be welcomed in the Crystal Palace!

Fifteen thousand contributors, from all parts of the civilized globe, had sent in their specifications, and their claims for space. Waggon after waggon-load of goods were thronging the entrances. Mass after mass of raw material, such, for instance, as a column of coal from North Wales, sixteen tons in weight; a block of twenty-four tons, ditto material, from Derbyshire; obelisks and columns of granite; slabs of Portland and other stones; grind-stones, flag-stones, mill-stones, huge filters, gigantic cisterns, anchors, chimney-cans, drain-pipes, and similar productions, more useful than ornamental, were, one after another, taking their "patient stand," on the spots assigned them outside the building; to the amazement of a crowd of spectators of the humbler classes, who stared at them open-mouthed, wondering, like the Jack Tar, after he had been blown up at a pantomime, by an accidental explosion, and landed safely down again, "what would come next." Not that we mean to quarrel with the "raw material;" on the contrary, we agree with the *Athenæum*, "it was a happy decision of the Executive Committee to allow the exhibition of raw materials: it is most instructive to have under the same point of view, the manufactured article, and the stuff from which it was made—the cotton pod, and the calico and muslin—the hempen fibre, and the ship's cable and sails—the elephant's tusk, and the marvellous Indian carvings in ivory—the iron ore, and the Sheffield blades. To us these raw materials, ranged side by side, just as they were picked from the lap of nature, are full of interest. That 'Greek Slave,' now so suggestive of life and beauty, was once a block of marble—the Amazon, once metallic ore—those strings that utter delicious music, were parts of a living animal—the materials of those silken fabrics were all spun by caterpillars—the pearls on that diadem were formed by a shell-fish—those colours that dazzle on the fabrics of India and China are the produce of very humble plants. The distance between the raw material and the perfected work is the measure of the conquest of man over the external world—the record of that victory, which the Crystal Palace first celebrates for the whole human family."

Whilst the objects we have mentioned were attracting the attention of the multitude without, the multitude within were running to and fro, as busy, and almost as numerous as ants in an ant-hill. There were packages opening, goods examining, classing, describing, numbering, ticketing, placing; scaffolds were disappearing, rubbish removing, outer packing cases clearing away, fittings of all kinds going on; excavations for fountains, pedestals for statues, foundations for machines; and tables, counters, partitions, and glass cases rising rapidly around. The monster organ was beginning to try its pipes, *sotto voce*, from the western gallery. In the great central avenue was the Amazon of Kiss, levelling her spear at the tiger, neck or nothing, who has seized upon her horse; further on was a mailed Crusader, of colossal dimensions, about to charge upon his foes; whilst, utterly guiltless of any such warlike propensities, Lord Eldon, and his brother Lord Stowell, were peaceably seated, in effigy, side by side, as if gazing in placid admiration upon the busy scene before them, within the operations of which assuredly Lord Elgin's favourite motto "*Festina lente*" had nothing to do.

But still the work of the building was going on. Still the hammer and the chisel, the saw and the plane reverberated through the long aisles, and interminable galleries; the pipes for the supply of water and gas had still to be finished; the ventilation to be controlled; some acres of canvas to be spread over the roof; the chief of the internal arrangements and compartments to be made, and in short, to many it would have appeared as if there were the work of two years to do, instead of as many weeks.

But masters and men were alike indefatigable. Mr. Fox was on the ground every day, from seven in the morning until ten at night. It was calculated that at this period not fewer than ten thousand persons were engaged, some way or other, in the service of the Exhibition. One week, two thousand two hundred and sixty workmen were actually employed in and about the building itself; and it was in keeping with all the rest of the business details, that the system of payment was so admirably arranged with regard to exactitude and celerity, that out of this number, two thousand received their wages at the close of the day, in one hour, without confusion, noise, or mistake of any kind.

And now rapidly congregated on British ground the representatives of the different nations, with their respective productions and wares, who had been invited to take their place in the great industrial mart, one of the avowed objects of which was to draw all the families of the civilized world together, in bonds of amity, for their mutual benefit and enlightenment. Thus were these families typified by an ingenious writer, with equal truth of discrimination and playfulness of fancy :—

"First on the lists were the kingdoms of Arabia and Persia; with their caravans freighted with rich tissues, and the work of delicate looms from Mushed and Tehran; with myrrh and frankincense from Hadramaut, 'musk from Khoten,' pearls from the sea of Oman, and *attar gul* from the gardens of Shinar. Then came 'small-eyed China;' sending her fragile porcelain, her painted screens, her snow-white and crimson silks, her gold and silver stuffs, her paper made of rice, her ivory fans, so curiously carved, and her mother-of-pearl ornaments, so laboriously and exquisitely graven. Brazil and Mexico were ready with diamonds and rich ores, and many-tinted flowers, whose hues were borrowed from the ruby throats and emerald wings of the *colibri*. Turkey held out her jewelled weapons, with their Damascus blades, her perfumed skins, gaudily dyed, and stamped with rare devices, her splendid caparisons, her fragrant and richly ornamented pipes, her costly variegated carpets. Greece, no longer able to astonish the world with the sculpture of Phidias and Praxiteles, or the marvels of Appelles' art, could vie with her former rulers in the beauty and elegance of her mountain costumes, and the elaborate workmanship she bestowed on weapons now little suited to her hands. Egypt, under the impulse of a newly awakened industry, had drugs, and dyes, and perfumes, soft cottons, and cloths of finest texture, the plumes of the ostrich, and raiments of the camel's hair. Italy was prepared to display her manufactures from the fertile plains of Lombardy to the sunny cliffs of Sorrento : Genoa, rich in velvets and embroidery; Bologna, decked in the gayest silks and ribands; Rome, proud of her cameos, her mosaics, her false pearls, and her *hats ;* Venice, stil famous for her glass, though its occult virtues are flown; Leghorn, renowned for its everlasting straw-bonnets; Fabriano, with a paper reputation, not yet torn to pieces, and Ancona, whose waxen images tempt the 'decoratives' to St. Peter's, and whose tapers light them on the way. Spain and Portugal came next, suggestive of every produce that the earth hides in its bosom, or spreads over its surface, though not of the means by which its wealth may be turned to account. Yet who could think of Spain without conjuring up the thousands of interesting objects with which the world's bazaar might be studded? Who would not expect from Andalusia specimens of the fans and mantillas which the women use with so much dexterity, and wear with so much grace; the splendid dresses of the *majos ;* the guitars which are in every man's hand, and the castanets which are common to both sexes? From Valencia—that true paradise on earth—those curious silver-gilt combs which adorn the Valencian beauties; those silks and bombasines which form part of their attire; those beautiful azulejos, or coloured tiles, the art of making which was bequeathed, with so many other secrets, by the Moors? From Granada, and throughout the southern coast, the rich marbles and minerals susceptible of being wrought into every form of grace or purpose of utility? From Murcia, the fatal *cuchillo,* and the gailey-striped silken manta? From Cordova, the silver filigree-work that still keeps its old renown? From Toledo, those wondrous blades, welded out of a steel whose temper has no equal? From Barcelona, those goods which (if they do not really come from Manchester), may shame the Manchester manufacturers? In a word, who would not look from every province of Spain for some rich or rare production which might show, that where nature has been so bountiful, man has not been altogether idle?

" Nor could the mineral and vegetable wealth for which Portugal is famed, and which, despite of her poverty, she has the will to fabricate, pass unrepresented. Her marbles, her antique silks, heavy as armour, her cloths and carpets, even her curiously manufactured snuffs, were all ready for exportation. Switzerland followed, with her muslins and gold watches, and her countless specimens of that ingenuity, with which every summer-tourist returns laden, when he delights the family-circle by producing from the depths of his knapsack, now a *châlet* entire, anon a milking-pail; then an egg-cup, a drinking vessel, a salad-spoon, or the costume of every canton, faithfully carved in cherry-tree and boxwood. France—but what does the skill of man create that is gorgeous in colour, graceful in form, rich in substance, delicate in texture, beautiful in pattern, ingenious in construction, or faultless in execution that France might not send forth? To name her chief towns, is to name a competitor for every great prize in the struggle for art's supremacy. The bronzes, the *bijouterie,* the mirrors, and the *meubles* of Paris— the silks, the satins, and the velvets of Lyons—the flaxen threads and linens of Lille— the lace of Valenciennes—the carpets of Beauvais and Aubusson—the prints and muslins of Mulhausen—the watches of Besançon—the porcelain of Sevres—the enamels of Limoges—the cottons of Amiens and Rouen—the gossamer scarfs of Bareges—the point of Alençon—the broad cloths of Elbœuf and Louviers—the soaps of Marseilles—the dyes and perfumes of Carcasonne, Montpelier, and Hyères—to say nothing of the thousand creature comforts which find no place in the Exhibition itself, though truffled turkeys, Chartres, Perigueux, and Strasbourg pies, Orleans quinces, Tours plums, and many a delicacy besides, are not prohibited in the refreshment rooms; while the vintages of Burgundy, Champagne, the Rhone, and the Garonne, are not to be had any nearer than Monsieur Soyer's monster *restaurant ;* all these things, whether to delight the eye or please the taste, might reach the Palace of Industry from all-producing France !

" Belgium, in many things the formidable rival of her southern neighbour, succeeded, decked like a bride, in Mechlin and Brussels lace, or richly arrayed, like a burgomaster's wife, in the ponderous silk of Antwerp, and beneath her feet the priceless carpets of

Tournay, in whose soft fabric those feet were completely buried. She pointed to Ghent for her cotton manufactures, to Vervier for her cloths, and gazed with pride on Liege, as the emporium of her cutlery and fire-arms, where the attributes of Sheffield and Birmingham are united. Holland, the elder sister of Flanders, moved onward with dignified, but measured pace, proud of her rich spices, strong waters, and rare cordials, and prouder still of the gorgeous tulips in her garden, for which her sedate money-making husband has given, in hard guilders, more than a king's ransom.

"Germany next presented herself under three different aspects :—the northern division bearing her own name—a vast conglomerate called the Zollverein—and Austria, resolute in keeping aloof, unless she could cast her net over everything else, from the shores of the Baltic to the banks of the Po ; and dictate one universal law to Germans and Italians, Sclaves, Croats, Czeeks, and Hungarians. Manifold are the productions of the Teuton and Sclavonian races.

"Berlin has wealth of iron, fit metal for a people so warlike ; Eberfeld dresses half the world in its dyed cottons ; Cologne displays her *flacon;* Solingen balances the foil, and proves the well-tempered blade of the ' Schläger,' renowned in the 'renownings' of Germany's bellicose students ; Magdeburg modestly appeals to her various merchandise ; Bremen takes upon herself the task of preparing the tobacco which all the rest of Germany smokes; and Dresden paints the bowls of all the German pipes ; Leipzig manufactures books which this year nobody will have time to read ; Meissen gives birth to the shepherds and shepherdesses who exist only on consoles and chimney-pieces ; Frankfort has her own fair, but that attraction must cease for a time ; Nuremberg still vaunts her toys, though the marvellous works of Kraft, of Adam Vischer, and of Wentzel Jamitzer, belong to a past age ; Munich has sculpture, and bronze, and stained glass, and glowing frescoes, and bright mosaics ; and the simple Tyrolese rivals the Switzer's patient labour on the long winter nights, when all other occupation ceases. Surely the things we have spoken of, and more, the things we have left unnamed, were to be gathered in Germany.

"There are yet more names on the list. Scientific Denmark, with her accurate instruments for measuring time and space. Learned Sweden, a hortus siccus in her hand, and a medallion of Linnæus on her breast. Half-civilized Russia, with a Paris bonnet on her head, a bearskin on her shoulders, in the midst of which blazes a diamond star, and beneath which shines a brazen cuirass, a long cut-and-thrust sword by her side, seven-league boots, well garnished with spurs, on her lower limbs, in either clutch grasping a knout and a pair of curling-irons, and her own person reflected in one of her own looking-glasses, before which she admiringly stands. She is rich in gold and platina, and malachite ; in furs, in tallow, and in hemp, and through one or other of these media, is prepared to contribute to the world's industry.

"Of foreign lands America comes last. Follow the course of her rivers, examine her sea-board, track her footsteps across the prairies and rocky-mountains—follow her into the Far West, amidst falling forests and flying Indians,—cross her immense lakes, whirl with her through her swamps and savannahs, or pause amidst her rising and risen cities, and ask what variety of manufacture exists which the enterprise, and toil, and acuteness of the United States cannot supply, with little to fear from the result of universal competition.

"To give the rest of the world its chance, the British colonies had their assigned space ; every zone of the earth, and every temperature beneath the sun, received the command to exhaust their riches and lay them at the feet of Queen Victoria."

But whilst poetic minds were thus revelling in the anticipations of the probable, practical ones were no less busy with the actual. All London was to be " repaired and beautified," according to the memorials of the churchwardens. The names of streets were all to be repainted, with directions at the corners, and hands significantly pointing out, every finger stretched to the utmost of its powers of extension, to denote leading here, leading there, for the peculiar edification of foreigners; lest they should become bewildered among the mazes of Leicester-square, or the more aristocratic, and, to those who cling to old associations, dreadfully monotonous, and coldly genteel straight lines of Hyde Park Gardens. Nor ought we to lose sight of the truth, that these directions are just as much required for "country cousins," wandering about St. Paul's, in search of the Houses of Parliament; or honest gentlemen-farmers, threading, or trying to thread their way from Smithfield to the Bank, as for the numerous host of whiskered foreigners, who stare about them in the great city, divided between admiration of its vastness, and disgust at the difficulties it presents to those unused to "Life in London."

"The plot, moreover," continues the lively narrator, "began to thicken. Shabby shop-fronts were removed, and bronze and plate-glass supplied the place of painted wood and dingy panes. The boot-makers made models of their customers' favourite legs, and paraded them in tops and buckskins, in gigantic wide-mouthed tubes that passed for hunting-gear, and in delicate silk and French polish for evening parties. The tailors, who were very particular in stating that *there* they spoke every language under the sun— Français, Deutsch, Espanol, Italiano and Cherokee—got up the most bewildering dressing-gowns, the hairiest and most poodle-like paletots, the sportingest waistcoats, the tightest and most expansive ladies' habits, the most elaborate dress coats, and the most impossible waistcoats. They took it into their heads that the inhabitants of France and Germany were coming to London in the costumes which their ancestors wore when they fought with Cæsar and Agricola, and filled the columns of the *Times* and *Morning Chronicle* with advertisements, setting forth, in elegant French, the fact that 'des commis, réunissant le tact et l'intelligence aux bonnes manières, sont constamment a la disposition des visiteurs;' or in less palatable German, the similar assurance, addressed to the 'Publicum und Fremde,' that 'zu jeder zeit stehen tüchtige und verständige Assistenten bereit jede Auskunft über alle Geschäft betreffenden Gegengtände zu ertheilen,' to receive and execute the orders they might be favoured with.

"As a sign of the times, the Hôtel d'Italie, in Sherrard-street, painted its doors and window-sills sky-blue, and prepared for a most terrific gastronomic campaign; the Sabloniere announced its *table d'hôte* at six o'clock, and inwardly resolved not to give a new coat of paint to anything; while the Provençe Hotel gave out the startling intimation that '*restauration à la carte*' was incessant in that establishment. Even the old-fashioned chop-houses in the Strand and Haymarket began to look about them; the 'Boars' and 'Castles' whetted their tusks, and threw open their portals; the 'Belles Sauvages' looked amiable; the 'Queen's Arms' expanded hospitably; the 'Blue Posts' declared themselves fixtures; 'Williams,' who (perfidiously) came from 'Betsy's,' intimated his resolve to supply luncheons and dinners on his own account; and 'Mrs. Robertson,' who has been residing for the last century with 'Dr. Johnson,' in Fleet-street, abandoned the great lexicographer, and set up housekeeping for herself in Maiden-lane. Nor were the creature-comforts alone considered. The head was cared for, and the feet also: for the sake of the former, the St. George's Chess Club announced 'a grand chess tournament;' and for the behoof of the latter, a brigade of shoeblacks turned out from the ragged-school in Field-lane, in scarlet jackets of the most astonishing brilliancy.

"The interpreters began to look up, and those who had lodgings to let, not only looked up, but also very considerably ahead. They were right in doing so, for John Bull's preparations were not without a cause. It was no longer the Quadrant and Leicester-square that exhibited signs of the friendly invasion, but, in all directions, foreigners surged up, affording convincing proof of their anxiety to see the latest wonder of the world, to applaud the design of Prince Albert, render homage to the genius of Paxton, and admire the unwearied industry and zeal of Messrs. Fox and Henderson.

"Shoals of the 'Bruderschaft' also appeared; fervid Italians, in bands like brigands or opera singers, from every part of their genius-favoured land, hurried to London; and Switzerland emptied her valleys to inundate Regent-street.

"The *St. Lawrence* frigate not only brought her overwhelming contribution of dry goods, but something dryer still,—in the person of the president of 'The everlasting Gold Bluff Sand Company,' who had taken a passage in her from New York, and came —like his compeers from Paris—to see whether 'a pretty smart spekilation in dust' was likely to answer in Britain; and firmly resolved that it should'nt 'cave in,' if he could prevent it. Nor was his project by any means a solitary one; for whether he came from the 'diggings' on the Sacramento, was raised in pleasant Texas, or had served his time in the 'Tombs,' at New York, brother Jonathan helped himself on with his shiniest coat, and fetched across the Atlantic, to see whether he could'nt 'make a pile somehow' among the Britishers. Not a weekly steamer ran up the Mersey that did not bring a full cargo of strangers from every one of the unions waved over by the 'star-spangled banner;' not a packet showed its flag on the Southampton Water that was not crowded with a living freight of dusky Spaniards, and duskier Portuguese; of swarthy Moors, and swarthier Egyptians; of cane-coloured East Indians, and copper-coloured Tartars; of Mulattos, with complexions of a lively brown, and of Haytians, with countenances— such as Solomon loved—of a lovely black. At Dover and Folkstone, and eke at the Tower-stairs, steamer after steamer arrived with the bearded civilization of Europe. There was 'your straw coloured beard,' representing Russia, Norway, Sweden, and the whole of the north of Germany; 'your orange-tawny beard,' those who dwell on the Rhine and its tributaries; and your 'purple-in-grain beard,' our excellent democratic neighbours the French, who speak their own language so well, and every other tongue so badly. There was, in fact, an assortment of beards more than enough to satisfy the cravings of a dozen monopolists like Bottom the weaver, and these were to 'wag all' in the Crystal Palace, in the merry month of May."

In the meanwhile the "note of preparation" was busily and incessantly going on at the principal scene of action; "the sound of hammers closing rivets up" rang through the air "from morn till noon, from noon till dewy eve," startling the Dryads and Hamadryads among the venerable shades of Hyde Park and Kensington—the "busy hum of men" throughout the spacious interior of the rising wonder, was like the murmur of bees at their busiest season in their "waxen citadel;" and the rapidity and precision with which the combined labour advanced, outstripped the most sanguine expectations. The astonishment and delight of the public were unbounded; praises were lavished on all sides—on the projectors, the inventor, the architect, and the workmen employed; the name of Paxton was in everybody's mouth; all the journals, daily, weekly, and monthly, were eloquent on the subject. The all-engrossing theme found its way, through their medium, to every corner of the empire, to the remotest quarters of the globe. An eloquent writer in *The Times* thus describes the sudden and brilliant apparition:—

"The vast fabric may be seen, by any one who visits that part of town, in its full dimensions—an Arabian Night's structure, full of light, and with a certain airy unsubstantial character about it, which belongs more to enchanted land than to this gross material world of ours. The eye, accustomed to the solid heavy details of stone and lime, or brick-and-mortar architecture, wanders along those extended and transparent aisles, with their terraced outlines, almost distrusting its own conclusions on the reality of what it sees, for the whole looks like a splendid phantasm, which the heat of the noon-day sun would dissolve, or a gust of wind scatter into fragments, or a London fog utterly extinguish.   There, however, the Crystal Palace remains, a monument of the extent to which lightness of structure can be combined with permanence and strength— a building remarkable not less for size than for the beauty of mathematical proportions and rectangular outlines.   The varied dimensions and fantastic features of other edifices, there find no parallel.   Everything is done by the rule, and yet everything is graceful, and it might almost be said grand.   Wherever one stands no disagreeable effects present them-selves—nothing crooked, awkward, or out of place.   The subordination of parts to the whole is complete, and an expression of order and exactitude reigns throughout, not unaptly typical of the progress which the mechanical sciences have made in this country. But for that progress the Crystal Palace could never have been constructed ; and it certainly is curious to reflect, now that the work has been accomplished, and the great result stands patent to the world, that, with the facilities we possessed, glass and iron have hitherto been so little employed by our architects.

" Like many other structures which will readily suggest themselves to the mind of the reader, the Crystal Palace must be viewed from a distance to be appreciated.   Whoever would see a great mountain to perfection, must not survey it immediately from its base, and on exactly the same principle the new edifice in Hyde Park cannot be well viewed from the Kensington-road.   The drive along the Serpentine, and the bridge over it, are the best points for a spectator to select.   There the ground rises, and the vacant space enables the eye to reach over a large proportion of the building.   The trees partly shut out the prospect, but enough remains to astonish and to captivate.   The vast extent of area covered, the transparent and brilliant character of the structure, the regular and terraced elevations, the light airy abutments, the huge transept, with its arched and glittering roof shining above the great vitreous expanse around it, and reminding one of nothing that he has ever heard of before—all these things are worth seeing."

As the time drew near for the opening of the "World's Wonder," and the various products of various climes, as we have already stated, were pouring into the vast em-porium, the bustle and activity of the neighbourhood, nay, of all London and its vicinity, increased in ten-fold proportion ; carts, waggons, and trucks, loaded with every species of merchandise and manufacture, from the ponderous steam-engine, requiring sixteen horses to impel its course towards the park, to the most delicate manufacture of ornament or attire, thronged in apparently inextricable confusion all the avenues leading to the appointed place of rendezvous ; shoals of omnibuses, crammed to excess, inside and out, frequently got blocked up in immense masses, while the hapless drivers

> *   *   *   * " harder beset
> And more endangered, than when Argo passed
> Through Bosporus, betwixt the justling rocks,"

in vain endeavoured,

> " Through the shock
> Of fighting elements,"

to win their way.   So great was the occasional "hubbub wild," "the stunning sounds and voices all confused" that assaulted the ear, that many foreigners stood aghast, and were altogether unable to proceed, or even to understand in what direction to shape their course.   An Italian lady of our acquaintance, witnessing a scene of this kind in the neighbourhood of the Mansion-house, compared our metropolis to six enormous cities all conglomerated into one, and of which all the inhabitants were, at the same point of time, eagerly occupied in changing their lodgings.   To attempt at these periods to cross the streets was a hazardous and a bewildering task for the pedestrian ; many were the

THE OPENING OF THE GREAT EXHIBITION.

BY HER MOST GRACIOUS MAJESTY QUEEN VICTORIA MAY 1, 1851.

Engraved by H Bibby

JOHN TALLIS & COMPANY, LONDON & NEW-YORK.

"hairbreadth 'scapes" that we witnessed, and many the abortive attempts to "change sides"—relentlessly onward rolled the living tide, and waited not for individual accommodation. *Forward!* was the emphatic word that seemed to actuate the determination of every one in their pilgrimage westward; and how greatly this desire increased, and how greatly the multitudes augmented their forces on the eventful day of opening, we shall have occasion to show in our next chapter, which we accordingly propose to dedicate to that memorable event.

CHAPTER IV.

THE OPENING OF THE EXHIBITION.

THURSDAY, the 1st of May, the auspicious day, at length arrived—the day originally fixed upon for the great event arose with unwonted brilliancy; the sun, "rejoicing as a giant to run his course," had scarcely shed his earliest beams upon the countless towers and spires of the mighty metropolis, ere its myriad population were afoot, all eager for the long-anticipated spectacle, the brilliant pageant, when England's queen, attended by the noblest and proudest of the land, should in her own person open to the admiring world a palace more glorious than the sumptuous abodes of royalty—a palace devoted to the combined industry and art of every various nation upon the face of the habitable globe. May-day has ever been memorable in our island, and many are the eulogiums bestowed upon it by our native poets, from the time of old Chaucer and Spenser to our bards of modern date; but never did it witness a spectacle more imposing, a pageant more brilliant, or a multitude assembled in its honour more numerous and rejoicing. As early as six o'clock the whole town was in motion; from every portion of the suburbs, along every street and avenue leading westward, the countless thousands pressed onwards, in orderly and continuous march; every face was turned in one direction, and the incessant tramp of the joyous multitude, as they wended their way towards the spacious parks, was regular and unbroken.

In the more immediate vicinity of the Crystal Palace, the grand centre of attraction, every space was occupied where human foot could be planted; a sea of heads extended over the whole of St. James's Park, along Constitution-hill, through Knightsbridge, and Rotten-row, whose owners were all intent to catch a glimpse of royalty, and to testify their loyal feelings and their gratitude by repeated cheers and notes of gratulation. Every house that commanded a view of the procession was crowded with spectators; the very roofs teemed with life,—

"Each jutting frieze, and corner stone,"

supported its delighted gazer; and when the procession emerged from the arch at the top of Constitution-hill, enthusiastic shouts and animated cheerings rent the very air, while on every side the waving of innumerable handkerchiefs and hats saluted the gorgeous pageant as it swept proudly onwards.

At a quarter before twelve, the royal procession reached the northern entrance of the Crystal Palace, and was greeted with the national anthem of "God Save the Queen," from the band in attendance at the building. The scene at this moment became inexpressibly animated; the cannon stationed on the banks of the Serpentine, from their "brazen throats," sent forth a thundering welcome, emulated by the joyous shouts of the applauding multitude; while "the merry bells rang round," the union-jack was displayed in triumphant exultation, from every elevated point, to greet the entrance of her Majesty within the precincts of the glittering palace, and the royal standard was at the same time displayed floating proudly above the hundred-and-one flags of all nations, with which the building was decorated.

A popular journal gives the following description of the admission of the public within the favoured precincts :—

"The hour fixed for the opening of the various doors to the holders of season tickets was nine o'clock; but long before that time every possible point of access to the building was thronged with well-dressed persons—a great proportion of them ladies—eagerly waiting for admission. Considering the immense number who eventually were admitted—some twenty-five thousand or thirty thousand at least—the proceeding was conducted with wonderful order and regularity, and with much less personal inconvenience than generally attends the congregating of large assemblies. The first *coup d'œil* of the building on entering the nave was grand and gorgeous in the extreme: the vast dimensions of the building; the breadth of light, partially subdued and agreeably mellowed in the nave by the calico coverings placed over the roof, whilst the arched transept soared boldly into the clear arch of heaven, courting, admitting, and distributing the full effulgence of the noonday sun; the bright and striking colours and forms of the several articles in rich manufactured goods, works in sculpture, and other objects displayed by the exhibitors, dissimilar and almost incongruous in their variety, were blent into an harmonious picture of immense grandeur, by the attendant circumstances of space and light to which we have just alluded; and the busy hum, and eager and excited movements of the assembled thousands, infused the breath of life into a picture which, at the period of the crowning incident of the day, became truly sublime.

"The centre area of the intersection of the naves and transept was that set apart for the reception of her Majesty and her Court, and the other distinguished persons who were to take part in the interesting ceremonies of the day. At the northern portion of this area a daïs was erected, covered with a splendid carpet, worked by one hundred and fifty ladies for her Majesty, and graciously accepted by her; and upon this was placed a magnificent chair of state, covered with a velvet robe or mantle of crimson and gold. High over head was suspended an octagon canopy, trimmed with blue satin and draperies of blue and white. Before the chair rose the beautiful glass fountain, glittering as a precious stone in the morning beams. Behind rose the stems of the Oriental plants and the stately elm, one of the most agreeable and refreshing parts of the whole view. Along the galleries of the main western avenue, the department for British goods, a succession of the most beautiful carpetry was suspended, like bannerets, only more splendid, in a knightly hall of old. Along the foreign avenue everything stood revealed in its best; and the vista along the whole line was perhaps the most splendid and extensive, as a piece of art and human contrivance, ever presented to human view.

"As eleven o'clock approached, the hour at which the admittance of the public terminated, the inward tide became very heavy, and some little struggling at one moment was given way to, but only for a moment. The immense mass of spectators were settled down into their places, the ladies having seats in front, the gentlemen standing behind them, along the principal avenues, and in the galleries.

"The Duke of Wellington was early in attendance, arriving, with the Marchioness of Douro, about ten o'clock; and the knowledge that it was his grace's birthday, perhaps contributed to increase in volume and warmth the hearty cheering with which he was greeted as he passed to his place near the central area. Shortly afterwards, the members of the *corps diplomatique* and the foreign commissioners began to drop in, and after them the members of the Cabinet, a faint cheer being attempted for Lord John Russell, and another for Lord Palmerston; the latter, with true statesmanlike policy, thinking to ensure the harmony of his reception amongst the industrial representatives of the world, by walking up the transept under the portly wing of Lablache, who looked as good-humoured as ever. Nearly the latest of the arrivals at the north entrance were the Lord Mayor and Aldermen, with various civic authorities, all decked forth in their robes of office.

"By this time the honourable corps of Gentlemen-at-Arms, in their gay uniforms, had taken up their stations at the rear of the daïs, whilst the time-honoured body of Beefeaters were ranged along the outer line of procession. The trumpeters and heralds stood ready to proclaim the arrival of the Queen of these isles, and the heralds to marshal the order of her coming. Meantime, Sir George Smart stood, *baton* in hand, perched up in a small rostrum, in front of the north transept organ gallery, ready to beat time to 'God save the Queen,' for the five-hundredth time in his life. Meantime the Lord Chamberlain and his subordinate officers glided about, looking very well satisfied with all their arrangements, and Mr. Commissioner Mayne was here, there, and everywhere, smiling so good-humouredly as for the moment to rob even police law of its terrors. Everybody was on the tip-toe of expectation for the arrival of the royal personages who were to grace the day with their attendance.

" At half-past eleven the Duke of Cambridge arrived at the north door, but did not enter the area, awaiting the arrival of the duchess of Kent, who, accompanied by the Princess Mary of Cambridge, followed shortly after him. Their royal highnesses now entered the retiring room, which had been prepared for her Majesty's reception, an elegant little apartment, covered with tapestry, and lined with silk, pale blue and white, fluted, with a crown overhead in the centre. The Commissioners and foreign ministers now made their way down to the entrance hall, ready to pay their respects to her Majesty on her arrival. Exactly at ten minutes to twelve, the Queen and her Royal Consort, accompanied by the Prince of Wales and the Princess Royal, alighted from their carriage; and after repairing to the retiring-room, proceeded to enter the magnificent edifice, of the production of which his royal highness had been the chief promoter. The Queen wore a dress of pink satin, brocaded in gold; Prince Albert, a field-marshal's uniform; the Prince of Wales, a highland dress; and the Princess Royal, a white lace dress, with a wreath of flowers round her head. The royal party, especially the young Prince and Princess, appeared much struck and delighted with the stately grandeur of the scene which burst upon their view. A tremendous burst of cheering, renewed and prolonged from all parts of the building, greeted the announcement of the near approach of the Queen."

And, unquestionably, neither Eastern fairy tale, nor Arabian Night's wonder, could surpass, or even emulate the gorgeous reality that greeted the delighted gaze of the assembled spectators, as the royal party and brilliant *cortége* advanced through the bronzed and gilded gates that led into this hall of enchantment; fragrant exotics bloomed and shed their soft perfume around, crystal fountains threw up their sparkling waters, the choicest statuary formed graceful avenues of approach, while the clarion and shrill trumpet " brayed forth" " the triumph" of the hour. And when the Queen was seated in her lofty chair of state, surrounded by " the pride of all the land," nobles, dignitaries of the church, heroes, and statesmen, and attended by the representatives of " principalities and powers" from every quarter of the globe, the national anthem, from " the full-voiced choir," swelled upon the ear, and accompanied by " the pealing organ," floated in harmonious accord beneath the high vaulted and unrivalled dome.

After a speech from Prince Albert, as the head of the Commission, addressed to the Queen, explaining the nature and purposes of the Exhibition, and stating that it was the heartfelt prayer of the Commissioners that the undertaking, which had for its end the promotion of all branches of human industry, and the strengthening of the bonds of peace and friendship among all the nations of the earth, might, by the blessing of Divine Providence, conduce to the welfare of her Majesty's people, and be long remembered among the brightest circumstances of her Majesty's peaceful and happy reign;—and after the gracious reply from her Majesty, stating her entire satisfaction, and her increasing interest in their proceedings, together with her cordial sympathy in the good wishes they expressed, the Archbishop of Canterbury read the following prayer, or benediction :—

" Almighty and everlasting God, governor of all things, without whom nothing is strong, nothing holy, accept, we beseech Thee, the sacrifice of our praise and thanksgiving, receive our prayers which we offer up to Thee this day, in behalf of this kingdom and land. We acknowledge, O Lord, that Thou hast multiplied the blessings which Thou mightest most justly have withheld; we acknowledge that it is not because of the works of righteousness which we have done, but of Thy great mercy, that we are permitted to come before Thee this day with the voice of thanksgiving. Instead of humbling us for our offences, Thou hast given us just cause to praise Thee for Thine abundant goodness. And now, O Lord, we beseech Thee to bless the work which Thou hast enabled us to begin, and to regard with Thy favour our present purpose of uniting together in the bond of peace and concord the different nations of the earth; for of Thee, O Lord, and not of the preparation of man, it cometh that violence is not heard in our land, nor contentions nor violence within our borders. It is of Thee, O Lord, that nation does not lift up sword against nation, nor learn war any more. It is of Thee that peace is within our walls, plenteousness within our palaces, and men go forth in safety, and that knowledge is increased throughout the world. Therefore, O Lord, not unto us, but unto Thy name, be all praise. Whilst we survey the works of art and industry which surround us, let not our hearts be lifted up that we forget the Lord our God, or that it is not of our own power, or of the might of our hands, that we have gotten in this wealth. Teach us to remember that this store which we have prepared is all Thine own; in Thine hands it is to make great and give strength and honour. We thank Thee, we praise Thee, we entreat Thee to overrule this assembly of many nations, that it may tend to the advancement of Thy glory, to the increase of our prosperity, and to the promotion of peace and good-will among the different races of mankind. Let the many mercies we have received dispose our hearts to serve Thee more and more, who art the author and giver of all good things. Teach us to use those earthly blessings that Thou hast given us so richly to enjoy, that they may not withdraw our affections from those heavenly things which Thou hast prepared for them that love Thee, through the merits and mediation of Thy son Jesus Christ, to whom, with Thee and the Holy Ghost, be all honour and glory, world without end. Amen."

At the conclusion of this prayer, Handel's magnificent Hallelujah Chorus thundered its powerful harmonies to the gratified ear, and completed the solemn and religious character of the ceremony, which, to those who were gratified in witnessing it, will not readily be effaced from their memory.

The Royal procession was then formed in the following order :—

Heralds.

Architect, Joseph Paxton, Esq.   Contractor, Mr. Fox.

Superintendents of the Works—C. H. Wild, Esq.; Owen Jones, Esq.

Financial Officer, F. H. Carpenter, Esq.

Members of the Building Committee—I. K. Brunel, Esq.; Charles Cockerell, Esq.; Professor Donaldson.

Members of the Finance Committee—Samuel Peto, Esq.; Sir Alexander Spearman, Bart.

Treasurers—Baron Lionel de Rothschild, William Cotton, Esq.; Sir John William Lubbock, Bart.; Arthur Kett Barclay, Esq.

Secretary to the Executive Committee, Mathew Digby Wyatt, Esq.

Executive Committee—George Drew, Esq.; Francis Fuller, Esq.; Charles Wentworth Dilke, jun., Esq.; Henry Cole, Esq.; Lieut.-Colonel William Read, Royal Engineers, C.B.

FOREIGN ACTING COMMISSIONERS.

Austria—M. C. Buschek, Chevalier de Burg.	Holland—M. Goothens, M. J. P. Dudok van Hal.	Sweden and Norway — M. Charles Tottie.
Bavaria—Professor Dr. Schafhault, M Theobald Boehm, M. Haindl.	Northern Germany—M. Noback.	Switzerland--Dr. Bolley, M. Eichholzer.
Belgium—M. Charles Caylits, M. de Broucken.	Portugal—M. F. J. Vanzeller, M. Antonio Valdez.	Tunis—Signor Hamda Elmkaddem, M. Santillana (interpreter and secretary).
Denmark—Regnar Westenholtz.	Prussia—Baron Hebeler.	
France—M. Sallandrouze de Lamornaix.	Rome—Signor Carlo Trebbi.	Turkey—M. Edward Zohrab.
	Russia—M. Gabriel Kamensky.	Tuscany—Dr. Corridi.
Grand Duchy of Hesse — M. Rossler	Sardinia—Chevalier Lencisa.	United States—Mr. Edward Riddle, Mr. N. S. Dodge (secretary).
	Saxony—Dr. Seyffarth, L.L.D.; M. Gustavus Dorstling.	
Greece—M. Ralli.	Spain—M. Man. de Ysasi, M. Ram. de la Sagra, M. Ram. de Echivarria.	Wurtemburg—Mr. C. Brand.
Hanse Towns—M. Piglheim.		Zollverein—M. Banrath Stein.

Secretaries to the Royal Commission—Edgar A. Bowring, Esq.; Sir Stafford H. Northcote, Bart.; J. Scott Russell, Esq.

Special Commissioners--Dr. Lyon Playfair; Lieut.-Colonel Lloyd.

HER MAJESTY'S COMMISSIONERS.

Mr. Alderman Thompson.	John Shepherd, Esq.	Sir Charles Lyell.	Sir. C. L. Eastlake.
R. Stephenson, Esq	Philip Pusey, Esq.	Sir R. Westmacott.	Rt. Hon W. E. Gladstone.
Wm. Hopkins, Esq.	John Gott, Esq.	Rt. Hon. H. Labouchere.	Lord John Russell.
T. F. Gibson, Esq.	Wm. Cubitt, Esq.	Lord Overstone.	Lord Stanley.
Richard Cobden, Esq.	Thomas Bazley, Esq.	Earl Granville.	Earl of Ellesmere.
Charles Barry, Esq.	Thomas Baring, Esq.	Earl of Rosse.	Duke of Buccleuch.

Her Majesty's Master of the Ceremonies.

Foreign Ambassadors and Ministers.

F. M. the Duke of Wellington, K.G., Commander-in-Chief.   F. M. the Marquis of Anglesey, K.G., Master-General of the Ordnance.

Her Majesty's Ministers.

His Grace the Archbishop of Canterbury.

White Wands : viz., Comptroller of the Household.
Treasurer of the Household.
Vice Chamberlain.
Lord Steward.   Lord Chamberlain.
Garter Principal King of Arms.
His Royal Highness Prince Albert, leading Her Royal Highness the
Princess Royal.
The Queen, leading his Royal Highness the Prince of Wales.
His Royal Highness the Prince of Prussia.
Her Royal Highness the Duchess of Kent.
His Royal Highness Prince Henry of the Netherlands.
Her Royal Highness the Princess of Prussia.
His Royal Highness Prince Frederick William of Prussia
Her Royal Highness Princess Mary of Cambridge.
His Serene Highness Prince Edward of Saxe-Weimar.
His Royal Highness the Duke of Cambridge.
Mistress of the Robes.
Lady of the Bedchamber, Marchioness of Douro.
Lady of the Bedchamber in Waiting.
Maid of Honour in Waiting.   Maid of Honour in Waiting.
Bedchamber Woman in Waiting.   Lady Superintendent—Lady Caroline Barrington.
Foreign Ladies, and Lady in attendance on H. R. H. the Duchess of Kent.
Gold Stick in Waiting.   Master of the Horse.
Groom of the Stole to H. R. H. Prince Albert.
Captain of the Yeomen of the Guard.   Captain of the Gentlemen-at-Arms.
Master of the Buckhounds.
Lord of the Bedchamber to H.R.H. Prince Albert in Waiting.   Lord in Waiting to the Queen.
Groom of the Bedchamber to H.R.H. Prince Albert in Waiting.   Groom in Waiting to the Queen.
Clerk Marshal.
Equerry to H.R.H. Prince Albert in Waiting.   Equerry to the Queen in Waiting.
Gentleman Usher.   Gentleman Usher to the Sword of State.   Gentleman Usher.
Silver Stick in Waiting.   Field Officer in Brigade Waiting.
The Gentlemen in attendance upon their Royal Highnesses the Duchess of Kent, the Duke of Cambridge, and
the Prince and Princess of Prussia
Heralds, &c.

Our journalist continues as follows :—

" The royal procession went up to the west end of the nave by its north side, returning to the east end of the nave by its south side, including the south end of the transept; and coming back to the centre along the north side of the nave, all present were thus excellently well enabled to see her Majesty and the procession.

" During the procession, and at the Queen's approach, the organs in the British division, built by Messrs. Willis, Walker, and Hill, of London, and those by foreign importers, Du Croquet (Paris) and Schulze (Erfurt), were successively played.

" On her Majesty's return to the platform, the Queen declared 'the Exhibition opened!' which was announced to the public by a flourish of trumpets and the firing of a royal salute on the north of the Serpentine. The barriers, which had kept the nave clear, were then thrown open, and the public were allowed to circulate, which they by no means appeared disposed to do, as they were all crowding towards the glories of the transept.

" Her Majesty then returned to Buckingham Palace by the route by which she came, and all the doors, which had been closed at half-past eleven o'clock, were again opened.

" Throughout the whole of the Queen's traverse of the building, her face was wreathed with smiles and pleasant looks, and her Majesty evidently took a more than common interest in the brilliant spectacle which everywhere attracted her notice. The Queen wore a rich embroidered pink satin dress set with precious stones, and a tiara of diamonds on her head. Prince Albert wore a field-marshal's uniform.

" The Duke of Wellington and Marquis of Anglesea attracted much attention, the duke supporting himself on his more aged companion, while both seemed highly gratified in their tour of inspection. We must also remember the droll Chinese mandarin amongst the foreign ambassadors and ministers, who swayed along from side to side, those before and those behind him, leaving a pretty full berth for his comical progress.

" Let our last words respecting this truly national festival be commendatory to those who originated and perfected it. No event—not even the coronation of our monarch—had ever more strongly called forth public expectation; and none, we will at the same time affirm, has ever more completely fulfilled it.

" The ceremonial was one, it may be said, without precedent or rival. The homage paid by the sovereign of the widest empire in the world to the industry and genius of both hemispheres, will not fill a page in history as a mean and unsubstantial pageant. While the race of man exists, this solemn and magnificent occasion will not readily fade away from his memory like the baseless fabric of a vision;'

it commences an era in which the sons of toil shall receive honour and reward; and, in accordance with the spirit of the day, it stimulates the energies of man to conquer 'fresh domains,' and discover new faculties of nature and her products, for the well-being and use of his fellow-creatures.

" Of itself, as a passing display of state, pomp, and power, we cannot speak too highly; for even Oriental gorgeousness fades in comparison with the glories of the unequalled temple which enshrines the Exhibition of all Nations in Hyde Park."

CHAPTER V.

PREPARATORY ARRANGEMENT—REFRESHMENT ROOMS—" MONSTER" LODGING HOUSE—PRICES OF ADMISSION—THE FOUR GRAND SECTIONS.

HAVING accompanied our readers through all the pageantry we have described in the preceding chapter, and conducted them safely through the toils and glories of the day, we shall now take a more leisurely survey of the wondrous structure, and proceed to examine into the various accommodations and arrangements that were made, as well for its numerous visitors, as for the reception of the treasures of industry, art, manufacture, and native produce, that were destined to flow into its mighty reservoirs from every portion of the habitable globe.

As all the world received cards of invitation to " assist," as the fashionable phrase is, in the grand parties that diurnally were expected to assemble within the ample area of the Crystal Palace, and as every facility was afforded, even for the humblest classes, to travel up and down from all parts of the empire, to gratify their longings to participate in the view of the " World's Wonder," it became a point of necessity that sufficient accommodation should be prepared within its hospitable walls for rest and refreshment for all, and more particularly for those who had travelled far from their homes, and whose limited time, as well as means, would not permit them to wander backwards and forwards in search of such necessary " creature comforts" as are indispensable for the support of our natural bodies, even when we are engaged in the delightful toil of making a business of our pleasure. " Ample space, and verge enough," were therefore granted for extending, at a very moderate remuneration, the rites of hospitality towards those who either through necessity or choice, were inclined to participate in them. Moderation, however, was the motto that was adopted; for the commissioners very properly thought that it would be inconsistent with the nature of the Exhibition, to allow the building to assume the character of an hotel, tavern, or dining-room. Wine, spirits, beer, or intoxicating drinks, were expressly forbidden; but then tea, coffee, chocolate, cocoa, lemonade, ices, ginger-beer, seltzer and soda-water, were allowed to circulate in abundance; and in more solid requirements, cold meats, sandwiches, patties, pastry, fruits, with humbler bread and cheese, were liberally provided.

That these " dainties" were not expected to be unacceptable to the thirsty throats and keen appetites of the multitude, is evident from the tenders made for their supply. For the privilege of vending refreshments, together with soda-water, *et hoc genus* of potables, Messrs. Schweppe and Co. paid the sum of £5,500! Upwards of 2,000 dinners were daily calculated upon in the various spacious areas destined for the hungry guests, whose fare, however, was limited to cold meat and steamed potatoes, as cooking was strictly prohibited in every part of the building. These areas were three in number: the central, the eastern, and the western; the space occupied by the first of these divisions, including all the passages, lobbies, &c., was not less than 17,756 square feet. The eastern refreshment court contained 19,008 square feet, and the western 12,096 square feet. And yet, so small was the actual extent of these capacious halls, in comparison with the vast proportions of the whole edifice, that many parties frequently wandered about, "with fainting steps and slow," a considerable time before they could find, among the intricacies of the building, these festive courts, and often required the friendly aid of some kind policeman to guide their erring steps.

Although the influx of visitors from all parts of the kingdom was expected to be enormous, and preparations were made accordingly, still the reality, contrary to usual experience in such cases, far outstripped the ideas of the most sanguine calculators. The millions that thronged to the banks of "Old Father Thames" were unheard of, undreamed of. Had the result been really made known beforehand, how would the danger of congregating so vast an assemblage in a metropolis like ours been predicted and commented on! As it was, many an old lady and timorous gentleman anticipated nothing but riot and disorder; some spoke of famine, others of chartism, and perils of that kind; but, to the wonder and almost consternation of all such evil-foreboders, the utmost tranquillity and harmony prevailed. Even the great Iron Duke, who snuffed mischief in the breeze, and talked of cannons and gunpowder, and encampments in the park, was compelled to admit, with astonishment, and we are disposed to believe with pleasure also, that all the parade and display of "gun, blunderbuss, and thunder," would be very much out of place. A more peaceful "gathering" never mustered its forces beneath the broad light of the sun. Amity and brotherly love actuated not only those of a kindred tongue, but appeared to unite all nations—

> ———— Embassies from regions far remote,
> In various habits; some from farthest south,
> Syene, and where the shadow both way falls,
> Meroe, Nilotic isle; and, more to west,
> The realm of Bocchus to the Black-moor sea;
> *   *   *   *   *   *
> From India and the golden Chersonese,
> And utmost Indian isle, Taprobane,
> Dusk faces with white silken turbans wreathed;
> From Gallia, Gades, and the British west;
> Germans and Scythians, and Sarmatians, north
> Beyond Danubius to the Tauric pool,
> All nations   *   *   *

And London, whose "great revenge had stomach for them all," received into her cordial embrace all these kindreds and people, and would have done so, had even twice the number demanded her hospitality; aye, and given food and shelter to them all. The Commissioners were therefore wise in leaving the accommodation of the strangers to the care of the town itself, and innumerable were the various residences that opened their doors to those that sought a temporary abode. All found a fitting *gite*, from the luxurious noble to the humble peasant, the hardworking mechanic, whose scanty purse rarely sufficed to maintain its owner beyond a single night in his "unaccustomed lair."

Among other accommodations that were provided, through the speculation of spirited individuals, we may notice a "monster" establishment for the reception of the working-classes, projected and registered by Mr. Thomas Harrison, of Ranelagh Road, Pimlico, which was really so gigantic that we cannot forbear presenting a description of it to our readers, were it only to show the promptitude, and the effectual manner, in which the necessities of the public can be provided for in our wealthy and flourishing land.

The building we are about to describe, was in the immediate vicinity of Mr. Cubitt's Pimlico Pier, to which steam-boats arrive from the city every ten minutes. It occupied a space of two acres, was bounded by roads on three sides, was airy, and well ventilated.

It contained two sleeping-rooms, comprising an area of 25,000 feet, and two other dormitories of half the size. These four rooms were calculated to accommodate 1,000 persons per night. Every lodger had his own bed-room, separated from the others by a partition seven feet high, ensuring perfect privacy to the occupant. Efficient warders were appointed to watch over the dormitories, which were well lighted with gas during the night. These rooms were open at the top, for the purpose of ventilation. In each room was a good bed, and the lodgers kept the keys of their own dormitories. Each of these rooms was five feet wide, and six and-a-half long. The dining-room, the reading-room, and the smoking-room, had each an area of 2,000 feet. The news-room was well supplied with newspapers, magazines, and all works relating to the Exhibition, and other sights of London, free of charge. A band of music enlivened the reveries of the smokers in their cloudy apartment. On the summit of the edifice was a lantern 1,500 feet square, from which visitors were enabled to enjoy an excellent view of the moving panorama of the river and the adjacent country. Hot rolls were baked upon the premises, and a good breakfast provided for 4d., and a dinner for 8d. The price of the lodging, with all the agrèmens and advantages, was 1s. 3d. per night, which also included soap, towels, and every convenience for ablution. "Boots" performed his duty for a penny each, and a barber looked after the heads and chins of the guests. A surgeon was also in daily attendance at nine o'clock. A penny omnibus was attached to the service of the institution, and every precaution was taken to ensure the comfort and welfare of every one, even to providing for the care of such as, in the joyousness of their hearts, and their unaccustomed liberty, should have indulged a little too far in their libations to the "jolly god."

All were abundantly gratified, from the Queen herself, the mistress of the revels, to the meanest of her subjects who participated in them—revels, not of the senses merely, although great was the delight inspired by so many objects of beauty and of art, but of the understanding also, in the contemplation and admiration of the progress and advancement of human knowledge and human industry.

The charge for admission to the World's Grand Show, was not arranged without a good deal of discussion. It was proposed by Mr. Paxton, to "throw open the doors of the world's Exhibition to the world's citizens," but this visionary scheme was overruled, and the Commissioners finally determined that the charges for admission should be as follows:—

Season Ticket for a Gentleman . . .	£3 3	0
Season Ticket for a Lady	2 2	0

These tickets were not to be transferable, but were to entitle the owner to admission whenever the Exhibition should be open to the public.

The Commissioners reserved to themselves the power of raising the price of the season tickets when the first issue should be exhausted, should it be deemed advisable.

On the first day of Exhibition, it was determined that season tickets *only* should be available, and no money received at the doors that day.

On the second and third days the admission price would be, each day . .	£1	0	0
On the fourth day of Exhibition	0	5	0
To be reduced on the twenty-second day to	0	1	0
On Mondays, Tuesdays, Wednesdays, and Thursdays, in each week . .	0	1	0
On Fridays	0	2	6
On Saturdays	0	5	0

To avoid confusion and delay, no change was to be given at the doors.

It was suggested by Prince Albert, in his first conference with the original projectors of the Exhibition, that there should be four grand compartments, which, as far as possible, should be devoted to the reception of the following specimens. In the first, all raw materials; in the second, machinery and mechanical inventions; in the third, manufactures; and in the fourth, sculpture and plastic art.

With respect to the productions of Great Britain, this arrangement was strictly carried out. Various reasons rendered it advisable to allow each foreign nation to fill up its own space in its own manner. A strong argument in favour of this deviation from the original plan was found in the circumstance that without such concession the arrangement of the Exhibition would be indefinitely delayed until the last package from the most distant country had arrived.

Nothing could more clearly prove how well his royal highness had studied the problem he had undertaken to demonstrate than his suggested arrangement of raw material, mineral, vegetable, and animal, upon which the skill and industry of man is exerted to grow and manufacture; machinery, by which, from raw material, the greatest results may be obtained, at the smallest cost of time and toil; manufactured articles, in which the result of man's industry, applied to the gifts of a gracious Providence, may be seen and compared; sculpture and plastic art, from which the manufacturer and the consumer may alike learn to value that perfection which can only be attained by the union of beauty and proportion with useful manufacture.

Under one or other of these heads, an illustration of every material aid to the commerce, the agriculture, the manufactures, the sustenance, and the education of civilized communities, will be found. No matter to what country, or pursuit a visitor may belong —peasant or peer, duchess or dairymaid—soldier, sailor, or man of science—miner or miller, farmer or engineer—under some one or other of the subdivisions of this classification we will undertake to find something which shall interest, amuse, instruct, and profit him.

Each of these four principal compartments was divided into as many parts as were necessary for particular classification. The first, which included "raw materials," contained all ores, and non-metallic mineral products, and also what related to mining and quarrying operations, as well as geological maps, &c. The second had relation to all chemical and pharmaceutical products, and processes generally. The third, all substances used as food, both vegetable and animal; and the fourth had reference to all vegetable or animal substances, used in manufactures, or as implements or ornaments.

The second grand compartment "machinery," was also variously subdivided into classes; the first containing machines for direct use, such as steam-engines, water and windmills, and various other prime movers, together with railway carriages, objects of naval mechanism—and all carriages, public or private, carts, waggons, &c.; the second, for manufacturing machines and tools, as well as the manufactured articles themselves. A third was dedicated to civil engineering and building contrivances; designs and models of bridges, tunnels, docks, harbours, lighthouses, and beacons; plans of waterworks, gas-works, sewerage, ventilation, &c., &c. A fourth comprised all relating to naval achitecture, and military engineering; ordnance, armour, and accoutrements. A fifth had relation to the more peaceful labours of the husbandman, and displayed every variety of agricultural and horticultural machines and implements. A sixth led the philosophical inquirer to the contemplation of all instruments connected with science, as well as to every variety of musical, horological, and surgical instruments, adapted for the relief or cure of every malady of form or structure which " flesh is heir to."

Then came the compartment "manufactures," which also had its numerous subdivisions, for articles fabricated from cotton, silk, woollen, flax, hemp, from the mere simple thread, to the most elaborate dimities, cloths, gauzes, ribbons, fancy silks, velvets cambrics, down to rough cordage, &c. &c.

I

" There is nothing like leather," was the motto of the fabricator of this article, as he exhibited the skill with which he had contrived to render his "raw material" subservient to the gilded chariot of the monarch, and the war-horse of the knight, in rich trappings and embossed furniture, at the same time that he descended to the manufacture of the "clouted shoon" of the laborious peasant. In the same department with this worthy, were to be found the dresser of skins, the furrier, the feather-maker, and the hair-worker, who severally supplied their various stores for use or ornament.

The paper manufacturer was not behind-hand in his contributions to this compartment, and had his appropriate division wherein to arrange the manifold proofs of his industry, ingenuity, and skill, from the material in its raw state as it leaves the mill, to all articles of stationary, specimens of *cartonnerie*, and the perfection of bookbinding.

The tapestry weaver also, and the embroiderer, claimed their allotted space, and rich was the display of elaborate hangings, variegated carpets, elegant fringes, and rare needlework; while the unrivalled lace, and the unparalleled tamboured muslins, elicited unbounded admiration from the numerous groups of the fair sex, who thronged in delighted amazement in the sphere of such irresistible attractions. They who dealt in clothing, too, from the renowned Moses to the gentle man-milliner, also made their inviting appeal to the lounging dandy and the fashionable belle, in every variety of tempting display fitted to distinguish and adorn.

All these, however, were cast into the shade by the splendours of the gold and silversmiths, and the jewellers, whose department glittered like the sun with all "the wealth of Ormus and of Ind," and would have been unrivalled, had not the glass-manufacturer dazzled all eyes by the superior brilliancy of his workmanship. He could boast, too, of the large share he had had in the construction of the Crystal Palace itself, to say nothing of the superb fountain that formed the chief ornament of the transept, and served as a trysting place "to many a youth and many a maid" who had wandered up from the country to enjoy a sight of the "World's Wonder," as well as a point of general rendezvous for those who were desirous to meet their friends at "the appointed hour." Moreover, in point of glitter, as far as that quality is valuable, the superb candelabras he exhibited outshone the far-famed diamond of Runjeet Singh, the Koh-i-Noor, and all the sparkling treasures that

> " ——— The gorgeous east, with richest hand
> Showers on her kings barbaric."

The porcelain division, in which the upholsterer, the house-decorator, and the japanner, also exhibited their wares, was well worthy of attention; as was that wherein the worker in wood, in straw, and in grass, together with the artificial flower-maker, and similar operatives, deposited the proofs of their industry and skill. The marble-cutter, and the manufacturer of artificial stones, had likewise their allotted space; while, in the last division of this most comprehensive compartment, were amassed all the endless "contrivances," from caoutchouc and gutta percha, together with infinite examples of the utility of ivory, tortoiseshell, bone, horn, &c. &c.; to say nothing of umbrellas, parasols, walking-sticks, fishing-tackle that would have enraptured "Old Izaac;" and, in short, every possible invention, "*et quibusdam aliis*," for the use and convenience of civilized man.

The last, but by no means the least interesting, of the four grand compartments was devoted to "Sculpture, Models, and Plastic Art." A large proportion of the sculpture, however, was judiciously disposed in prominent positions throughout the naves and transepts of the building, and greatly conduced to the beauty and general effect of the whole. We shall not at present enter upon a description of the objects comprised under the

HIS ROYAL HIGHNESS PRINCE ALBERT.

HER MOST GRACIOUS MAJESTY THE QUEEN.

Engraved by G.Greatbach, from a Drawing by H Mason.

IVORY THRONE

EXHIBITED BY HER MAJESTY

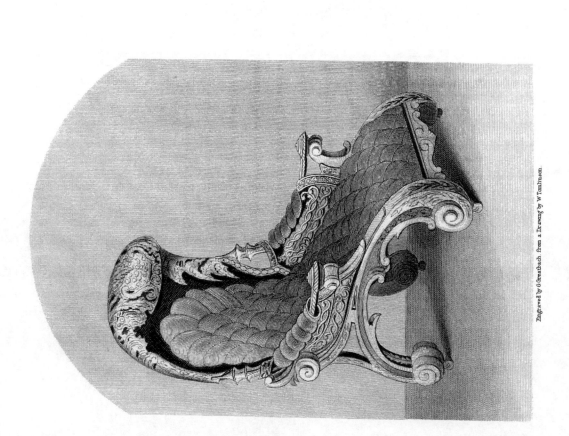

Engraved by G.Greatbach, from a Drawing by W.Tomkinson.

ORIENTAL CHAIR

MANUFACTURED BY JENNENS & BETTRIDGE

above head; the subject would be too comprehensive for immediate consideration. We shall, however, from time to time, as we conduct our readers through the intricate mazes before us, select and criticise what we may deem most worthy of notice. Many of the choicest specimens of artistic excellence, the "gems" of the Exhibition, will also be presented to them through the medium of the daguerreotyper and engraver, the excellence and fidelity of whose combined exertions have already enabled us to present to our subscribers, in our first number, besides the general view of the Exterior of the Crystal Palace, the Equestrian Statues of the Queen and Prince Albert, and the "Happy and Unhappy Child," which we trust will be found to unite the utmost delicacy of execution with the most perfect fidelity of resemblance.

CHAPTER VI.

COLONIAL DEPARTMENTS—INDIA.

As the arrangements we have described in the foregoing chapter have solely reference to the British department, as connected with our own islands, we shall now proceed to offer a few details with respect to our colonial possessions, at the head of which "India" indisputably stands pre-eminent. The riches of the East have long been proverbial, and the contributions that were forwarded from our Indian possessions were well worthy of their renown in that respect. A large proportion was sent in by "the Company," some were exhibited by her Majesty, and not a few were tributes offered on the occasion by native princes and other *magnates* of the East. They comprised natural products, native manufactures for domestic use, models, and a wondrous display of the richest articles of jewellery and luxury.

A magnificent chair, or rather "throne of royal state," of carved ivory, elaborately and exquisitely finished, the back and seat covered with green velvet, richly embroidered with gold, was one of the chief objects of attraction among the treasures of this unrivalled department. It was sent as a present from the Rajah of Travancore, and at the closing of the Exhibition, was used by Prince Albert as President of the Royal Commission. The next article of interest that awakened the curiosity of the spectator was contained in a glass case, enclosed within an iron railing, and attracted general attention, from the extraordinary richness and brilliancy of some large undefined object placed at the top, which, on examination, proved to be the gorgeous coat of a Sikh chief, presenting to the astonished gaze, a mass of gold embroidery covered with pearls, and loaded with the finest rubies and emeralds. Each epaulette alone, attached to this most extraordinary garment, was valued at £5,000; other portions of military attire and trappings were laid about in rich confusion. All this lavishing of wealth upon mere articles of dress, upon that of a soldier too, strikes us as a notable instance of "wasteful and ridiculous excess." What a prize the wearer of it would have been to the fortunate wight that should be lucky enough to capture him, with the ransom of a kingdom on his back! Our Queen's state drawing-room, with all its bevy of courtly dames and lords in waiting, might have been be-jewelled and bedizened from the spoils of this single coat. What a proof of a barbarous state of society is this taste for inordinate decoration; and after all, the humming-bird, or the golden beetle, is more splendidly attired than was this doughty hero; and in point of glitter and show, a tinselled harlequin in a pantomime outshines him. Pope tells us of the vanity of the nobleman of his time, who because his dress-coat did not satisfy him—

———-" His taylor turned away
Who stitched a star that scarcely threw a ray."

But what was his ambition to be fine, compared to that of this egregious Sikh? After all, there is but a poor satisfaction to the mind, that is gifted with a ray of intelligence, in the contemplation of these glittering toys, and more especially so, when they are too bulky or too precious for use. Witness the great Koh-i-Noor, imprisoned like a robber in his own iron cage; the tribute of admiration bestowed upon which was not equal to that elicited by the most trivial piece of machinery, that was applicable to the use or service of man. We shall however continue our description of these priceless treasures, in a brief notice of the most prominent objects, among the most conspicuous of which were a pair of "moorchals," or emblems of dignity, used only by a few of the Indian potentates, when in the presence of the Governor-general. These emblems consisted of hollow cases, of about two and-a-half feet in length, and about six inches in diameter at the upper end, tapering down to a handle of two inches in diameter. The whole was formed of pieces of pure gold, most curiously fastened together by gold thread, and were intended for the reception of the feathers of the beautiful birds of paradise. Of the beauty of the *tout ensemble*, which this specimen of Eastern magnificence presented, it would be difficult to convey any adequate idea.

A princely girdle of gold, studded with nineteen emeralds, each an inch and-a-half square, and bordered with diamonds, next attracted our view, surpassed, however, by a pair of armlets, decorated with three enormous rubies, in comparison with which, the largest in the most celebrated jeweller's possession, would shrink into insignificance. Then we gazed on the famous Lahore diamond, the "Durria-i-Noor," or sea of light; then on the splendid necklace containing two hundred and forty Oriental pearls. But we should never have done, were we to describe the number and variety of these valuable "gawds"—vases, cups, bowls, jewel boxes, and brilliants of every sort and description were displayed on every side, till the wearied spectator was ready to exclaim "*jam satis!*" and to turn his attention to objects less costly, but more satisfying to the intellect.

Leaving therefore these jewels to repose in their own caskets, within their strictly guarded prison bars, we will make mention of specimens of Indian magnificence, in the shape of thrones, canopies, howdahs, trappings for elephants on state occasions, all which travelled across the desert, bound on their pilgrimage to the "world's fair," and were chiefly presented to her Majesty by the renowned Nawab Nizam of Bengal, a short account of whom, as a magnificent contributor, may not be unacceptable to our readers, and which, in the language of a contemporary writer, we here present for their edification.

" The present Nawab's ancestors ruled for several centuries as independent sovereigns over the districts of Bengal, Behar, and Orissa, and their residence—at least for a considerable time previous to the British conquest of India—was the city of Moorshedabad, which is situated on the banks of the Hooghly, about 150 miles north of Calcutta. It occupies a perfectly level site, and is destitute of fortifications. Its streets are narrow, irregular, and dirty, and the houses, for the most part, are only one storey high, and of mean appearance. Of these the majority are built of earth mixed with chopped straw, and thatched with dried grass, and are called *kutcha*; others are constructed of mud and bricks—a kind of masonry which is styled *pukka kutcha*—while some, called *pukka*, are built entirely of brick. The city contains many curious old mosques, but the only public edifices of any magnitude and architectural beauty, are the Emaumhara, or House of God—to the construction of which the British government contributed £15,000—and

Engraved by Crickmore from a Drawing by Mason.

CHESSMEN IN IVORY,

BY STAIGHT OF WALBROOK.

Engraved by Crickmore from a Drawing by Mason

MODEL OF AN INDIAN STATE BARGE,

EXHIBITED BY THE HON.BLE EAST INDIA COMPANY.

the new palace built for the late Nawab. The latter is a spacious edifice in the Doric style, and was erected from the plans and under the superintendence of General Duncan Macleod, at the cost of £66,000. There is a large model of it in Hampton Court Palace, which occupies a pretty large room. The population may be estimated at about 150,000, the bulk of whom are employed in the cultivation of rice and indigo, and the various processes of silk manufacture. Of the numerous factories and filatures, those of Messrs. Lyall and Messrs. Watson are the most extensive, many thousands being daily employed by those houses in spinning and hand-loom weaving. Moorshedabad is also an important mart for cotton, and many of its native merchants have acquired great wealth.

The late Nawab, who died in 1837 or 1838, was the last person on whom the Guelphic order of knighthood was conferred. His successor, the present Nawab, attained his majority four or five years ago, and is now about twenty-three. He has a son by each of his three wives, with whom he lives in his harem, about a quarter of a mile from the new palace, which is only used on *durbar*, or levee days. Of these there are six or eight yearly. On such occasions he is generally borne by eight men in a palkee, or howdah, with poles, like that presented to her Majesty, and is escorted by the principal officers of his household on foot, while he is followed by a numerous train, mounted on elephants, camels, and horses, all gorgeously caparisoned. Those who have seen the rich elephant-trappings at the Exhibition, will be enabled to form some idea of the magnificent spectacle presented by fifty elephants in full state equipment, followed by about a score of camels, and a similar number of horses, with housings of corresponding splendour. The sumptuous canopied couch in which his highness reclines on reception-days, was accurately represented by that at the Exhibition, of which we have already given a detailed description. The natives who attend the *durbar* leave their shoes at the entrance of the reception-hall, and, with head covered, according to the Eastern custom, advance with a series of salaams to his highness, who is surrounded by his attendants and guards, and on whose left, the place of honour in the East, sits the agent for the governor-general. They then present him with a mohur—a gold coin £1 12s. in value—and if the person offering it enjoys his favour he accepts the coin, and pours a few drops of attar of roses on his handkerchief. After this ceremony it is the custom to retire backwards with a repetition of the salaams. Besides the respect and affection with which the present Nizam is regarded on account of his personal qualities, he is also held in great consideration as the head of the sect of Sheahs, who are much looked up to in Lower Bengal.

We will now take a survey of another court or division appropriated to our East Indian Colony; and here again were divers articles of state and luxury—superb couches, royal bedsteads with richly-embroidered curtains; marble slabs and carved furniture, in wood and ivory; together with a vast variety of ornaments; fruit and flowers in wax; carved boxes and ornaments in sandal-wood from Mangalore; embossed paper and illuminated writings, sent by the King of Oude; together with a large assortment of manufactured articles illustrative of the wonderfully-exact and patient industry of Hindoo workmanship. The most striking feature, however, in this collection, was an apartment completely furnished in the style of an Indian palace, in which was realised all that the Arabian Nights, and other romances, have detailed with respect to their gorgeous and costly luxury.

Around the exterior of this room were arranged a number of figures illustrating the various trades and castes of the Hindoos, together with a rich assortment of shawls, carpets, matting, &c. &c. Various objects, also, of natural produce from different parts of our vast Indian Empire were distributed around this interesting compartment.

Beautiful carvings in ivory were also to be seen, one representing the procession of a native Indian prince, another a state barge, with its bank of agile rowers. At the same time, proofs of their attention to rural economy were to be found in many

K

curious models of agricultural tools and implements, which appear to be precisely of the same form and description as were in use among the ancient Egyptians, as is evident from drawings and manuscripts that are still in existence. Hydraulic machines, on which tropical cultivation so greatly depends, were also exhibited, of various and original construction. The mode of manufacturing sugar was likewise exemplified, and a rude process it was—two grooved rollers of wood, placed face to face, were turned by two men with handspikes, while two or three sugar canes were thrust between them; this imperfect force serves to extract but a small quantity of juice, and yet we receive a good quantity of sugar from our East Indian possessions.

To turn from these peaceful occupations to the business of "grim-visaged war," we will now direct the attention of our readers to the "pride, pomp, and circumstance" of military operations, as carried on among the dusky tribes of our Eastern colonies.

In one of the bays of the East Indian department the counters on each side were entirely occupied with a splendid assortment of arms and military equipments, comprising magnificent matchlocks (inlaid in silver or mounted with gold), blunderbuss-like guns, used by our fierce enemies the Sikhs; and brass-swivels, used by Malay prahus, with mortars from Lahore, and cannons from Mysore, swords and sabres, and spears, of all shapes and sorts—all keen, glittering, and sharp weapons—used by the Scindians and the Sikhs, the Mahrattas and the Burmese; some with blades of dark steel, and others with light, inlaid with gold; some with hilts entwined with pearls, or exquisitely enamelled, or otherwise beautifully decorated. Nor was it only the weapons of modern warfare that were here, but those also which illustrate the mediæval history of India, and which may have been wielded by the chivalry of the East amidst the gleaming battle-hosts of Nadir Shah or Genghis Khan. Here, in short, were to be seen the armouries alike of Tippoo and Tamerlane. Here hung the glittering scimitar and tapering lance. Here we found the small circular shields suited to a former age of warfare; and here were suspended the fine chain-worked coats of armour, almost as flexible and light and yielding to the form as the beautiful coats of linen or silk of similar shape, exhibited in the cross avenue of the compartment opposite, reminding one of the chain armour of our ancient Norman chivalry. Here, again, were the bows and arrows, and the javelin (also recalling the ideas of our own early military history), arranged tastefully in circles, presenting all around a terrible close array of keen-looking points. Here likewise was the battle-axe—most beautifully inlaid—and a superb suit of steel armour inlaid with gold, together with a shield of deer-skin, transparent, and with enamelled bosses. And lastly, here were some curious specimens of most murderous ingenuity: such as a shield, with gold bosses, every boss concealing a pistol; a double sword dividing at pleasure into two longitudinal or lateral sections, each constituting a complete weapon; and strange conical caps, having round them sharp-edged *discs* of brass, hurled most dexterously and dangerously by some tribes as weapons of offence— little knives and daggers being very engagingly stuck all round, and giving an appearance to the whole far less graceful than grim.

Many specimens of bows, those most ancient of weapons, were also exhibited in this department, some of extraordinary length, and rude enough, in comparison with the more modern implement; others were short, carved, and curiously ornamented, probably the real Scythian bow which has for many long ages been in use among the Asiatic tribes, a bow of singular construction, deriving its chief elasticity from animal tendons, bound tightly upon the wood.

As we shall probably again have occasion to refer to the "East India compartment," we shall close our notices of it for the present; not, however, without paying our respects to its great lion, the KOH-I-NOOR. And in order to give it "honour due," and to impress our readers with a befitting sense of its high dignity and value, which perhaps from a mere inspection of the royal relic of Eastern grandeur they might be disposed to question, we shall give a few particulars with respect to its " ancient and modern history."

The Koh-i-Noor, then, our readers must be informed, is one of the most valuable diamonds that are known to exist in any part of the globe; two others only are supposed to be of greater value—the Russian sceptre-diamond, valued at the enormous sum of £4,800,000! and one belonging to Portugal, uncut, but supposed to be of still greater value. The Koh-i-Noor, however, has been long celebrated both in Asia and in Europe, and lays claim to our respect for its traditionary, as well as its historic fame. Hindoo legends trace its existence back some four or five thousand years, and mention is made of it in a very ancient heroic poem, called *Mahabarata,* a circumstance which gives us reason to suppose that it is the most ancient of precious stones that have come down to modern times. The poem states that it was discovered in the mines of the south of India, and that it was worn by Karna, the King of Anga, who was slain in the great Indian war, the date of which there is good evidence for believing to be in the year 3001 before Christ, consequently nearly five thousand years ago. A long silence then takes place on the subject of this jewel, which is not again mentioned in fable or in history till fifty-six years before Christ, when it was stated to have been the property of the Rajah of Nijayin, from whom it descended to the Rajahs of Malwa, and was possessed by them until the Mahommedans overthrew their principality, and swept away this priceless gem, and other spoils of immense value from the subjugated territory. The Mahommedans, in their turn, were obliged to bow their necks to their fierce invaders, for we find that in the beginning of the fourteenth century, they were constrained to yield up the territory they had won, the noble diamond and all their spoil, to the victorious armies of Ala-adin, the Sultan of Delhi, in whose dynasty the diamond remained for a lengthened period.

The modern history of this precious stone may be said to commence about two hundred years ago, when an eminent French traveller, skilled in diamond lore, visited India with the object of effecting purchases in those matters, and being favourably received at the court of Delhi, he was allowed to inspect the imperial jewels, and the account he gives of the one that surpassed all the rest in size and beauty, warrants the supposition that the diamond he describes was actually the great Koh-i-Noor. We next trace it to the possession of Baber, the Mogul emperor, through the right of conquest, and eventually to that of the ruling family of Kabul. Nadir Shah, on his occupation of Delhi in 1739, seized upon all that the imperial treasury contained, and also compelled his poor vanquished foe, Mahommed Shah, who wore this precious gem in the front of his head-dress, to exchange turbans with him, pretending to do so in testimony of his exceeding friendship and regard. It was at this period that it obtained the name of the Koh-i-Noor. After Nadir's death, it is generally believed that Ahmed Shah, the founder of the Abdali dynasty, prevailed on the young son of Nadir Shah to show him the diamond, and then kept possession of it, the youth having no means to enforce its restoration. The subsequent history of this diamond is free from all doubt and mystery; it descended to the successors of Ahmed Shah, and when Mr. Elphinstone was at Peshawur, he saw it on the arm of Shah Shoojee, surrounded with emeralds. The fortune of war drove the unhappy Shah to seek the hospitality of Runjeet Singh, who treacherously made him his captive, and partly through importunity, and partly through menace, in the year 1813, wrested from him his diamond, presenting the wronged monarch with a paltry sum in alleged consideration. So that after all, the gem has in it the greatest possible flaw, that of having been dishonestly obtained,—

> " Asleep and naked as an Indian lay,
> An *honest* factor stole his gem away;"

and were we disposed to play the part of Cassandra on the occasion, we should venture to predict that the enjoyment of it would not be without its corresponding alloy. O! for those days of chivalry and honour, when the glittering bauble would be restored to its rightful owner, even at the expense of the paltry millions at which its worth might be estimated.

But to return to our history. The traitorous Runjeet, on the principle, we suppose, that "stolen waters are sweet," exhibited on all occasions, and with the greatest satisfaction, his ill-gotten gem, which he wore as an armlet on all state occasions. Death, however, who, as Sancho says, levels all distinctions, threatened him at last with the loss of his stolen jewel, and there were not wanting Hindoo jesuits about him, who endeavoured to persuade him that he might quiet his conscience by bequeathing it to the great Indian idol Juggernaut. The sick monarch appeared to be struck with the idea, but he was too far gone to articulate, and could only signify his assent by nodding his head. As, however, no other warranty could he produced in favour of the grim idol, the king's successors kept fast hold of what they had got. With the ordinary quick transition of property in these countries, the gem next became the property of Rhurreuk and Shu Sing; and after the murder of the latter, also a frequent occurrence among Indian princes, the jewel remained in the Lahore treasury, until the annexation of the Punjab by the British government, when the East India Company contrived to get possession of it, on the plea that it was right and proper to seize upon all the property of the state, in part payment of the debt alleged to be due by the Lahore government, and also for the expenses of the war. It was then agreed that the Koh-i-Noor, being a state jewel, and not easily convertible into cash, should be presented to the Queen of England, which was accordingly done. Such is the history of this extraordinary jewel; but, besides these various acts of rapine and fraud, a more sanguinary deed, in cool blood, is connected with its history; for it is related that the Italian lapidary by whom it was cut, having performed his task in a manner unsatisfactory to his employer, he was forthwith ordered to immediate execution. True it is that the facets of this diamond are cut in a very unartist-like manner. The situation, too, in which it was placed, and the crimson cloth with which it was surrounded, were very unfavourable for a full display of its beauty and splendour.

In taking our leave of India for the present, which we do somewhat reluctantly, we shall close our remarks with a citation from the learned and eloquent discourse of Dr. Whewell, illustrative of the difference between the arts and manufactures of the countries called barbarous, and the productions of our own more civilized land.

"We call these nations," says the talented lecturer, "rude and savage, and yet how much is there of ingenuity, of invention, of practical knowledge of the properties of branch and leaf, of vegetable texture and fibre, in the works of the rudest tribes! How much, again, of manual dexterity, acquired by long and persevering practice, and even so, not easy! And then, again, not only how well adapted are these works of art to the mere needs of life, but how much of neatness, of prettiness, even of beauty, do they often possess, even when the work of savage hands! So that man is naturally, as I have said, not only an artificer, but an artist. Even we, while we look down from our lofty summit of civilized and mechanically-aided skill upon the infancy of art, may often learn from them lessons of taste. So wonderfully and effectually has Providence planted in man the impulse which urges him on to his destination—his destination, which is, to mould the bounty of nature into such forms as utility demands, and to show at every step that with mere utility he cannot be content. And when we come to the higher stages of cultured art—to the works of nations long civilized, though inferior to ourselves, it may be, in progressive civilization and mechanical power—how much do we find in their works which we must admire, which we might envy, which, indeed, might drive us to despair! Even still, the tissues and ornamental works of Persia and of India have beauties which we, with all our appliances and means, cannot surpass. The gorgeous East showers its barbaric pearl and gold into its magnificent textures. But is there really anything *barbaric* in the skill and taste which they display? Does the Oriental prince or monarch, even if he confine his magnificence to native manufactures, present himself to the eyes of his slaves in a less splendid or less elegant attire than the nobles and the sovereigns of this our Western world, more highly civilized as we nevertheless deem it? Few persons, I think, would answer in the affirmative. The silks and shawls, the embroidery and jewellery, the moulding and carving, which those countries can produce, and which decorate their palaces and their dwellers in palaces, are even now such as we cannot excel. *Oriental* magnificence is still a proverbial mode of describing a degree of splendour and artistical richness which is not found among ourselves.

"What, then, shall we say of ourselves? Wherein is our superiority? In what do we see the effect, the realization, of that more advanced stage of art which we conceive ourselves to have attained? What advantage do we derive from the immense accumulated resources of skill and capital—of mechanical ingenuity and mechanical power—which we possess? Surely our imagined superiority is not all imaginary; surely we really are more advanced than they, and this term 'advanced' has a meaning; surely that mighty thought of a PROGRESS in the life of nations is not an empty dream; and surely our progress has carried us beyond them. Where, then, is the import of the idea in this case? What is the leading and characteristic difference between them and us, as to this matter? What is the broad and predominant distinction between the arts of nations, rich, but in a condition of nearly stationary civilization, like Oriental nations, and nations which have felt the full influence of progress like ourselves?

" If I am not mistaken, the difference may be briefly expressed thus :—That in those countries the arts are mainly exercised to gratify the tastes of the few; with us, to supply the wants of the many. There, the wealth of a province is absorbed in the dress of a mighty warrior; here, the gigantic weapons of the peaceful potentate are used to provide clothing for the world. For that which makes it suitable that machinery, constructed on a vast scale, and embodying enormous capital, should be used in manufacture, is that the wares produced should be very great in quantity, so that the smallest advantage in the power of working, being multiplied a million-fold, shall turn the scale of profit. And thus such machinery is applied when wares are manufactured for a vast population—when millions upon millions have to be clothed, or fed, or ornamented, or pleased, with the things so produced. I have heard one say, who had extensively and carefully studied the manufacturing establishments of this country, that when he began his survey he expected to find the most subtle and refined machinery applied to the most delicate and beautiful kind of work—to gold and silver, jewels, and embroidery: but that when he came to examine, he found that these works were mainly executed by hand, and that the most exquisite and the most expensive machinery was brought into play where operations on the most common materials were to be performed, because these were to be executed on the widest scale. And this is when coarse and ordinary wares are manufactured for the many. This, therefore, is the meaning of the vast and astonishing prevalence of machine-work in this country—that the machine with its million fingers works for millions of purchasers; while in remote countries, where magnificence and savagery stand side by side, tens of thousands work for one. There Art labours for the rich alone; here she works for the poor no less. There the multitude produce only to give splendour and grace to the despot or the warrior, whose slaves they

L

are, and whom they enrich; here the man who is powerful in the weapons of peace, capital and machinery, uses them to give comfort and enjoyment to the public, whose servant he is, and thus becomes rich while he enriches others with his goods. If this be truly the relation between the condition of the arts of life in this country and in those others, may we not with reason and with gratitude say that we have, indeed, reached a point beyond theirs in the social progress of nations?"

CHAPTER VII.

SCULPTURE.

It is not our intention, in threading our way through the inexhaustible variety of objects presented to our view in the Crystal Palace, to attempt any scientific or classified enumeration of its wonders. That herculean task has been already fully and ably executed in the vast and voluminous catalogue, of which we are told, "that if the whole of the earlier editions had been consigned, in one vertical column, to the bottom of the Pacific Ocean (a computed depth of 6,000 feet), the present improved and corrected edition would still form a lonely peak rising to the height of Chimborazo or Cotopaxi, exactly 18,000 feet above the level or the censure of the ordinary inhabitants of this earth." Our time and limits, indeed, would not permit us to examine a tithe of what was spread out before us; we shall, therefore, confine our remarks to the consideration of the most useful, the most astonishing, the most ingenious, the most interesting, the most beautiful. And in our discursive flights, we shall not profess to be bound by any rigid plan of proceeding from first to last, as those unimpassioned visitors of an exhibition who begin at No. 1., and never suffer their eyes to wander till they have coldly examined every picture upon the walls, in the exact series and order in which they are enumerated in the catalogue. We, on the contrary, shall stray through the gay parterre, at our own free will, stopping only to examine and describe, as our captivated fancy may impel and direct; through the vast *embarras de richesse*, we shall pass from one subject of interest to another, "from grave to gay, from lively to severe," in the true spirit of liberty and unrestrained enjoyment.

Having premised thus much, and feeling ourselves, for the present, somewhat overpowered by the contemplation of all the Oriental magnificence, the "barbaric pearl and gold," which formed the subject of our preceding chapter, we shall "let Euclid rest and Archimedes pause," and suddenly removing, as with the touch of an enchanter's wand, the scene we so lately beheld, transplant our readers to the halls of sculpture, and call their attention, for a time, to the consideration of what the Plastic Art contributed towards the embellishment of the world's great emporium of industry and talent.

It will be the business of our engraver, whose art has been put to its utmost stretch of excellence, to compete with the elaborate and exquisite detail of the daguerreotype, to present our readers, from time to time, besides the general views of the interior of the building, with such specimens of individual talent among the numerous sculptors, both British and foreign, who contributed their offerings, as our impartial judgment may select, and which we shall accordingly forthwith proceed to describe.

In compliment to our foreign contributors, we shall commence with the colossal group of the "Amazon attacked by a Tigress," by Kiss of Berlin, which was one of the marvels of the Great Exhibition, and received more tributes of unqualified praise than

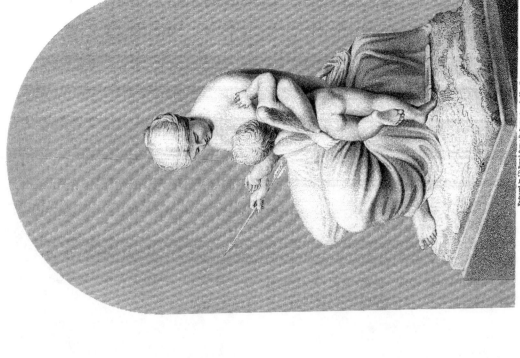

VENUS AND CUPID.

FROM THE ORIGINAL BY E. DAVIS

Engraved by J.D.Freud from a Daguerreotype by Mayall

AN EPISODE IN THE HISTORY OF THE WAR BETWEEN
THE AMAZONS AND THE ARGONAUTS.

FROM THE ORIGINAL BY J ENGEL

Engraved by J.D.Freud from a Daguerreotype by Mayall

perhaps any other single object in the Crystal Palace. It was certainly a very masterly production, and in a style which was almost new to sculptors of our day; though at the same time, from the nature of the subject, not entitled to rank with works in the highest class of sculpture. It was more animal than spiritual; the conception more startling than poetic. The Amazon was a figure of tremendous energy. The manner in which she was represented, as having thrown herself back out of her ordinary seat, in order to get beyond the reach of the tiger, whose claws were already deep dug in the neck and flanks of the horse, whilst she took deliberate aim for a single and critical blow at the head of the savage monster, was admirably conceived and carried out; the face, with its mixed expression of terror and determination, was of itself a study sufficient for an entire work in sculpture. The horse and tiger were both master-pieces in their way, but unfortunately they more than divided the interest with the human subject. This work was a copy in zinc, bronzed, from the original in bronze, erected in 1839, at the foot of the steps before the Museum at Berlin; having been made a present to the King of Prussia by a society of amateurs. We should like to see this group in the place for which it was originally designed, as its position in the Exhibition, owing to its narrow limits, and its proximity to gaudy paraphernalia, considerably injured its effect as a whole.

Another group, of Theseus and the Amazons, in the south transept, the production of Engel, an Hungarian, also attracted a good deal of attention, partly, perhaps, from its being the property of Prince Albert, as well as from its own intrinsic merit. We had frequent opportunities of seeing this work in progress in Rome, where it was executed during the troubles and commotions that agitated that most unfortunate and most injured city, at the period of its treacherous usurpation by Republican France. The artist, nevertheless, with unchecked application and industry, achieved his laborious task sufficiently in time for its being conveyed to our hospitable shores for exhibition.

More graceful than energetic, the composition of this group wanted a little of the fire that characterized the production of Kiss; the story, moreover, was not very clearly told, and the draperies were deficient in smoothness and naturalness. At all times among ancient sculptors these lady-warriors were especial favourites, and their well-contested battles with the Athenians are to be seen among the terra-cottas in the British Museum, as well as on the friezes of the temples of Theseus at Athens, and of Apollo Epicurus on Mount Cosylion, near the ancient city of Phigaleia, in Arcadia.

"Fine subjects do not always make fine pictures," was the remark of a sage academician of our acquaintance; neither do they always make fine groups in marble. Our Lord's charge to Peter, "Feed my Lambs," was deficient in dignity and expression, and too literally understood. Seldom, indeed, have scriptural subjects been adequately treated: rarely has the figure or the countenance of the Saviour, "full of grace and truth," been worthily delineated. Even Michael Angelo failed in his celebrated statue in the Church of the Minerva, at Rome, in representing the august majesty of "The Incarnate Deity." Before attempting such a task, the artist would do well to bear in mind the beautiful invocation of Milton, at the commencement of his noble poem :—

> "—— And chiefly Thou, O Spirit, that dost prefer
> Before all temples the upright heart and pure,
> Instruct me, for thou know'st—   *   *   *
> *   *   *   *   * What in me is dark,
> Illumine; what is low, raise and support."—*Paradise Lost.*

On pursuing our investigations among the crowded marbles that throng the sculpture court—

> "Thick as autumnal leaves that strew the brooks
> In Vallambrosa"

we discovered a fine statue of the calm and philosophic Flaxman, by Watson; a Prometheus, by Theed; and an Ino and Infant Bacchus, graceful and joyous. We next recognised our old acquaintance, Whittington, the runaway apprentice, and subsequent Lord Mayor of London, apparently listening to the melodious bells that augured to his youthful fancy his future greatness. There was a great deal of truth and nature in this little figure; but perhaps we have been too much accustomed to see the sculptor's art employed on higher subjects, to relish its adoption in those of more humble and common life. Before we quit this department, we must not omit to cast a glance of admiration and pity upon the fair Ophelia, about to hang "her coronet weeds" upon the fatal willow. A pastoral group, too, by Kirk, was deserving of our notice—simple, natural, and illustrative of the golden age from which its happy subjects were selected. In the transept, setting aside the majestic elm, "star-proof," and the noble fountains, we confess we found no pre-eminent object to exclusively engage our attention, always, of course, excepting the personifications of our august Queen and her royal Consort, to whose intelligence England is indebted for the original idea of this mighty gathering of nations—these "embassies from regions far remote." The statuary was too much on a par to excite individual notice.

We will next notice "The Boy attacked by a Serpent," and "The Deliverer," by Lechesne, a young Frenchman of great promise. The first of these groups represented a child attacked by a large serpent, and defended by a dog, which generously interposed between the reptile and its object of attack. The fear of the child, and the watchful and angry zeal of its four-footed protector, were exceedingly well given; and in the companion group, in which the headless snake testifies to the victory of his canine antagonist, the gratitude of the boy, and the placid satisfaction of the noble animal, were equally well represented. We understand this pair of subjects was to be executed in marble for Prince Demidoff.

As we sauntered down the nave, we next came upon a fine group by Pierotti, who gave us the "Binding of Mazeppa upon the back of the Wild Horse," from the vigorous verse of Byron. The action of the untamed animal, the fierce and remorseless bearing of the executioners of the tyrant's vengeance, and the hopeless resignation of the victim, were not unworthy of the poetic description of the noble bard himself.

We wish next to direct the attention of our readers to a fine group by Jerichau, a Danish sculptor, and no unworthy successor to his great fellow-countryman, Thorwaldsen, whose style he appears to have followed. It represented "Adam and Eve after the Fall." Never were the different characteristics of the masculine and feminine nature, psychologically considered, depicted with more truth and feeling. The man appeared to suffer with all the force of his intellect; not only fully aware of his own altered and awful situation, but already beholding, by the clearness of his perceptions, all the dismal calamities to his descendants, in consequence of his transgression. Deeply were the effects of his view, turned inwards upon himself, and his prescient glance into futurity, and what it had in store through him, for generations yet to come, marked in his countenance. No trait of merely human regret was to be found in it. He was astounded at his own state, but evidently submitted to it, from the conviction that his sentence was the decree of Almighty Justice, which cannot err, and that he had brought it upon himself; but it was the effect of it upon others, which roused all his powers of thought, all the extent of his comprehension; and it was the finding his utmost grasp of mind unequal to the fulness of the terrible reality, that imprinted despair upon his "fair large front." In the woman, the form and essence of love, we saw the suffering of the affections. Never was Milton's beautiful line—

"He for God only, she for God in him,"

Engraved by Hollis from a Daguerreotype by Beard

THE BOY ATTACKED BY A SERPENT.

FROM THE ORIGINAL BY LECHESNE

Engraved by Hollis, from a Daguerreotype by Beard.

THE DELIVERER.

FROM THE ORIGINAL BY LECHESNE.

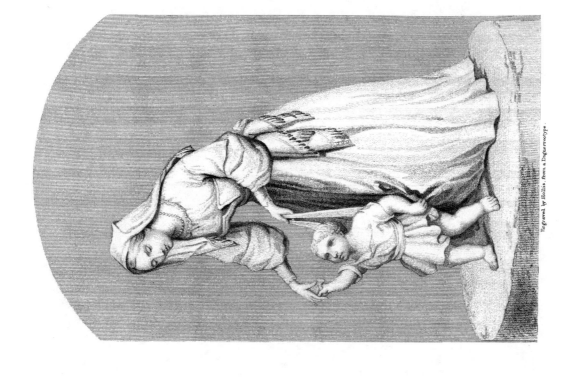

THE FIRST STEP.

THE ORIGINAL BY F. MAGNI, MILAN

Engraved by Hollis from a Daguerreotype.

THE BASHFUL BEGGARS

THE ORIGINAL BY D. GANDOLFI, MILAN

Engraved by Hollis from a Daguerreotype.

THE CIRCASSIAN SLAVE AT THE MARKET.

Engraved by Hollis from a Daguerreotype by Beard.

FROM THE ORIGINAL BY RAFFAELLE MONTI, AUSTRIA.

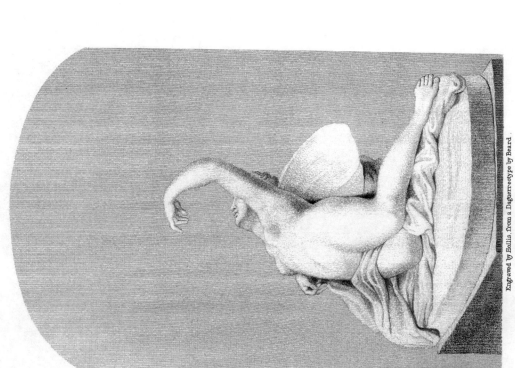

PSYCHE CALLING ON CUPID FOR HELP.

Engraved by Hollis, from a Daguerreotype by Beard.

FROM THE ORIGINAL BY C.A. FRAIKEN, BELGIUM.

Engraved by D. Pound, from a Daguerreotype

THE VEILED VESTAL

FROM THE ORIGINAL BY RAFFAELLE MONTI.

JOHN TALLIS & COMPANY LONDON & NEW YORK.

more admirably illustrated. We saw she was not thinking of the decree against herself, though including all the trials most grievous to her nature: deep, indeed, and touching, was the penitence and grief with which her whole frame seemed penetrated; but we saw, we felt, that her penitence was for the act by which she had brought ruin upon him she loved and reverenced, her "glory," her "perfection:" her sorrow for the sad reverse of the boon by which she had thought to impart additional good to him; a good in which, though first to taste it, she yet found no relish until he could share it with her. It is this sweet womanhood in our "general mother," that Mr. Jerichau has expressed with a feeling worthy of Milton himself, to whom we are indebted for the most perfect portraiture of feminine excellence and loveliness that ever was depicted by the aid of words; and the contemplation of this group will give rise to many a musing and many an aspiration in the mind of the thoughtful beholder, pure and lofty as its theme.

Not, however, to extend our remarks on this subject beyond its due limits, we will now turn our attention to the *Austrian* sculpture, as in its wonted spirit of usurpation, that government termed the productions of the Milanese chisel; and at the very point of entrance to the apartment, doubtless much to the gratification of the artists whose works are arranged withinside, the stern Radetzky was planted in full military display—the rugged serf elevated to the dignity of epaulettes and the marshal's baton. The equally celebrated Hainau might have formed a fit companion to this worthy, in the "sentinel watch" he appeared to hold over these unfortunate sons of genius; but we do not think the British public would have relished the appearance of the hero of Breschia within those peaceful walls. For our own part, we will leave the *par nobile fratrum*, the tools of despotism, to their unenviable notoriety, and endeavour to forget the reminiscences attached to their names, in the contemplation of the lofty and poetic fancies which gentler minds and more amiable spirits spread around these favoured limits.

"A veiled Vestal," and a "Slave in the Market-place," by Monti, were the great objects of attraction in this apartment. In both works the illusion, at a little distance, was very remarkable, and until the spectator came nearer and examined the figure, he did not discover what may be termed the ingenious trick, which pretended to represent two surfaces at once the one under the other, in the untractable marble; an impossible feat, however, as far as truth in the representation of either of the surfaces was regarded, as was evident on a close inspection. The latter of these pieces was purchased by the Duke of Devonshire.

Leaving, however, these subjects with their *ad captandum* merit, we will draw our reader's attention to a work of more sterling excellence by the same artist, "Eve after her Fall," a graceful and beautiful personification of our "original mother." We did not, however, approve of the little Cupid peering up from a cluster of roses behind, a trivial and unworthy conceit.

Three works by Antonio Galli, of Milan, were deserving of especial notice: "Jephthah's Daughter," simple, elegant, and full of expression—"A Youth on the Sea-shore," and "Susannah at the Bath," graceful and chastely voluptuous, in her surprise. Marchesi's "Eurydice" also demanded commendation; but, unquestionably, the "Hagar and Ismael," by Max, of Prague, in this so-termed Austrian apartment, was the most impressive and touching, full of nature, dignity, and truth. We must not, however, deny its just tribute of praise to the "Ismael" by Signore Strazza, of Milan, a wonderful performance, and full of terrible pathos in its death-like agony.

It is only of late years that sculpture has descended to the lower range of poetic imagining. Painting, indeed, had frequently illustrated incidents of domestic and ordinary life, and dealt largely in *tableaux de genre*, but sculpture rarely sought inspiration beyond the page of holy writ, poetic fancies, or the graceful imagery of classic befal. Monumental tributes, indeed, she did not deem unworthy of her genius; but then the "storied urn and animated bust" were chiefly devoted to the memory of the great, to the hero, the poet, or the scholar. She has now, however, begun to trifle with her art, and adopt subjects of lesser importance, familiar or domestic. Roubilliac appears to have been one of the first who began to clothe his figures in the costume they usually wore, a practice we should like to see generally adopted. It has been so arranged with respect to the drama, owing to the good taste of the late John Kemble; for the time was when Cato wore a modish court-dress, bag-wig, ruffles and all; and Garrick performed the parts of Macbeth and Othello in a full suit of modern regimentals. "Reform it altogether," as Hamlet advised, and if our statesmen and orators must strut in marble, let them not figure in a Roman toga, with the incongruity of a shaven chin and military whiskers. We remember seeing in an artist's studio at Rome, to our great astonishment, a full length of Prince Albert as a Greek warrior! *Risu teneatis?* But to return from this digression. The sculptor Cibber, the father of the poet, has shown, in his admirable statues of the two maniacs over the portico of Bethlehem Hospital, how much may be done in marble to illustrate passion and emotion in ordinary life; and Thom, in his Tam O'Shanter and Souter Johnnie, long afforded diversion to the town, and furnished an additional proof, that it is not alone in the stately, the solemn, or the classical, that the genius of sculpture can display its excellence.

We make these remarks, to introduce to the notice of our readers two subjects of this grotesque description, which attracted a good deal of notice from the visitors to the Crystal Palace; more favourable notice, indeed, than the gigantic Crusader by the same artist, who "towered above his sex" in the same locality. The subjects we allude to were known as the Happy and the Unhappy Child; the first a little urchin, stretched at length and at his ease, was admiring the *outre* physiognomy of a punchinello with which he was playing; while the other was blubbering over the drum he had, probably through excessive energy in beating it, most unluckily broken. We will now pay our respects to the "Greek Slave," by Hiram Power, an American sculptor, of great talent, who has been for some years past a resident in Florence, where he has executed many admirable works, several of which have found their way to this country. The modest dignity expressed in this figure, its beauty, and the delicacy of its execution, are deserving of the highest praise. The talented Frederika Bremer bears the following testimony to the excellence of this piece of statuary :—"This so-called Greek Slave, this captive woman, with her fettered hands, I had seen many times on the other side of the Atlantic, in copies of the original—cold weak copies of that original which I saw here for the first time. The copies had left a cold impression on my mind. The original seized upon me with an unusual power, as no other statue in marble had done. This noble woman, with her bound-down hands, who so quietly turned her head with its unspeakably-deep expression of sorrow and indignation—scorn is not a sufficiently noble word—against the power which bound her; that lip which is silent, but which seems to quiver with the tumult of wounded feeling, with the throbbing of her heart;—I wonder whether Power himself comprehended the whole of its significance!" Gibson presented us with a "Greek Hunter," and a fine basso-relievo representing the "Hours leading forth the Horses of the Sun." Both of these were noble and spirited productions, and may fairly take their places among the most celebrated works of antiquity. Not far from these, we noticed a "Narcissus," by Theed, a graceful and classic figure. He was represented leaning upon a boar-spear, gazing upon the fountain which was supposed to reflect his beauteous image, while the flower which bears his name and perpetuates his memory, was springing up at his feet. A "Prodigal Son," by the same artist, was

From a Daguerreotype by Beard

THE UNHAPPY CHILD

From a Daguerreotype by Beard

THE HAPPY CHILD.

Hiram Power. Sculptor.   Daguerreotyped by Mayall.

THE GREEK SLAVE

Hiram Power. Sculptor.   Daguerreotyped by Mayall.

THE GREEK SLAVE

RINALDI AND ARMEDA.

Engraved by D.Pound, from a Daguerreotype by Beard.

CUPID AND PSYCHE.

Engraved by D.Pound, from a Daguerreotype by Beard.

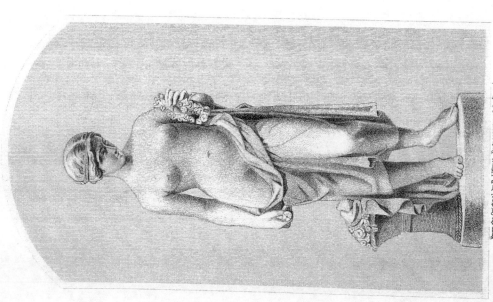

From the Original by R. J. Wyatt. Daguerreotyped by Beard.

CLYCERA

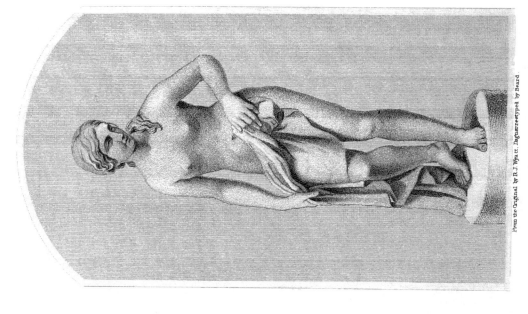

From the Original by R. J. Wyatt. Daguerreotyped by Beard.

A NYMPH.

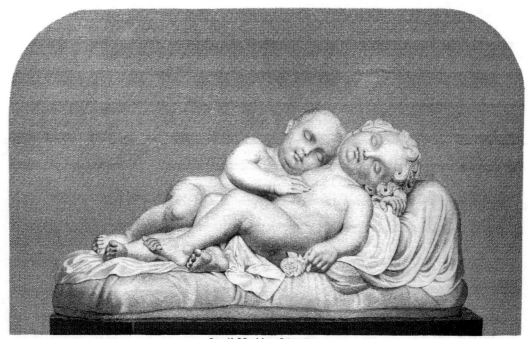

Engraved by D. Pound, from a Daguerreotype.

INNOCENCE

BY S. GEFFS

Engraved by D. Pound, from a Daguerreotype.

STATUETTE,

IN PARIAN MARBLE BY H. MINTON & C°

remarkable for the tenderness of the sentiment it inspired, and for its just illustration of this beautiful and touching narrative in Holy Writ. Thrupp, in his charming figure of "Arethusa;" and Behnes, in his personification of a "Startled Nymph," were equally deserving of commendation. "Una, with her Lion," has always been a favourite subject with artists—the gentle Una, whose beauty, as Spenser tells us, when she was lost in the recesses of the forest, "made a sunshine in that shady place." The sculptor represented her seated on the lion's back; but we cannot say that the effect was very happy: indeed, we overheard a country critic express his opinion, that the Lady Godiva was before him. Mr. Bell succeeded better in his "Dorothea"—the beautiful vision by the brook that greeted the ravished eyes of the Knight of the Sorrowful Countenance and his companions, in the inimitable romance of Cervantes. This, too, is a subject that artists love to delineate; as is also that of the "Babes in the Wood," which was ably treated by the same hand. We remember, many years ago, to have seen this simple story beautifully illustrated by Stodhart, whose magic pencil imparted to it a romantic grandeur and solemnity which, after a period of full forty years, still, in vivid colours, is present to our imagination.

In the Roman department there were but few evidences of the intelligence and genius which the Italians undoubtedly possess. Nor can we wonder at it, oppressed and enslaved as they are by their priests, through the unjust interference of France. Moreover, passports were either altogether refused to many artists, or the hint was given to them, that if they left the country they might find it difficult to return. Nevertheless, a stray object or two found its way within the walls; but the sculptors of Rome were poorly represented, while the works of Tenerani and other magnates of the Eternal City withheld their contributions. Among those which did arrive, we particularly noticed a "Cupid and Psyche," by Benzoni, very beautifully treated; also "Innocence defended by Fidelity," and "Gratitude," a young girl extracting a thorn from the foot of a dog, by the same artist, equally deserving attention. These are the property of Captain Leyland, a munificent patron of art, who was also fortunate enough to secure two admirable specimens from the chisel of the late lamented Richard Wyatt, entitled "The Nymph Glycera," and "A Nymph," executed with wonderful delicacy and grace. In the death of this artist, Rome has to deplore the loss of one of the most talented of her adopted sons; one, too, who would have risen to the highest walk in his profession, for, diligent and studious, he was ever improving in his art, as his later productions sufficiently testify. We shall, perhaps, resume our remarks upon the sculpture exhibited in the Crystal Palace at a future opportunity. At present let us pause—

"To-morrow to fresh fields and pastures new."

CHAPTER VII.

CHAUCER'S DREAM—THE TRANSEPT—THE WESTERN NAVE—CANADIAN TROPHY—RUSSIAN SUSPENSION BRIDGE—MODEL OF LIVERPOOL DOCKS.

WE invite such of our readers as, unfortunately, have not had an opportunity of inspecting the "World's Emporium" in person, to take a glance at the elaborate view of "The Nave of the Great Exhibition, looking west," which we presented to them in our first number, preparatory to their following us in our description of that splendid avenue. Before we enter upon it, however, we must request leave to be allowed to make a short digression in honour of one of England's eldest and most renowned of bards, whose prescient muse appears to have had a sort of foreknowledge of what was to take place in our favoured isle, when Science, Industry, and Art, should combine their united efforts, throughout the whole earth, to produce among us the unrivalled display of talent and advancement to which an admiring world has just borne witness; for the vast variety that was contained in the wondrous House of Glass, as well as the building itself, wherein every nation found room to treasure up their stores, and to congregate their countless thousands, were, indeed, matters of admiration and astonishment to all the world. Sober-minded people, a few years ago, would have scouted the idea as absurd and visionary, and even the most enthusiastic would never have dared to hope in its realization. What judgment and reason, however, never anticipated, it appears that poetry imagined; for we find in the writings of Chaucer, eldest of British bards, a sort of prophetic announcement of the future Wonder, in his Introduction to the " House of Fame," which he describes as a vision, and speculates upon the causes of dreams, stating his inability to decide whether

> " Spirits have the might
> To make folks dream o' night,
> Or if the soul of proper kind
> Be so perfect as men find,
> That it wote what is to come.
> As I slept,"   *   *   *   *

he goes on to say,—

> " I dreamt I was
> Within *a temple made of glass*,
> In which there were more images
> Of *gold*, standing in sundry stages,
> In more rich tabernacles,
> And with *jewels*, more pinnacles,
> And more curious *portraitures*,
> And quaint manner of figures
> Of gold work, than I ever saw."
>   *   *   *   *
>
> " Then saw I stand on either side,
> Straight down to the doors wide,
> *From the dais, many a pillar*
> *Of metal*, that shone out full and clear."

> " Then gan I look about and see
> That there came entering in the hall
> A right great company withal,
> *And that of sundry regions*,
> *Of all kinds of conditions*
> That dwell on earth beneath the moon,
> *Poor and rich*."
>   *   *   *   *
>
> " *Such a great congregation*
> *Of folks as I saw roam about*,
> *Some within and some without*,
> *Was never seen nor shall be more*."
>   *   *   *   *   *

But to proceed. Passing through a pair of richly-gilded iron gates, the visitor entered

THE TRANSEPT,

when its full glories burst upon his view, heightened and magnified by the narrow dimensions of the external roof and vestibule. A vast hall was before him, lined on either hand with sculptured forms. In the centre arose, like some fantastic stalactite or splinter from an iceberg, a transparent crystal fountain, glittering with all the colours of the rainbow, which, towering from a solid base up to a point, poured down upon an overflowing crystal basin an unceasing stream, with a delicious bubbling sound. Beyond the fountain stood the chair of state—a throne of crimson and gold, commanding the grand avenues both east and west. On the left of the throne, at the head of the eastern avenue, the great Indian diamond, the Koh-i-Noor, glittered in a golden cage or prison. Other statues, another fountain of huge spouting stone tritons, a mass of broad-leaved tropical plants, and lofty, smooth-barked palm-trees, another pair of gilded gates, and over all a mighty elm, spreading its full-leaved branches far and wide, and touching the very summit of the lofty roof, completed his first impression of the scene—but not the scene itself, for every glance revealed some new effect, gorgeous or graceful. His eyes travelled at one moment to the semi-transparent roof, with its delicate arches of blue and white, and spider-like

THE TRANSEPT OF THE GREAT EXHIBITION.

LOOKING NORTH

Engraved by W. Lacey, from a Daguerreotype by Mayall.

THE NAVE OF THE GREAT EXHIBITION.

LOOKING WEST

Engraved by T. Sherrat. from a Daguerreotype by Mayall

diagonal bracing-lines; then they rested upon the pendant tapestry above the galleries, the rich carpets and brocades; or followed the crimson lines of the gallery rails, till they wearied with the luxuriance of colour, animate and inanimate; for all this time, silk, satin, and velvet, plumes and flowers, borne by gazers as curious as ourselves, were streaming all around. At length he reached the ground, and was recalled to the real purpose of this Fairy Palace by the word "India" at the head of the British, and "Egypt" at the head of the Foreign Avenue; both making a rich display of arms—the first manufacture of semi-barbarous nations.

THE WESTERN NAVE,

East and west, next challenged attention, and, as the *Illustrated London News* has aptly observed, "were it possible to attain to that state of dual individualism which would have enabled one to visit two places at once, it is probable there would quickly have been a complete duplication of visitors, one half going east and the other west." We shall at present confine our notice to the western side, into which, with the aid of our daguerreotype, we shall forthwith penetrate. Proceeding then, from that crystal marvel, Osler's Glass Fountain, we must lead our visitor to the extreme west; the various objects arranged in the centre striking the eye in rapid succession, from the silk trophy of Messrs. Keith and Co., to the great mirror at the end under Willis's grand organ. This silk trophy was a novelty, and stood as the type of the textile fabrics of Great Britain and Ireland. It was originally intended that, as each trophy would represent a particular class or manufacture, exhibitors in those departments should unite to form a complete type of their trade. Thus, the silk trophy was intended to have been contributed to by the various manufacturers of Spitalfields, and would thus have been a fitting representation of the silk trade in all its branches. Practical and technical difficulties, however, had to be overcome, in bringing together products so varied as those of the loom, even in one material; and Messrs. Keith and Co., as manufacturers of the largest kind of silk goods for furniture damasks, undertook the whole work, the construction and arrangement of which was based on a suggestion and sketches made by the superintendent of textile fabrics, Mr. George Wallis, and subsequently improved upon and extended by Messrs. Laugher, Dwyer, and Co., of Poland-street, to whom the merit of the practical realization in its complete form was due. The whole was hung with the richest silk damasks, brocatelles, tabarets, &c., to the height of upwards of fifty feet; the sides of the base being filled in with mirrors of the largest dimensions, reflecting, at certain angles, the draped arrangement, and surmounted by flags and a banner, the central one being emblazoned with the royal arms. In order to effect the regular rearrangement of the whole at stated periods, the structure was so contrived, that, by ladders placed inside, the requisite work could be effected with comparatively little trouble in a short space of time. This trophy stood between two bronzes of very different character—the statue of the Duke of Rutland, by Davis, and a very clever group of a "Horse and Dragon," by Wyatt, intended, we presume, to typify the triumph of the intellectual powers over the lower and more sensual propensities of our nature, since the horse is the symbol of the one, and the traditional dragon that of the other. As, however, notices of individual works belong to the future portion of our task, attention only is called to these objects. The Colonial or Canadian trophy, which we shall more particularly notice hereafter, was the next object of interest, and was formed of specimens of the timber with which our North American colonies supply us. These examples were cut into such slabs as might at once show their wrought and unwrought character, one side of each being duly finished and varnished, or polished. Among these specimens were two contributions by a fugitive slave, settled in Canada. This group of raw products was placed in the midst of the colonial department; and the materials, though interesting from their utility, were certainly very unpromising ones for the formation of a trophy having any pretensions to symmetry or artistic effect; but the difficulty was got over much better than might have been expected, and the whole was surmounted by a small canoe.

Passing the large mirror, with its elaborately ornamented framing and gilding, the spandril from Hereford Cathedral, placed at the back, could not fail to attract the attention of the lover of ecclesiastical decoration. Mr. Thomas's fountain, the subject of which is the story of Acis and Galatæa, stood next, and was a work of no mean excellence. To do it justice, however, a recurrence must be made to it in future notices. A beautifully carved mediæval cross, designed by Pugin, came next in order. The subjects of the relievi were beautifully appropriate, and the whole was an excellent example of stone carving. The next object was a kindred one, being a Gothic screen executed by the Patent Machine Carving Company (Jordan's); and grouped at the sides were excellent examples of the results of the same process as applied to general decoration. The "Eldon and Stowell" group, two colossal portrait statues of those eminent brothers, the late Earl of Eldon and Lord Stowell, was well placed in the central avenue, as the work was a bold and massive one. The draperies were grand in their arrangement, and there was a repose in the whole subject which was highly satisfactory. The artist, the late M. L. Watson, was not known or appreciated to the extent which this work and another we shall take occasion to notice when visiting the sculpture, proves he ought to have been. This, alas! is the old story; and his talent is now fully recognised, when it is no longer available to us, or of any value to him. The specimen of Honduras mahogany, several large pillars of alum, and some examples of chemical products, astonished the curious in those matters; whilst Dent's turret clock, and the Sheffield trophy—a grand group of cutlery, &c., by the celebrated house of Rogers and Sons—formed admirable contrasts to those huge productions of nature and science. The Coalbrook Dale dome—a conspicuous object from all parts of the building, commanding a view of the central avenue—as an example of constructive metal casting, was worthy of all praise. We wish we could say as much for the design as a work of art, although in many parts there was much to admire. The statue of the "Eagle Slayer," by John Bell, was placed in the centre; but as this is one of those works to which, as a whole, recurrence must be made at some future period, we pass on, after calling attention to Mr. Bell's ideal statue of Shakspere, which was placed on the eastern side of the dome —a pleasing work, but of more pretension than power. An equestrian group, representing a "Dead Crusader, his Horse and Mistress," illustrated a painful episode of bygone times; whilst the great telescope placed next to it as distinctly illustrated the glorious pursuits of modern science, her aims and triumphs. The glass cases containing splendid selections of furs by Nicolay, and feathers by Adcock, were attractive to thousands. The former was a remarkable example of ingenuity in arrangement, the case being supported round the base by preserved animals. At this point, too, the magnificent furs suspended from the galleries attracted the attention of the visitor.

The use of terra cotta as a decorative adjunct in building, was admirably displayed by the model of a church in the decorative style, the whole idea being well and thoroughly carried out, and the application of this material as a constructive agent very fully exemplified. Having seen and examined a church so constructed, near Bolton, Lancashire, built by the contributors of this model, Messrs. Willock, of the Lady Shore works, we can bear testimony to its excellence in many respects, although, like all artificial materials, it has its disadvantages. For garden decorations, there is no material better adapted for general use; and with the progress made of late years, particularly by the enterprising firm to which we were indebted for this example of skill, it is wonderful that the many elegant decorations adapted to ornamental grounds are not more generally used than they are, since we find elegance combined with cheapness, and, under all circumstances, with durability also. The next object, a model made by Mr. Jabez James, of Broadwall, of a suspension-bridge erected over the river Dnieper, at Kieff, in South Russia, designed by Mr. C. Vignolles, was the most perfect thing of the kind in the building. A similar model to the one exhibited was made for the Emperor of Russia, and cost upwards of £12,000. The scale was one-eighth of an inch; all the details were imitated with such nicety, even in the size of the nails and the threads of the screws, that from it a perfect copy of the original bridge might be executed on a full scale, without any written description. The abutments take to pieces, to show the construction of the masonry and the chambers for the chains. It contains 6,880 pieces of wood, and 87,097 pieces of metal. Before the construction of the suspension-bridge at Kieff, a bridge of boats was in use, the river being 1,200 feet wide. Mr. James, the modeller, received a ruby and diamond ring, valued at £200, from the Emperor, on the arrival of the first model, which is now set up in the Winter Palace at St. Petersburgh. The model of the Britannia Bridge, although less elaborate, was equally exact in scale. Between the two stood a model of Mr. Brunel's bridge over the Wye at Chepstow. The large and massive fountain, by Seeley, constructed of artificial stone, astonished and delighted a large number of visitors. The whole work was at once an example of skill in construction and fitness of design. The model of the Lord Mayor's state barge, by Searle, had its admirers, particularly in those who delight in civic decorations. In this rapid sketch of the leading objects in the western side of the central avenue, the revolving lights have been overlooked.

The very elaborate and costly model of the Liverpool Docks and the commercial part of that town, was a remarkable example of the extent to which the œconomy of our great cities may be illustrated and permanently recorded. This admirable work originated in a desire on the part of certain patriotic gentlemen of Liverpool, that this great port, the outlet of so large a portion of our trade, and the scene of so important a part of the commercial transactions of this country, should be fairly represented in the Exhibition. As, however, Liverpool has no staple trade, properly so speaking, but exists and owes its importance to the diffusion of the products of other localities, rather than the productions of its own, the suggestion that the extent of its means for promoting the great purposes of international communication should be illustrated was a very happy one, and was most admirably carried out by its originator and designer, Mr. John Grantham, C.E., a gentleman who acted as honorary secretary to the Exhibition committee at Liverpool, and spared no pains to do honour to this great occasion. Upon a scale of eight feet to a mile, we had, then, an accurate representation of the docks of Liverpool, and the most important commercial part of the town, including St. George's Hall and the Railway Station, the Town-hall, Custom-house, St. John's Market, and several of the churches; the shipping lying in the docks, or floating, to all appearance, on the surface of the Mersey, which was represented by the silvering or coloured glass. The model was supported on an appropriately designed base formed of elephants, cast in iron, from the backs of which the columnar supports of the roof arose; pediments, filled with appropriate decorations in imitation of bas-reliefs, being at the ends and centre. Our limits will not allow us to describe more minutely this great and important contribution—a work which did honour to the merchant princes of Liverpool, and which was intended to be eventually deposited in St. George's Hall, as a record of this assemblage of all which constitutes the basis of its greatness, its wealth, and practical utility. A specimen of plate glass of extraordinary size was placed against the columns supporting the cross at this end, and the whole scene through which we have so far journeyed was reflected with great effect.

Standing at this point the whole length of the building was seen, and the result was in the highest degree impressive and beautiful. It was to be regretted, however, that the sides of the central avenue were not kept more clear of projecting objects, as in many instances one or two of these projections interfered with the whole range, and were anything but sightly. As a whole, however, more was done in this direction than could have reasonably been expected, since each exhibitor endeavoured to display his own contributions in the very best possible position, and had as little regard to those around him as the regulations would permit. To our mind the British side was a wonderful exemplification of British character, and the notions each man entertained of his own freedom and independence of action. Like our street architects, each ran up his own erection in his own way, and it was only by a constant supervision, that anything like an *ensemble* was obtained. Bedposts and conservatories, glass cases, iron rods, and sign-boards, appear to have formed the stock notions of the best mode of construction, and these were only worked into a presentable form by a variety of modifications. Again, the substantial character of many of these erections was evident at once. If the whole Exhibition was intended to remain *en permanence*, and the exhibitors contemplated that their great-grand-children would display their industry and their genius in the space assigned to themselves to-day, they could not have more effectually provided for such a contingency. These fittings, therefore, formed a remarkable contrast to many of those on the foreign side, which were remarkable for lightness, elegance, and fitness for their purposes.

CHAPTER VIII.

FOREIGN AND COLONIAL DEPARTMENTS—*continued*.

CEYLON—CANADA—AUSTRALIA—VAN DIEMEN'S LAND—THE CAPE.

It has been ably observed by a popular writer, that "the great social lessons suggested by the completion of the Exhibition of the Industry of all Nations, were not less valuable than the educational." Of all European countries, England certainly had been the least visited by foreigners: they admired our industry, they purchased our solid manufactures, they dreaded our prowess and ambition; but the climate, the expenses of travelling, the absence of popular amusements, deterred them from visiting our shores, or drove them away before they had an opportunity of fully appreciating those personal qualities, which, when known, inspire respect, confidence, and permanent good-will. But they came at length; and before proceeding further, we shall do well, perhaps, to enumerate the nations which co-operated with us, and filled with specimens of their industry, the eastern wing of the Crystal Palace.

France and Austria stood first in the number of their contributions, although Prussia carried off the palm in sculpture, with Kiss's vigorous poetical Amazon, already described. We had also Norway, Sweden, and Denmark, Holland, and Belgium; the Hanse Towns and Northern States of Germany; several of the minor states of the Zollverein, Saxony, Bavaria, Wurtemburg; the republics of Switzerland; the kingdoms of Piedmont and Sardinia; Tuscany; and the Papal States. The kingdom of Naples alone, to the eternal disgrace of her government, refused to have any share in contributing to the universal mart, and therefore tacitly declined to rank among civilized nations. Then came Russia, Spain, and Portugal; Mahommedan Turkey, Egypt, Persia, and Tunis; Pagan Western Africa, and the converted islanders of the Pacific. The American Continent answered us from New Granada, Mexico, Peru, Brazil; and, although last, not least, the United States aided us in this great work. In addition to our foreign friends, whom courtesy compels us to name first, our colonies and dependencies, of which many, although much talked of, are less known to us than foreign states, made up a goodly array. Among these, Canada, Nova Scotia, and New Brunswick, corn and timber-bearing, held a foremost rank, grouped with the barren sheep-walks of the Cape; the great emigration-fields of New South Wales, Port Phillip, and South Australia, famous, too, for minerals; Van Diemen's Land, the alpine island of Australasia; New Zealand, the most romantic, healthy, and unprofitable of all our settlements; Bermuda, where the name of the chairman of the Executive Committee will ever be revered as the re-introducer of agriculture and horticulture. The Bahamas, famed for pine-apples, turtle, and shells; many West Indian islands; and St. Helena, chiefly remembered as the prison-house of a great captive; Ceylon, also, and the fortress of Malta, joined for that time together. Ceylon is prolific in fibrous materials, many of which may be well employed as substitutes for flax and hemp. Some of these were shown in the raw and manufactured state. The earthenware of the Cingalese is more curious than valuable; the art of pottery with them being, in all probability, not more advanced than in the time when Ptolemy and the Arabian navigators first visited

"The utmost Indian isle, Taprobane."

The same remark will apply with equal truth to their agricultural and manufacturing implements. The Cingalese women may still be seen grinding their corn, "two at one stone," as described in Scripture. The bows and arrows employed by the wild Veddahs of the Ouvah and Bintenne districts, in the hunting of deer and buffaloes, were remarkable for little beyond their simplicity and diminutiveness. The coffee, the cinnamon, and the cocoa-nut of Ceylon, are articles well known in the commercial world: they are equal, if not superior, to the production of any other country. There were also to be found models of the buildings, machinery, and implements employed in coffee plantations in Ceylon. Models of the Cingalese fishing-canoes, of very singular and beautiful construction, unlike those of any other country, were displayed with their nets and gear on a proper scale. First, in value and importance, were specimens of *cinnamon*, a spice highly prized from long antiquity, and peculiar to the "utmost Indian isle." Java has in vain attempted to produce cinnamon that should rival the fine spice of Ceylon, and the rough coarse bark grown on the Malabar coast cannot be compared with it. Cinnamon is the bark of the *Laurus cinnamomi*, freed from its outer cuticle, and removed from the sticks in long narrow slips: these pieces of bark are rolled into *pipes* or *quills*, in layers of three or four, and are dried gradually first in the shade, and then in the sun. A cinnamon plantation of 800 acres will produce annually 400 bales of spice, of 100lbs. each. The present consumption of cinnamon of Ceylon growth is about 3,500 bales per annum, of which not more than the 500 are used in this country; the remaining 3,000 are taken chiefly by France, Spain, and South America. Of far more recent date, though equally important as an article of commerce, is coffee. Twenty years ago, the *Caffea Arabica* was scarcely known in Ceylon. It was not until the years 1832 and 1834 that a very few Europeans commenced the cultivation of the coffee-bush. There are now 300 estates, comprising 50,000 acres of land, all under coffee; the shipments amounting to 350,000 cwt. annually. This article is all grown inland, at various alti-

o

tudes, the best being from the highest estates. Coir fibre and rope is made from the outer husk of the cocoa-nut: the kernel of the nut yielding a most useful oil by pressure, which is exported to Europe in large quantities. *Paddy* is rice with its natural skin upon it, and in this state is given to all sorts of cattle and poultry. The rice of Ceylon is not nearly so fine as that brought to this country from Carolina and Bengal, but it has very nutritious qualities, and the Cingalese and many Europeans prefer it to any other description. The woods of Ceylon are scarcely inferior to those of any other country, and exist in great variety. There are upwards of four hundred kinds, of which one-half are employed for a variety of purposes, the remainder being useless. The ornamental woods are ebony, calamander, satin, cocoa-nut, peyimbeya, teak, tamarind, jack, palmyra, &c. The most abundant of the woods used for house and ship-building, of which specimens were sent, were halmanilla, teak, morotto, dawete, mangoe, keena, hall, and horra. Besides *coir*, there are several fibrous substances in Ceylon, capable of being turned to useful purposes. Amongst those forwarded to the Exhibition were fibres, both in their natural and prepared state, from the pine-apple, bibiscus plantain, *Sanseveira zelonica*, and Adam's needle. There were a number of gums and resins unknown in this country, most of which are employed medicinally by the native practitioners. Besides these, a collection of medicinal plants, roots, and seeds, in a dried state, were found. Many of them possess valuable properties, well known in Ceylon, in the removal of fever, dysentery, liver complaint, and cholera. The Dutch and Cingalese doctors seldom have recourse to any but vegetable medicines, and these are often found to succeed where European remedies have failed. The collection was forwarded by Mr. T. Piries, of Kandy.

Under the head of Machinery, Implements, &c., we found three models of the various works and their fittings, as employed on coffee estates. First, there was the *pulping-house*, with its *pulpers, cisterns*, &c., for removing the outer red husk of the coffee berry, and afterwards washing the mucilage from it. Next was the stove, and moveable trays running on wheeled platforms, whereon the washed coffee is exposed to the sun in its inner covering of parchment-skin. When thoroughly dried to a flinty hardness, the berries are removed to the adjoining building, the peeling-house, where a pair of copper-covered wheels are revolving in a circular trough, under which the parchment rapidly breaks, and becomes detached from the coffee beans. Near these we observed another model of a stove for curing coffee. This was of peculiar construction, and fitted up according to a process which had been patented by the ingenious inventor, Mr. Clershew, of the Rathongodde estate. It was formed on the principle of curing the coffee whilst in the *parchment*, by means of a current of hot air, to be used during weather when out-of-door drying would be impossible.

The models of Cingalese palanquins might be regarded rather as curiosities than as specimens of fine work. Too much praise, however, can scarcely be accorded to the construction of the three Cingalese boats, which were unique, not only as specimens of handicraft, but as models of very singular and beautiful vessels. The long sailing canoe, to be fully admired, should be seen in full sail when going at a speed of fourteen miles the hour, which it frequently does. The flat-bottomed fishing dhoney, with its nets and accoutrements, was a very pretty thing. The large dhoney was such as is employed in the coasting trade of Ceylon, for the transport of rice, tobacco, salt, betel-nuts, &c.: they vary in size from 30 to 200 tons; and not the least singular feature about them is, that not one iron nail is used in their build, nothing but wooden pegs and coir string holding the planks and beams together. The plough, harrow, and rake of the Cingalese agriculturist attested the little improvement effected in their operations, which have, no doubt, remained unchanged during the last 1,800 years.

Amongst the manufactured articles, the most attractive was, undoubtedly, a table and stand of ebony, richly carved, and beautifully inlaid with the many-tinted woods of Ceylon. We also noticed a desk composed of porcupine quills, a carved ebony box, an ivory stand in imitation of a cocoa-nut blossom, and some other trifles. These formed but a tithe of what might have been exhibited, had time permitted. There were some rather grotesque specimens of native pottery, the only one worthy of notice being a painted teapot used by the King of Kandy. There were a number of specimens of cordage, &c., woven from the fibres previously named; also a pretty Kandian mat, and several ornaments displayed by the Kandian kings on state occasions, made from fibres, and dyed with indigenous roots. The Veddah bows and arrows were such as are actually employed in the present day by a wild and almost unknown race of Cingalese, in the pursuit of deer, buffaloes, and wild boars. This singular caste of aborigines dwell entirely amongst rocks, or perched in trees like monkeys, living chiefly on roots, seed, and a little deer or buffalo flesh. The manufactured oils of Ceylon were numerous, though most of them are at present unknown in this country. They may be divided into medicinal and commercial. Many of the former are said to possess valuable properties, yet, with the exception of the castor oil, they are not known to any but native practitioners. These were forwarded by Mr. Piries, of Kandy. Of the oils of commerce, the cocoa-nut, cinnamon, lemon-grass, citronella, and kekuna are tolerably well known, the first being highly useful for burning in lamps; the second is chiefly employed in medicine and confectionary. Arrack is a spirit distilled from the fermented juice of the cocoa-nut tree, called *toddy*, and has long been known in England as forming the chief ingredient of Vauxhall punch. The sample sent was very curious, having been upwards of thirty years in bottle, and coming originally from the cellar of the last Dutch governor of Ceylon.

CONTRIBUTIONS FROM CANADA.

By crossing the breadth of the avenue we travelled from Ceylon to Canada, and were within sight of the Cape of Good Hope, Van Diemen's Land, and the produce of the three Australian colonies of New South Wales, Port Phillip (or Victoria), and South Australia. Canada made the best display, as was to be expected from the energetic character of the people, the means they had of obtaining early intelligence, of conveying their goods to this country, and obtaining the cooperation of the governor, the earl of Elgin, and their local authorities. The Canadians held a preliminary exhibition of native produce, and selected from that exhibition the best, as specimens of raw produce and manufactures. The most prominent object was a fire-engine from Montreal, which carried off the first prize at the Canadian exhibition of industry, and was sent, by subscription among a few patriotic Canadians, to show what the mechanics of that fine colony could do. As a carriage, it was extremely handsome. The panels were adorned with paintings of Canadian scenery, views of a great fire at Montreal, the principal churches, banks, and other public buildings, and figures of an Indian in snow shoes in winter costume, of a fireman, &c., executed with a spirit and feeling of reality which raised them above the class of ordinary coach-painting. The body was of copper, from the rich copper mines of Lake Superior, lined with wood. The tool-box was of mahogany. The mechanical arrangements seemed good, and the finish of both the wood and metal work was most creditable to Canadian workmen. It was followed by a hose-box on two wheels, to carry 300 feet of hose, and weighed altogether 25 cwt. It would pump up water from a depth of 27 feet; and according to the statement of the gentleman who manufactured it, would throw 170 feet high from 300 feet of hose. Fire-engines throughout both British and republican America are drawn by men, and not by horses.

They are usually the property of young men associated into voluntary companies, who take great pride in adorning their respective engines. Hence the profusion of painting and other ornamental decorations. Over the fire-engine was suspended a canoe of white birch, which presented no especial difference from canoes we have seen a hundred times, except its size; but this canoe was actually paddled 3,000 miles of lake and river navigation, with a crew of twenty men, before being placed on board a steamer for England. It was the same description of canoe employed by the Hudson's Bay Company in their annual journeys to the vast preserves of fur-bearing animals under their command. We should have been pleased if it had been accompanied by one of the *voyageurs*, whose gay costume, and songs, and semi-savage manners, have been described in the book of Sir George Simpson, late resident governor of Hudson's Bay, or as it is now officially named, Rupert's Land, and several North American travellers. A piano, a large French bedstead, a set of tables and chairs, all elaborately carved out of Canadian black walnut, next came under our notice, as remarkable specimens of a wood as yet little known in this country. In colour, size, beauty of grain, and polish, it was equal, if not superior to the best specimens of French and Italian walnut. A slab, which formed part of the Canadian trophy in the central avenue, was cut from a tree which made 27,000 feet of available timber. The workmanship of this furniture, although very fair, offered nothing remarkable for praise or blame. We liked the emblematic beavers carved round the edge of the table; but not the same animals crawling like rats on the cross bars of the legs. Among the chairs were a set unpolished, and fashioned after some introduced into America by the earliest settlers. It was reported that her majesty had condescended to accept them. One Canadian gentleman was under the impression that the originals had been imported from England in the sixteenth century, by Sebastian Cabot; but that is unlikely, because, although Cabot discovered Labrador, there is no evidence that he formed any settlement in Canada at all. The originals are probably of French origin, and not older than the time of Louis Quatorze. Around the fire-engine were arranged a set of Canadian sleighs. The white one was a cutter for one horse; the next, an elegant long carriage of very graceful curves, was a tandem sleigh; the largest was for a pair or four horses, and was made after the fashion approved by the Military Tandem Club. With the sleighs, we must notice a set of harness that hung on the wall, the saddles covered with bells, and adorned with pendent plumes of blue horse-hair: white plumes of the same material were arranged to wave from brass spikes between the ears of the prancing horses. On a bright winter's day we can imagine no prettier sight than the whole turn-out, with its blood horses, ringing bells, fair ladies wrapped in furs, and dashing fur-wrapped driver, careering across the hard snow or the sounding ice of a frozen river. Furs, skins, horns, and Indian curiosities filled up the interstices of the Canadian collection. The head and wide-spreading horns of a gigantic moose, or elk, might be compared with the European variety of the same species, from the Lithuanian forests, exhibited in the Russian section.

Before we quit Canada, however, we must not omit to make mention of the enormous Canadian timber-trophy, and of the importance of the timber trade in this valuable colony. The Canadas are almost entirely divided by the Ottawa or Grand river, which forms the great highway of the timber trade, on which from eight to ten thousand men are constantly employed; an army waging continual war with the denizens of the forests. The white and red pine have as yet formed the chief timber exports of Canada, which are floated on immense rafts down the Ottawa and the St. Lawrence, a distance of from six to seven hundred miles, to Quebec. A single raft frequently has a surface of three acres, and appears at a distance like some landslip, or island, huts and all, sailing down the river; broad thin boards serve for sails. Some of the white pines yield planks

Engraved by G. Greatbach, from a Drawing by H. Mason.

SLEDGE FROM THE CANADIAN COURT

Engraved by G. Greatbach, from a Drawing by H. Mason.

SLEDGE FROM THE CANADIAN COURT

five feet in breadth, and the largest red pine will give eighteen-inch square logs as much as forty feet long. Of the pine order was the hemlock, a ship's futtock of which was shown in the trophy; and close by it was a thick plank of a beautifully-feathered and highly polished dark wood, from the fork of a black walnut. The tree from which this plank was obtained was a hero of the forest, probably of more than a thousand years' growth. Its circumference at the ground measured 37 feet. The whole tree was cut up into 23 logs, and yielded more than 10,000 feet of timber. Another furniture wood in the trophy was the curled maple, little inferior to satin wood. A bird's-eye maple veneer was also shown. The other timbers in the trophy were more generally known. The last however we noticed was a little log near the floor, with light edges and a dark centre, marked iron wood,—of no earthly use, said our native informant, " It won't float, it's the contrariest wood in creation; if you want a straight piece, and half break your heart with hard work to get it, it will twist itself crooked in no time, and if you mark out a crooked piece, as sure as sunshine it will stretch out as straight as a line; it's as hard as iron and as heavy as lead, and as obstinate and cranky as an old mule, and never worth either letting grow or cutting down." We have a word of advice, in view of this timber trophy, to give our Canadian friends; it is, that they begin to build ships of their better woods. Their firbuilt craft stand but four years A. 1. on Lloyd's list. They do right well to send a cargo of timber to England to help to pay their cost, but are not profitable afloat. We have to face the world now with our ships. Canada has no longer any advantage, and can only hold her place in ship-building, whether for sale or trade, by aiming to build as seaworthy and durable vessels as the Northern and United States. Cheap run-up ships are the dearest in the end; try, therefore, your walnut, red oak, hemlock, and rock elm, and use the pine only where pine is best, and where first-class vessels use it.

The total value of the export of timber from Canada in 1849 was £1,327,532, of which not less than £1,000,000 worth came to England.

AUSTRALIAN CONTRIBUTIONS.

The colonies of Australia, although among the most important of our possessions as producers of raw materials required for our staple manufactures, as large consumers of our manufactures, and as great fields for emigration, had nothing very new or very showy to exhibit. New South Wales, Port Phillip, and South Australia, all sent barrels of fine wheat and flour, which were satisfactory as proving that the intending colonist might depend on cheap bread in those distant regions. Australian wool and tallow are to be seen in such quantities in the warehouses of London and Liverpool, that we need not dwell on those great and annually increasing sources of wealth. The timber, although much of it was good, especially from Van Diemen's Land, and some specimens very ornamental, is not likely to become an article of commerce with this country. The distance is too great to enable it to stand the competition of countries nearer at hand. Van Diemen's Land sent the jaws of a sperm whale—another source of colonial wealth—often hunted down from the shores of that island.

South Australia supplied specimens of the rich copper mine of Burra Burra, which restored the fortunes of that colony, and rendered it one of our most flourishing possessions, at a time when, under the ruinous results of an empirical system of land-jobbing and colonization, it had sunk into the lowest state of depression and stagnation: abandoned by men of enterprise or means, it was on the point of becoming a mere sheep walk. It is a curious fact, that although the copper exports of South Australia exceed a quarter of a million sterling per annum, no copper mine in that colony has paid a dividend except the Burra Burra, but that pays 1,500 per cent. On the walls of the

South Australian section hung a set of clever water-colours, representing the country round this Aladdin's lamp of a copper-mine, and various Australian scenes, bullocks in drays and stockmen riding after cattle. On the wall appropriated to New South Wales, was a beautiful view of Camden, where Macarthur first introduced the fine-woolled sheep, which has proved a living mine of wealth to the whole continent of Australia. Our colonial brethren, who know well how they are appreciated in the City, will excuse us from dwelling on sources of greatness which are more felt than seen : there is nothing picturesque in a sack of wheat, though the grain be "heavy and bright-coloured ;" there is nothing interesting in a tin of preserved Australian beef, excellent though it be, unless to a hungry man ; little variety of "tone or colour" in a fleece fine enough to make the fortune of a Yorkshire manufacturer ; and, as for copper ore, the worst specimens are often the most sparkling. Bottles of Australian wine informed those who were before ignorant, that wine is as easily grown in that country as cider is here.

There was a melancholy tribute paid in the Van Diemen's Land department to its now extinct aborigines. In our forty-years' possession of that settlement we have utterly destroyed them, by as atrocious a series of oppressions as ever were perpetrated by the unscrupulous strong upon the defenceless feeble. Yet these poor people had tastes and industry too. Their bread appears to be worth reviving as a new truffle for soup by the gourmands of Hobart Town. The specimens of the root exhibited weighed 14lbs. They obtained a brilliant shell necklace by soaking and rubbing off the cuticle, and gained various tints by hot decoctions of herbs. They procured paint by burning iron ore, and reducing it to a powder by grindstones. They converted sea-shells and sea-weeds into convenient water-vessels ; they wove baskets, and they constructed boats with safe catamarans. All these things were exhibited. Surely, then, the men whom their greedy supplanters admit to have done this, and whom the least possible pains ever bestowed on them proved to be capable of much more, ought not to have been hunted down, as we know they were, and then almost inveigled to be shut up in an island too small for even the few remaining.

The New South Wales contributions offered no sign of the aborigines' works, and probably the country contains no longer any trace of the people. As Newfoundland contributors do not pretend to an interest in the works of the lost people who once inhabited it, New Brunswick seemed to have nothing to show but the pretty models of an Indian family, the kindness of whose character was attested by having protected two maiden ladies, whose father emigrated from the United States after the American war, and settled among the tribe some seventy years ago. The remnants of the Indians and the remains of the royalists must have had many subjects of sympathy, and many feelings in common, to have maintained so long a career of mutual respect. The whole amount of aboriginal articles exhibited was much smaller than it would certainly have been, but for circumstances deserving of notice. Of late years the political condition of the aborigines connected with various civilized nations, has been a subject more than usually interesting to the public. The emancipation of our negro slaves in 1834 having in a great measure settled that question, the attention of philanthropists was free to be directed to the persecutions suffered by the aborigines of our colonies. This was an extensive inquiry, and some reforms took place. Then a reaction occurred ; until at length the old law of force and oppression extensively recovered its influence. In this state of things the Exhibition was planned, upon the principle of an universal invitation of the nations of the earth to bring specimens of their industry and art under a common inspection. The commissioners made no exceptions ; but it was impossible that they should grant a privilege, or any special advantage, even to the least favoured in actual condition. The collection of articles to be exhibited was necessarily left to the cost and activity of the contributors and their various supporters. France was to take care of her people, Germany of hers, America of hers. The peculiar claims of the less advanced aborigines for aid were discussed; but all that could be done was carefully to make known in various quarters that the Exhibition would be open to them. The result has been, that the same circumstances which render them inferior to civilized men in accumulated property and in acquired knowledge, have operated to leave their show of industrial development in the Exhibition somewhat meagre, whatever equality of capacity may be conceded to them, and however acute their natural intelligence.

The Cape of Good Hope sent one article deserving special notice—the ivory of an elephant's trunk, of 163 lbs., which must be a fine specimen. Ivory is chiefly bought of the natives; and, from Mr. Gordon Cumming's account of his own trading, its mystery may be interpreted to mean extraordinary hard dealing on our part. He had carried into the interior muskets, for twenty of which he had paid £16, and obtained ivory in exchange at a profit of 3,000 per cent., which, as he was informed by merchantmen, was "a very fair profit." To be sure, the manner in which the black chief, of whom he bought the ivory, had obtained it, by oppression inflicted on the Bushmen who killed the elephants, invites little consideration for that chief: but the whole story furnishes a fresh argument in favour of the civilization which we, consumers of this beautiful product of the desert, are bound to use all means to substitute for its existing barbarism. The South African assortment of *karosses*, or cloaks made of the skins of wild animals skilfully dressed, ostrich feathers, and ivory, represented the aboriginal produce, for which the Cape traders carry into the wilderness to the native tribes, beads of many colours and sizes, brass and copper wire, knives and hatchets, clothing, guns, ammunition, &c.

CHAPTER IX.

NUMBER OF VISITORS—SOLIDITY OF THE BUILDING—AMUSEMENTS—ORGANS—PIANOFORTES—
BEES—MOONLIGHT EFFECT.

WE have promised our readers that, in the record of our retrospective visits to the Crystal Palace, we should depart from the dull routine of ordinary description—the methodical precision of the pedant, who never leaves a subject till he has hunted it fairly down, till he has exhausted the patience of his listeners in never-ending disquisition on every possible variety, from class A to class Z, that in all imaginable profusion, culled from every quarter of the globe, was crowded within the bounds of the fairy structure. We shall, for a short period, altogether leave the contemplation of these matters, and revert to a renewed admiration of the building itself; its extraordinary lightness, both aërial and architectural, its matchless solidity and strength, and its wonderful adaptation for the reception of the selected treasures of the whole earth, as well as of the congregated thousands of its inhabitants that crowded in daily-increasing numbers to gaze upon and enjoy them. Indeed, the human tide that, from the very day of the opening of the building—from the 1st of May, 1851,—an epoch that will be celebrated in every future age—flowed with increasing force into the interior of the palace, was greater than even the most sanguine expectation had anticipated; every week the numbers rose to a higher figure, every week the stream of wealth that flowed into its exchequer was more deep and copious. It was at one time proposed to limit the number of visitors to 60,000, but the continual tramp of these 60,000 shook not in the slightest degree the solidity of the building; the galleries, the stairs, the floors, were all as buoyant, as elastic as ever; and, although full and free limit was finally afforded to as many thousands more as chose to enter, still there was "ample verge and space enough," and the fairy structure stood unshaken and unharmed. From the country the rural population, in many instances headed by their pastor, or their chief magistrates, came in admiring throngs, clad in their smock-frocks, "all lily-white," thronged the agricultural departments, and took their fill of wonder and delight; the population of our manufacturing towns besieged, *en masse*, the departments of mechanic art and invention, and greedily devoured the mental feast that was presented to their eager gaze. The very schoolboys, too, and youthful maidens, had their holiday trip within these precincts, which often resounded to their clamorous and innocent mirth, and re-echoed to the sound of castanets, and merry feet that beat the ground in jocund hilarity.

In the meanwhile, to delight the more imaginative ear, at stated intervals the solemn organ, from various parts of the edifice, breathed its magnificent harmonies around, for there were several of these noble instruments within its walls. The most celebrated among them, the Leviathan, which reared its lofty structure at the western end of the gallery, was of the largest class of church organs, and its size and extent may be judged of from the synopsis which we shall give of its contents. It was built by Mr. Willis, a young London organ-builder, who doubtless sought to make his fame by this great effort; and he certainly deserved high praise for the boldness and spirit of his enterprise, by which the Exhibition was put in possession of a specimen of far greater magnitude and costliness than it would otherwise have boasted. The instrument referred to, which was constructed somewhat after the German model, had three rows of keys (or claviers) —the great organ, the choir organ, and the swell, the compass of each being from C C (in the bass) to G in alt., 56 notes. It had two octaves and-a-half of pedals; and seven coupling stops, by means of which the three rows of keys could be united in various ways, and the pedals brought to act on each of the three claviers at pleasure. The pedal organ contained 14 stops, the total number of pipes being 576. The great organ had 20 stops, numbering in all 1,456 pipes. The choir organ, consisting of 14 stops, contained 760 pipes. The swell organ, with 22 stops, commanded 1,682 pipes. The total number of stops, including couplers, was 77; of pipes, 4,474. This organ had the application of the pneumatic valve, the invention of Mr. Barker, and first applied, we believe, by Mons. Cavaillé, the French organ-builder. The effect of this movement was to lighten the touch, which, in instruments of great magnitude on the old system, was usually so deep and heavy as to fatigue and distress the player, and render difficult or impossible any passages of rapid execution. With the pneumatic valve, however, the touch of the largest organ is rendered almost as facile and agreeable as that of a pianoforte. The principle consists in connecting with the movement of each key a small reservoir, into which, on the pressure of the key, the wind rushes from the main bellows of the instrument with such force as to relieve the finger of the performer from that effort which would otherwise be necessary. The same principle has been also applied by Mr. Willis to the mechanism for drawing the stops, which, in addition to the old method of registers placed on each side of the performer, he effects by means of little brass knobs placed over the keys, so that the player may, by an instantaneous touch of his thumb, while playing, effect the desired change. The organ was what is technically termed a 32-feet instrument, which signifies that the deepest-toned pipe is nominally 32 feet in length—giving the note which the Germans distinguish as C C C C, in other words, two octaves lower than the fourth string of a violoncello. Besides the English organs, of which there were several remarkable specimens, there were two of foreign manufacture, and of considerable magnitude, one from Germany, the other from France. The former

Engraved by G. Greatbach from a Drawing by W. Tomlinson

REGISTERED PIANOFORTE WITH IMPROVED JOINT,

MANUFACTURED BY J. BRINSMEAD

Engraved by G. Greatbach, from a Drawing by W. Tomlinson.

WALNUT TREE WOOD — COTTAGE PIANOFORTE,

MANUFACTURED BY J. ALLISON

was the work of Herr Schulze, of Rudolstadt. It had 16 stops, two rows of keys and pedals, and was suitable for a church or chapel of moderate size. Some of the stops, particularly the flutes and the labial metal stops, were of very good quality, having that peculiarly plaintive tone which is scarcely ever met with but in the German organs. The chorus or mixture stops, as in most German instruments, were somewhat shrill and harsh to English ears. The French organ was well placed in the main avenue, and stood in an oak case, some 30 feet or more in height. It was the production of Monsieur Ducroquet, of Paris, and contained 20 stops, two rows of keys, and two octaves of pedals. Mr. Barker's pneumatic valves were also applied here, and the mechanism generally appeared to be exceedingly good. The quality of the instrument was also worthy of praise—being brilliant without harshness in its full power, and delicate but not feeble in its solo stops. The reeds (for which the French have long been celebrated), were of excellent quality. In addition to the soul-entrancing symphonies that were poured forth by this king of instruments, the more brilliant notes of the piano, touched by a master-hand, failed not to draw a crowd of delighted listeners within the magic sphere of its influence, and imparted a sort of drawing-room festivity to the place, graced as it was with the loveliest forms of beauty and fashion, and adorned with every object that the combined efforts of science, of industry, and of art, could lavish to enhance its perfection, and support its unrivalled claim to the admiration it elicited from all quarters of the globe. We will here pause awhile, and allow our readers to indulge their imagination in a retrospect of the pleasures they doubtless enjoyed in their visits to this renowned temple of industry and art; for who, save and except the gallant and eccentric legislator, whose sayings and whose doings the inimitable *Punch* has delighted to record and to celebrate—who, we ask, that could command "a splendid shilling," failed to pay their respects to the Crystal Palace. Distance, however remote, presented no obstacle to the adventurous traveller; perils by land and sea were disregarded, mountains were scaled, deserts passed over, and the unfathomable deep was crowded with sails. Even extreme old age, and crippled infirmity, found ways and means to enter and enjoy the sight. Witness the marvellous old dame, from Cornwall, we believe, who, past her hundredth year, travelled up to town, and paced with willing feet through the various intricacies of the place, and gratified her aged eyes in beholding wonders, such as in her juvenile days had never been even dreamed of in the wildest flights of the most extravagant imagination. Tender infants, too, in maternal arms, were carried about, that in after times they might be able to say that they, too, had been within the walls of the wonder of the world. The scene, however, was not altogether an idle one. Industry on an extensive scale in the midst of all this mirth, bustle, and enjoyment, was steadily going on in more than one part of the immense fabric. Let not our readers be startled, when they are gravely assured, that an extensive manufactory of two of the most useful articles in domestic life was in full progress, perfecting its produce without hands, though not without living impulse—that more than 200,000 little animated beings were diligently engaged in their occupation, an occupation which man, with all his chymic lore, cannot imitate, uninterrupted by all the noise and confusion around them, and joining to the "busy hum of men," their own industrious murmur—that winged race, in short, which, as Milton beautifully relates—

> " ———— when the sun with Taurus rides
> Pour forth their populous youth about the hive
> In clusters; they among fresh dews and flowers
> Fly to and fro. or on the smoothed plank,
> The suburb of their straw-built citadel,
> New rubbed with balm, expatiate and confer
> Their state affairs :"   *   *

Q

There were indeed several interesting contributions of bees and beehives, and contrivances for securing swarms, not only from various parts of the United Kingdom, but also from France, Germany, and the United States of America. Among the most interesting were those of Mr. Milton and Mr. Neighbour. The inhabitants of Mr. Milton's " mansion of industry," which, with his " Royal Alfred hive," and the " unicomb hive," occupied a large space close to the wall of the north transept gallery, the whole being enclosed in a large glass case, forming, in fact, a very fine apiary, consisted of four swarms of bees, the first of which was hived on the 20th of July, 1850; the second and third on the 23rd of the same month, and the fourth on the 31st. As hiving the bees after swarming is one of the operations which requires the greatest care and attention on the part of the bee-keeper, it may be as well to mention the mode adopted by Mr. Milton, of successively hiving the four swarms of bees within a few days of each other, and uniting the whole together, "without any trouble or fighting about queens,' the immense population, amounting, according to Mr. Milton, as we have before stated, to 200,000 strong, continued to work harmoniously together, after a residence of nearly four months in their apparently close quarters. The first of these swarms came out about three o'clock on the 20th of July, as above, and was immediately secured or hived in a wooden box, which was left in a shady place until eight o'clock in the evening, when it was removed to its intended position. The two swarms, which came out on the 23rd of July, were each hived in a common straw hive, and at eight o'clock at night a cloth was spread on the ground near to the box-hive, a brick being placed on the cloth, on which to rest one of the sides of the box, for the purpose of admitting the bees into the box. After being tumbled altogether into the cloth by a smart rap on the brick with one edge of the hive, the other swarm was treated precisely in a similar manner; both swarms were speedily underneath the box, which was left undisturbed till the following morning, when it was put back again to its proper position in the apiary. On the 31st of the same month the same process was performed with the fourth swarm. Contiguous to Milton's mansion of industry was the " Royal Alfred hive," named after his Royal Highness Prince Alfred, on whose birthday, the 6th of August, 1844, the first experiment of placing bees within this newly-formed hive was successfully made. The principal novelty in this hive appeared to be the inclined floors, by which the bees could easily ascend to any part of the hive, and the dead bees and other refuse, instead of remaining, as on level floors, necessarily fell to the bottom, and so were easily removed. There were, on the two upper sloping compartments, covered over with flaps hung with hinges, three bell glasses in each, which would hold altogether about eighteen pounds of honey. By means of windows, the whole of the interior could be inspected from time to time, without any risk or annoyance. The bees might be fed either at top or in front. Milton's revolving top hive, for which he received the Society of Arts' silver Ceres medal in 1846, consisted of a cylindrical case of straw, covered with two boards having corresponding holes in each, by turning the upper one of which the openings could be closed at pleasure. Bell-shaped glasses were placed on the top above the openings, which, when filled, might be readily removed, and fresh glasses substituted. Bees are easily hived by this arrangement, by placing the hive from which they are to be removed on the revolving board, taking care to leave only one opening, and the bees will severally descend into their new habitation without any trouble, the lower hive being prepared for their reception by washing its interior walls with a mixture of sugar and beer, or other suitable sweet liquor. Mr. Neighbour's apiary consisted of a large glass case, with parts of the sides covered with perforated zinc, for the sake of ventilation. This apiary also contained three hives: first, Neighbour's ventilating box-hive; Neighbour's observatory glass hive; and a two-storied square box-hive, with sloping roof. From this latter the bees decamped within a week after they had been hived, owing to some disturbance, or to the dislike taken by the bees to their new habitation. The ventilating box-hive was square, and had windows and shutters. The entrance was at the back, enabling the bees to go to Kensington-gardens, or other resort. In front, at bottom, was a long door hung with hinges, so that all dead bees and refuse could be easily cleared away. By means of a perforated metal slide in the floor, ventilation, which some apiarians contend for, was effected. Above the wooden box was placed a bell-glass, into which the bees ascended to work by means of a circular opening in the top of the square box. In the top of the bell-glass was an aperture through which was inserted a tubular trunk of perforated zinc, to take off the moisture from within. The observatory hive was of glass, with a superior crystal compartment, an opening being formed between the two. A straw cover was suspended over the upper compartment by a rope over a pulley, which cover was raised up by the attendant at pleasure. The larger or bottom compartment rested on a wooden floor, which had a circular sinking therein to receive the bell-glass. A landing-place, projecting, with sunken way, to enable the bees to pass in and out, completed the contrivance. These exceedingly curious little palaces of industry proved a great point of attraction to the labouring population, and drew many a group of honest rustics around them, not from England alone, but from other parts of the world as well, and much interest was exhibited with respect to the movements of their busy inmates. Her Majesty also, and Prince Albert, frequently bestowed their notice on the wonderful operations of the gifted little insects, whose undeviating attention to their own concerns, in the midst of all the various distraction of sound and sight that surrounded them, afforded an admirable lesson to those who suffer themselves to be led away from the more important concerns of life by petty and unavoidable annoyances.

In the immense variety of all these different objects of interest that solicited the attention of the curious spectator, whether scientific or otherwise, a lover of art, or a mere lounger, there was abundance of food to satisfy the appetite of all, and the daily increasing demand for it served at once to show how vast is the desire for information that influences all classes of the people; and the order and tranquillity that pervaded the moving masses, evinced not only their gratitude for the feast that was provided, but the great improvement that has taken place in the morals and manners of the lower classes, and how easily they may be led to the consideration of topics that are too apt to be regarded as belonging exclusively to the privileged few, to whom, through their adventitious advantages of hereditary rank or affluence, they are more readily accessible. The whole of every "live-long" day, then, within the walls of the Crystal Palace, was one continued scene of movement, bustle, and excitement, from the early dawn, when preparations were made for the reception of the innumerable guests that were expected to be in attendance—first and foremost amongst whom was our own gracious Queen, who in her repeated visits to the mighty emporium, may be considered to have gained as complete a knowledge of its various contents, as the most inquisitive among her subjects —from the hour, we repeat, when the gates were thrown open for the admission of the public, till the moment arrived for their final departure, when gradually as the lingering crowd retired, the continuous buzz arising from so many congregated thousands began to subside,—the Crystal Palace presented one unvaried aspect of delighted enjoyment and innocent festivity; and when the shades of night at length stole over the scene, when the silence was complete, and the moon arose above the trees in the park, and shed her pale lustre upon the glittering roof of the building, another picture presented itself to the contemplation of the curious spectator, which we shall gratify our readers with describing in the eloquent language of the *Times*, and with which description we shall close our present chapter.

THE CRYSTAL PALACE BY MOONLIGHT.

To those who had seen the interior during the daytime, filled with thousands of spectators, and agitated by all the bustle of sight-seeing, it was difficult to realize the aspect which the same presented when the crowds had departed, when the gates were closed, and the police had taken under their entire control that vast collection of the trophies of human industry. One could scarcely comprehend the strength of that confidence in the law and in the security of property which reconciled 15,000 exhibitors, gathered from every civilized country in the world, speaking different languages, and brought up under different forms of government, to trust the most valued evidences of their skill, their wealth, their enterprise, night after night, to a body of about fifty policemen, paid little above the ordinary wages of labour, and armed against dangers from without with no weapon more formidable than a bâton. A Russian jeweller was the only person we heard of as showing any uneasiness in the exercise of this confidence. He wanted to be convinced that his diamonds were safe, and accordingly he applied for an order to visit them by night. His request was granted, and he soon had a practical test of the watchful care taken of his property. Standing in front of his glass case, and satisfying himself that all was safe, he happened to turn round, and there to his astonishment he found that he had a constable at either elbow, superintending his movements, and by no means disposed, from their looks, to take his honesty for granted. We visited the Crystal Palace ourselves, but in a less sceptical spirit than the Russian jeweller, and for a different purpose. We wished to see the aspect of the interior under the influence of a fine clear moonlight, to observe how each object of interest varied in expression when looked at through a new medium, to contrast with the bustle and thronging excitement of the day the effects of silence, solitude, and darkness. Let the reader accompany us in our survey, and share in the impressions which it produced. In the centre everything was plainly revealed; the pinnacles of the crystal fountain appeared tipped with silver, and in the basin below, the ribs and sash-bars overhead and the sky beyond them, and portions of the adjacent galleries, and the occasional glimmer of gas-lights, were all reflected with marvellous distinctness. An air of solemn repose pervaded the vast area; the very statues seemed to rest from the excitement of the day, and to slumber peaceably on their pedestals. Some were enveloped in white coverings, which in the doubtful light gave them a ghostly appearance; others remained unprotected from the night air, and braved exposure to cold as they had already done to criticism. At one point of intersection between the nave and transept, Virginius under the flare of a gas-lamp from the China compartment, brandished the knife with which he had sacrificed his daughter. At another corner, and under a similar dispensation of light from Persia, a cavalier leaned upon his sword, and appeared to be calculating the number of people that had passed him during the day. Of Turkey and Egypt we could see only at the entrance the faint glitter of Damascus blades and of brocaded muslins and trappings. All beyond was buried in darkness and mystery. The shades of night, too, fell heavily upon Greece, Spain, and Italy, though behind them, through the open girders, gleams of unexplained light were seen rising. The zinc statue of the queen rested in grateful obscurity, and Lemonnière's jewel-case had cautiously been stripped of its attractions. On the metal pipes of Ducroquet's organ some struggling moonbeams played, though without evoking any sound. The colossal group of " Cain and his Family" looked well in a gloom which seemed suited to his expression of guilt qualified by the traces of human affection. So it was all down the eastern nave. The shades of night, which fell heavily on some points, were strangely relieved at intervals by gas, which carried the eye forward over intervening objects to those immediately around it. Instead of looking at those things which lay nearest, attention was directed to distant and out-of-the-way spots, brought into prominence by the light streaming upon them. Policemen in list slippers might occasionally be seen flitting noiselessly to a point whence the strangers might be reconnoitred, or suddenly emerging from behind some dark object where they had remained for a time cautiously stowed away. If a court was entered, or a divergence made to the right or to the left, the quick eyes and the scarcely discernible footfall of some member of 'the force' followed. Over the whole interior a profound silence reigned, broken only at intervals as the clocks of the building rang out slowly the advancing hour. Turning towards the western half of the interior, huge envelopes of calico concealed most of the objects facing the nave, but the large trophies in the centre remained uncovered, and looked solemn and grand in the dim neutral light which prevailed. The Indian shirts of mail and the model prahus of the East were favoured by the beams of the moon. The chandeliers of Apsley Pellat and Co. caught the eye in passing, and glistened as if anxious to have their illuminating properties tested. Glimpses were again caught of remote galleries brought into prominence by gas-lamps. In some places light shone, though whence it came appeared a mystery. In others there was almost a Cimmerian darkness. The contributions to the carriage department were swathed in calico, while the gigantic locomotives disdained any covering, and rested in grim repose. The activity of mules, spinning-frames, and looms was hushed, the whirl of driving-wheels was silent, and amidst the whole of that usually noisy department dedicated to machinery in motion, the only sound we heard was that of a cricket chirruping away merrily amidst Whitworth's tools.

CHAPTER X.

FOREIGN AND COLONIAL DEPARTMENTS—*continued.*

FRENCH DEPARTMENT—RAW ARTICLES—LYONS MANUFACTURES—SCULPTURE AND FINE ART—DECORATIVE ART—FANS—VASES, ETC.—ARTIFICIAL FLOWERS—BELGIAN DEPARTMENT—FURNITURE—ARMS—LACE.

UNQUESTIONABLY the French collection, next to that of the United Kingdom, was one of the most attractive and extensive in the Exhibition. The lengthened and successful experience enjoyed by France in exhibitions of national industry, gave to the exhibitors an advantage not possessed by the majority of those contributing to the Exhibition, so far at least as concerned the arrangement and execution of necessary minor details. No class of the Exhibition was left unrepresented by our continental neighbours. The total number of exhibitors amounted to about 1,750, and the area they occupied was very extensive, both on the north and south sides of the main eastern avenue and in the galleries. In raw materials, the beautiful specimens of raw and thrown silk attracted universal admiration; and an interesting specimen of cocoons in the frames, in which the silkworms are reared and spin, gave a good idea of the manner in which the culture of these insects is carried on. Hemp, wool, and other textile materials, were also interesting, as well as those more delicate chemical preparations in which the French more particularly excel other nations. Specimens also of metals were not wanting, and articles of food were largely exhibited. Machinery was likewise displayed in fair proportion, though here the superiority was decidedly in favour of the British collection of similar objects. Still considerable ingenuity was evinced in philosophical instruments, and in various kitchen contrivances; matters, indeed, in which our continental neighbours have been long accustomed to claim a fair right of precedence.

Among the manufactures, we are bound to notice as the first in importance, the gorgeous productions of the silk-looms of Lyons, which were arranged in cases in the gallery. The cotton, wool, and linen manufactures were also interesting, and the skilful arrangement of these articles added greatly to their attractiveness. The splendid and justly celebrated tapestries of the Gobelins, and of the manufactory of Beauvais, certainly formed one of the most interesting features of the whole collection. The manufacture of Sèvres too, in richness, rarity, and costliness, was unrivalled. Much talent was also displayed in the design and execution of useful and ornamental furniture, and a vast profusion of articles of *bijouterie, virtû,* &c., and jewellery were heaped around. Photographs, both talbotype and daguerreotype, were exhibited, and various objects of sculpture and of the fine arts added to the interest of the collection. We would more particularly notice among the sculpture, a very masterly group of " Eve," by De Bay, exhibited in the Gobelins room, the idea of which struck us as both poetical and picturesque, and ably carried out. The first mother appeared to be lost in a reverie as to the future destinies of her offspring, the principal incidents of which were foreshadowed to the spectator in the bas-relief sculpturings of the pedestal. All things considered, we should be inclined to pronounce this to be one of the finest works of sculpture that the Exhibition contained. Some have given it the fanciful title of the " First Cradle," or " Nature's Cradle ;" but as that does not do justice to the poetic mystery involved in the conception, we prefer the simpler title by which we have denoted it. We cannot bestow similar commendation on M. Le Seigneur's colossal group, in plaster, of "St. Michael overthrowing the Dragon," which stood in the east nave, a specimen of the more exaggerated school, which prevails to an alarming extent amongst our French neighbours. Vicious in composition, it disturbed the eye with innumerable angular projections. In fine, it had all the vice of ill-studied and incomplete action, whilst there was nothing in the character or expression of the principal figure (whose costume was absurd) to redeem the more glaring defects of the composition.

Let us return, however, to the more graceful and lighter productions for which the French are so justly celebrated, and which reveal an activity of imagination indicative of a highly developed social and political vitality—a universality of gracefulness in every article, for the use even of the poorest, demonstrating the spread of those sentiments which make taste a humble luxury for all, if not an indispensable accessory to the enjoyment of life. Throughout the French compartment no one could fail to notice the Protean shapes and styles in which the same objects presented themselves. One Sèvres vase was oriental : another was antique ; a third recalled the breakfast-table of Mesdames Pompadour or Du Barri ; a fourth intimated the Majolica of Guid' Ubaldo of Urbino ; a fifth recalled the tazze of Jean Courtois or Liotard. One fragment of ornament was Pompeian, another pure Italian, another Louis Quinze ; and thus the flowers of all time were combined in the modern Parisian bouquet. All this variety of style—springing rather from impressions and floating recollections than from any desire to copy with servility—bears testimony to the spread of a popular knowledge of the history of art ; and it could only become universal in a country in which models of art had been popularized through every imaginable variety of graphic reproduction. So long as France is likely to retain her title of " Queen of Fashion," so long must she continue to be the cleverest adapter and remodeller of old designs. The vivacity of her artists checks any approach to fac-simile copying ; and so skilfully are her revivals made, that, while they seldom fail to recal a pleasing original type, they yet possess all the freshness of novel and generally appropriate design. Thus, in the ebony cabinet exhibited by Ringuet le Prince, the mind was carried back to some of the charming pieces of furniture still to be met with here and there in the old palaces of Italy—and yet the whole was composed and modelled with so much taste and freshness, that no doubt was entertained as to the cleverness of the artist, or his merits as an original designer. Again, in Marcelin's imitation of Indian inlaying in minute mosaic work, there was just sufficient departure from the original (principally in point of colour) to determine the work to be very clever French, instead of oriental. To cite examples of a similar nature would be an almost endless labour; it may suffice generally to notice, as illustrative of the principle, the revivals of enamelling on copper in the Sèvres collection—the reproduction of the processes of Florentine and Milanese mosaic work by Theret—the examples of quasi-Indian embroidery of Billecoq; and the revivification of the spirit of Ghiberti and his Florentine successors in the "bronzes artistiques" of Barbedienne, and many others. It is a fact almost peculiar to France, of all the nations of the earth, that there appears to be scarcely a style or a process ever naturalized upon her soil which the Frenchman of to-day cannot produce in as great or greater perfection than that to which his ancestors were wont to carry it. In the stained glass of Gerente, Mareschal, Laurent G'sell, Hermanowska, and Lusson, the old glories of Suger and the Sainte Chapelle are still transmitted to us. In the productions of Ponssilgne Russand, Villemsens, and Rudolphi, the Limoges enamels, with which France supplied the world in the thirteenth and fourteenth centuries, are still elaborated with a spirit equal to their prototypes. In the royal manufactory at Sèvres every variety of preparing and painting enamel on copper, which was in use in the sixteenth and seventeenth centuries, by Leonard Limousin, Jean Courtois, Penicault, Luzanne Court, Nouailhier, &c., down to Toutin, and Petitot of Bordier, is still performed with a zeal and spirit worthy of the industry and talent of the great Limousin. The charming vases, dishes, and figures in "faïence," with which the indomitable Bernard de Palissy was wont to gladden the eyes of his royal master, the great Francis, are reproduced in the highest perfection, by Avisseau. Many a frequenter of the old curiosity shops on the Quay Voltaire has been taken in by the modern ivory carvings of Normandy, which simulate the the mediæval *retables*, triptics, and *cors de chasse*, with a spirit and exactitude calculated to deceive all but the most knowing in such matters. Again, in silks and ribbons, and in paper-hangings—while nature generally furnishes the base—flowers and other objects are indicated so gracefully, and relieved from one another with such delicacy in each case, as to convey no sensation of imperfection. It is in the almost universal exercise of a judicious taste, retaining for each object its peculiar and appropriate style of treatment, that the great strength of the French artist-manufacturers (for so they must be called) consists. Taking, for example, so common an object as the rose, how gracefully we shall find its treatment varied! On a Sèvres vase it was painted up to nature—or to Constantin (for they are nearly the same thing). On a paper-hanging of Mader's, or Delacourt's, a few bold touches of "chique" served, at a little distance, to convey almost as perfect an idea of the flower as was given by the elaboration of the China painting. The flower transferred to Lyons silk was the same in form, but changed in chiar'-oscuro—the dark was gone, and all was light and brilliant. On a ribbon of St. Etienne the form was simplified; delicate white lines marked the separation of the rose leaves from each other, and the ultimatum of conventionality was attained: carried but one step further, the thing would become a meaningless red blot.

To descend to still more graceful trivialities, Duvelleroy has made a *specialité* of fans, in the production of which he is perhaps without a rival. His fame extends not only over Europe, but has made its way to remote quarters of the globe. Even the Chinese, so famous for their fans, so unwilling to learn, and jealous of change, have copied his designs. It would be rather difficult to describe the truly gorgeous fan which this celebrated artist has made for the Emperor of Morocco. It is a fan of wonderful magnificence, and, to say nothing of the painting and general enrichment, the diamonds and jewels alone have cost more than £1,000. He exhibited also a set of fans illustrating the stories of the " Arabian Nights," which had been made to order for the Sultan of Turkey. But our present business is with the *éventail royal*. In this little work of art, her Majesty and Prince Albert were represented sitting in the drawing-room at Buckingham Palace, surrounded by their royal children, after a picture by Winterhalter. The handle was of mother-of-pearl, and the medallions in carved gold. In the centre of the handle were the royal arms of England, carved in alto-relievo, in the thickness of the mother-of-pearl: the lion and unicorn supported the 'scutcheon; and the two mottoes, *Honi soit qui mal y pense*, and *Dieu et mon droit*, appeared in letters of mother-of-pearl on a ground of gold. Each of the radiating branches was terminated by a royal crown, and the two principal branches bore, chiselled in the mother-of-pearl, and richly gilded, portraits of the Queen and her Royal Consort. We understand that M. Duvelleroy employs upwards of two thousand men. This is easily accounted for, when we state that he makes fans as low as a half-penny each, and that even these have, every one of them, to pass through the hands of fifteen workmen. Before we quit the French department, which for the present we are about to do, and enter upon that of Belgium, we must not omit to notice the display of ornamental and sculptured silver by M. Froment-Meurice, which was, taken altogether, the handsomest on the foreign side of the Exhibition, some of the works displaying an amount of artistic feeling and executive power worthy of the days of Cellini. A very handsome vase was exhibited which had been presented by the city of Paris to M. Emmeny, an engineer of eminence, to whom the Parisians are largely indebted for their present water supply. The sculpture was by Klagmann, and was partly done *en repoussé*, or by punching, and partly cast; the whole richly chased and engraved. The little groups on either side were two out of twelve representing the months, or seasons—very elegant little works, about ten inches high, and all done *en repoussé*. Another attractive and beautiful object in the French department was the case containing Constantin's artificial flowers. We wish we could, within our limits, do justice to the exquisite truth and delicacy exhibited by M. Constantin in an art which he may fairly be said, if not to have created, at least to have brought to a point of excellence which it had never reached before. We may briefly observe, that these productions were hardly to be called artificial flowers, in the every-day sense, being in beauty and in almost everything but smell, identical with those of nature. Roses, lilies, hot-house plants, ivies, and endless other varieties, were here before us, as it were, *in propriâ personâ*, and not always in full bloom, but occasionally represented, with most truthful effect, in their way of declining and withering, with the canker-worm at the core, and blight upon the face. All these wonderful realizations were produced in one material—cambric; and very high praise is due to the artist who has achieved what he has done with it.

THE BELGIAN DEPARTMENT.

In close conjunction with republican France we had the little constitutional kingdom of Belgium occupying the bays on both sides, and a portion of the northern galleries of the eastern nave, and its contributions included specimens of almost every branch of industrial occupation; agriculture, commerce, manufactures, mining, and fine arts, were all creditably represented. For more than four centuries this flourishing state has maintained its manufacturing and agricultural position, notwithstanding the various con-

SHIELD AND ARMS.

BY GUÉYTON.

SHIELD AND ARMS.

BY LEPAGE & DELACOUR.

flicts of which it has been the battle-field, of revolutions and political changes which it was doomed to undergo, until its final establishment as a limited monarchy. As far back indeed as the days of imperial Rome, the Flemish cities were celebrated for their manufactured goods. In the latter part of the fifteenth century, Brussels, Antwerp, Louvain, and Ghent, employed an immense population in woollen manufactures. Ghent alone had upwards of 30,000 looms; and the weavers of that city mustered 16,000 men in arms. Mechlin and Brussels originated the thread lace of inimitable texture:

> " With eager beats his Mechlin cravat moves,"

sung the mellifluous Pope in his celebrated town pastorals, bearing testimony to the undiminished value of that highly prized article in his own time; and the black silk of Antwerp still preserves its high renown among the votaries of fashion. With only forty miles of coast, and with only two indifferent ports, Belgium struggled through many difficulties to establish a foreign trade, which at length her net-work of railroads enabled her to accomplish, and to present to the world the varied exhibition we are about to describe. And here we may observe that the arrangement which rendered France and Belgium next door neighbours in the Crystal Palace, as they are when at home, suggests a question which the minister of commerce would be rather puzzled to answer.

Between France and Belgium there is a war of custom-houses and an interchange of smugglers, chiefly in the shape of large dogs, which carry Belgian tobacco and lace into France, and bring back French silk or some such article. Every French *douanier* is provided with a thick volume of instructions on the art of stopping, seizing, detecting, poisoning, and shooting Belgian smuggler dogs. Nevertheless, day and night—especially at night—large packs of contraband hounds, heavily laden, rush past the bewildered officers. Now, when Belgium was part of the French empire, its manufactures, its coal, its cattle, its corn, were all freely admitted into France; nothing was taxed, nothing was prohibited; since the disjunction everything that is not taxed is prohibited, and yet the line of division between the two countries is purely imaginary, and the people who, under Napoleon, were free to interchange their goods, must have had just the same wants the day after the custom-house division made it unlawful as the day before. Why, then, was interchange useful before Napoleon's last campaign, and baneful after his dethronement? But to begin our walk through the Belgian territory in the Crystal Palace. We first entered the southern bay, where we found a varied display of textiles of every kind, which seemed very little visited by the curious crowd, although, no doubt, our manufacturers in the same line gave them a close examination. There we also found the cheap mixed fabrics of woollen and cotton, the fine kerseymeres in which the Belgians can undersell our Gloucestershire and West of England men; also capital stout canvass and damask linen from districts of Flanders which grew flax and wove linen long before Belfast was founded; printed silk handkerchiefs in praise of which nothing could be said, and woollen shawls of very dull, dowdy patterns. In this department almost every kind of woollen and mixed woollen was to be found. The sides of the next section were hung with carpets from the Royal Belgian Manufactory of Tournai, which, like the French Gobelins and Beauvais manufactories, is carried on with government money. An imposing stand of arms next attracted our attention, evincing the warlike disposition of the people; then we passed through a vast collection of saddlery articles, of boots also and of shoes, and of sportsmanlike gaiters for the service of those who shoot in woodland districts. The collection of arms was chiefly furnished by Liege, and presented specimens of the commonest *Brummagem*, as well as of the most expensive and finished article, both military and sporting. Rifles, too, were there of the Swiss fashion, over which a paper was affixed, stating that one of the rifles, fired from a rest, at a mark

s

four inches in diameter, at a distance of 110 yards, made 95 hits out of 100. Behind these engines of destruction were arranged those subservient to peaceful occupations, agricultural and mineral, in all their useful variety, to processes connected with the culture and weaving of flax, hemp, and silk, in all their various branches.

Crossing the grand avenue, we observed several splendid carriages, and a profusion of furniture, carved and richly covered with velvet. Two oaken cabinets particularly struck us, of a grave and ecclesiastical character, ornamented with figures of angels. On ascending to the galleries we found, at the top of the stairs, three figures, of life-size, in embroidered ecclesiastical robes, that far outrivalled all the glittering wardrobe to be seen at Madame Tussaud's. These represented the Archbishop of Paris, Affré, who was killed in the last revolution at the barricades; St. Carlo Borommeo, an Italian saint and archbishop, whose embalmed body, enclosed in a glass-case, we have seen at Florence, in the costly chapel dedicated to his memory, enriched with gold and precious stones, which is annually opened on a particular day, that the benighted bigots of that city may worship at his shrine. Our English Thomas à Becket was the last of these worthies that greeted us on mounting the staircase. At a later period of the Exhibition, however, the French Archbishop Affré gave place to Fenelon, whose *Telemaque* was so familiar to our schoolboy days; and the Italian saint, a good man, by the by, had also disappeared to make room for another French worthy, but the renowned St. Thomas à Becket stood his ground to the last. All these three lay figures, however, for some reason or other, wore white gloves, instead of the purple gloves of the archbishop, and the bright scarlet of the cardinal. While examining the embroidery of these robes, which the maker warranted to wear a hundred years, and *then clean*, we found ourselves side by side with two gentlemen actually wearing, the one *scarlet*, and the other *purple gloves;* such were the strange coincidences of the Exhibition! They proved to be Cardinal Wiseman and one of his bishops examining the costume of Thomas à Becket!

In the same galleries were cases of medals, cameos, bronzes, a shield and dagger, and other ornaments richly chased in iron, all displaying very considerable taste and executive skill; but, to own the truth, neither statuary, nor lay figures of archbishops, nor the large display of Roman catholic works, nor any object connected with art, science, or literature, excited half the sensation among the ladies, as did the tempting outspread of delicate lace, from Brussels, Mechlin, and other districts, for ages celebrated for its production. It was curious to witness the enthusiastic admiration with which the various articles of dress, robes, flounces, veils, collars, &c., fabricated out of the fine spun thread with more than Arachnean delicacy, were regarded by the numerous female visitors who absolutely haunted the enchanted spot, devouring with their eager eyes the coveted spoil; while exclamations of the most enraptured delight burst from their ruby lips. This love of dress may be considered inherent in the sex; from the unenlightened savage to the courtly duchess, all are swayed by its influence. We remember an amusing story by Peter Pindar in evidence of its supremacy, in which he relates how on a visit of some country female cousins to the great metropolis, when he thought equally to astonish and delight them by a first sight of St. Paul's, which was breaking on their view as they paced up Ludgate-hill, the eyes of his fair companions were suddenly attracted by a rich display of ribbons, laces, and shawls in a mercer's window, from which no argument or inducement held out by the disappointed bard, could for a long time prevail on them to withdraw their eager attention.

The Belgian diapers and damasks, although somewhat coarse, were serviceable, and of tolerably good design; we cannot however commend those which had the human figure introduced in them; one in particular was intended to represent the king of the Belgians on horseback, the effect of which was exceedingly ugly and inappropriate.

In the way of machinery, the great establishment at Seraing for the manufacture of steam-engines, and all kinds of machinery, which was founded by Cockerell, under the patronage of Napoleon, and afterwards supported with capital by the father of the late king of Holland, sent several specimens of heavy work of a respectable character. The steady-going pace approved of on the Belgian railroads, viz., fifteen miles an hour, with sundry stoppages, by no means demands the flying engines we impatient Englishmen require. M. Presmany, writing his opinion of England in the Paris journal *La Patrie*, says, " An Englishman never saunters, but always rushes forward like a mad dog." Probably the facetious journalist never in his younger days sauntered down Bond-street himself; had he done so he might have seen specimens of lounging and idle *nonchalance* quite equal to anything of the kind to be met with on the Boulevards or the Tuilleries of his own most delightful capital of fashion, and the *dolce far niente*.

CHAPTER XI.

FOREIGN AND COLONIAL DEPARTMENTS—*continued*.

THE UNITED STATES.

THE number of articles sent from the United States to the Exhibition was neither what was expected of them, nor, we believe, did it adequately represent their capabilities. There were, nevertheless, many things in their collection which presented features of peculiar interest, and which did credit to their industry, ingenuity, and skill. Foremost among the articles displayed in this division of the Exhibition were a coach, three or four waggons, " a buggy," technically so called, and a trotting " sulkey." We call these " foremost," because, both by the prominent place they occupied, and on account of the real merit of the vehicles themselves, they were really so. The coach—styled by the exhibitor a " carriola"—was a very creditable piece of workmanship, of good design, apparently most thoroughly well built, and finished with great regard to good taste. There was nothing of the gewgaw style about it. The colour, decorations, mountings, finish, and ornaments, were all rich and neat. The carvings upon it were admirably well executed, and for symmetry and good keeping in every part, from the step of the footman to the board of the driver, it deserved high commendation. The wheels were much lighter than in carriages of a similar kind in England. This is claimed as a decided improvement. Certainly the appearance of the vehicle is improved by the absence of that bulkiness which gives a lumbering aspect to many an English carriage; and if the roads of our transatlantic brethren are not too rough to deal fairly with such wheels, we know not why they should be considered unsafe upon English turnpike roads. The other vehicles exhibited were respectively entitled a York waggon, a Prince Albert waggon, a slide-top buggy, and a trotting sulkey. The chief characteristic of all these was their extreme lightness of weight, when compared with their size. They were richly finished within and without, and beautifully carved; the upholstery being done in exceedingly good taste, with constant regard to the comfort of the rider, and exhibiting very considerable artistic merit in design. The wheels were made from carefully-chosen materials, the joints exactly fitted, the felloes (two in number, instead of the usual five or six, for greater strength), confined by a steel insertion and bolts, and the axletrees exceedingly neat and strong. It is claimed for these axletrees (an American invention), that, in loss of friction, strength, freedom from all noise in motion, and cleanliness, they are superior to any in England. Several of these lighter carriages are now in use in this country, and give great satisfaction; and several more of a similar manufacture have been recently ordered from New York. Indeed, it is not difficult to understand why they should become favourites out of London; nor how reluctantly a lover of quick driving would return to the heavier vehicles of city manufacture. There were several rich sets of harness which deserved notice, in particular that which was exhibited by Messrs. Lacy and Phillips. It was made from leather of the finest quality, and with perfect thoroughness of work. The mountings were of solid silver, with appropriate and graceful designs. In this, as in all the other harness shown, there was remarkable lightness and airiness, and an obvious endeavour to do away with all super-abundant weight.

The great use of oil in the United States has necessarily led to many improvements in lamps, as was evident in those exhibited from the manufactory of Messrs. Cornelius and Co., in Philadelphia, especially in those upon the solar principle, as it is called, where increased draught is made to bear upon the combustion, which are unknown among us. Unpretending as these lamps appeared, it was stated that they would give an amount of light greater, by one-half, than any others in use. The chandeliers that hung above them were graceful, and of extreme purity of glass, and beautifully cast. The branches, formed by arabesque scrolls, profusely ornamented with birds and flowers, delicately sculptured, or in bold relief, with centres of richly-cut glass, claimed universal approval for their elegance and lightness of design. This manufacture is among the latest intro-duced in the United States, it being scarcely fifteen years since every chandelier, girandole, mantel-lamp, and candelabra used in that country was imported from Europe; and it argued considerable enterprise and perseverance on the part of the manufacturers, that they attained so much excellence as to be willing to vie in the Exhibition with the oldest and most celebrated houses in the world. On the south side of their portion of the building, the contributors from the States exhibited, under the general classification of raw material, many very excellent specimens. There were among these a large variety of articles, such as Indian corn, ground, hulled, and in the ear; rye, oats, barley, wheat, rice, cotton, tobacco, minerals, chemicals, woods, brooms, beef, pork, lard, hams, and almost everything else identified with the productions of that country. Next in order were to be seen daguerreotypes, paintings, herbaria, and prints, with some samples of stained glass suspended from the galleries, and cottons, carpetings, wrought quilts, calicoes, and needlework, tastefully displayed around. Considering the distance from which these had to be conveyed, not only across 3,000 miles of ocean, but often from little short of that distance inland; and considering, too, that it is not in her manufactures that America makes her chief impression upon the world, we regard this portion of her exhibition with great interest. In pianofortes there was a show highly creditable to the manufacture of musical instruments in the United States. Pierson exhibited a seven-octave grand pianoforte; Chickering a semi-grand, and other instruments of less preten-sion but of much merit. There were two from the manufactory of Conrad Meyer, of Philadelphia, in neat and very unpretending cases, combining all the best qualities of the highest rank of pianos. In breadth, freedom, and evenness of tone, in promptness and elasticity of action, and in a combination of everything that is rich and sweet in this description of instrument, he claims to be unsurpassed.

Among cordage, boats, oars, and models of favourite ships, were exhibited two ship-ventilators, by Frederick Emerson, of Boston. These are intended to supersede the ordinary wind-sail now in use for sending pure air into the recesses of ships. The inventor has given much attention to the subject of ventilation, and his success has been honoured by several gold medals in the United States. How far this application of his invention may be superior to the methods now in use for the same purpose is uncertain. In the minds of sailors there is always an objection to fixtures above deck, which would be likely to impede their general introduction.

Together with daguerreotypes, before alluded to, there were exhibited camera obscuras by C. C. Harrison, of New York, the results of which, in the pictures that hung above them, were exceedingly favourable. There were shawls from the Bay State mills, of beautiful colour and a high perfection of manufacture; white cotton goods, which, in bleaching, finishing, and putting up, appeared equal to Manchester products; some very beautiful flannels, single-milled doeskins and wool-black cassimeres of thorough fabric; tweeds, well mixed and of good colours; a salamander safe, well made; Newell's improved bank lock, ingenious and well constructed; a patent paying-machine for pitching the seams of vessels, the box being provided with a ventricle wheel, which receives the hot melted material, and applies it neatly, economically, and directly to the seam to be covered; an air-exhausted coffin, with glazed aperture at top, a most whimsical idea, but whether for the benefit of the defunct to look out, or the survivors to look in, we were at a loss to determine. Next came a host of "notable things." Car wheels for railroads, wood and cork legs, clocks, watches, dentists' tools and works, India-rubber goods of various forms, mathematical and solar instruments, a self-determining variation compass, trunks, boots and shoes, hats, specimens of printing and binding, together with pistols, rifles, and other weapons of offence and defence. Of these rifles, manufactured by Robbins and Lawrence, it is but just to say that they are among the best, if not *the* best, of any rifles manufactured in the world, the Americans claiming to excel in this species of manufacture. They are made from the best selected Copake cold-blast forge iron, and are of an unpretending style, but remarkable for a plain, substantial, and perfect finish; they are strong, simple, and thorough in their workmanship, and eminently adapted for real service.

Two bell telegraphs, exhibited in the central avenue, very deservedly attracted much attention. The bell telegraph, otherwise called an "annunciator," is an invention made to supersede the awkward array of bells in houses and hotels. It is an extremely neat and beautiful article, and indicates whence the bell was rung, by uncovering a number corresponding to the number of the room; and this, too, for any length of time afterwards, until, by the touch of a spring, the number is re-covered. In the large hotels in the United States, and in many private residences, it is much used.

In the moving machinery department, among other objects of interest from the United States, was a machine exhibited by Mr. Charles Morey, called a stone dressing machine. A machine for dressing stone by power has long been regarded as a great desideratum, and has been the object of many expensive, though unsuccessful experiments. One great difficulty has been found in making the cutting tools of a quality to stand the action of stone, unless at such cost as to render their use unprofitable. This difficulty is overcome by the present invention, which consists in the employment of chilled cast-iron burrs, or rolling cutters. Iron, as is now known, may, by a peculiar process of chilling in casting, be converted to a diamond hardness, that perfectly fits it for reducing, with great facility and economy, the surface of stone. The burrs made in this way retain a sufficient degree of sharpness for a long time, and can be maintained at a small cost, being wholly formed and finished in casting. In dressing circular forms, the stones are made to revolve, when the burrs, which are mounted in sliding rests, are brought into action. For straight surfaces, however, the stones are laid upon a transverse bed, and the cutters, mounted upon a revolving cylinder, are placed above them. The burrs or cutters are so arranged as to turn freely on their axis when brought in

T

contact with the stone, and as they roll over it, they crush it away in the form of scales and dust. By varying the shape and arrangement of the burrs, ornamental surfaces may be produced.

Among the agricultural implements exhibited, which claimed the attention of agriculturists particularly, were reaping machines, ploughs, cultivators, fan mills, and smut machines. The American reapers are worked by a single span of horses abreast, with a driver and a man to rake off the grain as it is cut down by moveable knives. On land free from obstructions, these reapers will cut from twelve to twenty acres of wheat in a day, depending somewhat upon the speed of the horses and the state of the grain.

In taking our leave, for the present, of our transatlantic neighbours, we have the pleasure to inform our readers, that they have so far profited by the example we have set to them, as well as to other nations, as to contemplate an Exhibition of Industry at New York, which, indeed, it is publicly announced will take place in the ensuing year. A company, it appears, has been formed in America which is represented in this country by M. Charles Buschek, Austrian commissioner for the Exhibition of 1851, and Mr. Edward Riddle, commissioner for the United States, to whom the whole management of the design has been confided. A large building is about to be erected, which, when completed, will be considered as a bonded warehouse. The contributions from England are to be conveyed in first-class vessels, free of expense, and if they remain unsold, will be returned to the exhibitors without cost. This arrangement cannot but be considered as extremely liberal. There can be no doubt of the success of such an enterprise, if carried out by a body of trustworthy persons. We hear of several English firms as likely to accept the friendly invitation thus held out to them.

CHAPTER XII.

WOOD CARVING—ROYAL TROPHY—PRINCE OF WALES'S COT—GROUP OF FLOWERS—THE KENILWORTH BUFFET—BUFFET BY FOURDINOIS—PANEL BY LIENARD—HOLLAND'S BOOKCASE—PALACE OF TARA—SWISS CARVING—ELIZABETHAN AGE—AUSTRIAN CARVING, ETC., ETC.

AMONGST the decorative arts, wood carving has a distinct and legitimate position, and confined within due limits is always effective. Still its province is restricted, or ought to be, to the ornamentation of material when applied to a useful purpose; it can never assume the dignity of art *per se*. To usurp the place of sculpture, it has hitherto been, and will always continue to be, utterly incompetent, inasmuch as the material upon which it employs its skill, is altogether, both in colour and texture, inferior to marble, and utterly inappropriate to represent the human figure or the human countenance. In corroboration of our assertion, we would recal to the recollection of our readers the extremely objectionable representation of the Crucifixion in the Fine Art Court, the head of Her Majesty, or the human lineaments in any work of wood carving in the Exhibition, and compare their relative truthfulness of effect as to contour and colour with that of other objects, such as flowers, foliage, and fancy devices, and they will at once admit the principle for which we now contend.

There were several very beautiful specimens of this class of subjects by Rogers and Wallis, closely approximating in elegance and delicacy of finish to the celebrated productions of Grinlin Gibbon, that prince of carvers, whose works serve to decorate so many of our old ancestral halls and country residences. The first-mentioned of these

Engraved by D.Pound, from a Daguerreotype

MAHOGANY SIDEBOARD

MANUFACTURED BY MESSRS JOHNSON & JEANES, BOND ST

Engraved by D.Pound, from a Daguerreotype

THE KENILWORTH OAK BUFFET

DESIGNED & MANUFACTURED BY MESSRS COOKES & SON.

artists, Rogers, besides a number of charming devices, exhibited two larger subjects, on which he appeared to have lavished all his resources,—a royal trophy, carved in lime-tree, representing the crown as the chief power, the source of all titles and dignities—the patron and promoter of the arts, sciences, &c., in illustration of which an elaborate group which occupied the centre, displayed all the insignia of rank, and every means and appliance of science and art. In the lower part were medallion portraits of royal personages. The whole was encircled with a border composed of groups of game, fruit, flowers, fish, and shells. A trophy emblematical of Folly was also worthy of high praise. The carved boxwood cradle, moreover, by the same artist, exhibited by her majesty, must not be passed unnoticed, although we by no means participate in the wild admiration which it excited amongst the numberless mothers and daughters of England, who gazed enviously at it. The shape itself was not elegant, being heavy, and more like a sarcophagus than a cradle; and the decoration, though doubtless appropriate as "symbolising the union of the royal house of England with that of Saxe-Coburg and Gotha," was neither picturesque nor interesting in a general point of view, whilst the execution, though exquisitely neat, was perhaps a *tant soit peu* tame. Wallis, likewise, exhibited some productions of surpassing merit in the same style. One, a group of flowers, &c., emblematical of Spring, elicited general admiration; it was carved out of a solid piece of lime-tree, five feet high by two-and-a-half wide, and projecting thirteen inches. Spring was allegorically represented by the grape-buds and apple-blossoms, of which there were no less than 1,060 buds, and 47 varieties. A blue-cap titmouse was picking insects out of an apple-blossom; another was taking food to its young, which were partially concealed in their nest, and here and there caterpillars were dragging their slow length along. A shepherd's crook and lamb's head were added, symbolical of the season. The whole of this work was copied from nature, and executed expressly for the Great Exhibition.

The most magnificent object, however, in this department of art, was unquestionably "The Kenilworth Buffet," by Cooke, of Warwick, and which we shall proceed to describe in an abridged account from that given by the makers themselves. The wood from which this buffet was made, we are informed, was obtained from a colossal oak-tree, which grew near Kenilworth Castle, and of which we believe a view was given in *Strutt's Deliciæ Sylvarum*, published some years ago. The tree measured ten feet in diameter, and contained about 600 cubic feet of timber, and was cut down in 1842, and afterwards purchased by the exhibitors. The subject of the design was the Kenilworth Pageant of 1575, in honour of Queen Elizabeth's visit to the Earl of Leicester, described by Laneham and Gascoigne, two attendants on the Queen in this "royal progress," and vividly reproduced by Sir Walter Scott. The design of the centre panel, carved out of one solid block of oak, represented Queen Elizabeth entering Kenilworth Castle in all the pomp usually displayed on these occasions. The cavalcade was seen crossing the tilt-yard, and approaching the base court of the building by Mortimer's tower. Leicester was bareheaded, and on foot, leading the horse upon which his august mistress was seated, magnificently arrayed. The Queen, then in her forty-second year, wore her crown, and had around her neck the enormous ruff in which she is always represented. Two pages and a long train of attendants followed the Queen and her host, composed of ladies, statesmen, knights, and warriors—some on foot, others on horseback. In the distance were soldiers and a mixed multitude of people. A portion of the castle was seen in the back-ground. At one end was Mortimer's tower, through which the cavalcade was about to pass; the remains of this tower are still in existence, and considerably heighten the romantic beauty of the Kenilworth ruins. At the opposite end of the panel, the Earl of Essex, Leicester's rival in the favour of Queen Elizabeth, was conspicuously seen, mounted on a charger. On the table underneath the centre panel was displayed the Tudor rose, and surmounted by the royal crown, with the famous motto of Elizabeth, *semper eadem*, on a ribbon. On the spandrils, supported by water flowers and rock-work pendentives, were marine subjects taken from the " Pageant," namely, a triton on the mermaid, and Arion on the dolphin, connected with Mike Lambourne's mishap, in the novel of *Kenilworth*. The panel on the right or dexter side of the buffet, recalled the scene in the same work, where Elizabeth meets Amy Robsart in the grotto, in the grounds of the castle. The subject of the left panel of the buffet represented the interview of Queen Elizabeth and Leicester, after the exposure of the deceit practised upon her by the latter, and his marriage with Amy Robsart. Leicester was shown in a kneeling position, with one hand on his breast, and the other extended towards Elizabeth, as if appealing to her sensibility. The four statuettes at the corners were emblematical of the reign of Elizabeth. At the extreme corner of the right was Sir Philip Sydney, the nephew of the Earl of Leicester, whose character combined all the qualities of a great poet, warrior, and statesman. He died in 1586. The shape of Sir Philip's sword (which is still preserved at Penshurst) was singular, the handle being about sixteen inches long. On the opposite side of the same pedestal might be recognised Sir Walter Raleigh, who attained eminence in almost every branch of science and literature. He was arrayed in a courtier's dress, and the figure represented him in a thoughtful attitude, with a pen and scroll in his hand. Raleigh was beheaded on a charge of high treason, in 1618. On the left pedestal, at the inner side of the buffet, was a figure of Shakspere, who was shown in a reflective mood. The last figure was that of Sir Francis Drake, the first Englishman who circumnavigated the globe. An anchor was appropriately introduced, emblematic of his naval career; and the costume chosen was that of a court dress. The ragged staff mouldings of the Kenilworth buffet were imitations of the best examples in the Beauchamp Chapel, Warwick, where the Earl of Leicester was interred. The supporters to the projecting shelves also represented the proud crest of this splendid noble, the bear and ragged staff, borne by the earls of Warwick from the most remote times. The small panels of the buffet, behind the Leicester cognizance, contained monograms of the date of Queen Elizabeth's visit to Kenilworth Castle, and the eventful year 1851, with the cipher of the reigning monarch, designed to record the era of the Great Exhibition of all Nations. Around the door-panels of the Kenilworth buffet were copies of architectural details still seen on the gate-house. The upper part, above the shelf of each pedestal of the buffet, displayed the monogram of the Earl of Leicester, encircled by the insigna of the order of the Garter, and surmounted by his coronet. The decorations on each side were specimens of Elizabethan ornaments, designed by the proprietors. An important feature in the production of this work was the introduction, by Mr. Walter Cooper, of *pointing*, the process adopted by sculptors in stone and marble, and by which greater accuracy is secured.

Next in importance to the magnificent piece of workmanship we have just described, and equal to it in beauty of execution and finish, was the elaborate buffet by M. Fourdinois, of Paris; and it is in such peaceful rivalry and friendly competition alone, that we wish to see the two nations opposed to each other; a contest in which the advantages of victory,—for

" Peace hath her victories no less than war—"

are counterbalanced by no misery or deprivation on the part of the vanquished; and it is to such a state of beneficial intercourse between nations, hitherto opposed to each other in hostile array, that such an exhibition as we have just witnessed must eminently

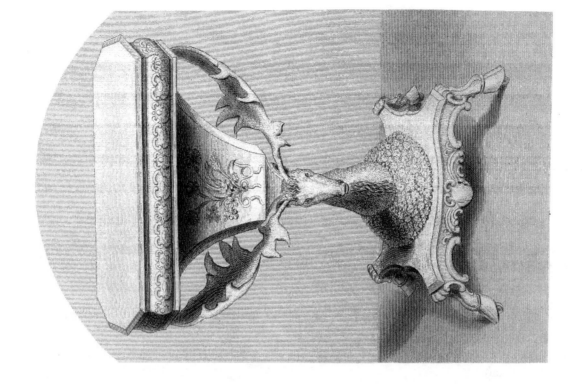

BOG WOOD — LADY'S WORK TABLE .

A JONES DUBLIN

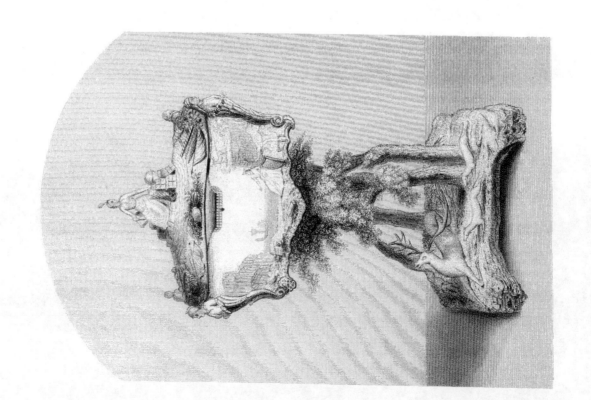

BOG WOOD — TEAPOY .

A JONES, DUBLIN

tend to lead. Let us, however, return from this digression, and describe the "stately sideboard" of M. Fourdinois. The design of the French artist very judiciously aimed at rendering the ornamentation of his work entirely subservient to its intended use. Consequently, in order to express the general temperament of the banquet, four female figures, representing the four quarters of the globe, were bearing in their hands every delicate variety of food, the produce of their several climes, whilst around them were heaped in rich profusion—

> "Meats of noblest sort
> And savour; beasts of chase, or fowl, or game,
> *   *   *   *   all fish from sea or shore,
> Freshlet or purling brook, or shell or fin,
> And exquisitest name, for which was drained
> Pontus, and Lucrine bay, and Afric coast,
> With fruits and flowers from Almathea's horn."

At either end were figures representative of hunting and fishing. Above was a female figure emblematic of Plenty, supported by two charming groups illustrative of the corn-field and the vineyard. Even the chained dogs, which have been censured by some, placed as supporters at the lower part of the sideboard, we consider as appropriate—the chase was over, the game ready for culinary operations, and for a time, at least, the faithful animals were at rest beneath the trophies of their prowess. The centre of the sideboard was occupied by a painting in gay colours, representing a combination of various fruits and flowers, surmounted by a large American aloe. We cannot too highly commend the great fidelity with which the various objects in this elaborate performance were copied from nature, the graceful manner in which each part was made to blend with its neighbour, the taste, skill, and patience of the workman, the care bestowed upon the minutest details, or the originality of conception and beauty of finish in the whole work,—the *tout ensemble* was worthy of the country which produced it, and the occasion which called for its exhibition.

Another work of Parisian manufacture, by M. Lienard, was also deserving of notice— a pair of large panels of exquisite workmanship, one of which, illustrative of the sports of the field, we shall forthwith describe. The first compartment represented a group of foxes in search of prey, the last a family of partridges in a corn-field, while in the centre, in all the serenity of safety, reposed a trio of deer, the noble old buck looking out upon the scene in the very luxury of idleness. But the choicest *bits* of carving were in the animals, birds, and foliage which surrounded the frame, emblems of the noble sport.

Of a totally different character from the preceding, was the massive book-case exhibited by Messrs. Holland, in the style of the Renaissance, with natural forms finely introduced. The design was furnished by Mr. Macquoid, architect. Regarded artistically, it might have been considered rather too architectural in its style, but it was certainly a splendid piece of workmanship, and well suited for the library of a great castle or baronial mansion.

We will now make mention of a contribution from "the Emerald Isle," in the form of a music temple, carved in bog-yew, by Arthur Jones, of Dublin. As in all periods of their history, the Irish have been passionately fond of music, the decorative piece of furniture embodying this characteristic, was certain to acquire importance and promi-nence; and, therefore, the ancient Palace of Tara was selected as the proper theatre in which to display this subject, its halls having been celebrated by the ancient Irish bards, as the frequent scenes of music and festivity. A statuette of Ollamh Fouhdla, the founder of the Irish monarchy, and also of the Palace of Tara, naturally surmounted the temple. He was represented in his capacity of monarch and lawgiver, delivering

U

the laws to the Irish nation, holding forth the beechen boards, on which were inscribed passages from the Brehon laws, engraved in the ancient Irish character :—

> "Seven things bear witness to a king's improper conduct:
> "An unlawful opposition in the senate.
> "An overthrow of the law.
> "An overthrow in battle.
> "A dearth.
> "Barrenness in cows.
> "Blight of fruit.
> "Blight of seed in the ground.
> "These are the seven candles lighted to expose the misgovernment of a king."

He was seated on the Lia Fail, or enchanted stone, said to be deposited in Westminster Abbey; he sat in the centre of a platform, representing all Ireland mapped out under him. The panel in front represented, in relief, the opening of the triennial convention at Tara, in the reign of Cormac "Ufalda," or "Long Beard," in the early part of the third century, anterior to the introduction of Christianity into the island. Cormac sat in the centre of the hall, surrounded by ten principal officers of state, who always accompanied the monarch on state occasions. The opposite panel represented the harpers in Tara Hall performing before the monarch and his queen; a canopy formed by the fossil antlers and skull of the giant deer, supported the drapery, an opening in which discovered the undulating hills of Tara. Four statues at the corners personified vocal music, warlike, pastoral, dramatic, and devotional—or, in other words, the camp, the field, the stage, and the sanctuary. The whole subject formed a sort of chronological series, commencing 700 years B.C., the date of the foundation of the Irish monarchy—touching the flourishing state of the kingdom under Cormac—passing through the chivalrous age of the Crusaders—and ending with the present agricultural age of Ireland.

The Swiss department contained several specimens of wood carving, in decorative furniture and otherwise, which were interesting for the great amount of executive skill displayed upon them, and for the truthful homeliness of the subjects represented in them. They were, indeed, for the most part, sculptured bucolics, exhibiting the pastoral life of happy Switzerland, in all its various phases; whilst a few illustrated other points of nationality, as the costumes of the twenty-two cantons, still kept remarkably distinct amongst the rural population; or some spot dear in the memories of Swiss men, as the chapel of William Tell, at Altdorft. There was something very charming in the simple devotedness to a beloved nationality thus evidenced by a brave, industrious, and primitive people, in their contributions to the world's great and glittering fair. The escritoire, by Wettli, of Berne, in white wood, and intended for the use of a lady, was well deserving attention; it was so contrived that it could be used either in a sitting or a standing posture. The embellishments, as already stated, comprehended various passages in the industry, field sports, and amusements of Alpine life. The general style of this piece of furniture, considered as such, was light, and by no means inelegant. The small table, by Schild, of Berne, was also extremely pretty, and both were well suited for a lady's boudoir in the retirement of a rural hour.

To return, however, to our native productions: we were reminded by the "Kestral Hawk" of Mr. Batsford, and the Elizabethan contributions by the Duchess of Sutherland, of that Augustan age of England, when poetry and the fine arts had arrived at their zenith—when carving in wood, a branch of the latter, profusely adorned the houses of the wealthy and the noble. The finer specimens of this class of art are scarce, and in great demand among collectors, dealers, and antiquarians. In chapels and cathedrals, what elaborate specimens are to be found of this somewhat neglected art!—witness the

Engraved by G Greatbach, from a Daguerreotype.

WALNUT TREE BEDSTEAD.

MANUFACTURED BY MESSRS ROGERS & DEARS, HYDE PARK CORNER

Engraved by G Greatbach from a Daguerreotype.

THE AUSTRIAN BEDSTEAD

MANUFACTURED BY C. LEISTLER & SON VIENNA

PURCHASED BY HER MAJESTY.

LARGE LOOKING GLASS AND CONSOLE TABLE,

ORNAMENTED AND GILT.

Engraved by D Pound from a Daguerreotype by Beard

MANUFACTURED BY C. MC.LEAN. FLEET STREET.

CABINET MADE OF WALNUT WOOD

CARVED WITH PANELS OF RAISED EMBROIDERY

Engraved by D. Pound from a Daguerreotype by Beard

DESIGNED & MANUFACTURED BY J. STEEVENS. TAUNTON.

noble structures of Westminster Abbey, Lincoln, Durham, and York. Nearer our own times, too, we have had some rare examples of excellence, from the chisel of Grinlin Gibbon, already mentioned by us, and of whom Walpole justly observes, " that there is no instance of a man before Gibbon, who gave to wood the loose and airy lightness of flowers, and chained together the various productions of the elements, with a free disorder natural to each species." And so delicate was the workmanship of Gibbon, according to the same authority, that a carved pot of flowers in a room shook, as though they were natural, by the mere motion of the coaches in the street. The Chapel at Windsor, and the Choir of St. Paul's, contain some foliage by Gibbon, executed in the most artistic manner. His heads of cherubs possess a sweetness of expression and an angelic loveliness which, as long as they exist, will render them the admiration of all lovers of ideal beauty ; and his picture-frames, where dead game, flowers, and foliage, almost deceive the eye into a belief of their reality, are equally marvels of the art. Many other specimens of the taste and skill of our English carvers were to be found in the various recesses of the Crystal Palace. In the Mediæval Court stood a massive oak sideboard, the production of Mr. Crace, of Wigmore-street, elaborately and richly carved, and intended for the new dining-hall at Alton Towers, the seat of the Earl of Shrewsbury. A sideboard by Snell and Co. also merited attention ; the design of the sculpture was given by Baron Marocheti, the workmanship of which was equal to the best examples in the Exhibition, and elicited universal approbation. An elegant commode or cabinet of walnut wood, was exhibited by Hanson and Sons, highly ornamented, for china, bronzes, &c., with oval carved frame for a mirror, representing a variety of British birds arranged in a pleasing manner around the glass. The carved work on the lower part of the commode represented stags in a recumbent posture, and the pillars were ornamented with well executed heads of boars and deer. Two elaborately-carved brackets for flower-stands, served to complete this elegant and useful piece of furniture.

We will now, however, take a look at the contributions in this department of art as supplied by Austria, the most conspicuous among which was the huge BEDSTEAD, with its pillars, its niches, its screens, its groups of angels, champions, sprites, and saints—cathedral-like in its design and decoration. Architectural in character, it appeared like a vast temple dedicated to sleep ; so grand in conception, so massive in proportion, so deeply rich in carved glories, so evident an invocation of the artist, and so resolute an abnegation of the mere upholsterer, it was a real triumph of the artificer, who must have been " sleepless himself to make his patrons sleep." Next in magnificence was the GOTHIC BOOKCASE, sent over as a present from the Emperor of Austria to her Majesty. The superbly-bound books which ornamented some of the shelves were also the gift of his Imperial Majesty. The material was oak. The design, which was Gothic, was by Bernardo de Bernardis, an architect of eminence, and J. Kraner, both of Vienna. It was rather too architectural in its arrangement, and the introduction of the statuettes in all directions, was not to be approved on the score of taste or propriety. The executive department was very creditably carried out ; but at the time it was exhibited the joining business had not been completed, and we understand several workmen belonging to Messrs. Leistler's establishment are now engaged upon it, and will be so for some months, at Buckingham Palace. A Prie Dieu, also by Leistler, was worthy of notice ; Gothic in its structure, like the bookcase, and very richly carved. In the central panel was a painting of Christ bearing the cross ; on either side were angels holding tablets, on which were inscribed the date, " Anno 1851." A set of tables, too, in another part, awakened the especial admiration of the lovers of the gastronomic art, which, in their hospitable breadth and expanse, spoke volumes in favour of the geniality of their designs. The wood of these was extremely beautiful ; the guests had only to look beyond their glasses to see their joyous countenances correctly mirrored, while the substantial legs and sup-ports, in buttresswise, entirely banished the idea that the tables they supported could ever *groan* under whatever weight of good cheer might be placed upon them.

From Belgium the most important contribution in this style of art was in the shape of a GOTHIC CHAIR, an elegant and elaborate piece of aristocratic furniture executed in carved oak, entirely gilt, and cushioned with the finest crimson velvet. The ornamental portion of the chair gave it a very light and chaste appearance. The seat was supported by figures of griffins in a sitting posture, and the elbows and tracery work beneath the seat were in admirable keeping with its other decorations. The chair was modelled after the decorated Gothic style of architecture, and formed a portion of a finely-finished set of furniture in dark wood, consisting of a Gothic rosewood bookcase, bedstead, and étagère, and oak and rosewood tables and chairs, which were well worth the attention of the visitor. The whole had been designed by a very clever artist, A. F. Roule, of Antwerp, and numbered 419 in the Belgium department of the Great Exhibition.

In concluding our present remarks on carved work, we must not omit to mention that Tuscany, that old field of classic art, exhibited several specimens of exquisite beauty by Barbetti and others. Greece also, amongst her sixty-one contributions, sent two works in the Byzantine style, executed by the Rev. Triandaphylos of Athens, namely, a carved cross, and a carved picture of the "Annunciation." These works were remarkable as specimens of a style of art now almost extinct, being a remnant of the Byzantine period, and which still lingers in some of the convents of Greece, and particularly at Mount Athos. The carving, which was done with graving instruments, was very minute, in slight relief, upon the plane of the wood—a boxwood which is abundant in Greece, and appears to be of a very fine grain. The crucifix, which did not measure more than a foot in its largest dimensions, was covered on both sides with scriptural subjects, fourteen on each side, so that each subject occupied only from an inch to a couple of inches of the surface. In the carving representing the "Annunciation," the figures were larger, and the form oval, the band being surrounded with twenty-five heads of saints. The government of Greece has of late years done a good deal to promote this style of illustration, in a School of Arts established at the cathedral at Athens.

CHAPTER XIII.

DISCOVERY OF GLASS—GLASS BLOWING—CRYSTAL FOUNTAIN—CANDELABRA—THE GLASS KOH-I-NOOR—SUPERB CHANDELIER—ETRUSCAN VASES—DIOPTRIC APPARATUS—BOHEMIAN GLASS —ENGRAVING ON GLASS—PRESSED GLASS, ETC.

THE manufacture of glass is one of great and daily increasing importance in this country, the application of this material to many uses heretofore unthought of being daily on the increase; thanks to the liberal policy which a few years ago abolished those fiscal bur-thens which had operated as a bar to enterprise and progress. The subject is one of peculiar interest in connexion with the Great Exhibition of Industry of 1851, as but for the enfranchisement of the glass manufacturer, the building in which that unrivalled display was held could never have been constructed.

The time at which glass was invented is very uncertain. The popular opinion upon this subject refers the discovery to accident. It is said (Plin., *Nat. Hist.*, lib. xxxvi., c. 26), "that some mariners, who had a cargo of *nitrum* (salt, or, as some have supposed, soda) on board, having landed on the banks of the river Belus, a small stream at the base of Mount Carmel in Palestine, and finding no stones to rest their pots on, placed under them some masses of nitrum, which, being fused by the heat with the sand of the river, produced a liquid and transparent stream: such was the origin of glass." The ancient Egyptians were certainly acquainted with the art of glass-making. This subject is very fully discussed in a memoir by M. Boudet, in the *" Description de l'Egypt,"* vol. ix., Antiq. Mémoires. The earthenware beads found in some mummies have an external coat of glass, coloured with a metallic oxide; and among the ruins of Thebes pieces of blue glass have been discovered. The manufacture of glass was long carried on at Alexandria, from which city the Romans were supplied with that material; but before the time of Pliny, the manufacture had been introduced into Italy, France, and Spain (xxxvi., c. 26). Glass utensils have been found among the ruins of Herculaneum.

The application of glass to the glazing of windows is of comparatively modern introduction, at least in northern and western Europe. In 674 artists were brought to England from abroad to glaze the church windows at Weremouth, in Durham; even in the year 1567 this mode of excluding cold from dwellings was confined to large establishments, and by no means universal even in them. An entry then made in the minutes of a survey of Alnwick Castle, the residence of the Duke of Northumberland, informs us that the glass casements were taken down during the absence of the family, to preserve them from accident. A century after that time the use of window-glass was so small in Scotland, that only the upper rooms in the royal palaces were furnished with it, the lower part having wooden shutters to admit or exclude the air. The earliest manufacture of flint-glass in England was begun in 1557, and the progress made in perfecting it was so slow, that it was not until near the close of the seventeenth century that this country was independent of foreigners for the supply of the common article of drinking-glasses. In 1673 some plate-glass was made at Lambeth, in works supported by the Duke of Buckingham, but which were soon abandoned. It was exactly one century later that the first establishment of magnitude for the production of plate-glass was formed in this country, under the title of "The Governor and Company of British Cast Plate-Glass Manufacturers." The members of this company subscribed an ample capital, and works upon a large scale were erected at Ravenhead, near Prescot, in Lancashire, which have been in constant and successful operation from that time to the present day.

At an early period of its history in this country the glass manufacture became an object of taxation, and duties were imposed by the 6 and 7 William and Mary, which acted so injuriously, that in the second year after the act was passed, one-half of the duty was taken off, and in the following year the whole was repealed. In 1746, when the manufacture had taken firmer root, an excise duty was again imposed, at the rate of one penny per pound on the materials used for making crown, plate, and flint-glass, and of one farthing per pound on those used for making bottles. In 1778 these rates were increased 50 per cent. upon crown and bottle-glass, and were doubled on flint and plate-glass. These rates were further advanced from time to time, in common with the duties upon most other objects of taxation, and in 1806 stood as follows:—On plate and flint-glass, 49s. per cwt.; on crown and German sheet-glass, 36s. 9d. per cwt.; on broad glass, 12s. 3d., and on common bottle-glass, 4s. 1d. per cwt. In 1813 those rates were doubled, and, with the exception of a modification in 1819 in favour of plate-glass, then reduced to £3 per cwt., were continued at that high rate until 1825. In that year a change was made in the mode of taking the duty on flint-glass, by charging it on the weight of the fluxed materials, instead of on the articles when made, a regulation which did not affect the rate of charge. In 1830, the rate on bottles was reduced from 8s. 2d. to 7s. per cwt. The only further alteration hitherto made in these duties occurred in 1835, when, in consequence of the recommendation contained in the thirteenth report of the Commissioners of Excise Inquiry, the rate upon flint-glass was reduced two-thirds, leaving it at 2*d.* per pound, a measure which was rendered necessary by the encouragement given under the high duty to the illicit manufacture, which was carried on to such an extent as to oblige several regular manufacturers to relinquish the prosecution of their business.

Since the alteration in the tariff, the manufacture of glass in this country has received an immense extension, and in several branches of the art we have outstripped the foreigner, who a few years since maintained against us a flourishing competition. In the preparation of the raw material, with one or two exceptions, we occupy the highest place, and have acquired this advantage by our large capital, by our improved chemical knowledge, and by the indomitable energy of our character. Even the foreigner acknowledges our superiority in these respects, and in taste and colouring he also admits that we have made considerable progress. "For a long time," says M. Stephane Flachet, "England has excelled us in the manufacture of glass, especially crystal glass. The precise cause is not known; it does not appear in the mode of fusing the materials; more probably it may be attributed to the purity of the lead which they use. We know how poor France is in this important respect, having imported, for several years past, from fifteen to sixteen millions of kilogrammes of that metal, principally from Spain. *   *   *   *   *   * The French glass is inferior to the English in point of colour, and changes much sooner when exposed to the air. Our manufacturers declare that this difference does not arise from an inferiority of workmanship, but from the limited means which we possess of purchasing the article, and which in a great measure may be attributed to the *minute division of the soil.* In order to reduce the price of glass to the condition of the purchaser, our manufacturers have recourse to an extra infusion of alkali, which, being slowly absorbed by the atmosphere, causes the glass to lose its transparency."

Glass may be regarded, generally speaking, as an admixture of three kinds of ingredients—silica, alkali, and a metallic oxide. The silica is the vitrifiable ingredient, the alkali is the flux, and the metallic oxide, besides acting as a flux, imparts certain qualities by which one kind of glass is distinguishable from another. If silica be exposed to the strongest heat it will resist fusion; but if it be mixed with an alkali, such as potash or soda, and the mixture be then submitted to the same temperature, a combination will ensue which takes the form of a liquid, and when cooled becomes transparent. The quality of glass mainly depends on the proportions in which the silicious matter and the alkali are combined, on the temperature to which they are exposed, and on the skill with which the entire process is performed. When a perfect combination of the materials is not secured, the glass is covered with dark spots or particles, and other inequalities, which are called *striæ.* There are three kinds of glass in ordinary use—crown-glass, plate-glass, and flint-glass. The silicious sand, which forms the base of the manufacture of each, is principally derived from Alum Bay, in the Isle of Wight; from Lynn, in Norfolk; and from Aylesbury, in Buckinghamshire. The materials for flint-glass are nearly as follows:—One part of alkali, two parts of oxide of lead, three of sea-sand, and a small portion of the oxides of maganese and arsenic. The oxide of lead is employed as a powerful flux; it also imparts a great lustre to the metal, and causes it to be more ductile when in a semi-fluid state. The manganese renders the glass perfectly colourless. When these ingredients are mixed it is called the *batch,* and the mixture is generally of a salmon-coloured hue, the red tinge being given by the oxide of lead.

"Who," says Dr. Johnson, "when he first saw the sand or ashes by a casual intenseness of heat melted into a metalline form, rugged with excrescences and clouded with impurities, would have imagined that in this shapeless lump lay concealed so many conveniences of life as would, in time, constitute a great part of the happiness of the world? Yet by some such fortuitous liquefaction was mankind taught to procure a body at once in a high degree solid and transparent; which might admit the light of the sun, and exclude the violence of the wind; which might extend the sight of the philosopher to new ranges of existence, and charm him at one time with the unbounded extent of material creation, and at another with the endless subordination of animal life; and, what is of yet more importance, might supply the decays of nature, and succour old age with subsidiary sight. Thus was the first artificer in glass employed, though without his knowledge or expectation. He was facilitating and prolonging the enjoyment of light, enlarging the avenues of science, and conferring the highest and most lasting pleasures: he was enabling the student to contemplate nature, and the beauty to behold herself.' Owing to the injurious operation of the excise duty upon glass, as already stated—since happily abolished by Sir Robert Peel—the English manufacture was long inferior to the French for plate-glass, and to the Bohemians for coloured and ornamental glass. Since the exciseman was released from his attendance at the glass-house, the English have been gradually improving themselves in the manufacture of every variety of this beautiful article; adopting processes new to England, but which had been long in use in other countries, where the manufacturer was not impeded by the operation of impolitic laws. Among these new processes, that of the manufacture of plate-glass is one of the most interesting. When the Messrs. Chance, of Spon-lane, near Birmingham, took the contract for the supply of the large quantity required for the Crystal Palace, amounting to nearly 400 tons, they found it necessary to import a few foreign workmen, in consequence of a scarcity of English hands sufficiently skilled and experienced to complete the order within the time specified. The process of production is very simple and beautiful, but requires a steady and practised hand. When the requisite weight of "metal" is taken from the furnace by the blower, it is blown into a spherical form in the ordinary manner. It is then, after having been reheated in the furnace, swung above the head and below the feet of the workman, until it assumes the form of a cylinder. The workman stands upon a stage opposite the mouth of the furnace, with a pit or well beneath his feet, six or seven feet in depth. He swings and balances the molten metal—firmly affixed to a knob of glass at the end of a long iron bar, or blowing-tube—first above and then beneath him, until it gradually expands to the size which the original quantity of metal was estimated to produce. The slightest miscalculation of his power of swinging it, or deviation from the proper course, might dash the hot glass either against the side or end of the pit or well, or against the wall of the furnace —or, worse than all, against the body of a fellow-workman or of a spectator. No such accidents ever happen, though the stranger unaccustomed to the sight is for a while in momentary dread of some such result. When swung to the proper length, the cylinder is about four feet long, and twelve inches in diameter. The next operations are to convert it into a tube, by disconnecting it from the blowing-iron, and removing the bag-like extremity. These processes are performed by boys, with strings of red-hot glass, which easily cut through the yielding metal. The boys then take the tubes under their arms, and remove them to another part of the building, where they stand on end, like chimney-pots, to await the operation which shall convert them into flat sheets of glass. This is also very simple. The tube is cut down the middle, and in this state placed in the "flattening-kiln," where the moderate application of heat, aided by a gentle touch from the attendant workman, brings it flat upon a slab or stone. It is then gently rubbed, or smoothed, with a wooden implement, and passed into a cooler part of the kiln, where it soon hardens. It is then tilted on edge, and the manufacture is complete.

We offer no apology for the length to which we have extended the foregoing remarks. The subject to which they introduce us is unquestionably the most important of any connected with the history of the Great Exhibition, not only as respects the building itself, whose fairy structure owed its chief attraction to the surprising adaptation of so glittering and fragile a material to the combined purpose of lightness and solidity, but also in the vast variety of articles it contributed, useful alike to science, to the fine arts, and to domestic comfort and adornment. Indeed, it is quite certain that however we may be inclined to yield the palm to the foreigner for beauty of design and delicacy of workmanship in other branches of ornamental manufacture, the British workman need fear no competitor in the various applications of glass, that most beautiful of chemical combinations. The gallery devoted to the work of his hands glittered like a fairy palace, and was every day visited by increasing crowds, more particularly of strangers, who were all unqualified in their admiration. In noticing the articles in this class, the place of honour belonged of right to the Messrs Osler, whose far-famed Crystal Fountain was the gem of the transept, and won for itself a European celebrity.

The basin of concrete in which the fountain itself was placed, was some 24 feet in diameter, and afforded a goodly surface for the falling spray. The structure of glass stood 27 feet high, and was formed of columns of glass raised in tiers, the main tier supporting a basin from which jets of water could be made to project, in addition to the main jet at the top. As the structure arose it tapered upward in good proportion, the whole being firm and compact in appearance, and presenting almost a solidity of aspect unusual with glass structures. A central shaft with a slightly " lipped" orifice finished the whole, and from this the water issued in a broad well-spread jet, forming in its descent a lily-like flower before separating into a spray, which in the sun-light glittered and sparkled in harmony with the fountain itself. Altogether this was a unique and magnificent work, and many difficulties of construction had to be overcome before the structure presented itself in its perfect form. The principal shaft was strengthened by means of a rod of iron passing through it, but concealed from observation by the refracting properties of the fans. Upwards of four tons of crystal glass were used in the construction of this fountain. The principal dish was upwards of eight feet in diameter, and weighed previous to cutting nearly a ton. The shafts round the base weighed nearly 50 lbs. each prevous to cutting.

The same firm also exhibited a magnificent pair of candelabra, in richly cut glass, each to hold fifteen lights, and standing eight feet high. Her Majesty was the purchaser of these truly regal ornaments, and it was by her gracious permission they were exhibited. The other contents of Messrs. Osler's case were, a large crystal candelabrum, supported by three griffins in dead or frosted glass, the figures of which struck us as being well executed, considering the material; some richly mounted lustres; and several portraits in frosted glass, including those of her Majesty, Prince Albert, and some of the national literary and political celebrities. The collection was handsomely arranged in a large glass case, and afforded every facility for inspection. Next in rotation, but second to none in excellence or beauty, came the beautiful specimens of Mr. Apsley Pellatt. This gentleman, not contented with carrying on his manufacture merely as a trade, has devoted much time and attention to vitreous chemistry, and to the history of glass from the time of its apocryphal origin on the coast of Syria down to the palmy period of Venetian art, and thence to the processes and discoveries of the present day. The results were the beautiful Anglo-Venetian services in gilt glass, which had all the fragile delicacy of form so much prized by connoisseurs—whether they have the imputed quality of detecting poison is a question which it is happily not necessary to discuss at the present day. Mr. Pellatt also made a bold attempt at restoring the lost Venetian art of frosting glass,

THE QUEEN OF SPAIN'S JEWELS.

BOUQUET, &c. IN DIAMONDS, PEARLS AND RUBIES.

MANUFACTURED BY LEMONNIERE, PARIS.

Engraved by G Greatbach from a Drawing by H Mason

THE QUEEN OF SPAIN'S JEWELS.

HEAD DRESS AND SHOULDER KNOT IN DIAMONDS, PEARLS, RUBIES AND EMERALDS.

MANUFACTURED BY LEMONNIERE, PARIS.

Engraved by G Greatbach from a Drawing by H Mason

and certainly the articles exhibited had a wonderful resemblance to ice, the thing intended to be represented. A curious feature in this collection was what the manufacturer called the Koh-i-Noor," consisting of several lumps of the purest flint glass, cut diamond-wise, and quite rivalling in brilliancy the two million original down stairs. We are certain that if the largest of these specimens had been placed on the velvet cushion, surrounded by an iron railing, and attended by a reverential policeman, it would have received a much larger meed of public wonder and approbation than the real eastern gem. As a specimen, however, of the purest and most beautifully cut flint glass, it afforded an excellent opportunity for observing the difference between that material and the true diamond. It had the advantage of the gem in entire absence of colour, and produced the prismatic changes with nearly equal effect. But it was deficient in specific gravity, and in that wondrous power of radiating light which gives to the diamond its value, and is its unique peculiarity. The mode of cutting these specimens proved the workmen to be first-rate lapidaries. The other prominent feature in this collection was a magnificent centre chandelier in highly refractive cut glass, which glittered like the valley of diamonds. It was of graceful and original design, and the purity of the glass might at once be detected by contrast with other specimens in the neighbourhood. This magnificent ornament was 24 feet high, and adapted for 80 lights. It was a prominent feature in the Exhibition, being easily seen from the nave below, and reflecting the sun's rays (on fine days) with extraordinary brilliancy. There were other chandeliers in coloured glass, in what the manufacturer pleased to call the Alhambraic style; but the taste of these was questionable, at least in our opinion, and rather marred the effect of the chandeliers, which were constructed solely with a view to prismatic effects. The remainder of the collection consisted of Etruscan vases ornamented with fine and delicate engraving, some carved incrustations, and numerous articles of lesser importance, but all affording ample reward for a lengthened inspection. Bacchus (Birmingham) appropriately employed himself in the fabrication of wine-cups, glasses, and decanters, in coloured and cased glass. The collection was not large, but well designed and executed. A flower-stand, with vase and cornucopia, had a very pretty effect. The delicate twisted stems of the champagne glasses were novel and chaste, but we fear for their continuity after the third "fire." Harris and Son, of Birmingham, exhibited a large collection of coloured glass, adapted to the various uses of the table. Fine effects of colour were here produced, and many of the shapes possessed novelty and grace. The articles exhibited by these and other manufacturers in coloured glass would seem to intimate that the Bohemians are not long to enjoy their monopoly. Specimens of the beautiful silvered glass lately become so fashionable, and which has formed so ornamental a feature at various public banquets, were exhibited by Messrs. Varnish, of Berners-street. The silvered globes were already familiar to the public, but there were various other articles, such as a chess-table, goblets, curtainpoles, &c., which showed the great adaptability of the material to ornamental purposes. Perry and Co. (New Bond-street), had an immense chandelier for 144 candles, of most elaborate workmanship. The design, however, is rather confused, and the quality of the glass does not appear so pure as is the case with Mr. Pellat's chandeliers. Perhaps it wanted cleaning, as the intricacy of the pattern afforded innumerable receptacles for dust; but, whatever may be the cause, it looked rather dull beside its more brilliant neighbours. There were various smaller collections of glass, among which good taste and good workmanship were generally discernible There was not, however, sufficient variety to require particular notice. Messrs. Chance and Co., who supplied the glass for the Exhibition building, were also exhibitors of an article which, until the removal of the duty, was scarcely ever attempted in this country. One of the specimens of dioptric apparatus for light-houses, in the western nave, was from their manufactory; the other was constructed by Mr. Wilkins, of Long-acre, for the Trinity Board. This optical apparatus was itself a distinguishing feature of our improvement in glass manufacture. Hitherto all the lenses of this order had been supplied from the Continent. The light-houses on our own shores could only be rendered effective by the use of French and German glass. Here we had, however, the most interesting proof that we can make these beautifully arranged lenses and catadioptric zones for ourselves. Fresnel claims the merit of this last improvement, by which a total reflection of all the light is effected; but at the same time it must not be forgotten that the experiments and suggestions of Sir David Brewster, during the investigation of the commissioners appointed to report on the northern light-houses, were the starting point of the inductive process from which this final deduction was derived. Messrs. Apsley Pellatt and Co. exhibited all the materials employed in the manufacture of flint glass, together with models of the glass-house furnaces, and examples of the purest crystal, particularly as employed for candelabra and chandeliers.

The exhibition of these various objects sufficiently proved the perfection of this branch of manufacture. It is not merely in its transparency and in its freedom from colour that the beauty of flint glass, or crystal, consists—it is in the diamond-like property of sending back the rays to the eye in greater brilliancy than it receives them; and in this respect much of that which was shown in the Exhibition was very perfect. The English were not formerly successful in giving colour to their glass; there was always a want of that brightness which distinguished the works of the Germans, and particularly of the Bohemians. The colours are given in nearly all cases by metallic oxides, and these vary not merely in tint, but actually in colour, by the quantity of heat to which the fused mixture is exposed. In the Bohemian glass, a ruby, in particular, was produced of far greater beauty than anything which our manufacturers could accomplish. This colour is due to oxide of gold, although reds of much brilliancy can be produced by copper, and also by iron. Some examples of the reds produced by these metals were found amongst the productions of British exhibitors; and upon examining the examples of Bohemian glass, it became apparent that we can now produce glass in every respect as brilliant and as intense in colour as that which has rendered our continental friends so long celebrated. In the articles exhibited by Mr. Varnish and Mr. Mellish, these colours were well shown. Most of the glass exhibited by them was manufactured by Messrs. Powell and Co., Whitefriars, and this itself presented a noticeable peculiarity. All the glass was double, the object of this being to enable the patentees to fill the inside with a solution of nitrate of silver, to which grape sugar was added, when all the silver held in solution was deposited in a beautiful film of revived silver over every part of the glass. This *silvering* on the interior wall of the glass (globes, vases, and numerous other articles were shown to be susceptible of the process) has the property of reflecting back through the glass all the light which falls on the surface—whereas ordinarily some is transmitted, and only a small portion reflected. This exalts many of the colours in a striking manner, and not only does it exalt the colours, but the dichromism of the glass is curiously displayed. Much of the red and yellow glass thus assumes an opalescent tinge of blue, which, in some examples, is not unpleasing. We greatly admired some of the coloured examples of this process, but we cannot think that the pure white glass—the beauty of which is its transparency— is in any respect improved by silvering.

The illustrations of engraving on glass were numerous, and many of them exceedingly beautiful. We particularly admired some of the specimens by Mr. Kidd of his new process of illuminating, embroidering, and silvering flat surfaces. All the designs were

Engraved by G.Greatbach, from a Daguerreotype

GROUP OF BOHEMIAN GLASS VASES

EXHIBITED IN THE AUSTRIAN DEPARTMENT

Engraved by G.Greatbach from a Daguerreotype.

CHANDELIERS IN COATED GLASS.

EXHIBITED IN THE AUSTRIAN DEPARTMENT.

cut on the under face of the glass, and then being silvered, were thrown up in a very pleasing manner, producing an optical deception of an interesting character. In many of the engraved specimens we had the very beautiful effect of cutting through several surfaces of coloured glass, down to the translucent body. The opaque glass coating, which may be produced either by mixing oxide of tin or arsenic with the glass, is first laid over the crystal; then on this is applied the ruby glass, and where the ruby has been produced by gold the result is most satisfactory. These being cut through, present the three surfaces in any way which may be decided on by the artist. Rice Harris and Son's pressed glass was of the greatest interest. By pressing into moulds, this elegant material is produced to the public in useful and symmetrical forms, at prices considerably below those at which cut flint glass could possibly be offered. Many of the specimens of pressed glass exhibited, had a degree of sharpness in all the ornamental parts, which rendered it difficult, without a close examination, to say whether or not they had been subjected to the operation of the glass-cutter's wheel. Among other new applications of this process of pressing glass into form, Messrs. Powell and Sons, of the Whitefriars Glass-works, exhibited their patent pressed glass for windows. There is much novelty and ingenuity in this. The pattern is pressed in the glass, and then, by a subsequent process, glass of another colour is flowed into it; the whole is then ground down to a uniform surface, and the result is an inlaid pattern of glass of one colour, in glass of another. The windows formed in this manner were very effective; and it appeared to us that they realized the results which in stained glass are only obtained by the long-continued action of the atmosphere and light. None of our modern church windows realised that " dim religious light" which is peculiar to those older fanes standing as memorials of the piety of our forefathers. The light permeating the modern windows suffers ordinary chromatic analysis, and falls upon the floor in well-defined colour, and the outline of the design can be easily traced. In those of olden time the colours fall blended; there is a general diffusion of tones, no one colour coming out more decidedly than another. Upon examining old glass windows it will be found that the utmost pains had been taken to secure this effect; the glass is often purposely roughened; frequently pieces of different colours are blended; but still the action of time and the abrasion of the exposed surface is the important agent to which the harmonious effect is due. Messrs. Hardman and Co. have had glass manufactured purposely to endeavour to imitate the required condition of the mediæval styles, and in many of their windows they have been eminently successful. The antiquity of pressed glass is very remarkable. The Assyrians, the Egyptians, the Greeks, and the Romans, all adopted the process of pressing or squeezing the glass, when it was in a pasty state, into moulds. Some fine examples of this will be found amongst the glass series in the Museum of Practical Geology. The examples of plate-glass were exceedingly good. The Thames Plate Glass-works exhibited at the western end of the building the largest plate glass hitherto manufactured. The examples of British plate which were found in the Spitalfields trophy were beautiful specimens of this class of manufacture. On the whole, the glass manufacture of the Exhibition—commencing with the sands, alkalies, and models, and terminating with the great Glass Palace itself, and its fancy fountain—was exceedingly complete, and of the highest interest.

CHAPTER XIV.

PRECIOUS STONES—MR. HOPE'S COLLECTION—THE DIAMOND, SAPPHIRE, EMERALD, GARNET, ETC.
—QUEEN OF SPAIN'S JEWELS—THE JEWELLED HAWK—PEARLS.

THE high estimation that in all ages has been bestowed upon jewels and precious stones, is perhaps sufficiently to be accounted for, when we take into consideration their essential qualities of light, and colour, and durability; and the correspondence which, in consequence of these valuable attributes, they possess with respect to the more elevated principles in the world of mind. Frequent mention is made of them in Holy Writ, from the breast-plate of Aaron described by Moses, to the sublime account in the Apocalypse of the wonders of the Holy City, its shining courts, and its gates of pearl, in all which description there is doubtless involved some mystic meaning connected with the future glorious destiny of the church, not obviously apparent to the merely superficial or general reader. In the world of poetry, too, constant recurrence is made to the different qualities of precious stones, and their reference to various physical endowments. Mental acuteness, and brilliancy of imagination, are invariably likened to the radiance of the diamond, whilst constancy and truth are equally represented in its unchangeableness and its durability. What can be more appropriate or beautiful than the lines of Collins, where, in illustration of the playfulness of wit and repartee, in one of the characters in his Ode to Music, he says—

"The jewels in whose crisped hair
Were placed each other's beams to share."

And with respect to personal beauty, who among all the votaries of Apollo ever neglected, in speaking of the brilliancy of his mistress's eyes, to compare them to the lustre of the diamond, her teeth to orient pearl, or her lips or her cheeks to the glowing ruby? The treasures of the secret mine have indeed been an inexhaustible source of comparison and metaphor, from the days of old Anacreon to those of his great rival and imitator, of Hibernian celebrity. Pliny, and other early writers on the subject of gems, attributed various occult qualities and miraculous powers to precious stones in general; they were also supposed to possess rare medicinal qualities, an opinion sanctioned by our own great philosopher Boyle, in whose time were to be found in the Materia Medica such compositions as the *Electuarium e Gemmis, Confectio de Hyacinthis,* &c., with which the more opulent of our forefathers endeavoured to ward off the stroke of death. The diamond more particularly enjoyed a high repute for these and other hidden virtues; it was considered as an infallible specific in many diseases, and a test of conjugal fidelity, a reconciler of domestic strife, and an amulet of highest power against poisons, insanity, witchcraft, incantations, nocturnal goblins, and evil spirits.

Never before in the history of the world was there so large a collection of valuable gems and exquisite specimens of the lapidary's art collected in one building as was exhibited in the Crystal Palace. The Exhibition contained the finest diamond, the finest ruby, and the finest emerald known to the world. For a sight of a single one of these stones an adventurous voyager traversed enormous distances two centuries ago, and by dint of extraordinary influence, audacity, and fortune, was enabled to record himself as the only European who had ever succeeded in the attempt. That stone was lately placed in Hyde Park, and might have been seen by any working man in the country for a shilling. The richest collection of treasures ever known was formerly to be found at Dresden. Its existence was due to a singular succession of wealthy and acquisitive

Engraved by G. Greatbach, from a Drawing by S. Mason.

THE EMPEROR OF RUSSIA'S JEWEL CASKET,

IN EBONY, THE FRUITS, &c. IN PRECIOUS STONES.

Engraved by G. Greatbach, from a Drawing by S. Mason.

HER MAJESTY'S JEWEL CASE,

NQUE CENTO STYLE BY ELKINGTON – DESIGNED BY GRUNER.

princes, in an age which favoured such fancies; its preservation, to an impregnable fortress within a few miles of the capital. It was deposited with extreme care in the vaults of the royal palace, and was only to be seen on the payment of a considerable fee, and after compliance with stringent conditions. Travellers and travellers' guides were full of the magnificence of these " Green Vaults," of the matchless splendour of their contents, and the unparalleled cost of their ornaments. Yet, if the "Green Vaults" could have been transferred bodily to Hyde Park, they would not have constituted either the richest or the most curious of the hundred compartments of the Crystal Palace. In objects of historical interest they would, of course, surpass what professed to be an exhibition of modern industry alone; but in singularity and value the collection would be altogether excelled by the contributions around it. Of the splendid and unpurchaseable diamond called the " Mountain of Light" we have spoken in a former chapter.

A most valuable and interesting addition had been made to the department of gems and precious stones in the Exhibition, by Mr. A. J. B. Hope, M.P., who deposited therein a portion of his valuable collection. They were placed upon a pedestal firmly secured to the floor, and covered with a circular iron frame, made by Mr. Chubb, similar in form to that which contained the priceless Koh-i-Noor. In this collection of Mr. Hope was the largest known pearl in the world; its length was 2 inches, its circumference $4\frac{1}{2}$ inches, and its weight 3 ounces, or 1,800 grains. Near this splendid specimen was placed a very beautiful Hungarian opal $1\frac{5}{16}$ inch in length, by $1\frac{5}{16}$ in breadth. A third specimen was the handle of the favourite weapon of Murat's, " the handsome swordsman," the hilt of which was formed of a single beryl or aquamarine. A rough beryl deposited near it showed its original condition. " Le Saphir Merveilleux"—a sapphire of an amethystine colour by candle-light—was viewed with interest by every admirer of the delightful productions of Madame de Genlis, one of whose most charming tales is founded upon this very stone, which was formerly in the possession of Philippe Egalité; with many other specimens of equal interest.

Among the minerals employed for personal decoration, the diamond evidently occupies the most prominent position, both on account of the beauty of the gem itself, and also because of its immense commercial value. The diamond, like charcoal, is composed of carbon; and, in a chemical point of view, differs from it only in being perfectly free from traces of the earthy and other impurities with which the latter substance, even when most carefully prepared, is to a considerable extent contaminated. This mineral, although principally used in ornamental jewellery, is likewise applicable to many other purposes; in consequence of its extreme hardness it is now extensively employed for making the pivot-holes of the better description of watches; it has also been used in the formation of holes through which very fine metallic wires are drawn, besides furnishing the only convenient tool which can be employed for cutting glass.

The countries in which this gem has been as yet discovered are far from numerous, the only localities in which it is found being the Indian peninsula, Brazil, the island of Borneo, and Siberia, on the western side of the Ural mountains. Its geological position appears to be among diluvial gravel and conglomerate rocks or pudding-stone, consisting chiefly of rolled flint pebbles and ferruginous sand. India has from the most remote ages been celebrated for the beauty and magnitude of its diamonds, the largest and most valuable of which are obtained from the mines in the provinces of Golconda and Visapoor. The tract of country producing these gems extends from Cape Comorin to Bengal, and lies at the foot of a chain of mountains called the Orixa, which appear to belong to the trap-rock formation. The diamonds obtained from even the richest localities are rarely procured by directly searching the strata in which they are found, since they are commonly so coated with an earthy crust on the outside, as not to be

z

readily distinguishable from the various other substances with which they are associated. For this reason the stony matter is first broken into fragments, and then washed in basins for the purpose of separating the loose earth; after which the residual gravel is spread out on a level piece of ground, where it is allowed to dry, and where the diamonds are recognised from their sparkling in the sun—thus enabling the miners readily to discriminate between them and the stony matters with which they are associated.

Among the other minerals much prized by the jeweller, many specimens of which were found in the Crystal Palace, may be mentioned the sapphire, which, when perfectly transparent and of a good colour, is as highly esteemed as the diamond. This gem is almost entirely composed of alumina, the various colours of different individual specimens being occasioned by extremely minute admixtures of the metallic oxides. Those having a blue colour are known as Oriental sapphires, whilst others not having the same oxides in combination are differently coloured, and consequently receive various distinctive names. When red, they are called Oriental rubies; when yellow, Oriental topazes; when violet, Oriental amethysts; and when they are hair-brown, adamantine spar. The finest blue specimens of this gem have been procured from Ceylon. The most esteemed red varieties come from the Capelan mountains, in the kingdom of Ava; and the smaller stones of the same kind are occasionally met with in Saxony, Bohemia, and Auvergne. Amethysts are principally brought from the Carnatic, on the Malabar coast, and elsewhere in the East Indies.

The emerald is a precious stone of a beautiful green colour, valued next to the diamond, and in the same rank as the Oriental ruby and sapphire. It occurs crystallized in regular six-sided prisms, and has a specific gravity of 2·70. In composition this gem may be considered as a double silicate of alumina and glucina, mixed with variable small portions of iron and a little lime.

The garnet is a vitreous mineral belonging to the cubic system, and of which the predominating form is the rhomboidal dodecahedron. Its constituents are silica, alumina, lime, and protoxide of iron. It is usually found disseminated in the primitive formations, and frequently occurs in gneiss and clay-slate. Garnets are abundantly met with in many parts of Europe, particularly in Germany; but those of Pegu are the most esteemed. Quartz, or silicic acid in a crystalline form, is also frequently cut for ornamental purposes, and, when limpid and entirely free from flaws, is a very beautiful stone. When existing in the form of calcedony, and variously coloured by metallic oxides, the substance receives the name of cat's-eye, plasma, chrysoprase, onyx, sardonyx, &c. It has a vitreous lustre, a conchoidal fracture, and a specific gravity of 2·69. The chrysolite, called "peridot" by Haüy, and the French mineralogists, is probably the topaz of the ancients. It is the softest of the precious stones, being scratched by the file or a fragment of quartz. Among the numerous examples of this mineral, as adapted for ornamental purposes, may be mentioned various very beautiful stones from Cairngoram, in Aberdeenshire, both cut and in the natural state. A case containing some specimens of peculiar briliancy was exhibited by Mr. Jamieson, of Aberdeen, near the western extremity of the space allotted to mineral productions. Some fine specimens in their natural state were to be seen in the Highland stall of Mr. M'Dougall, in the gallery on the south side of the transept. Opal, or uncleavable quartz, has a conchoidal fracture, with a resinous or vitreous lustre, accompanied by a strong play of colours. It occurs in kidney-shaped or stalactitic concretions, and has a specific gravity of 2·091. Hungary was long the only locality of precious opal, where it occurs in connexion with common opal in a sort of porphyritic formation. Lately, however, some very fine specimens of this substance have been discovered in the Faroe Islands; and most beautiful ones, sometimes quite transparent, are obtained near Gracias a Dias, in the province

Engraved by G Greatbach, from a Drawing by S Mason

DIADEM,

CONTAINING 1800 BRILLIANTS, WEIGHING 260 CARATS, AND 1750 ROSE DIAMONDS, 11 OPALS, AND 67 RUBIES,

ALL THE STONES BEING SET EN GRIFFS, VALUE £ 4800.

MANUFACᵈ BY MESSʳˢ BALIN & AIN Sᵗ PETERSBURGH

Engraved by G. Greatbach, from a Drawing by S. Mason.

DIAMOND AND RUBY STOMACHER,

CONSTRUCTED TO SEPARATE INTO SEVERAL DISTINCT PIECES OF JEWELLERY, AS BOUQUETS, &c.

MANUFACTURED BY MOREL, LONDON.

of Honduras, in America. The red, yellow, and other coloured varieties of opal, are chiefly found near Limapan, in Mexico. In modern times, fine opals of moderate dimensions have frequently been sold at prices nearly equal to those obtained for diamonds of the same bulk. They are especially esteemed by the Turks, and are usually cut into a convex shape. The value set on this stone by the ancients appears to have been very extraordinary, as Nonius, the Roman senator, preferred banishment to parting with his favourite opal, which was coveted by Mark Antony.

The turquoise, or calaite, is a massive mineral found only in the neighbourhood of Nichabour, in Persia, and is highly prized as an ornamental stone in that country. Its colour is greenish-blue, but those varieties are most esteemed in which the blue predominates. It is composed of alumina, oxide of copper, oxide of iron, and phosphoric acid, and has a specific gravity varying from 2·83 to 3·00. There is also another totally different variety of this substance, known by the name of bone turquoise, which appears a phosphate of lime more or less coloured with phosphate of copper. Malachite, or green carbonate of copper, is also frequently used for personal decoration; numerous specimens were to be found in the Russian department, worked up into a variety of splendid objects. Besides the Hope Jewels, already noticed, there was a magnificent display belonging to the Queen of Spain, exhibited by M. Lemonniere, of Paris, consisting principally of diamonds, pearls, rubies, and emeralds, the diamonds greatly preponder-ating. They were, perhaps, the best specimens of well-set gems that were exhibited. In point of radiance and gorgeousness, however, the "Diamond and Ruby Stomacher" by Morel, was a powerful rival to the most splendid of all these costly adornments—a truly sumptuous production, upon which the jewellery trade of England might be bold to stake its reputation in the face of the world. It was originally intended and designed as a bouquet, but was equally, perhaps more appropriately, available as a stomacher; moreover, it was so constructed as to separate into several distinct pieces of jewellery, according to requirement. The diamonds were all of the finest water, and the rubies were described as "a unique collection." The setting was contrived with springs, resulting in a waving or slightly oscillating motion when in use, which displayed to the fullest extent the brilliant colours of the stones. Messrs. Hunt and Roskell were large contributors to the splendours of this department. The principal and all-attractive object among the various treasures they exhibited was a magnificent diamond bouquet, a perfect specimen of the art of diamond setting. The flowers (comprising the anemone, rose, carnation, &c.) were all modelled from nature. This brilliant structure was divided into seven different sprigs, each perfect in design; and the complicated flowers, by mechanical contrivances, were so arranged as to separate for the purpose of effectual cleaning. In the production of this costly work nearly 6,000 diamonds were employed, the largest of which weighed upwards of ten carats, whilst some of the smallest, in the stamens of the flowers, did not exceed the thousandth part of a carat. We also observed from the same party an ornament for the head, composed of branch coral, orna-mented by leaves of enamel and gold, enriched with diamonds, a very elegant production, of chaste effect. There were also several brooches, bracelets, and other ornaments, enriched with diamonds and other precious stones, not the least curious amongst which were some specimens of ear-rings in emeralds, diamonds, carbuncles, &c., after the sculptures from Nineveh. Messrs. Paravagna and Casella, from Genoa, also sent a variety of ornaments of the same material. We may here remark that red coral has, from time immemorial, been used in jewellery, in all parts of the world, in beads, brooches, drops, bracelets, charms, studs, and fancy contrivances. The price varies from one shilling up to £5 and £20 per ounce. The best colours are considered a bright red or pale pink: the latter is most scarce. We must not confound with this substance the coral reefs found by mariners, as they are nothing but a spongy white rock, having no analogy whatever with the real red coral. The fishery of the real coral is carried on in the Mediterranean Sea. The largest samples are taken along the Barbary coast, but not the darkest colours. Along the coast of Spain a considerable quantity is taken annually, of a deep red colour, but sometimes rather wormy. The pink and deepest red, but in comparatively small branches, are taken in the Straits of Bonifacio, between Corsica and Sardinia. The amount annually taken varies from £100,000 to £200,000, the principal stations for the fishing-smacks being La Torre del Greco, near Naples; Leghorn; and Santa Margherita, near Genoa. This article is supposed to give employment to from 10,000 to 20,000 hands.

Not, however, to weary our readers with too lengthened an account of these " glittering gauds," we shall for the present close our caskets of diamonds with a brief notice of the Jewelled Hawk, the property of the Duke of Devonshire, in the Netherlands department, whose history is not without interest. It rejoiced in a name proper, being the " Knyp-hausen Hawk," and was made, many a long year ago, to commemorate the reconciliation of two noble Dutch families which had been long at variance. It contained within its gay plumage the identical gold drinking-cup which was used by the rival counts upon the auspicious day of their reconcilement, and which was discovered upon removing the head of the bird. The wings and body were chiefly covered with rubies; turquoises, emeralds, and other precious stones, were displayed in other parts. The bird stood about a foot high, more or less, and had a very stately appearance. We must now be allowed to make a few remarks upon pearls, since, although they cannot exactly be classed among precious stones, they must still be included under the head of "jewels;" indeed without them the richest casket on the toilet of the duchess would be considered as incomplete. We shall on this head avail ourselves of the following observations of an able contemporary in the pages of the *Westminster Review*. And first, with respect to mother-of-pearl. " The brilliant lustre and gleaming irridescence of its shelly envelope are not always destined to remain hidden in the depths of the ocean, or immured within mountains of rock. The painted savage appreciates its pearly charms, and plunges beneath the waves to seek the living joints of his simple necklace and armlets, or to supply his civilized brother with highly-prized materials for more elaborate ornaments. Mother-of-pearl, as it is called, is the nacreous portion of the shells of certain molluscs belonging to very different orders. Its charming colouring is not due to pigments, but caused by the arrangements of the layers of membrane and solid matter of which it is composed. The nacreous shells which furnish it are now sought for greedily wherever they can be obtained in sufficient quantity, and form articles of considerable import. From our own seas, or rather from the sea around the Channel Isles, we procure the Haliotis, or sea-ear, to use in the decorations of papier-maché work, and other and larger kinds of the same curious genus are brought from the shores and islands of the Pacific Ocean for the same purpose. They furnish the deep-coloured and richer-hued dark-green and purple mother-of-pearl; the brighter and paler kinds are derived from the shells of the pearl-oysters, almost all inhabitants of tropical regions. The nacre of pearls themselves is identical with the substance of these shells. These jewels of animal origin, so highly prized for their chaste beauty, are only the rejected or superabundant secretions of a shell-fish, consisting of concentrically-disposed layers of animal matter and carbonate of lime. In most instances they are consequences of the attempts of irritated and uneasy molluscs to make the best of an unavoidable evil; for, rendered uncomfortable, their peace of mind and ease of body destroyed by some intruding and extraneous substance—a grain of sand perchance, or atom of splintered shell—the creature incloses its torturing annoyance in a smooth-coated sphere of gem-like beauty. Would that we bipeds could treat our troubles so philosophically, and convert our secret cankers into sparkling treasures !"

Shakspere has observed that—

> " To gild refined gold, to paint the lily,
> To throw a perfume on the violet,
> Were wasteful and ridiculous excess,"

and we might equally suppose that any attempt to impart an additional value to the priceless commodities we have been describing in the present chapter would be just as hopeless and unavailing. Nevertheless the hand of Art has not laboured upon them in vain. Engraved gems are among the most valued treasures in royal and national museums. "Gems," says Hartley Coleridge, "always remind me of the enchanted rings and amulets of romances, of Gyges, and the Barmecides, and those marvellous crystals in whose translucent water necromancers beheld the face of things that are to be."

The earliest mention of engraving upon stones, as of carved figures, is to be found in Holy Writ. We are told, in the Book of Genesis, that Judah gave his signet and his bracelets to Tamar, and that Pharoah took his signet-ring from off his own hand and put it on that of Joseph. We are also informed in Exodus, that Moses was commanded to engrave the names of the children of Israel on two onyx stones, "with the work of an engraver in stone, like the engravings of a signet." To the Egyptians, who loaded their obelisks, the columns and walls of their palaces, temples, and tombs, with figures and hieroglyphic characters, the transition from tracing them on metals and precious stones was natural and easy. Their favourite productions in their commencement of this branch of art were stones cut in the form of the scarabeus, an insect venerated by them as the symbol of the sun, the principle of reproduction of all things, with attributes of their gods or heroes engraved upon the back. They regarded these stones as preservatives against disease and mischance; ornamented them with the images of their divinities, and the garments of their priests; bestowed them as marks of honour upon the living, and endeavoured to impart their beneficial influence even to the dead, by placing them upon their bodies in the tomb. After the Egyptians, we must look to the Etruscans for engraved gems; in which, as in sculpture, their first efforts were rude and stiff, as those of their predecessors. It is not however with the early efforts of this exquisite branch of art that we wish to detain our readers; we would rather introduce it at once to them as it existed in Greece at the same period when all the other arts attained their full perfection, that is to say, in the time of Alexander the Great. The Greeks paid equal attention to the minute as to the colossal. Size was no criterion to them, in their scale of excellence; and, as in the world of nature, the wisdom and goodness of the Deity are as evident in the organization of an ant as in that of an elephant, so in the world of art they could display as much grandeur of thought and purity of design within the circlet of a ring, as in the decoration of their majestic temples, and stately porticoes. Hence it is that their engraved gems are still and ever will be considered as among the choicest treasures of antiquity. In them are presented to us every subject of god and hero, allegory, and emblem; religious, historical, poetical, or mystical, that comes within observation or tradition; to them the most precious stones, the emerald, the ruby, the amethyst, the chalcedon, the cornelian, the topaz, were consecrated; and in them, as Pliny admiringly says, "we see nature in all her majesty, condensed within narrow compass."—*Hic in unum coacta rerum naturæ majestas.*

Were it possible to collect in one cabinet a complete series of ancient gems, we should possess in fairy editions an entire and most comprehensive library of materials for the history of every thing connected with Greece and Rome, in their "most high and palmy

2 A

state;" no wonder, then, that those which have actually come down to us should afford an incessant subject of inexhaustible gratification to the poet and the artist, the historian and the philosopher.

The earliest Greek engraver of precious stones, whose name has been recorded, is Theodorus of Samos, who flourished 750 B.C. He engraved for Polycrates, tyrant of Samos, a lyre for his signet ring, upon an emerald of such value that it was deemed by its owner a fit offering to the marine deities, to propitiate the evils that he feared might be in store for him, to counterbalance the unmixed good fortune of his life up to that period. Accordingly, he threw it into the sea, as we are told by Herodotus; but according to that same graphic historian, he was not to be deprived of any thing he possessed; for lo! on sitting down to table, when a fish of extraordinary size and superior quality was served up to him, he beheld again in its stomach his own identical ring, which it had caught from his hand upon the surface of the wave. The art of engraving upon gems was carried, as we have already remarked, to the highest perfection among the Greeks at the same time that they attained their utmost excellence in sculpture. The first devices upon them were simple, consisting of some single object, as the lyre, in the ring of Polycrates; or an animal, as the lion, which was worn by Pompey in a ring, out of compliment to Hercules, with whom he loved to claim affinity. But they soon came into request for portraits, of which the Greeks, as well as the Romans, were passionately fond, insomuch that few families of note were without statues of their relatives and friends. Alexander the Great was so exclusive on this point, that he allowed only one sculptor, Lysippus, to mould his statue; one painter, Apelles, to paint his portrait; and one engraver, Pryrgotoles, to engrave his likeness. One of the most important features, however, connected with engraved gems, was the beautiful moral lessons inculcated in the mythological subjects they continually present —subjects in which modern eyes seldom discern anything beyond the mere outline of some fabulous incident, of which they retain an imperfect recollection from their school days' learning; but to the mental view of those who looked deeper into them, they revealed truths equally beneficial for practice as for meditation. How, for instance, could an exhortation to temperance be given more pleasingly than it is conveyed in a fine sardonyx in the Orleans collection, showing the youthful Bacchus dancing hand-in-hand with three water-nymphs, in illustration of the caution observed by the wiser Greeks, the anti-Anacreonites, to mix three parts water with their wine, prettily alluded to by Enenus in an epigram thus rendered by Merrivale :—

> " 'Tis young Bacchus' chiefest pleasure
>   To move with Naiads three, in linked measure,
>   'Tis then he is good company
>   For sports, and loves, and decent jollity:
>   But when alone, avoid his breath!
>   He breathes not love but sleep—a sleep like death."

But it would far exceed our limits to enter upon even the briefest view of half the interesting subjects and their important meanings, that are to be found in the engraved gems of Greece. Such was the magnificence and taste of the ancients, that they not only employed engraved gems for seals, rings, bracelets, armlets, ear-rings, necklaces, buckles, clasps and girdles, but ornamented their robes, and even their sandals with them. Nor did the warrior disdain to place them in his helmet, breast-plate, and buckler, the hilt and scabbard of his sword, nay, upon his saddle also and the trappings of his horse. Thousands and thousands of intaglios and cameos were set in the gold and silver cups, vases, and plates, which the rich and luxurious consecrated as ornaments of their sideboards, or which pride or bigotry deposited in the temples of their divinities. With a similar profusion, even large cups, goblets, vases, and urns were made of solid onyx, sardonyx, and rock crystal, externally ornamented with relievo work by great and eminent masters. Calculation is astounded at the enormous expense and the immense time and labour that must have been bestowed upon this branch of art. Some idea of it, though a very inadequate one, might have been formed, by the examination of a small cup of rock-crystal in the Crystal Palace, the setting of which, we were informed, had cost three hundred pounds; though undoubtedly the materials of which that setting is composed fall far below in actual value that of many of the *tazze,* which may be seen in the British Museum. The art of engraving on precious stones gradually declined among the Romans from the time of Augustus to the beginning of the seventh century, when it disappeared entirely in the long night of barbarity and ignorance, justly designated by the appropriate term of the dark ages.

Michael Angelo, Raphael, the Carraccis, Poussin, and other celebrated painters, have borrowed largely from the gems of Greece : the sculptors the same. Some of Gibson's finest productions—and where can finer be found?—have originated in the ideas they have suggested to him. The Amazon defending her horse from the attack of a ferocious tiger, by Kiss, of Berlin, so much admired in the Crystal Palace, was taken from an antique gem ; and the veiled figures of Tuscan (we will not say Austrian) workmanship, which excited equal wonder and admiration, were probably suggested by the exquisite gem by Tryphon, of the marriage of Cupid and Psyche, wherein the bridal pair are represented linked together by a chain of pearls, and covered with the nuptial veil, through which their features are seen in all the beauty of youth and innocence—a masterpiece of art, of which no imitation is to be found, save in the half-veiled head of Ptolemy Auletes, on a gem in the Orleans collection, and that of the Empress Sabina on another, formerly in the Crispi collection, at Ferrara. The art began to revive, however, in the fifteenth century, and its present state, in the skilful hands of such an artist as Girometti, of Rome, warrants us in the assertion that, although neglected for so long a period, it now bids fair to emulate the high and well-merited reputation it anciently enjoyed. The artist we have just mentioned, we are informed, had prepared a magnificent sample of his skill for the late Great Exhibition; the difficulty, however, of finding a safe conveyance for so precious a gem, and his being prevented from visiting our shores himself, proved, unfortunately for the lovers of art, insurmountable obstacles to his design. We have hitherto chiefly spoken of the art of cutting subjects on gems in *intaglio,* or indenting, a simpler and easier process than relieving the work from a ground ; we will now make a few remarks upon the more elaborate mode of *relievo,* or relief. There has been much unsatisfactory discussion respecting the origin and exact meaning of the word *cameo,* or *camaieu,* as it is sometimes written. In the language of art, it is usually applied to gems or stones, and latterly to shells, that are worked in relievo ; and strictly speaking, it refers to such stones only as have strata or grounds of different colours. It is impossible to describe works of this sort, containing so much fine detail, with sufficient accuracy to convey a just idea of their merits. They must be seen, and examined with care, to be properly appreciated ; but it will not be amiss to notice a few of the most celebrated camei that are preserved in the museums of Europe. One of the finest is the Apotheosis of Augustus, in the collection at Vienna. It represents Augustus, his wife Livia, as Rome, accompanied by her family, with Neptune and Cybele ; another is of an Imperial Eagle ; also a Ptolemy and Arsinoe, &c. &c. In the French collection, the sardonyx or Tiberius is one of the best known : it exhibits the Apotheosis of Augustus, and the princes of the house of Tiberius ; a Jupiter Ægiochus is a very fine specimen : to which may be added the Apotheosis of Germanicus, and one of Agrippina and Germanicus ; with others, particularly some portraits of great interest. We possess in this country some camei of first-rate excellence, but they are chiefly in private collections. The workers in cameo not only exercised their skill in the cutting or engraving, but also in so arranging their subject, and the composition of its details, as to make the different colours or zones of the stones answer for parts of the design; as, for example, in relieving fruit, flowers, or drapery in colour, while the other parts, as the flesh of a portrait or figure, were left white; or, cutting the subject entirely in white, and working no deeper into the stone than the first layer of colour, thus making, or rather leaving, a natural dark back-ground for the design. These irregularities are sometimes taken advantage of so skilfully, that it is very difficult to decide whether the variety is the effect of art, or really the natural colour of the stone. The ancients so greatly admired this variously-coloured work, that they even imitated the material in glass, and we possess in this country a fine specimen of their skill in the Barberini or Portland Vase, in the British Museum, the execution of which is of the first quality. This celebrated vase was a few years ago purposely dashed to pieces by one of those lunatics who seek to gain notoriety by some great act of malevolent mischief. It has been, nevertheless, completely repaired, and restored to its original beauty. The practice of working camei on shells, *conchylie*, is of comparatively modern introduction in Italy. It is now, however, particularly in Rome, practised with considerable success, and we may be allowed to hope it will be more practised by our own gem engravers. The subject is worked in relievo in the white or outer portion of the shell, while the inner surface, which is of a darkish hue, is left for the ground. In the Roman department we observed several very good specimens of these camei, by Saulini, one of the best workers in that line of art.

CHAPTER XV.

MOSAIC WORK — ITS HISTORY — ANCIENT MOSAICS — ROMAN MOSAICS — FLORENTINE MOSAICS — THE CHEVALIER BARBERI — STAINED AND PAINTED GLASS — MARECHAL AND GUGNON — CHANCE, BROTHERS, ETC. ETC.

MOSAICS are a kind of picture, executed with small pieces of glass or wood, pebbles, enamel, &c., fixed upon any given surface by means of mastic. Although this branch of art was well known and much practised by the ancients, Pliny has spoken of no express style, nor has he particularized any of the artists who wrought in it. We can only judge, therefore, by the appearance of antique relics of this kind, and by comparing them with modern performances, the method of executing which is known to us. When an artist commences a work in mosaic, he cuts in a stone plate a certain space, which he encircles with bands of iron. This space is covered with thick mastic, on which are laid, conformably to the particular design, the various substances meant to be used. During the whole of his work, the artist must have his eye constantly fixed on the picture which it is his object to copy. The mastic, in time, acquires the consistency of stone; it is susceptible of a polish like crystal. However, as the brilliancy thus acquired is injurious to the effect of the design itself, which is not clearly perceived through it, those mosaics which are applied to the adornment of cupolas, ceilings, &c., are generally less elaborately polished, the distance from which they are viewed preventing the spectator from detecting the inequalities of surface, or the interstices between the pieces of which the work is composed. The means have been discovered of giving to the colour of glass so many different shades, that it has been found to serve the purposes of all the various descriptions of painting. The artist in mosaic has all his various materials ranged before him in compartments, according to their several tints, in much the same way as the printer arranges his different letters. To Pompeo Savini, of Urbino, has been attributed the art of executing mosaics in relievo.

The origin of mosaic work must, apparently, be sought in the East, the rich carpets of which were imitated in hard stone. It is probable that the art was known to the Phœnicians, but to the Greeks its perfection and glory are to be attributed. From Greece it passed, with the other ornamental points of knowledge, into Rome, towards the end of the republic; the Italian conquerors of Greece transporting from that country into their own the most beautiful specimens in the shape of pavements, &c., which they could discover. Sylla was the first Roman who caused a piece of mosaic work of any magnitude to be executed for the temple of Fortune at Præneste (now Palæstrina); which mosaic, at least a great portion of it, still exists. At first they ornamented in this manner the pavements of buildings merely, but after a while the walls and arched ceilings also. The tents of the generals, in time of war, were also paved thus, to keep off the humidity of the ground, as Suetonius reports of the tent of Julius Cæsar. The invention of coloured glass was a great discovery for the purposes of mosaic work. When the dark ages had driven the elegant arts out of Italy, mosaic work, as well as painting and sculpture, was preserved a considerable time amongst the Byzanthian Greeks, who used it to adorn the altars of their churches. Towards the conclusion of the thirteenth century, an Italian of the name of Tafi learnt to work in mosaic of a Greek called Apollonius, who decorated the cathedral of St. Mark at Venice, where is still preserved an admirable pavement executed by him. But, in general, these works are wanting in design, are in bad taste, and equally bad in colouring. Since then the art has been brought in Italy to a very high degree of perfection. Pope Clement VIII., at the commencement of the seventeenth century, contributed much to this end by adorning in mosaic all the interior part of the dome of St. Peter's. Among the earliest artists employed thereon were Paul Rossetti and Francis Zucchi. One of the greatest advantages of mosaic is its power of resisting all those things which ordinarily affect the beauty of painting, and another the facility with which one can repolish it without at all hazarding the brightness and effect of the colouring. At the same time, as it can only be worked slowly, and requires great exertion, it can never come into such general use as painting: nor would it have attained the degree of perfection which it did at Rome and Florence, had ·not the respective governments of those two states made a point of encouraging it. Among the most beautiful mosaics preserved in the pavements or walls of ancient buildings, we may particularize that found in a chamber in Hadrian's villa, near Tivoli, and the Palæstrine mosaic, before alluded to, which is remarkable for the light which its delineations throw on the history, local and natural, of Egypt. In the villa Albani is also a beautiful mosaic discovered in the territory of Urbino, which represents a school of philosophers, and another depicting the history of Hesione, daughter of Priam. In 1763 was found, in a villa near Pompeii (probably that of the Emperor Claudius) a mosaic representing three females with comic masks, and playing on various instruments. The name of the artist (Dioscorides, of Samos), was engraven thereon in Greek letters. There are, besides, a very great number of others which have been at sundry times dug up, and which present a greater or less degree of beauty and of excellence in the art.

Among the mosaics exhibited in the Crystal Palace was a magnificent table, by the Chevalier Barberi, executed for the Emperor of Russia. In that style of art it was a work of consummate excellence. The principal cities of Italy contributed to form its border.   Rome brought forward her glorious old Coliseum and her mighty dome of St. Peter's; Florence her Palazzo Vecchio, the old feudal residence of her former princes; Venice displayed her church of St. Mark; Milan her magnificent cathedral, that splendid wonder of Northern Italy, rearing its beautiful marble pinnacles of purest white towards the azure vault of heaven; Genoa, *la Superba*, gave her ample port and her noble amphitheatre of hills; Naples, its *pezzo de cielo caduto sul terra*, as its inhabitants term its glorious bay, over which Vesuvius reared its inauspicious head; while Palermo, with her Duomo, completed the magic circle.   The rich tone of colour, the accuracy of delineation, and the perfect finish that were found in this admirable work, could not have been surpassed by the delicacy of miniature oil painting; so great, indeed, was its perfection, that the spectator might almost have required a microscopic examination to satisfy himself that the work of art before him was not the production of pencil and pigments, but of materials widely different.

There was another mosaic to which we would also direct attention, if it be not invidious to particularize where all were excellent of their kind; but we mention it, partly because it was a copy of a *chef-d'œuvre* of Italian art—Guercino's "John the Baptist"—and partly because it had been produced in the great parent school of Roman mosaic art, the studio of the Vatican.   It was the work of Signor Raffaelle Castellini. Although the *Studio de Mosaici* in the Vatican, which is maintained at great expense by the Papal government, chiefly for the purpose of decorating churches with mosaic copies of the masterpieces of Italian art, must be regarded as the great parent school, which has developed to its present state of perfection the art and mystery of mosaic working, there are, nevertheless, private establishments which produce works of great beauty for the decoration of mansions and palatial residences, and of these the mosaics in the Exhibition were beautiful specimens.   Besides those already referred to, there were two handsome tables by Signor Boschetti, and others by Luigi and Domenico Moglia, presenting views of the Roman Forum, the Coliseum, the temples of Pæstum, &c., which stood the test of close inspection, being very admirable works.   Although the table above referred to, by the Chevalier Barberi—a name of European celebrity—was a most exquisite specimen, and well worthy of his fame, it is very much to be regretted that he had not been allowed to exhibit to the admiring eyes of all nations in the Crystal Palace a *chef-d'œuvre* which he had just completed for the Emperor of Russia, and which he had been obliged to transmit immediately to St. Petersburg; viz., a large octagonal pavement, containing twenty-eight figures, the central piece being a colossal head of Medusa, and the whole being surrounded by a border of fruits and flowers.   The design was copied on a reduced scale from an ancient pavement in one of the rooms of the Vatican museum; but it would be impossible for any one thing to surpass another to a greater degree than that to which Barberi's copy excels the original in drawing, colouring, and style of execution generally.   He was aided in his work by his Russian pupils, who were placed in his studio by the Czar for the purpose of learning the art of mosaic decoration, with a view to founding a school of mosaic at St. Petersburg.

The improvements in the mechanical parts of the operation of mosaic painting which have been introduced by Barberi are so great, that a work which would require upwards of four years for its completion in the Vatican studio, can now be executed by him in less than a year and-a-half.   A remarkable instance of this celerity of operation was recently manifested at his studio, where a copy in mosaic of the St. Nicholas in the church of St. Peter, was made in something less than two years, although a similar work at the Vatican occupied from four to five years.   The pavement above referred to took three years and-a-half in its execution.   But these are works on the grand scale, to which the mosaics in the Exhibition only bore the relation of miniatures to full-length paintings. The latter, however, were well calculated to impress on a mind hitherto unacquainted with mosaic works, a correct idea of this peculiar and beautiful branch of art.

The Florentine mosaics are very different in structure from the Roman, being composed of the most valuable marble, jasper, chalcedony, agate, lapis lazuli, &c., from which thin layers are cut out of such portions as can be made to represent leaves and flowers, in which form they are inlaid into a solid slab of black marble. This constitutes the ground; the pattern generally consists of wreaths of lilies, roses, vine leaves, or any other graceful or beautiful objects which require soft shades and delicate tints of colour. We have seen, at Florence, a table made in this manner, which was valued at several thousand pounds. And no wonder, for the pattern inlaid was of vine leaves exquisitely shaded, and the grapes were of rubies and amethysts. In the Pitti Palace, the residence of the Grand Duke, there are several of these splendid articles of furniture, fit adornments for so sumptuous and regal an abode. Its collection of pictures, too, is one of the most choice and faultless that is to be met with in all Italy. The finest specimens of Florentine mosaic were, in all probability, too costly and too easily injured to be sent for mere exhibition, for the specimens that were to be seen in an apartment adjoining to the Roman were very inferior to what we had seen in Florence, where we spent nearly a whole day in the manufactory, inspecting at our leisure the whole process of cutting the marble, and placing the thin pieces which formed the pattern in their appropriate places in the slab. The specimens in the Exhibition, however, showed very distinctly the plan of the work, and there was one sprig of roses in the centre of a round table, which might have been mistaken for the most exquisite painting, and which was more rich and mellow in its effects than any that could be produced by the mere laying on of colour. Great use is made in this work of a kind of green marble, the soft shades of which are often so managed in the cutting out, as to represent the folding over of the edge of a leaf, or the light side of one resting upon the darker surface of another. The landscapes in this style of art, of which there were two or three exhibited of a rather large size, we do not altogether consider as very successful. The materials employed are too untractable and rigid to admit of a free or graceful pencilling; neither in mosaic work, as in painting, can one hue be passed over another, to impart that rich transparency, or that aerial mistiness which is so beautiful in nature, and which the practised hand of a master, with all the appliances afforded him in a well-arranged palette, can alone hope to imitate. But in graceful and even elaborate representation of foliage, fruit, flowers, and ornamental work, such as may fitly adorn the chambers of royalty itself, it is that the art of the mosaicist displays its utmost beauty and perfection.

We will now for the present dismiss our mosaics, and take up the kindred subject of

STAINED AND PAINTED GLASS,

which in lengthened display extended its brilliant and kaleidoscope hues throughout the half of the upper gallery above the nave, and attracted a general and admiring notice. Few of those who visit either our own cathedrals, or inspect the interior of continental churches, ever think of investigating the merits, much less examining the subjects, of the

" ———— Storied windows, richly dight,
Casting a dim religious light,"

and which shed such a beautiful and mysterious glow over the structure. It was therefore a rare satisfaction to be enabled to scan closely the merits of those productions, whose principal claim to our attention was avowedly that of being an imitation of bygone arts. Although the art of staining glass is lost in antiquity, its adaptation to pictorial purposes is comparatively recent. Doubtless the mosaics of the Egyptians and Romans originally suggested the idea of transparent glass pictures; for, indeed, the earliest attempts were entirely composed of small pieces of glass of various colours, united by thin strips of lead, as may still be seen in old churches and cathedrals. The first records of pictorial glass work extant, date from about the year 800, in the days of Pope Leo III., when so many magnificent ecclesiastical edifices were erected, commenced, and designed.

Venice was chiefly famous for the manufacture of stained glass, the use of which was brought to high perfection with the pointed style of architecture in England. Fine specimens of the art may be seen in York Minster, the collegiate halls and chapels, and especially in the chapel of King's College, Cambridge. It is evident that the art of painting on glass may be divided into two perfectly distinct operations: firstly, the artistic design with reference to the capacities of the materials; secondly, the mechanical or rather chemical preparation and application of the materials themselves. Unlike most other descriptions of painting, in which vegetable as well as mineral colours are freely used, glass requires the exclusive use of mineral colours. The oxides of metals, such as gold, silver, cobalt, &c., are chiefly employed. These colours are, as it were, burnt into the glass. Some of them stain the whole substance, and are quite transparent; others mix with a substance called flux, and vitrify on the surface. These last are more or less opaque or semi-transparent, according to the mode in which they are applied.

Now, the ancients being more moderate in their demands on such a means, were more primitive, and perhaps more successful in their effects, whilst the moderns have progressed in an artistic point of view, but at the expense of the transparency, breadth, and simplicity of their ancestors. As a general rule, the modern paintings on glass are too much paintings in the strict sense of the word, too opaque in their shadows, and, in fact, too much shaded altogether. Whereas, painting on glass, to be really effective, should be almost entirely outline and colour, and as free from nontransparent, that is black shading as possible, for it must be remembered that all non-transparent colour becomes mere neutral tint when opposed to light in a window, and that the depth of the tint is mainly regulated by its transparency; hence the somewhat muddy character of the majority of modern paintings on glass. Where, however, the nature of the material is sacrificed to real excellence in the design, we are inclined to make great allowances; but, unfortunately, either most manufacturers of stained glass grudge the expense of employing competent artists to draw for them, or artists of merit consider it beneath their dignity, or lastly, the patrons of the art themselves regard it in too mean a light, and do not offer an adequate remuneration for the production of such painting on glass in their churches, &c., as we should desire to see, and seeing, to admire. Yet there are plenty of young artists who would be glad to make coloured designs for glass windows for a very moderate remuneration, and who are perfectly capable of good composition, correct drawing, and judgment in the arrangement and distribution of the colours. Upon those more especially, who, from the spur given to the art by the late Exhibition, may speedily be called on to fulfil the above requirements, we would impress the following suggestions, which we venture with all humility to advance for the guidance of adventurers in a new or revived domain of pictorial creation. In the first place it must be borne in mind that a stained glass window is not a mere painting, but a means of admitting light, modified and tempered, it is true, but still light, into the building to which it pertains. Hence an additional reason for the all-importance of transparency in glass window-pictures. Secondly, it must be remembered that these pictures are generally seen at a considerable distance; therefore, the boldness breadth, and above all, the harmony of the effect is far more vital to its success than any minuteness of detail. Thirdly, it must be invariably present to the mind of the artist that he is not producing a work for isolated exhibition, but is labouring in combination with the architect of the edifice which his design is to adorn, and with which it is expected to fall in and harmonize—not to jar and contrast by painful and violent uses of light and shadow, such as, we are sorry to say, the late collection very plentifully offered. Actual white and black (that is, opaque shadow) ought to be almost entirely excluded from works of this kind. In a word, the window ought never to lose for an instant its character as a window, that is, an admitter of light, which is its absolute and æsthetic relation to the walls, columns, and domes of the building it illuminates. It is certain that the practical art of staining glass, which flourished in such perfection during the thirteenth century, has been in a great measure lost, and, notwithstanding all the efforts of modern chemistry to equal and surpass it in purity and brilliancy of colour, it remains unrivalled. On the other hand, painting on glass, when carried out by artists such as form the exceptions to the strictures above made, is decidedly pushed much further than in former times, as far as mere pictorial excellence is concerned. Whether it has advanced in its legitimate mission, that of an harmonious adjunct to architectural effect, we doubt. A new era has, however, commenced in the art, and we must take it as we find it, merely considering its merits with reference to the object intended to be attained, and not criticising it according to any abstract causes of glass window-painting, which, right or wrong, may form a part of our artistic conscience. In proceeding to notice the works in this department displayed in the Great Exhibition, we would premise that we are not amongst the devotees to this mode of decoration as a vehicle for high art; and consequently, must be prepared to view the various candidates as copyists of the art as developed at the early period when it was in vogue. The following observations therefore will be considered to be written with a feeling for "mediævalism." As a general fact, we have to admit, that the English glass-stainers did not take the first rank in this branch of national competition. On taking a first and cursory view of the long range of stained glass windows and medallions in the northern galleries of the Exhibition, our attention was forcibly arrested by the striking works of MM. Marechal and Gugnon, of Metz, which, in almost every requisite quality, artistic composition, harmony of colour, and mechanical execution, excelled all the productions of their competitors. In the "Portrait of a Bourgemestre," the richness of the dark yet transparent drapery was very remarkable. Perhaps the head was a little too bright a contrast to the deep background and dress. But in the large painting at its side no such defect was visible. "St. Charles Borromeo giving the Sacrament to the Victims of the Plague," was remarkable as a restoration of mediæval life and sentiment. The drawing of the figures, rude and unsatisfactory, *per se*, was combined with a devotional sincerity in the expression and attitudes, and a local historical truth in the peculiar cast of feature, which denoted the revival of an obsolete art in a kindred spirit. The blue sky in the background admirably relieved the warm group of earnest figures in front, and the colouring was of a beauty which reminded one of the early Italian painters. Nor was it in pictorial effect and drawing only that Marechal of Metz excelled. His medallion of the thirteenth century style was an excellent specimen of colour and design. It harmonized with the rest of his paintings, and though simple in its outlines and its colours, it was rich both in chromatic harmony and general effect. Marechal is, in fact, the one great glass painter and stainer of the present day in Europe. His works have been long known and appreciated in France as the first in that line of art. His paintings in the windows of the church of St. Paul, at Paris, which were furnished some years ago, raised him at once above all his competitors in France, both as a glass stainer and an artist. Without dwelling on the minute grada-

tions of merit in other glass-stainers and painters, we now pass on to a general examination of the works most worthy of attention in the late collection.

Messrs. Chance, Brothers, of Birmingham, exhibited a variety of paintings, amongst
which we noticed a Virgin in a green robe, well contrasted with some rich crimson
drapery. There was much breadth and simplicity about this figure. We also observed
a landscape, which would have been very well, but for the excess of green in the
arrangement of its colour. And here we may pause to mention a very curious fact as
to the glass paintings exhibited, viz., that each manufacturer or artist seemed to have
a peculiar love for one particular colour, in the production of which he succeeded better
than in others. Thus Messrs. Chance's greens were pre-eminent for brightness and
transparency; whilst, as we shall presently have occasion to remark, other glass-stainers
excelled in other colours, and affected them more exclusively.

Mr. Edward Baillie exhibited a painting of " Queen Elizabeth listening to the reading
of Shakspere," which surpassed all his rivals in the violent contrast of its lights and
shadows, and in the impenetrable opacity of the latter. We cannot say much for the
faces or drawing in this group. However, the Queen's white satin robe was very
brilliant; and the carpet was really so well executed, that we could have wished the
remainder of the picture up to the same level. Mr. W. Wailes was enterprising in
design, and displayed considerable brilliance of colour and transparency, but there was
a rudeness and harshness about the paintings which were not pleasing. The St. Helen's
Crown, Sheet, and Plate-glass Company sent a large painting of " St. Michael and
Satan," in which the tail of the arch-enemy was prolonged to an indefinite degree.
There was some spirit in the drawing, but the execution was lamentable in every respect.
Some lions and unicorns by Tobay, the former yellow, and the latter white, were not very
wonderful productions, nor in any respect likely to outshine the ordinary lions and
unicorns of every-day life.

Messrs. Hetley and Co., of Soho-square, sent a very fine painting of the " Ascension."
In this work the rich colour in the foreground contrasted well with the lightly managed
atmosphere, against which the figure of the Saviour was seen in a " glory" very spiritually
conceived and executed. M. P. Lafaye was doubly unfortunate in being placed by the
side of Marechal, to whose works his specimens served as a foil. They were muddy in
colour, and very inferior in design. Henri Fougue sent some curious specimens of
mezzotinto transparencies, produced by glass or china, carved or modelled so as to
produce the different gradations of light, shade, and tone, in a manner remarkable
for its softness and purity of effect. M. Thibaut Dallet had a very brown monk,
effectively drawn, but deficient in transparency. His " Judith and Holofernes" was a
fierce piece, of strong expression, and somewhat crude but rich effect. Red is evidently
the predominating and favourite colour with this artist. The " Lord's Supper" was
more transparent, but with little merit either in design or colour. Herr Geyling, of
Vienna, had a female figure leaning on a window-sill, which resembled an oil-painting in
effect. The flesh of the face and hands, and the white chemise, as well as the dress,
were well executed; but the opaque background was objectionable. As a work of art it
reminded one, on the whole, of Jullien's coloured lithographs. We consider this a strong
example of success in a line which ought never to be attempted by a glass-stainer.

M. Thevenot was chiefly noticeable for a blue turn of mind in his colouring. He
had, however, some very tolerable saints on pedestals, which were edged with gold, most
effectively rendered by transparent yellow glazing. His " Radegona" was a severe figure,
with much depth and richness, yet too opaque for real brilliancy of effect. The small
Gothic window, by M. Martin of Troyes, was remarkable as a quaint imitation of the old
style, as regards artistic treatment and brilliancy of colour. Upon these grounds, it was

one of the most curious specimens in the Exhibition to lovers of the ancient glass-stainers and their peculiar characteristics.

The painted window by Mr. Gibson, of Newcastle, contained subjects illustrative of various passages in the life of St. Peter. It was in the Norman style, and consisted of six geometrical forms upon a richly ornamented ruby background, embodying the principal events from the apostle's life. The centre medallion was Christ's charge to Peter; the others respectively contained the Angel delivering Peter from prison; Peter denying Christ; Christ calling Peter from the ship; Peter's want of faith; and in a small quatrefoil was the martyrdom of St. Peter; the whole surrounded by an elaborately worked and richly coloured border. The colours of the glass were rich and full-toned, and judiciously combined. It is a subject for regret, however, that, in reviving this ancient art, as a medium, it should be considered necessary to imitate the barbarous style of drawing of the Gothic ages. We have thus glanced at a few of the most meritorious, or rather, to speak conscientiously, of the least sinning, amongst the exhibitors in the stained glass gallery. On a future occasion we shall return to the subject, when we shall give some account of Bertini's famous Dante window. Before taking leave of this subject, we would draw this general conclusion from the examples we have been examining. We would once more impress upon the improver and enterpriser in this branch of decoration, that simplicity, transparency, and moderation in light and shade, are the three great requisites after harmony of colour.

CHAPTER XVI.

AN EARLY MORNING VISIT—A NOON-DAY STROLL—PEACEFUL CROWDS—PLEASING ADMIXTURE OF RANK—A GREAT DAY AT THE CRYSTAL PALACE—BRITISH HOSPITALITY—ENTERTAINMENT IN GUILDHALL TO THE QUEEN.

WE will now, for a short period, dismiss all particular criticism on the various productions of human industry and genius, and indulge in a retrospect of one of those calm and quiet days, which were frequently devoted by the assiduous visitor, satiated with curious examination, to a general and leisurely observation of what was passing in the busy microcosm around him. Our readers must be informed that it was the privilege of the "writers for the press" to wander unrestricted through the avenues of the glorious Crystal Palace, long before the general public were admitted—a privilege shared only with industrious exhibitors' attendants, and sundry busy gentlemen in red coats, known as sappers and miners. From one of these favoured votaries of the quill we are indebted for the following graphic description of its appearance at "early dawn," and the feelings it was calculated to awaken in the reflective mind. "It is scarcely possible," observes our writer, "for those who have not visited the wonderful Glass House, to conceive the curious effect its vast size and exquisite perspective have upon the mind. Its solitary grandeur at this hour can be likened to nothing of which we have hitherto had experience. It was like a forest in its stillness, but the songs of birds or hum of bees greeted not the listening ear—it was like a cathedral in its vastness and solemnity, but no masonic pillars, or heavy sculptured walls were there to break the light, and give the 'dim religious' air, so potent in its grandeur—it was like a fairy palace, in which a hundred thousand sleepers might have dozed away their lives, but that we knew it to be filled with the works of men's hands—it was like a dream of beauty, and light, and power, but that a passing footstep awakened us up to reality and life—it was like—like nothing but itself, unsurpassable, indescribable, unique, amazing, real! The sun broke out, and added new beauty to the painted line of girder and column stretching far away. We gazed upward in never-tiring wonder and admiration, and caught new glimpses of beauty in the glass roof of the beautiful transept, tinted with all the colours of the rainbow. We looked around, and found the light reflected in glass and silver and bubbling water—for the hour was passing, and the hitherto silent fountains had begun to play.   *   *   * Day had fairly set in, and where a solitary visitor was erstwhile standing, little knots had gathered; little knots, which, as the clock struck TEN, had become groups, which speedily swelled into assemblages, which presently became inconveniently close, and were at length a mass, a crowd, a mighty peace meeting. A throng, indeed; but there was wonder, and pleasure, and kindness on every face. We stood a minute in the corner of the gallery, beneath the ladies' carpet, and gazed upon the well-known spectacle. The sight of thousands in the Glass Palace was one worth seeing indeed,—for where the million is, there is love, and hope, and human passion. O, amazing thought! The GREAT GOD was in the midst!"

The interior of the Crystal Palace had now assumed that state of pictorial completeness in which it remained during the whole summer. Nothing more seemed wanting to it. Each day had added something to its picture, as well as to its uses; and we were never weary of repeating how in this wondrous edifice all had been so successfully contrived that every sense was satisfied. At every turn the eye was fed with beauty. In the fervid mid-day hours a delicious coolness filled the atmosphere. The low plash of falling fountains sent whisperings through the ears that were like sounds heard in a dream. Even the sounds which in ordinary buildings would produce discords, between the walls and under the roof of crystal combined into a strange and palpitating music. Few things in the mighty edifice were more remarkable than this effect. Great as was the daily concourse of people, the hum of voices seldom rose above the deep and trembling monotone produced by conversation in the open air. The talk of the fountains and the tones of minor musical instruments died on the ear at the shortest distance. The organ notes rolled but faintly down the naves, as they would have done along a line of forest trees,—the high swell and cadence falling gently on the unresisting medium in which they passed away. Even the click and whizz and whirl of machinery did not strike the ear with that sharp and semi-painful effect produced by them in close brick buildings. There were no echoes, reverberations, arrested or broken sounds. The noises passed away through the glass roof as freely as the light and sunshine entered by it.

Our holiday-makers from the country—the tens of thousands who poured into London from every great town of industrial England, were amongst the first to see the palace in its perfected beauty. The peasant's shilling in June returned him more than the peer's guinea did to him in May. Russia was then shut up in her frozen rivers,— Tunis had not quitted her burning sands,—Hindustan was out at sea,—France in great measure lay in her packing-cases,—America had barely stretched her limbs in her vast spaces,—Turkey was but preparing to transport herself from the Bosphorus,—Persia, for aught that could be ascertained to the contrary, was still in the heart of Asia. All these guests subsequently arrived. From China to Peru, from Norway to Arabia, the products, the art, the genius of all civilized nations, were at length in London. One nationality only was here unknown by name :—Naples furnished nothing to the industry of the world but a band of spies and secret police. The contribution was characteristic. Henceforth Naples is blotted from the list of civilized states.

The company assembled in the Crystal Palace day after day was scarcely less interesting than the collection of articles. During the whole of May the number of foreign visitors was comparatively low. Where were the Germans, Americans, French, Italians, and other strangers?—was a question on every lip. They were not there. The passenger traffic across the Channel did not visibly increase. The artistic fancies which in multiplied prints had filled the parks and thoroughfares of the West-end with Spanish mantles, Turkish robes, Greek tunics, and other gorgeous dresses, seemed to have had no foundation in reality. A few days, however, rapidly developed this picturesque feature. The scarlet-robed Tunisian was not the only wearer of a bright costume in the Crystal Palace. The Andalusian cloak, the French blouse, the slouched hat of the Rhine, the turban of the East, the scull-cap of the Morea, and several other varieties of human envelopment might be seen there. It was curious and interesting to notice the wonder and delight of the wearers of these foreign garbs at all they saw and learned. Nothing, however, seemed to strike these strangers so much as the building itself,—so marvellously new, graceful, and imposing,—erected in a space of time so incredibly short, and with casualties so remarkably few for so vast a work. Next to this, the cotton and flax machinery seemed to fill them with most wonder. The rapid increase of provincial visitors was still more remarkable. Agricultural implements, during the first month of the Exhibition hardly glanced at, now obtained a large share of attention from scientific and practical men. The Essex or Devonshire farmer, somewhat impatient of mediæval courts, chiselled marbles, and Byzantine mosaics, might be seen diligently studying the last hints and improvements in ploughs, spades, harrows, carts, flails, threshers, clod-breakers, and so on. The Lancashire mechanic might be found intently poring over some new contrivance of a London machinist,—the Yorkshire wool-grower busy with comparisons between the produce of the merinoes of Saxony and of Spain. A very visible change was observable in the aspect of the area. There was a strong determination of visitors to the transept,—that being the centre and the point of intersection; but a more general distribution of company over the galleries and recesses was obvious at a glance. The holders of season tickets were probably, for the most part, persons to whom the æsthetics of the place, its artistic arrangement, its beauty and satisfaction to the outward sense, were the chief attractions. To these it was first and foremost a lounge and a panorama unequalled for comfort, splendour and variety. For the details which occurred beyond the first reach of the eye, and which did not form a striking part of the spectacle as seen from any favourite point of view, many of these visitors cared little. The naves, the transept, and the front galleries—the points from which the pictorial effects could be best taken, and the artist-sense most completely gratified—were the positions chiefly frequented by them. But visitors from the country towns and hamlets, from workshop and farm, seemed to have a different object in view. Less sensible perhaps to the grace and beauty which came out in gleams of light and gushes of melody at every turn, they appeared to set themselves more resolutely to study the particular construction and contrivances which had for them a practical interest. This was very noticeable with the artizan, both English and foreign. The blouses of Brussels and Paris seemed to examine with intense curiosity the work in precious metals exhibited by the great London houses.

Education of eye and mind was going on at a thousand points at the same moment, directly and indirectly,—formally and informally—by example, suggestion, and illustration. It did not seem to us that even what were called the "idlers" of the Crystal Palace were altogether idle there. If they did not appear to examine minerals, compare the merits of rival ploughs, or pay much attention to the wool and cotton fabrics of the western nave, it would be a great mistake to suppose that their time necessarily passed away unimproved. The morals of the Palace did not all lie in its details. There is an education of the taste, a cultivation of that love of beauty which every one possesses in a greater or less degree, which may be more important in some cases than the acquisition of special knowledge. The most listless lounger in the Exhibition was there at school. Consciously or unconsciously, he received at every sense lessons which cannot be altogether without effect in after life. The apparent idler might undervalue neither the edifice nor its contents; he might wish only to enjoy them both in his own way. Some minds cannot endure particulars. The poetic imagination loves to take in the whole at a glance —to embrace the grand synthesis by a single effort—not caring to stay its action until it may find time to analyze and separate the component elements of the picture. In such an edifice, Shakspere or Raffaelle, though a thousand things would have arrested them at last, would probably not have descended to the examination of details for many a day.

Contrary to prognostication, the shilling people passed through the building without disorder. There was no crowd the first day, no *émeute* in Hyde Park, no cry for soldiers and police. The Palace did not come down like a house of cards. The aristocracy did not cease their visits because the hard-workers chanced to come " between the wind and their nobility." It was in this respect a very satisfactory circumstance to find that, along with the royal family, eight or ten thousand season tickets went in every shilling day—to see so many coronetted vehicles making their way through crowds of omnibuses to the doors—to observe how completely all social distinctions were for the moment merged in the general feeling of pride and admiration at the wondrous result of science and labour exhibited in the Palace of Glass. Never before in England had there been so free and general a mixture of classes as under that roof, and good results of many kinds it is to be expected will grow out of it in the future. Another circumstance surprised the would-be prophets. Instead of the artizans staying in the Crystal Palace all day long, as was expected, it was found that the shilling visitors remained on an average little more than half the time of the season-ticket visitors. Nor were the artizans, or the agricultural population, the only privileged persons among the lower orders who were gratified with a sight of the World's Fair. The Duke of Wellington having been from the first one of the most assiduous visitors of the Crystal Palace, bethought himself how the regiments under his command might enjoy the same satisfaction. For this purpose leave of absence was given by the commander-in-chief to all regiments at home, from the 1st of June to the 30th; one field-officer, half the captains, and half the subalterns to be allowed the indulgence each fortnight in the month. In the same spirit, the Admiralty gave leave to the officials of the royal dockyards to absent themselves under certain regulations; and the orders in which this permission was conveyed, at the same time announced that the officers visiting the Great Exhibition were expected to report to their respective superintendents any new invention in machinery, or improvements in articles in general use, tools, &c., that might attract their attention, or anything that might strike them as useful or advantageous to the public service. The order issued to the workmen of Portsmouth Dockyard, gave notice that the period of leave to be granted to them for the purpose of visiting the Exhibition was to be extended to six days—the first half of the workmen to proceed to London on her Majesty's birthday, returning on the Friday following; and the second half to proceed on the anniversary of her Majesty's coronation. The admiral intimated to the men, that in case the fares of the railway were not reduced to what might be considered a low figure, he would place a vessel at their disposal for the purpose of conveying them to the metropolis.

As early as the 18th of June the human tide began steadily to increase in its mighty flow towards the Crystal Palace, an account of which day, although far inferior in point of accumulated masses to many that followed, we shall forthwith present to our readers. Notwithstanding the fluctuating character of the weather, the visitors began to pour in at an early hour, so that at two o'clock the interior might be literally called the World's

Fair. The great increase of country visitors was becoming quite noticeable; and the foreigners, who formed a large ingredient in the company, were no longer exclusively of the stronger sex. French and German might be heard resounding through the building with a volubility which bearded lips would in vain strive to arrive at. From the subjoined figures it will be seen that the great body of visitors came between the hours of ten and two o'clock, and there was a fair presumption that those were the hours at which the provincial contingents would arrive. The three o'clock return gave the steady ticket-holders who came day by day, and examined the wonders, section by section, a task which was sadly interrupted; while the later hours' returns might be supposed to indicate the mere loungers who promenaded the nave or sat about the crystal fountain; and they, most of all, were incommoded by the myriads who came for the vulgar purpose of seeing and being instructed by the Exhibition. The numbers at the last return taken were 62,532, being nearly 5,000 less than the return of the previous day, but considerably beyond any preceding day's work, and the following was their order of arrival :—Eleven o'clock, 18,637; twelve o'clock, 17,715; one o'clock, 10,315; two o'clock, 5,913; three o'clock, 4,423; four o'clock, 3,366; five o'clock, 1,476; and six o'clock, 687: total, 62,532. At a quarter to seven the bell rang, and in an inconceivably short space of time the building was left to the tranquil possession of its nightly guardians. This process of clearing out was not the least remarkable feature of the Exhibition. Great military authorities had said that it would be easy to collect 60,000 people in Hyde Park, but not so easy to get them out again; but at the Crystal Palace the problem was solved every day without any coercive means, save the inherent orderliness and good feeling of the people. There was no rushing, no noise, no confusion. The tide receded as gradually as it had advanced, and the only trouble the police had was to control the curiosity of the ladies about the diamonds, and to make abstruse arithmetical calculations touching the ingress and egress. This admirable order, too, it must be observed, was the spontaneous result of an undertaking of which all manner of evil had been predicted, and, we may conclude, wished too, after the manner of prophets in general, according to the pithy remark of Dean Swift—

> " They'd rather far that you should die,
> Than their prediction prove a lie."

Nay, one wiseacre actually took the trouble to write a pamphlet under the title of *To-morrow,*—that the Great Industrial Exhibition was only the revival of its ante-type, the Tower of Babel, which was certain to realize in its effects the confusion of that never-finished structure, to which we owe so many different tongues, known and unknown, " the crash of Samson, the prostration of Dagon, the division of Solomon's kingdom, the handwriting on the wall, visible to all eyes, but comprehended by only one mind"—that one of course the author's.

In the meanwhile everything was done to do honour to the nation's guests by our willing countrymen. Besides a multitude of private hospitalities, dispensed with a heartiness that put the character for "pride and coldness," by which we have been generally known abroad, somewhat in peril. Concerts and receptions at the Palace, *soirees* at the rooms of the Society of Arts, entertaiments at the Guildhall, dinners at Soyer's Symposium, public breakfasts at the Inns of Court, evening parties at the meeting-places of the learned societies, followed each other in rapid succession. Peace was on every lip—welcome in every eye. To a degree that was scarcely conceivable before, we laid aside our insular airs, and became cosmopolitan under the mighty influence of the deed that we had accomplished. Like Pygmalion, we were inspired by our own work. Nor was this the only result. That which brought courtesy to the stranger, also brought calm to the house. Every unpleasant subject was kept down by the accumulating interest attached to the Festival of Industry. Politics were forgotten in the general excitement, and the demon of religious dissension, which had so long haunted with its presence so many firesides in the metropolis, seemed to have vanished into thin air. Sculptors and artists entertained their continental brethren, and sent them back to their own countries crowned with fresh laurels. Nor, while the manifestations of jubilee appeared in the higher circles of society, did the world of artizans allow the occasion to pass by without contributing its share to the general fund of hilarity. The overseers and chief workmen employed by the contractors of the Crystal Palace proposed to give a solid English dinner of roast beef and plum-pudding to the foreign artizans employed in arranging the contents of their several countries. The crowning act of demonstration, however, took place about the middle of the season, when a grand civic entertainment to celebrate the successful results of the Great Exhibition of the Industry of all Nations, was given in Guildhall to her Majesty, Prince Albert, and the Royal Commissioners, on the ninth of July.

To say that the streets were crowded by loyal and enthusiastic thousands; that the windows and the housetops all along the line of procession, from Buckingham palace to Cheapside, presented seas of pleasant faces; that the illuminations in the city were grand, brilliant, and appropriate; that gay flags and banners waved across the streets; that her Majesty and the Prince were received by the multitude, as only a beloved queen could be; that the carriages made their way through dense crowds of enthusiastic people—a body-guard, brave, loyal, and true—cheered and welcomed with true British fervour; that on the arrival at the ancient Gothic hall, the august party were received with all honour by the first man in the city; that the procession of the queen through living walls of loving subjects was the great event of the evening; that thousands bent the willing knee to royalty; that the old crypt, made gay and beautiful for the occasion, was honoured for the first time by the presence of the queen; that a ball afterwards took place in the Guildhall—one of the finest rooms in Europe unsupported by pillars; that the grand preparations which the citizens had made were worthy of their ancient fame for hospitality; that in that noble hall stood the representatives of almost every civilized nation under heaven; that the whole passed off with the greatest *éclat;* and that loyal crowds waited in the streets till long past midnight to escort their queen home again when all was over: to say all this, was only to repeat what was already familiar to every man, woman, and child in the three kingdoms.

But some other considerations arose out of this royal visit; some other thoughts came uppermost on reviewing the events of that auspicious evening. Of themselves, the royal procession and the civic entertainment were but gaudy pageants, in which soldiers and horses, and gaslights, and crowds, and well-dressed people, and notable foreigners took part; but viewed in connexion with the purpose for which the fête was held, it became a direct recognition of the claims of labour on the part of the highest personages in the realm, or indeed in the world. The royal visit to the city was an event of which we, as a nation, had reason to be proud; for of all the thousands whose productions filled the great Industrial Bazaar in Hyde Park, there was not one who might not have been said to have been represented in the Guildhall on the ninth of July. In the principal city of the civilized world the queen and her husband acknowledged, by their presence, their infinite obligations to the industrious classes. Both within and without the noble hall there was much to teach and interest our foreign guests and neighbours. "In the spectacle of the day," said an eloquent writer, "might be discovered a fair representation of that constitution and those institutions by the gradual growth of which Britain is what she is, while France and Germany are—what she is not. In the queenly yet domestic bearing of her Majesty, all might see what Britons love to see—that their sovereign is not only their queen, but the first matron and lady of the land : in the crowded yet peaceful streets of our capital many a smaller city of the continent be taught that there are other safeguards for the sovereign and the public peace, than bayonets, and other *vivats* more hearty than the simulated plaudits of a people ruled by fear and force. And, above all, we trust it is in no sanctimonious or self-righteous spirit that we express some confidence that it will be long before, as a great city of trade, we forget that lesson which we have inscribed permanently on marble, and on that night in letters of fire, above the portals of the Royal Exchange—" The earth is the Lord's and the fulness thereof."

CHAPTER XVII.

FOREIGN AND COLONIAL DEPARTMENTS—*continued.*

THE ZOLLVEREIN—ARTICLES OF FOOD AND CLOTHING—ARMS, CUTLERY, ETC.—FURNITURE, WALKING STICKS—CROCKERY—MACHINERY—OBJECTS OF VIRTU—STUFFED ANIMALS.

IT is now, however, time that we should continue our examination of the " Foreign and Colonial Departments." We will accordingly direct our steps towards Germany ; and, in the first place, we beg pardon of our friends in that quarter for any apparent neglect they may imagine we have been guilty of, in not noticing them at an earlier period. In the selection of the objects to which we have invited the attention of our readers, we have not been solicitous to follow any rigid systematic arrangement ; fancy and freedom, as we believe we have already stated would be the case, have been our guides in our various wanderings through the interminable mazes of the Palace, and we shall still continue our researches under their immediate influence and direction.

Our readers are probably aware that the Zollverein—a name which occupied a large portion of the foreign side of the Crystal Palace—is not that of any individual country. On the contrary, it designates a union of several states of Germany, under one common custom-house law, indicated in the term zoll (*duty*), verein (*union*)—a policy, not a country, which brings under one series of fiscal regulations, concerning import and export duties, the subjects of several states of Germany, having in other respects different laws, and lying widely apart. It embraces Prussia, Saxony, Wurtemberg, Bavaria, Baden, Nassau, the two Hesses, and all the minor states of the centre of Germany, and comprehends altogether somewhere about 26,000,000 people. Hanover, Brunswick, Oldenburgh, Bremen, Lubeck, Mecklenburgh, on the north ; Bohemia, Austria Proper and other German dominions of Austria, on the south, are not members of this union. Prior to its being formed, the thirty-seven states, large and small, into which Germany was divided, levied each its own duties and tolls on rivers and roads, and had its own custom-house officers to levy them. As the rule, no goods could be transmitted through any one of these states to another, or sent from one state to another, without being subject to all the vexatious delay of a custom-house examination at the boundaries of every state. The actual facts were still worse, for many noblemen and cities levied, till a very recent period, private tolls, and at their " bars" all goods were liable to a similar examination. The annoyance of this system, to say nothing of the accompanying annoyance of passports, which still continues, was immense, and far exceeded anything of which our people, long united under one government, and having amongst themselves internally a perfectly free communication, have ever practically had to form any conception of. To get rid of some of these vexations, the states above mentioned, under the influence of Prussia, united themselves commercially about twenty years ago into one body, abolishing all intermediate tolls and customs duties, and levying only duties common to all, at the one extreme boundary of the confederating states, and dividing the revenue accruing among the different states composing the union, in proportion to their size, population, consumption, previous revenue, &c. All states not comprised in the union, and preserving their own revenue laws, are, so far as trade and customs duties are concerned, considered foreigners. The reader will see, therefore, that the name Zollverein in the Exhibition was a mere political designation for a great part of Germany, separating it from Northern Germany on the one hand, and from the Austrian dominions on the other; and such products of the industry of the 26,000,000 people comprised in this Customs Union as they were pleased to exhibit, it is now our intention to describe.

The department of the Zollverein was in the eastern part of the Crystal Palace, approximating towards the centre. It extended on both sides of the nave into the galleries, as well as on the ground-floor, having Russia on the east, and Austria on the west. Intermingled with it, however, was the space appropriated to Northern Germany, an arrangement justified by the geographical relations of the two, but at variance with the political designations, and which became the cause of some confusion. In truth, disorder in arrangement, singularly enough for the methodical Germans, seems to us to have characterised their part of the Exhibition. Although Wurtemberg, Saxony, and Bavaria, had distinct exhibition rooms on the south side of the nave, in which to display their cloths and shawls and stockings, in the grand centre hall of the Zollverein on the north, some of their most distinguished products, and the most distinguished products of the other states, were mingled with the products of Prussia, which disabled us from forming a just appreciation of the industry of the separate people, or of the whole Zollverein. In the medley, we could not compare and contrast what had been done by the lively, vain, egotistical, and royal Prussian, with the productions of the more solid and somewhat duller Hessian; nor could we conveniently distinguish between the industry which is rooted on the Iser, and that which flourishes on the Elbe or the Rhine. For the above reasons the general remarks which follow will apply in a great measure to the industry of all the Germans, not excluding even the Austrians, though we shall describe separately the Austrian part of the Exhibition; and we must, therefore, make our readers fully aware of the number of people to whom they apply. The Zollverein comprises about 26,000,000; Northern Germany, about 4,000,000; and Austrian Germany, about 7,000,000. The tracts of land inhabited by these people extend from the Baltic to the Iser and the Rhine, from the German Ocean to the Carpathian Alps, and embraces a great variety of soil, surface, and climate. It is rich in minerals and raw products, and is traversed by numerous large rivers. It is the best and principal part of central Europe. For such a country and such a people, the exhibition of their industry struck us as comparatively poor and comparatively uniform. There was a sameness in it throughout, not met with in any other part of the Exhibition, of equal pretensions.

In one great natural quality Germany is deficient, and the want of it has been much aggravated, instead of being relieved, by the policy of its governments. It has comparatively a small extent of sea-coast. Denmark and Holland shut it out from a direct connexion and communication with two parts of the ocean. It has had, therefore, in relation to other states, a small and not fast growing foreign trade. The many small states into which it was divided, and the absurd fiscal regulations in each, added to the want of ocean communication, till very modern times, limited and hampered its internal traffic. The consequence was, that the subjects of each state were pretty much confined to their own products for subsistence; and comparatively little separation of employments, or little division of labour ensued, and, as a consequence, little variety in the industry of the people. The Germans rather pride themselves on the circumstance, that division of labour is not extensive amongst them—that they are what they call many-handed; but that is only an approach to barbarism, when every individual provided by his own means for all his wants. To satisfy the common demands for food and clothing they all necessarily adopted the same or similar arts; and the same causes continuing to prevent the separation of employments, they have continued the same or similar practices. In conjunction with this, too, the respective governments undertook to a degree unknown in England to guide the industry of their subjects; and as they were generally actuated by a similar policy, and had similar objects to attain, they generally directed the industry of the people in similar paths. After the wants of food and clothing were supplied, the great object of the different governments, besides the common desire of military power, was to have luxuries provided for courts, which for a long period borrowed their ideas of luxury from the French court as a common model. Accordingly, as you passed amidst apartments hung full of cloth and of damasked linen, with a profusion of swords and cutlery, walking-sticks, pipes, buttons, and common tools, models of old castles or modern residences, with some fine porcelain, some exquisitely carved ivory, some delicate bronzes, and some admirably stained glass, you found a great uniformity in the products of numerous distinct and different people, for which you were hardly prepared; nor was the impression removed by the appearance of some well prepared leather for different purposes, some valuable mineral and other raw products, several specimens of wool, and some splendid crystals and colours, the result of chemical arts, and a little well-wrought furniture. What is called Berlin-wool, raised carpeting scarcely fit to walk on, models of castles, dried fruits, a multitude of ornaments in cast iron, an abundance of toys, playing cards, much ordinary jewellery, piles of stockings and suspenders, with a few printed books, completed the miscellaneous assortment.

Many of the articles would excite surprise in any exhibition, but we were chiefly astonished to find them so many leagues away from the place where they were made. The Germans supposed they were to sell, as well as to exhibit; they looked on the Exhibition as a market, and thought that the cheapness of their hose, their cutlery, their common tools, and their cloth, would ensure them numerous customers. In fact, many of their articles had been exhibited avowedly only on account of their cheapness, not on account of their excellence, their rarity, or their beauty; and the exhibitors prepared and published a catalogue, in which the prices were marked, for the very purpose of showing that they can undersell the English, particularly in hose, cutlery, and cloth. Till the quality of the articles can be brought to a test, this appears to be possible. They imitate our patterns, and try to sell their goods as English. We noticed, and to our surprise, in the Saxon department, and amongst the hose, one or two pair marked very distinctly in good English letters, " Merino patent," an inscription which used to be stamped on a favourite English production. We had our doubts of the propriety of allowing such *contrefaçons* to appear in the Exhibition. They reminded us of what we saw on the Hartz mountains a great many years ago, where the shot cast at a celebrated lead manufactory were all packed up in bags, with the names and labels of English makers imprinted on them. We were told by an American gentleman in the Exhibition, " It is quite true the Germans have improved very much in making cutlery within a few years. I have had a great deal to do with them in the matter. They were anxious to sell their goods in our markets; but they were so clumsy, our people would not look at them. I then sent patterns of your best London and Sheffield makers to Solingen, and the Germans made their cutlery after these patterns, putting on them the name of Rodgers and Son, or some other celebrated English maker. The German cutlery looked very well, and was sold cheap; but, on being tried, it proved to be not half so good as that of the English, and I doubt whether the sale will increase." In various kinds of cutlery the Germans made a great show; but it is evident even here, that the bulk of their articles were made after English patterns. The display was intended, too, we believe, more for foreign markets, than for consumption here. If the Exhibition had been a mart, where the artizan could have bought a pair of pincers, the dandy a cravat, the housewife a jar of preserves or of potted larks, and parents Christmas presents for their children, it could scarcely have been richer in the supply of these and similar articles from Germany. With some exceptions, which it will be our business hereafter especially to notice, the products of German industry, taken as a whole, therefore, might be characterized as displaying little variety; and many parts of it were trivial, neither adding to national wealth nor helping forward national greatness. Admitting the fact, but implying that the Germans have a richer and more varied industry than they have shown, which we doubt, a German writer in the *Allgemeine Zeitung* states "that Germany is here exhibited to foreigners as small change." Who, then, is culpable for having kept back the large coins and the more precious ingots, if they exist? German industry is not only uniform; it is obviously imitative. There is as complete a want of independent thought in their art as in their political reforms.

France had its *bijouterie*, its exquisite ornaments, its unmistakeable graceful luxuries, its adornments for boudoirs and persons; England had its solid and compact machinery, often as neat and elegant in form, though rigid, as it was useful; the United States had their rocking and other chairs, their sewing machine, and their almost infinite application of caoutchouc; Russia had its furs, its hemp, its malachite; even Austria, with its Vienna furniture and its Bohemian glass, which are German, had something of its own. Nay, Tunis and India shone out conspicuous and peculiar. Only Germany, of all the nations of Europe, had nothing apparently in the Exhibition which could be said to be characteristic of it, but its toys, a few scull-caps, and some useful specimens of domestic wool manufacture. Borrowing its ornamental arts mainly from France, its useful arts from England, the things it exhibited were chiefly imitations, very often deficient in the grace, the lightness, the neatness, and convenience of the originals. Its productions were solid, substantial, sometimes cumbrous, and generally honestly made, but they were all in the main French or English, rather than peculiarly German. Perhaps those who had the ordering of the matter wished chiefly to exhibit the success of the Germans as rivalling other nations, and rather brought forward European than German productions. They exhibited no specimen of their durable but old fashioned furniture; of their *frachtwagen*, with their loads packed and secured to resist the jolting of bad roads, like the cargoes of ships, which move not when tossed about by the waves; no specimen of their multifarious vegetable productions on which the bulk of the people live, or of the useful and comfortable garments that their domestic industry still provides for the great multitude, all of which are at once peculiar and picturesque; they are sometimes, too, convenient. Germany has many peculiarities, but they belong to a past age, and the Royal Commissioners who have presided over the German part of the Exhibition, were not desirous to exhibit them. "I cannot deny," says a celebrated writer, "that, in general, the specimens of German industry in the Exhibition (the fine arts not included) have no peculiar character, and give me the idea of its having been the intention to avoid exhibiting what is national. German industry appears in every department to lean on something foreign, or to be an imitation, and nowhere to stand on its own feet. At one place we see the hand of England, and at another that of France. I may be mistaken, but this is my very distinct impression." If, indeed, we turned to the machinery exhibited we found it of little importance; and the principal objects, such as the vacuum pan and the Jacquard loom, very imperfectly improved, as compared with others in the building, were borrowed from England or France. The machinery exhibited, and generally, too, the tools and the cutlery, were imitations of those of England, and had nothing to recommend them but their cheapness.

The nature of German industry in general was brought into a strong light by the varied industry of Hamburgh, and the taste displayed in the exhibition of the articles sent from that city. It furnished no less than 123 ; while the rest of North Germany, the kingdom of Hanover, Lubeck, the two Mecklenburghs, supplied only 35. They consisted chiefly of useful and ornamental furniture, such as sideboards, sofas, chairs, &c., of a very superior description, clocks, musical instruments, specimens of oil-cake and refined sugar, charts, pianofortes, saws, rocking-chairs, looking-glasses, bird-cages, and a large assortment of walking-sticks. Here, however, instead of being merely hung against the wall, they were displayed in a cheerful tasteful manner, so that the Hamburgh room had a light and elegant appearance, superior to that of the central room of the Zollverein, in which were heaped together all the best and richest of its contributions. On entering the apartment, the spectator was much struck by a representation of the sun sending his rays on all sides, placed against the opposite wall of the apartment. It was composed of walking-sticks, chiefly from the workshops of C. A. Meyer, who employs several hundred persons, and exports walking-sticks to all parts of the world. In Hamburgh, as in London, it is a considerable trade ; and, being a source of wealth, is not inaptly typified by the sun. Herr Meyer, the founder of the house, is a good specimen of what trade does for men in Germany as well as in England. He arrived in the city from Thuringia, with no other wealth than his skill in carving wood ; and, by care, frugality, and an opportunity of exerting his talents, he has created a large establishment, and become one of the princely merchants of the city. He is an individual example of the general opulence and general industry and skill of Hamburgh. It was, and yet is, practically and truly free—not merely nominally a free city ; and the success of its industry as displayed in the Exhibition, in comparison with the industry of the many long-enthralled states of Germany, did honour to its freedom. As we have already adverted to the sculpture, and intend including that from Germany, we do not extend our present remarks to the latter. German sculpture took a high place in the Exhibition ; but that art, though treated successfully by the Germans, we need scarcely remark, was not peculiarly German.

With these first and general impressions, we now proceed to make a tour (from recollection) of the Zollverein department, commencing with that on the north side. Our attention was arrested at the entrance by an object which forcibly reminded us of the military character of the principal state of the Verein, and indeed of all the German states. Planted at the centre, as if to forbid entrance, or at least to allow it only on conditions, stood a remarkably well-mounted field-piece. The gun gave you an idea of solid and substantial work. At the same time it was highly polished ; and the plain varnished carriage was a perfect model, on a small scale, like one of Maudslay's engines, of compactness and neatness, combined with great strength. The workmanship had the finish of a jewel, concealing in the instrument the power of a demon. Beneath it were polished cuirasses and other instruments or emblems of war, destruction, and death. This was the shape in which an invention of a new process for the manufacture of one of the most useful things shown in the whole department, cast-steel, was exhibited. We admire Herr H. Krupp's skill, but should have thought better of him and better of Germany, had it been displayed in rollers such as are employed with great success at Munich, for grinding corn ; or surgical instruments, or something more appropriate to this peaceful age and to the Exhibition, than a model field-piece.

2 F

Close by it, however, inviting you to the confidence which the gun repelled, hung an altar-piece, in which were worked and emblazoned the words, " *Gott ist die Liebe; und wer in der Liebe bleibt, der bleibt in Gott, und Gott in ihm*"—(" God is love; and who dwells in love, dwells in God, and God in him.") There was not much in the article to admire, but the sentiment is very expressive of the affectionate kindly character of the Germans. The care they take to provide amusement and employment, as well as instruction for their children, as exemplified in one of their chief manufactures, and which a rugged hard people would have neither patience to begin nor the kindliness to continue, was another illustration of the same characteristic. The more one traces their kindliness in their manners, the more it is to be regretted that a contrary principle presides over their affairs, as typified by the field-piece. The softness of their character seems to allow a long dominion to a harsh political system; and a little more rugged energy amongst them would keep better in check the violence against which they now only direct a few enigmatic sentences.

Let us pass through the rows of arms, that were somewhat ostentatiously arranged in full display, and direct our attention to the various specimens of crockery, earthenware, or china, manufactured in the neighbourhood of Frankfort-on-the-Oder. It was clear, solid, and generally of pleasing forms, approximating more to our stoneware than to anything else that we are acquainted with, but was superior to that in its clear and uniform glaze. For neatness and utility, it was scarcely surpassed in the whole collection. The porcelain, both of Saxony and Prussia, was of course much more splendid; some of that was very much to be admired, and seemed to find numerous customers, for several of the articles of the Berlin manufacture were very soon marked, "disposed of;" but the porcelain, with its admirable paintings, came within the reach of a few, while the elegant and clean-looking *thonwaaren* was attainable by the many, and must contribute to the pleasures of all who use it. This ware is largely exported to countries with which England trades; and we are inclined, therefore, to suppose that it must be as cheap as our ordinary ware, and it is, generally speaking, more elegant, and appears less brittle. Combined with several other things which came from Frankfort-on-the-Oder, it gave us a much higher idea than we before had formed of that city as a place of manufacture. From the very circumstance that much of the cutlery, particularly that from Solingen, was made after English patterns, it appeared very good, and much superior to that which was formerly, and is still very much in use in Germany. Some of the surgical instruments, too, were very good—indeed they are said to be made better in Berlin than in any other part of the continent. Some of the common jewellery, the supply of which was large, was well set; but the bulk of it, as was to be expected from the quantity, was common, and rather tasteless. Germany abounds in metals; all the zinc in use comes from that country: but, with the exception of its being applied to roof a house, a model of which was exhibited, showing some very substantial workmanship, and for spouts, we noticed no other important application of this ductile, and now much used metal. Those who have visited Germany must be well aware that there are many uses to which it might be most advantageously applied: and it would unquestionably contribute to the health and comfort of the Germans, and the neatness of their houses.

Passing to the west and north, opposite the room for the machinery of the Zollverein, we observed two specimens of massive safes for money and papers. One was remarkable for the ease with which its heavy doors were moved, and the other for the impossibility of opening it without receiving instructions from the maker, and both for their many conveniences. Four of them, we have understood, have already been ordered from Germany, in consequence of their having been exhibited among us. The machine-room looked bare, and at least was quite spacious enough for the machinery the Zollverein chose to place in it. We believe that Germany is richer in such contrivances than the Exhibition showed. We should pronounce it very backward, were we to judge solely of the specimens that were sent. Cards for combing, made of imported materials, seemed to us very inferior to those made in Manchester. Engines for coining, punching, and milling were good, but nothing extraordinary. Civilization and the power of man are directly in proportion as he is enabled by skilful machinery to command the assistance of nature. As he makes the expansive power of steam, or the weight of the atmosphere, or the rushing of streams, work for him, he is strong and powerful. Machinery being generally private property, men cannot be constrained to display it when they fear that the secrets connected with it may be discovered; and hence the samples in the Zollverein were not specimens of the best machinery of Germany. If they were, we should form an unfavourable opinion of the past, and a very unfavourable augury for the future of that country.

Now coming back to the south, we enter the great centre room of the Zollverein, crammed full of the *bijoux* of German art, before describing which, let us direct the attention of our readers to a somewhat elegant pillar which stood on the western side. It represented a group of Amazons—they being apparently great favourites with the Berlin artists, the great Amazon in the nave being only one of many in the Exhibition—made of cast-iron, at the foundry of Berlin, but curiously inlaid with silver. It was remarkable for the simplicity of its form and the beauty of its workmanship. The striking characteristic, indeed, of most of the productions in the centre hall, where were collected the gems of the Verein, was, we think, beauty of form. The principal contents of the hall were statues, statuettes, painted glass ornaments, pictures, one or two cabinets or ladies' desks, porcelain, &c., all belonging to the fine arts, and all in general distinguished by this characteristic. Even the Berlin porcelain, which occupied a large space in the room, and part of which was copied from renowned works of antiquity, such as the Warwick vase, was as beautiful in form as it was in its ornament, and the designs on it, after Mieris, Vischer, and others, were as fine as art can produce. Less meretricious in ornament than the productions of Paris, and less encumbered with it than those of London, the artistic productions of Berlin, and indeed of all Germany, were chiefly agreeable from the beauty of their forms. Even the elaborate carvings in ivory from Darmstadt, particularly the large goblet, on which the great victory of Hermann or Arminius, from a picture in the possession of the Grand Duke of Baden, was carved in *alto relievo*, were as remarkable for their graceful shape as for their admirable execution. By crowding their finest room with almost innumerable articles of *virtù*, puzzling us to distinguish between them, and losing admiration for individual specimens in multiplicity, the Germans informed us that they set a high value on these comparatively trivial things. The production of them is what the influential government have chiefly encouraged; they have impelled the skill of the people in this direction, and we may expect therefore—or where shall we seek for the utility of royal or noble patronage?—that the arts which spring from them or grow up under their encouragement, shall be marked by superior taste. Amongst the ancient Greeks, and amongst the inhabitants of India, a keen perception of beauty of form seems to have been inherent, and is found almost equally in some of their earliest productions, which have descended to us, as in their latest. But, amongst the Saxon and Scandinavian tribes, judging from the rude figures of their old idols and earliest heroes yet extant, a perception of fine forms was not innate. It required cultivation, and has been cultivated by studying the examples of the people who were endowed with these perceptions. The highborn and well-educated, the opulent and the ruling classes, have been the means of extending that cultivation. They are conduits through which the old Greek perceptions have been conveyed to their unendowe and uncultivated countrymen. Thus we find their influence and the influence of courts more beneficial in these arts than in any others. Modern artists cannot boast of much novelty of conception. Their finest works, whether of sculpture, painting, or architecture, are generally imitations of the ancients. Nature is as pure and as free as in the times of the Greeks; but man's present perceptions are so mixed with ancient and derived knowledge, that they are confused; and artists are often the most graceful when they return to the original forms. For many years, even for centuries, European artists and their patrons, have aimed at little more than at diffusing amongst the rude people of the North a knowledge of the forms that sprang up intuitively in the minds of the Greeks, and that they have only acquired by a laborious process. By the Exhibition this species of cultivation was rapidly extended; and it seemed likely to do more, in a few weeks or months, to diffuse amongst our people a knowledge of graceful and artistic forms, than had before been done in ages. For the first time almost in our history, the common people of England were brought familiarly into contact with, and derived instruction from, the clear, definite, and brilliant conceptions of the Greeks, embodied in forms that have been preserved and spread by the influence of artists and courts through all Europe. Of our people, too, we are happy to say that the females share largely in the enjoyment and improvement. By a curious, and yet easily traced connexion, establishing a moral relation between the most ancient and most modern nations, the keen powers of perception of the beautiful in nature with which the old Greeks were endowed, and which were denied to the ancestors of our race, causing a great moral difference between them, are now made to subserve to the improvement of the English. By the Exhibition the bulk of our people were made familiar with form derived from antiquity, and of which they could otherwise never have attained a conception.

Among the articles of *virtù* exhibited by the Zollverein, the bronzes were well worthy of attention, particularly a statuette of Beethoven; we may also notice a large collection of miniatures on ivory, painted in a bold style, by a new method, by Hilder, a Wurtemburg artist. Amongst the articles of utility, the cloths, which were very abundant, took the first place in the Zollverein; and remembering that the manufacture of fine cloth is rather modern in Germany, and that homespun woollens, till very recently, formed the staple dresses of the bulk of the peasantry, the progress of the Germans in making fine cloth does them great credit. For some of that they may thank our restrictive laws, which partly force their industry into that channel, and compel them to grow wool and weave it, instead of growing corn and exchanging it for woollens. The damasks of Saxony and the linens of Silesia, the latter now not so highly honoured as they were wont to be, also occupied a large space in the halls and in the galleries, and they are very old and very favourite productions of Germany. In damask linens they excel; and the productions of Messrs. Proels, senior, and Sons, of Leipsic, in the Saxon department, may be mentioned as an excellent example of the produce of the German looms. Many of the woollens that came from Prussia were as remarkable as the celebrated Berlin wool for the richness of their dyes; and there were some common enough cloths at the end of the gallery of the Zollverein, on the south side, worth notice on account of the boldness and distinctness, and the meaning—for many of our patterns are utterly destitute of any meaning—of the designs which ornament them. We discovered, on referring to the catalogue, that the designs were copies of wood-cuts after Albert Durer, and we do not see why such things should not generally be reproduced, rather than unmeaning scrolls. We need say nothing of the patterns and the wool which were profusely displayed throughout the Prussian department, which has acquired a world-wide reputation as Berlin work, the delight of our wives, daughters, and mothers, and very often of no little comfort to ourselves in its results, if we are occasionally annoyed by it in its progress. Patterns, as well as the materials for embodying them in the canvass, abounded in almost every part of the Zollverein, together with carpets, rugs, table-covers, &c. In fact, the two circumstances of the splendid dyes and the excellent designs, for which Prussian workmen and artists are famous, have combined to make Berlin work so general a favourite. In damask linens, in fine cloths of various kinds, and in woollens of every description and for every use, the Zollverein was particularly rich. Taken as a whole, woollens were not only the most useful, but the most conspicuous production of German industry, and that in which they have attained the greatest excellence, and are making the most rapid advances. Connected, too, with them, we must add that there were numerous specimens of very fine wool, the produce of the German provinces and other flocks. Berlin has been famous, at least since the time of Diesbach, 1710, when Prussian blue was discovered, for its chemical products; and all through the eighteenth century, as well as before it commenced, some of the most distinguished names in the annals of chemistry were those of Germany. After the woollens, the chemical products of the Zollverein in the Exhibition ranked high. The specimens of beet-root sugar, which were perfect, and the product entirely of chemical art, the specimens of perfumery, of various salts and pigments, the crystals of several substances exhibited, all testified to the fact that the Germans continue on this point to deserve their well-acquired reputation.

In the vast and very miscellaneous productions which they sent us, we can only particularize a few more. We observed numerous specimens of types and of books, ornamented and plain, which did honour to German typography and their skill in illustration. Contrasting some of the books displayed there by Decker and others, with the ordinary books and newspapers of Germany, it is impossible not to wish that in the matter of paper at least some of the substantiality of the books exhibited might be imparted to the common productions of the booksellers. But it is probable, after all that is said of the durability of books, that the most flimsy are the best adapted for our transition age, as not likely long to stand in the way, either on our bookshelves or in our minds, of the improved works of which they are to be the parents. Connected with books, were many maps, geological as well as geographical, with a large globe to show the comparative elevation of the mountains of the earth, and other helps to diffuse knowledge. The Germans are not behind in applying papier mâché, which will take any form, and which, though made from refuse, is one of the products of human skill best adapted, of all those yet acquired, to various figured ornaments, as well as to many useful instruments and utensils. The Germans exhibited many specimens of their success in papier mâché, the name of which informs us that the art is neither of English nor of German invention. As we had specimens of our coal, so the Germans, particularly in the Hamburgh department, exhibited many specimens of their charcoals, of which they make great use, and which they apply in various forms to various purposes. They showed us, also, many of their mineral products, particularly from Nassau, from which little else had been brought than ores of lead, copper, zinc, manganese, iron, &c. Other things in which they excelled, or at least made a good show, were philosophical and musical instruments —characteristic of their harmony and their devotion to science. In the Hamburgh department, we found not only some excellent furniture, but veneers fifty-four plates to the inch: or the mahogany was cut into planks, each of which was only the fifty-fourth part of an inch thick. Till a recent period, when Sir Robert Peel abolished the duties on furniture woods, the inhabitants of Hamburgh had a considerable advantage over our furniture makers, and they sent great quantities of furniture over to various parts of America. They still carry on this profitable and useful business; but our people are now in a better condition to compete with them than they were, and, by the abolition of the duties, a valuable trade has been preserved to our country.

Here we must stop. Though the productions of German industry were by no means so numerous, so rich, nor so varied as those of French industry, with which, excluding Austria, they might be most appropriately compared—though the Germans were in the Exhibition remarkably deficient in machinery—their products were numerous and miscellaneous.   In general, except as to cast iron, bronzes, chemicals, dyes, and some woollens, German industry seemed a step below that of either France or England.   It is, however, plain, that the Germans have a great aptitude for improvement : we regard them as only recently aroused to a due sense of their relative position in knowledge, skill, politics, and morals, to the rest of Europe.   They occupy a noble country ; and as they become sensible of their wants, they cannot fail to achieve a commanding succcess.   In them we have great reason to be interested, and them we must wish to see strong, prosperous, and united. They stand between European civilization and Cossack barbarity ; and the hope we have that the latter will not be suffered to advance and prevail westward, rests on the Germans, and rests on the improving people as contradistinguished from their interfering, and, we are afraid, sometimes retrograde rulers.

Before we entirely take our departure from the Zollverein department, we must not omit to notice one very amusing and interesting feature it possessed ; we allude to the collection of stuffed animals, which were indeed so admirably got up, that they were worthy of the attention of Waterton himself, the great Nimrod of South America, of whose prowess in the savage wilderness, among the *feræ naturæ*, his own ancestral halls in the heart of Yorkshire afford ample testimony, and whose redoubtable arm slew, in single combat, every grim specimen he has therein collected and so skilfully preserved. Judging from the crowd that was always collected around the stuffed animals in the Zollverein department, it would seem to have been the most popular group of objects in the Glass Palace.   Doubtless, some part of its attractiveness was due to the predominance of family parties in the collection.   Quite independently of treatment, any artist who introduces the young of animals and the instincts of maternity in operation, is sure of attention.   Here we had partridges and their young, hawks and their young, a hooded owl protecting her nestlings from the onslaught of weasels, a female fox and her cubs awaiting their sagacious sire, who is bringing them a partridge to feast upon.   There were also groups in caricature.   Stoats and weasels, in sportsman-wise, pursued their game of young hares and rabbits.   A party of kittens were enjoying the pleasures of the tea-table, and various other amusing groups were exhibited, in which the artist had succeeded in throwing a most whimsical air of sentimental gentility.   The most attractive portion, however, of this display, consisted of a series of *tableaux* from the old poem of *Reynard the Fox*, a great favourite with the German children, and which we remember to have seen powerfully illustrated in the dark mysterious etchings of Roland Roghman. The incidents that were selected for representation were, the Cock receiving Reynard's confession of sin—Reynard leading the Hare to Court as a witness—Reynard at Home, carelessly reposing on a sofa, his tail resting on his left arm, and equipped with sash and dagger, *à la brigand*.   Our hero was next seen attacking the hare on his way to court, after which he was represented giving the cat a letter of introduction to court.   It was impossible to conceive anything better than the attitudes of all these animals, and they had just as much clothing put upon them as was necessary to produce a good effect.

Engraved by G Greatbach, from a Drawing by J. Mason. The Original by H. Plansuyer of Stuttgard

THE LAWYER

Engraved by G Greatbach, from a Drawing by J. Mason. The Original by H. Plansuyer of Stuttgard

THE MORNING WALK

Engraved by G. Greatbach, from a Drawing by Mason

THE SCHOOLMASTER AT HOME.

FROM THE COLLECTION OF THE COMICAL CREATURES FROM WURTEMBURG — BY H. PLOUCQUET

Engraved by G. Greatbach, from a Drawing by Mason

THE TEA PARTY.

FROM THE COLLECTION OF THE COMICAL CREATURES FROM WURTEMBURG. BY H. PLOUCQUET

CHAPTER XVIII.

LABORIOUS TRIFLES—INGENIOUS ABSURDITIES—THE ISLAND OF LAPUTA—DUNIN'S IRON MAN—
THE EARTH A LIVING CREATURE—THE MEDICAL WALKING STAFF—ARTICLES IN MUTTON
FAT—WONDERFUL ACHIEVEMENT WITH A PENKNIFE—CHINESE NICK-KNACKS—WILLOW WOOD
COTTAGE—ELABORATE CORKSCREW—SELF-ADJUSTING RAILWAY—WONDERFUL KNIVES AND
SCISSORS.

As the whole world was invited to display their talent, their industry, and their inventions, and to contribute to the vast display of human genius in the great show of the World's Fair, it was to be concluded that the public would occasionally have to put up with the productions of dreaming insufficiency, as well as to be gratified with the elaborate creations of scientific usefulness, and which, indeed, might serve as a foil to the more predominant examples of opposite excellence. And this was singularly the case. We will accordingly proceed to enumerate a few of the absurdities, which, in amusing variety, were brought before the eyes of the curious and astonished observer in the Crystal Palace.

> "There are more things in heaven and earth
> Than are dreamt of in your philosophy,
> Horatio,"

was the shrewd observation of the sagacious Hamlet, but we feel assured that even his philosophy never indulged in such wild speculations as were put forth in the ever-memorable year of 1851, to an admiring world, in the far-famed precincts of the wondrous House of Glass.

Philosophy in Sport made Science in Earnest, was the title of a little book which we recollect reading with very great pleasure some years ago; and, published at a time when the generality of the community had hardly begun to inquire "in earnest" into the important secrets of natural and physical science, now every day producing such useful practical results, the modest duodecimo in question did good service by awakening and inviting very many individuals to the pleasures and advantages of various branches of study, which they would otherwise never have dreamed of including within their province of intellectual observation. But "philosophy in sport" is not always "science in earnest," and industry, unguided by the unerring truths of philosophy and the essential demands of utility, is sometimes nothing better than industry "run mad." Industry is one thing, and caprice is another and a very different thing: in like manner, we may say that ingenuity is one thing, and whimsicality another; persevering good sense is one thing, and persevering folly a very different thing: so of workmanship and the production of a useful article, when compared with a prolonged waste of human labour in concocting and finishing a trifle, a toy, or an absurdity. These things all involve a different species of effort and result, and call for a very different sort of estimate. Amidst the innumerable examples of well-applied labour in the Great Exhibition, it must, nevertheless, be confessed that there were also a considerable number, amounting, indeed, to a motley variety of articles, in the construction of which we are bound to say that much thought, and yet more labour, have been grievously misapplied.

Foremost amongst these we must place Count Dunin's "Man of Steel," which is an invention of so singular and so puzzling a nature, that we feel convinced the author of it must have taken his degree in the academy of Laputa, among the celebrated professors there so admirably described by Swift. Indeed, as respects the utter inutility of his most elaborate production, he has gone far beyond the experimental philosophers of the Flying Island.   The worthy experimentalist who ingeniously attempted to extract sunbeams out of cucumbers, had at least some pretence towards a useful purpose ; and the learned and literary world would have had reason to bless, had it but succeeded, the projector of the noble idea, far superior to the wonderful calculating machine, from the aid of which "the most ignorant person, at a reasonable charge, and with little bodily labour, might write books in philosophy, poetry, politics, laws, mathematics, and theology, without the least assistance from genius or study."   We shall not attempt to enter into a description of this most desirable piece of machinery, but we think it might be worth the while of the ingenious inventor of "the great iron man" were he to carefully peruse the whole of the renowned Gulliver's account of the proceedings of these sub- lime philosophers of Laputa, nothing doubting that he would profit by many of the hints and descriptions he would there find detailed.   This piece of mechanism was in the figure of a man, and was constructed of seven thousand pieces of steel.   Most of them appeared to be either springs or slides, and they were so put together and arranged as to be capable of a graduated movement, by means of which the proportions of the whole figure might be expanded from the standard size of the Apollo Belvidere to that of a Goliath.   From these colossal proportions it might again be contracted at pleasure to any size between them and its original standard.   The mechanism was composed of 875 framing pieces, 48 grooved steel plates, 163 wheels, 202 slides, 476 metal washers, 482 spiral springs, 704 sliding plates, 497 nuts, 8,500 fixing and adjusting screws, with numerous steadying pins, so that the number of pieces was upwards of 7,000.   The only utility we ever heard suggested as derivable from this elaborate piece of mechanism, was its applicability to the various measurements of army clothiers or tailors, as it would serve for the figures of men of various sizes.   We do not know whether this was the purpose assigned to it by the inventor, as it seems a very absurd one ; the same result being far more easily attainable by the incomparably more simple means of half- a-dozen dummies, or wooden lay-figures.

But hold ! it behoves us to speak with deference and humility in this matter, seeing that the Council of Chairmen of Juries, the supreme heads of wisdom, to whom the dispensation of the Exhibition honours was intrusted, thought proper to reward the constructor of this huge mechanical toy with a "Council Medal."   Yes, hear it Troughton and Simms, who talk about novelties in astronomical instruments, to which a council medal was denied, though recommended by the jury ; hear it Claussen, whose newly-discovered, and nationally important processes in the preparation of flax received only a common medal ; hear it, Losely, whose compensating pendulum, one of the most ingenious and valuable improvements in horology in the whole Exhibition—hear it Applegarth, whose vertical printing machine—hear it all ye whose performances had to share the common fate of merit in "a certain degree ;"—the Jury in Class X. (" that of philosophical instruments, and processes depending upon their use,") awarded, and the Council of Chairmen confirmed to Count E. Dunin a council medal—"*For the extraor- dinary application of mechanism to his expanding figure of a man !*"   After reading this result, we began to be somewhat doubtful about all we set out with touching " philosophy in sport," and nice distinctions between " ingenuity" and " whimsicality" and so forth ; and in a moment of bewilderment and irritation, were almost upon the point of consigning the notes upon which the rest of this article will be composed to the fire. But fortunately, we were restrained from so doing, by an urgent application for " copy" from a quarter which is not used to be denied, and therefore we proceed with the task upon which we set out.   Still in the philosophical instrument department, we come upon " an apparatus of a peculiar construction, showing the ebb and flow of the tides," exhibited by a Mr. Ryles, of Cobridge, Staffordshire Potteries, who thus describes the novel theory it is intended to illustrate :—"The article I sent to the Exhibition, is an apparatus *to illustrate the idea of the earth being a living creature encased in a shell,* as a snail-house or sea-shell, and by the action of the heart, causing the tide to ebb and flow! Press down the blower, and the heart (as seen through the glass that is on the top of the shell), will contract, causing the tide to rise; let out the air of the shell, and the heart will expand, causing the tide to fall." He adds, "I want a patron that would enable me to show how *the tide causes the rotatory motion of the earth,* which only poverty prevents my doing." Mr. Ryles has *not* received a council medal, nor a prize medal, nor even "honourable mention," which, considering the honours heaped upon the "expanding figure of a man," we consider hard. The least Count Dunin could have done, would have been to have shared his council medal with Ryles, and, thrusting the model of the "living creature" constituting the earth, into his "extraordinary application of mechanism," exhibit its expansibility by revealing "the action of the heart" of the encased monster.

Dr. Grey invented a medical walking-staff, containing instruments, medicines, and other professional articles. Would not a small tin case have answered the same purpose far better, and far more conveniently, as it might be put into the pocket, where the "medicines," not being half so much "shaken" as in the walking-staff, would have less chance of fermentation or other injury? An "artificial silver nose" has been invented by Mr. Whitehouse. We will not pronounce rashly upon this; but it strikes us, that all artificial noses, both in shape, size, and the amount of nose required, will depend upon the amount wanting by an individual, and the size and shape, in fact, suited to his particular case; the material also of which the nose is manufactured would very often have to be regulated by the special circumstances.

Art-manufactures in *mutton fat* are certainly a novelty, and Mr. W. E. Hall, of Bideford, exhibited "a socle, or kind of vase," made of a mixture of mutton fat and lard. We should fear that in a hot summer, or in a cold winter, when a good fire is needed in the room, these articles would be extremely liable to a change of form not at all contemplated by the inventor; nay, there might be occasions on which they would "run away" altogether. Mr. M'Clintock, of York, exhibited a chain in regular links, the whole of which, we are informed, had been cut out of a solid block of wood: to what purpose, except to the unnecessary length of time such a performance must occupy, we are totally at a loss to conceive. Mr. M'Clintock has, however, been surpassed by a lieutenant of the navy, whose name has escaped us, and which we do not know where to look for in the Catalogue, who had achieved the same result from a block of wood, with the help of no other tool than a penknife. Will anybody endeavour to surpass them both, we wonder, by doing the same thing with a pin? We do not very well know what to say about the "ostracide," the instrument with a grand name for opening oysters, and bearing a close resemblance to a pair of sugar-nippers. It may be useful, or it may cut the oysters to rags in the operation; we hope not; but Messrs. Brown, of Newcastle, will excuse us if we hint, that, to avoid this, it may be necessary to practise opening oysters with the ostracide almost as much as with the old-fashioned oyster-knife.

"The semibreve guitar" of Mr. Dobrowsky was a good thought enough for a new name, and for a fresh attempt to prolong the sound of the notes of the guitar; but if the inventor would have us understand by the term "semibreve" that his instrument will sustain a note of any such duration, we must plead absolute scepticism to the possibility of any instrument of this kind being made to accomplish such a result. The enharmonic guitar, manufactured by Panormo, of High-street, Bloomsbury, claims for

2 H

its original inventor and designer no less a personage than the ingenious Colonel Perronet Thompson, M.P., who some years ago invented a new kind of organ. Of the enharmonic guitar lately exhibited, it was announced that it was "capable of being arranged in the perfect ratios for upwards of twenty keys." We do not doubt this; we accept it at once, not only from what we know of the scientific capabilities of a guitar, but of the great scientific attainments of Colonel Thompson: but after his enharmonic guitar has been "arranged" for any of these keys, what will be the effect of "playing" in them, amidst all this mechanical interference with the finger-board? So much for the impediments to execution, to say nothing of tone. We must say, in justice to Mr. Panormo, the manufacturer, that, being convinced his own simple guitars on the Spanish model have more tone in them than any other, we regret he should have employed so much labour in the construction of this very ingenious, learned, and impracticable invention.

Mr. Jones, of Lombard-street, exhibited "a silent alarum bedstead to *turn* any one *out of bed* at a given hour." This is certainly one of the most amusing inventions we ever heard of. It assumes a degree of density in the sleeper which no alarum can affect, or else a singular amount of luxurious weakness of purpose. The bed, therefore, acts the part of resolution for the sleeper; and having been " set" over night for a given hour in the morning, the said incorrigible sleeper finds the bed revolve so as to tilt him out; and a bath being placed by the bed-side, he may at once be relieved of all need for summoning a resolution either to get up or to take a plunge.

The Chinese have long been famous for their caprices of invention, and whimsicalities of workmanship, over each article of which the greater portion of the lives of several artizans appear to have been expended. They exhibited some of their celebrated ivory balls, richly carved outside, and containing another, a size less, inside, richly carved also, with open-work, to show you that there are balls within balls to the extent of twenty or more, each cut clear of the rest, and carved and capable of being turned round—the whole of these being produced by means of a variety of curious tools and instruments, out of the first solid ball. This, they assert, nobody else can do; and it may be true, for the Chinese are capable of wasting any amount of time upon any triviality. But the Chinese are not the only people who have a love for difficulties, for the sake of the unnecessary labour and time they involve, which give the articles so much additional value in their eyes. If Quang Sing, of Canton, carves and engraves upon peach-stones, and makes baskets and boxes with the stones of apricots and nectarines, Mr. Jacob, of Coventry-street, displays egg-shells with carvings and engravings upon them, and " views inside." If Shee-king, of Macao, delights in wasting his own life, and the lives of others whom he employs, in carving a nest of ivory balls out of one solid ball, instead of obtaining a similar result, (if the world *must* have these toys) by the regular tools and simple means of ivory workmanship, we find several of our own countrymen equally assiduous in substituting a common penknife in order to perform operations which proper tools would effect far more easily in a tenth, perhaps a hundredth part of the time. There seems, in fact, a sort of mania for this penknife-work. Mr. Aston, of Chelsea, executed a model of St. James's Church, South, in cardboard, with a penknife; Mr. Scollick, of Birmingham, exhibited a model of St. Paul's Cathedral; and Mr. Dickenson, of Waterloo-place, a model of York Minster, each in cardboard, and each employing no better instrument than a penknife. M. Schnitzer, of Jerusalem, exhibited two vases carved out of a species of sandstone found in Jerusalem, with a penknife, which the proprietor, Sir Moses Montefiore, gravely takes care to inform the world was " an ordinary penknife."

In like manner, we found an exhibitor who displayed a model cottage composed of

2,000 pieces of willow wood (these also were all carved with a penknife); and there was a table to be seen which was composed of 2,000,000 of separate morsels, all inlaid in mosaic-work. The practical philosophers and economists of modern times complain of the great waste of human labour in the construction of the Pyramids of Egypt—let them consider the same subject in reference to this table. Many of our readers were, doubtless, like ourselves, much struck with the model of a ship, made with bottle-corks, and rigged in the same fashion. The object of this "caprice" we cannot fathom. Mr. Cossens, of Holborn, exhibited a model made in elder pith; and Mr. Clifford, of Exeter, displayed models made "of the pith of the common green rush," which he carefully informed us was such as is "used in making rushlights." In one of Hogarth's prints there is a capital satire upon the expenditure of extraordinary means to produce a simple result. You see a pile of complicated machinery, which indicates that an operation requiring great power is about to be displayed. The skill of the artist in the design and the arrangement of light and shade causes the eye to travel about and examine the various parts of the machinery, in order to ascertain the work it is about to perform, when finally you discover, at the bottom of the great machine, an ordinary wine-bottle, the neck of which is corked, and the whole of this machinery is evidently employed in "drawing the cork." Of a similar kind of elaboration, in order to effect a very simple object, we fear we must class some of the new inventions in horns and flutes, to the former of which many complicated crooks and curves, and to the latter many scarcely practicable keys have been added, merely to enable the instrument to produce a certain note which might be omitted with no great loss, or produced by other means. Nothing injures tone more than a superabundance of mechanism. Vivier always plays on the old French horn, without any of the complicated improvements, and Nicholson used to play on a flute much simpler than many now exhibited, and we have never heard any performer who gave so much tone to the instrument.

An American inventor, of the name of Wood, exhibited a combination of the pianoforte and violin, with which he assumes that pieces can be played with the effect of these two instruments in concert. Something like this, no doubt, may be accomplished by giving an attachment to the piano, which shall produce a resemblance to the sound of a violin; but in the present instance the inventor has literally attached a violin, played upon by four bows, which are put in motion by a separate set of keys on a small upper fingerboard, which cause the bows to "saw" (as we may truly say) upwards and downwards, with an effect which we frankly confess to be indescribable. One might see the whole operation, and a more ludicrous thing, both to see and hear, it has seldom been our lot to experience. Moreover, there was nothing new in the contrivance. The " Philosophical" Jury, Class Xa, however, discovered some peculiar merit in it, and awarded the maker "£50 for the expenses incurred in constructing his piano-violin;" a slice of "solid pudding" (as *Punch* describes his imaginary award of £20,000 to Sir Joseph Paxton), far more acceptable than medal or "honourable mention."

An inventor exhibited "a model of a carriage," which supplied its own railway, laying it down as it advanced, and taking it up after the wheels had passed over. This was no doubt extremely ingenious, but, unfortunately, it *supposed* the existence of a level line for the operation, so that its utility becomes rather questionable. A drinking-glass was exhibited, with a partition for soda and acid, to be mixed separately, the junction of the two streams effecting effervescence only at the moment of entering the mouth. Few people could "stand this," we should think. In the windows of most of the great cutlers of London may be seen knives with an extraordinary number of blades; and on the ground-floor of the Grand Exposition was exhibited a large glass-case, as big as a handsome summer-house, full of all sorts of fine cutlery and other workmanship in steel, the most prominent features of which were several of these preposterous knives. Some seemed to have 50 blades, of all sorts of shapes and sizes, others 150 blades, and one or two of them, we felt assured, could not display less than 400 or 500 blades. To accomplish this capricious feat, the inventors were always obliged to have recourse to a strangely thick handle of an utterly impracticable kind as to all handling: and in the glass-case referred to might be found one in the shape of a cross, thus combining four handles, each one crowded with blades; another had the handle in the shape of a star or double cross, thus combining six handles, each one bristling with blades, and arranged at the end of each handle in the form of a fan of bright penknives and blades of instruments. But all these were surpassed in capricious ingenuity by a "knife," the handle of which, if we must call it so, is a combination of three handles, each in form of a cross, the largest being in the middle. The three crosses are combined by an upright shaft, and each of the three comprises four handles. Thus, we have twelve handles in one, and from each of the twelve there stuck out a shining fan-work of blades and steel instruments of all conceivable shapes, and all real or imaginary offices, not one of which could be put in operation amidst such a crowd. It was one of the most wonderfully useless things we ever saw. As to the number of blades and tools, they defied calculation. In the same case might be seen miniature knives, which were actually of the same kind, and presented numerous blades from a handle of an inch and-a-half in length. Also miniature knives and scissors of an inch long, of half an inch long, and of a quarter of an inch long; and, by way of completing the wonder, twelve pairs of miniature scissors, placed in little brass scales, which showed that the whole twelve only weighed half a grain. They required a microscope to be seen properly, when it became manifest that they were perfectly formed scissors. We suppose Messrs. Rodgers would say, in explanation of all this fancy-work, that the *use* of it was to show the world what Sheffield could do, not only in work, but in play.

CHAPTER XIX.

SCULPTURE—*continued.*

JOHN HAMPDEN—SHAKSPERE—FLAXMAN—THE ELDON GROUP—DR. JENNER—THE MARQUIS OF BUTE—BACCHUS—ARIADNE—VIRGINIUS—EARLY SORROW—EVE—THE LION IN LOVE—CUPID —PAOLO AND FRANCESCA—YOUTH AT THE STREAM.

OF all the forms of the beautiful, perhaps none excite the admiration and sympathy of the public mind in a higher degree than the products of the sculptor's art. To the uneducated eye, the human form, modelled in clay or chiselled in pure white marble, seems fraught with grace and vigour, and an unconscious education of the feelings is going on as it gazes on the wondrous symmetry of a Venus de Medicis, or beholds the agonizing throes of a Laocoon. To the man of taste and refinement the process of thought and appreciation is different, though the ultimate effect is the same;—to both there is profit. While the ordinary mind is absorbed, spell-bound, entranced in a kind of admiring awe, the educated man admires, criticises, appreciates. Though the art-education of both men has been conducted on different principles, the result arrived at is precisely similar, and both are equally informed and humanised.

The art of sculpture, with the kindred arts of modelling, carving, and casting, are of very remote antiquity. The ancients availed themselves of almost every known substance capable of being cut or moulded into form; and we find the remains of figures, architectural ornaments, vases, lamps, and pedestals, in marbles, woods, metals, ivory, bone, granite, porphyry, basalt, alabaster, stucco, wax, clay, and terra cotta, or baked earth. There is no reason to doubt that the art of sculpture was known before the flood; and we have certain evidence that it was practised in India and America by civilised races of men, known now only traditionally, and of whom no other traces remain. Indeed, the late discoveries of Mr. Layard in Nineveh, prove incontestably that the sculptor's art was practised, and arose to a remarkable degree of perfection, thousands of years ago. Universal as language, the art has risen from the rude forms of savage worship to the perfection in which we view it in our public buildings, our streets, and lately in the Crystal Palace. The productions in sculpture are either complete figures or groups, which may be viewed from all sides; or objects more or less raised, without being entirely detached from the back-ground with which they are connected. This is called *relief,* the kinds and degrees of which are defined by modern writers and artists by the words *alto,* or high relief, where the objects project so as to be nearly distinct; *basso,* or low relief, where the figure is slightly raised from the background; and *mezzo,* or half-relief, where not more than the face and half the figure is raised from the place on which it is sculptured. Examples of these were to be seen in the Exhibition, and there are some also in the British Museum. Nothing can be more simple than the mechanical processes of sculpture. As soon as the artist has conceived his subject, and made his drawing upon paper, a model in clay, or some soft material, is executed in *little.* In the production of the model it is that the artist-mind is displayed; if *that* be true and natural, its transference to stone or bronze is a matter of comparatively minor importance. Upon a frame of wood or iron, the figure is built up to the size it is to assume in the chosen material, and moulded by the hands and certain simple instruments in wood and ivory. Arrived at this stage, the drawing, or original idea of the future statue is reconsidered; and by the assistance of the human figure, minutely studied, is carried to completion. Statues are frequently modelled nude, and afterwards draped; and that accuracy of form, and gracefulness of outline may be obtained, draperies are commonly placed upon lay figures, the details of which are copied by the artist. When the clay model has sufficiently dried and shrunk, a mould is made of it by covering it with gypsum or plaster of Paris. When this is sufficiently hardened, the clay within is carefully removed, and there remains an exact mould of the model. This being carefully washed, and the interior brushed over with a composition of oil and soap, the mould is thoroughly filled in all its parts with a semi-liquid mixture of gypsum, which, in a few days, becomes sufficiently hard to allow the mould to be removed, and thus a complete cast of the model is procured. From this short description of the method almost universally pursued, it will be seen how the plaster casts in the Crystal Palace have been produced.

The model is to be executed in marble. The process of transference is a matter of mechanical rather than inventive skill. By means of a long steel needle, attached to a pole or standard, and capable of being withdrawn or extended, the exact situation of numerous points and cavities in the figure to be imitated are ascertained; and the statue is rudely blocked out and pointed. A superior workman, called a carver, then takes the marble and copies the more minute portions of the work by means of chisels, files, and rasps; and the statue being now in a sufficiently forward state, the final finishing touches are given by the sculptor himself. In the production of the model and harmony of effect, beauty of feature, variety of texture and surface, and consistency of detail in form and expression in the finished statue, the sculptor's skill is eminently displayed;

and while the ancients relied almost on the chisel for their effects, the modern artist in marble approaches the surface of his statue with extreme caution, and employs safer means of giving a perfect finish to what may bring him both fame and fortune. With this preface, then, we shall now proceed with our remarks on the sculpture in the Great Exhibition, and, in doing so, begin with a noble name, dear to Englishmen, and to every lover of freedom throughout the whole civilized world. We allude to the immortal Hampden, whose stalwart form in plaster cast, modelled for a statue in marble, which now is placed in the new palace at Westminster, formed a conspicuous and attractive object in the Crystal Palace. And certainly, when we consider the part its original played in the history of his country, we can conceive no better site for it than among the senators of Great Britain "in Parliament assembled." The contemplation of this fine statue failed not to recal to our minds the interesting actions of this noble man's life. Born in London, in 1594, he entered at an early age as a commoner at Oxford, which seat of learning he left for the profession of the law, studying for a short time in one of the inns of court. The death of his father, however, putting him in possession of an ample estate, he retired to Buckinghamshire, and for a while pursued his quiet career as a country gentleman. Events, however, arose, which called forth the natural energy of his mind. Cousin-german to Oliver Cromwell, he could not look calmly upon the usurpations, as they were considered, of Charles I.; and, therefore, he soon attached himself to the popular party. In 1626 he entered the House of Commons, and soon after married a lady of the Foley family. In Parliament he uniformly opposed the arbitrary practices of the kingly prerogative, and the illegal impost of ship money; and, being prosecuted for his adherence to the popular cause, and for the part he had taken *in reference to a contemplated emigration to New England*, he defended himself in person against the crown lawyers in the Court of Exchequer during a trial which lasted twelve days. Although he lost the cause, his defeat was looked upon as a triumph to the popular party. Henceforth he took a leading part in the contest between the Crown and the Parliament; and when at last an appeal was made to arms, he accepted the command of a regiment in the Parliament army, under the Earl of Essex. His military career, however, was short; but it was long enough to prove his courage and perseverance. Prince Rupert coming suddenly upon the Parliamentary troops, near Thame, in Oxfordshire, Hampden eagerly headed a few cavalry that were rallied in haste, and, in the skirmish that ensued, received a wound in the shoulder, which proved fatal. After lingering in much pain and suffering for six days, he died on the 24th of June, 1643. His death was as great grief to his own party as it was a source of joy and congratulation to the adherents of the crown. Time, the great leveller, has enabled us, however, to look with cooler judgment and clearer sight upon the great transactions in which Hampden and Cromwell were engaged. Party feeling on the subject of prerogative has died out, and all parties are in this day agreed to call the original of this fine statue by his ancient cognomen—"the patriot Hampden."

As we are now upon the subject of great men, we will advert to a name illustrative of all that is great and excellent in the world of poetry,—"Sweetest Shakspeare, fancy's child," to whose worth, all writers in every succeeding period, from the grave and philosophic Milton to the incomparable author of *Rasselas*, have delighted to bear testimony.

The former has summed up his eulogium in the following vigorous sonnet :—

> "What needs my Shakspeare for his honored bones
> The labour of an age in piled stones,
> Or that his hallowed relics should be hid
> Under a star-ypointed pyramid ?

P. MacDowell R.A. Sculptor.   Daguerreotyped by Beard.

VIRGINIUS AND HIS DAUGHTER.

J. Bell. Sculptor.   Daguerreotyped by Beard.

SHAKSPERE.

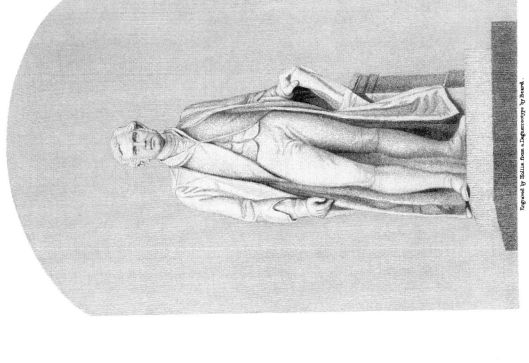

MODEL OF A STATUE OF HAMPDEN.

EXECUTED FOR THE NEW PALACE OF WESTMINSTER.

SIR WILLIAM FOLLETT.

FROM THE ORIGINAL COLOSSAL STATUE BY BEHENES.

Engraved by Hollis from a Daguerreotype by Mayall.

Engraved by Hollis from a Daguerreotype by Beard.

Engraved by J.Moore, from a Daguerreotype by Beard.

DR JENNER

ELDON   STOWELL

Engraved by J.Moore, from a Daguerreotype by Beard.

WILLIAM BARON STOWELL AND JOHN FIRST LORD ELDON

FROM THE ORIGINAL BY M.WATSON

Dear son of memory, great heir of Fame,
What need'st thou such weak witness of thy name?
Thou in our wonder and astonishment
Hast built thyself a live-long monument,
For whilst to the shame of slow-endeavouring art,
Thy easy numbers flow, and that each heart
Hath from the leaves of thy unvalued book,
Those Delphic lines with deep impression took,
Then thou our fancy of itself bereaving,
Dost make us marble with too much conceiving,
And so sepulchr'd in such pomp dost lie,
That kings for such a tomb would wish to die."

We have presented our readers with an engraving of a statue of our immortal bard, by Bell, which, from its graceful and dignified character, attracted considerable notice among the lovers of the plastic art.

Descending to more modern times, we must not forget to notice the statues of lords Eldon and Stowell, remarkable for the accuracy of the likenesses, and the calm dignity of the attitudes. These noble statues, executed by the late Musgrave Watson, were carved each out of a single block of marble, the whole weighing upwards of twenty tons. The admirable group, representing the brothers, John, first Earl of Eldon, who was nearly twenty-five years Lord High Chancellor of Great Britain, and William Baron Stowell, twenty-nine years Judge of the High Court of Admiralty, is the property of the present Lord Eldon, for whom it was executed by the above-named eminent sculptor. Alas, for the fame of the gifted! Mr. Watson lived long enough to achieve but not to enjoy fame. It is the old story over again: genius lives in obscurity and dies in poverty; and then all at once the world wakes up to the knowledge that a great spirit has gone from out its portals. Quite grieved and beside itself, the world of wealth wrings its hands in impotent regrets, and raises a monument to the memory of the genius which a little encouragement and a little sympathy would have kept alive. Let us pass on. Although we have already, in a former part of this work, paid the passing tribute of a word in favour of another statue by this lamented artist, which graced the sculpture court,—we again, to give him "honour due," bring the name of the illustrious Flaxman to the recollection of our readers, in order that such of them as had not an opportunity of admiring the exceeding beauty and tranquillity exhibited in the features of the talented artist during the late Exposition, may now be informed that they may still enjoy that privilege, by paying a visit to the Flaxman Gallery at the London University, where, through the praiseworthy exertions of a friend of the great artist, and the generosity of his near relative, besides the statue itself, an interesting collection of *bassi relievi*, and finished pieces of sculpture from the same talented hand, are placed in a handsome apartment, in lasting memorial of his immortal genius.

We next have to notice the fine models for statues of Dr. Jenner and the late Marquis of Bute, by Mr. J. Thomas. The names of both physician and peer are familiar to the public ear, the first as the discoverer of vaccine inoculation (a discovery of incalculable importance, considered in its proper light), and the last as being the descendant of the famous prime-minister under whom the peace of Fontainebleau, in 1763, was concluded.

In our description of the sculpture from Tuscany, we omitted to make mention of several pieces of merit which we shall in the course of these strictures duly enumerate. And first we shall direct the attention of our readers to a fine recumbent figure of Bacchus—

" Bacchus who first from out the purple grape
Crushed the sweet poison of misused wine—"

and a graceful and poetical representation it is of the joy-inspiring god, not the semi-Silenus of the drinking songs of our forefathers, but as he is invariably represented in the Grecian mythology, almost "*severe* in youthful beauty," and a fitting inamorato of the fair Ariadne whom he wooed and won. Even the grave and lofty Milton deemed him worthy of his muse in his poetical epistle to Diodate—

And why should revelry and wine
Be shunned as foes to song divine?
Bacchus loves the power of verse,
Bacchus oft the Nine rehearse;
Nor Phœbus' self disdains to wear
His berries in his golden hair,
And ivy green with laurel twine;
And oft are seen the sisters nine
Joining in mystic dance, along
Aonia's hills, with Bacchus' throng.
In frozen Scythia's barren plains
What dulness seized on Ovid's strains;
Their sweetness fled to climes alone
To Ceres and Lyæus known.

What but wine with roses crowned
Did the Teian lyre resound?
Bacchus with pleasing frenzy fired,
The high Pindaric song inspired;
Each page is redolent of wine
When, crashing loud, the car supine
On Elis' plains disjointed lies,
And soiled with dust the courser flies.
'Rapt with the god's all-pleasing fire,
The Roman poet strikes the lyre,
And in measure sweet addresses
Chloe fair with golden tresses;
Or his loved Glycera sings,
Touching light th' immortal strings.*

Whilst we are on this classic ground we must not forbear to notice the "Ariadne" by Kirk, who was represented sitting by the sea-shore, in melancholy-wise, after she had been deserted by the faithless god. Our readers will doubtless recollect the beautiful picture by Titian illustrative of the same subject.

"Virginius and Daughter," the production of P. Mac Dowell, R.A., next claims our attention. It was worthy of it; we all recollect the story of the stern old Roman who preferred plunging a dagger into his daughter's heart rather than she should become the mistress of a tyrant. How exquisitely was the idea rendered! The indignant father, with his dead child on his knee, raised his hand to heaven and denounced the base Appius Claudius, in a voice that was impressive enough to command for him sympathy and popular applause. Considered as an artistic performance this group might be pronounced first-rate. It stood in the south transept. Mr. Mac Dowell's "Early Sorrow," in the sculpture court, and his "Eve," in the south transept, were really fine, and second to, perhaps, no nude figure exhibited—not even excepting the famous Greek Slave.

"The Lion in Love," was a group in plaster, by S. Geefs, of Schaerbeck, near Brussels, and its place in the Exhibition was in the main eastern avenue, immediately before Simonis' famous equestrian statue of Godfrey of Bouillon. A small figure in marble, by the same artist, of Cupid, the God of Love, was sufficiently demonstrative of the graceful and poetic character of the sculptor's mind. With what almost human feeling the "brute enthralled" looked up into the face of its fair enchantress, and with what tender care the beautiful maiden tended her leoline lover! Really a fine conception, adequately worked out. Like Una, she had captivated the Lord of the Forest—

——————————"With those suppliant looks,
And voice more beautiful than poet's books."

Another group in plaster, "Paolo and Francesca," by Mr. A. Munro, next claims our attention. Mr. Munro, in this little group, sought to realize the incident described by Dante, or rather by his heroine, Francesca, for she is supposed to relate her own sad story to him, in the following passage, as translated by Cary:—

————————————"One day
For our delight, we read of Lancelot,

* *Milton's Latin and Italian Poems.* Translated by J. G. STRUTT.

Engraved by Hollis from a Daguerreotype by Beard

THE LION IN LOVE _ BY S. GEEFS

Engraved by Hollis from a Daguerreotype by Beard.

THE MOURNERS _ BY J. G. LOUGH.

THE TRANSEPT OF THE GREAT EXHIBITION.

LOOKING SOUTH

Engraved by W. Lacey from a Daguerreotype by Mayall.

Engraved by D.Pound, from a Daguerreotype by Mayall.

A YOUTH AT A STREAM.

FROM THE ORIGINAL BY J. H. FOLEY A.R.A.

Engraved by D.Pound, from a Daguerreotype by Mayall.

A YOUNG GIRL AT THE SPRING

FROM THE ORIGINAL BY W. F. WOODINGTON.

How him love thralled. Alone we were, and no
Suspicion near us. Oft-times by that reading
Our eyes were drawn together, and the hue
Fled from our alter'd cheek. But at one point
Alone we fell. When of that smile we read,
The wished smile, so rapturously kiss'd
By one so deep in love, then he, who ne'er
From me shall separate, at once my lips
All trembling kiss'd. The book and writer both
Were love's purveyors. In its leaves that day
We read no more."

We need hardly say a word to point out the difficulties which too obviously surround the treatment of such a subject in sculpture; at least, if it be attempted to represent *all* that the poet conceived of it. One point referred to in the passage, "the hue fled from our alter'd cheek," it is impossible to render through the medium of marble, because it is *never* colourable, and even to express the idea of strong emotion as conveyed through the eyes, is a thing not to be attempted in the plastic art. Nevertheless, Mr. Munro, who is a young artist of very considerable promise, produced a very pretty and graceful composition, though at the same time one which, costume, accessories, and all considered, would have been better adapted for a painting than a work in plaster. As regards expression, he certainly accomplished a great deal—much more than we should have been prepared to expect: the face of Paolo was earnest and impassioned in the extreme: it told of a devouring passion long pent up, first revealing itself; that of Francesca confessed a reciprocity of feeling, but with a modest hesitating reserve, which was admirably true to the more delicate poetry of the situation. Since this group was exhibited, we are glad to understand that Mr. Gladstone has commissioned the artist to execute it in marble.

"Girl Praying," by Mac Dowall. This very graceful production reflected the highest credit upon Mr. Mac Dowall's talent. The expression was extremely charming, and the attitude simple and effective. It stood in the southern transept, where it was greatly admired. The "Youth at the Stream," a statue in marble, by J. H. Foley, A.R.A., was one of the most attractive in the Exhibition. It stood in the transept to the east of the Glass Fountain. As a work of art it was extremely successful in its graceful and poetic character, while for ease of posture and delicacy of execution it might be said to be perfect. It has been remarked that the statuary in the Crystal Palace attracted much more attention from the general public than was expected. This was not surprising. The higher classes were familiar with the kind of sights to be seen in the Crystal Palace; but to the multitude they were new, rare, and surprising. The Exhibition was literally the greatest "sight" recorded in the history of the world, even if we attach to the phrase nothing but its commonplace import in the minds of idlers and "gadabouts." It was in this point of view that it supplied attraction, and, we should think, satiety to the wealthier or more listless class of visitors. Mechanics and operatives went naturally to the rival productions of their own competitors in various parts of the globe. Their observations took a turn of their own; nor would it have been easy, perhaps, to impress a man who had never travelled in search of "sights" with the prodigious magnitude of the specimen before him; but if our tourists and pleasure seekers will but reflect for a moment, they may discover that the capacities of an ordinary life have been just now concentrated into the experience of a fortnight. Not five years' travel nor a thousand pounds could have enabled a man to see what one shilling brought before his eyes; and one of the most striking morals of the Exhibition was that suggested by the astonishing influence which must have been exercised in amassing the collection. The spectacle was intended to be little more than a magnified "exposition" on the original French pattern. It turned out to be such a wonder as the world never saw. We read in Arabian fables that magicians could place before enchanted spectators the visible treasures of the universe. These very treasures were laid bodily at our feet by no other magic than that of national power. Every visitor carried away his own impressions, more or less profound, correct, or serviceable, as the case might be, but still distinct and characteristic; nor would it be easy to find two persons, even of the same abilities and station, who would give the same account of their sentiments or the same description of the show. There is an education which is not taught by books. It was working out its mission in the Crystal Palace.

From these classical subjects we now turn to one of stern reality, "The Wounded American Indian," by Stephenson. Those who have seen the inimitable representation of the Dying Gladiator, in the gallery of the Capitol at Rome, will, we think, trace in this work a remarkable similarity, both in character and attitude, to that most wonderful statue, which might indeed induce a belief that Mr. Stephenson had drawn his inspiration from that celebrated performance. Be that as it may, he has unquestionably produced a work of great merit. We were told the effort of the sculptor was to give a correct representation of the Indian races of North America. The figure was represented wounded and fallen, thereby typifying the race. While in the act of stringing his bow, he had received the wound; the moment the fatal arrow is felt, he relinquishes the effort and hurriedly pulls it from the wound. In the moment that succeeds, he realises his danger, and his left hand drops powerless, partially clinging to the fatal arrow, while a faintness creeps over him. The right arm instinctively supports the body, and prevents its falling. Beneath the right hand is his own arrow, in his ears are an eagle's claw and a small shell. Sufficient ornaments and implements only have been introduced to give character to the subject. It was the first statue ever executed in American marble. It stood to the north-east of Power's Greek Slave. Is it not suggestive that the Americans, proverbially a *'cute* people, should have so publicly drawn attention to slavery and the extinction of the aborigines of the Far West?

Mr. E. B. Stephens' group of "Satan Vanquished by St. Michael," which stood on the left in the South Transept, was a composition not without merit, though it certainly did not attain that high poetic character which we look for in works of that class. The subject was severely treated, without, however, its appropriate dignity; the Archangel stood erect, without any attempt at attitudinising, whilst the Enemy of man, whom he had just overthrown, crouched in the dust beneath his feet. There was a total absence of human passion in the expression of the face; a point in strict accordance, perhaps, with the heavenly nature of the personage represented, but which, on the other hand, would impose upon the artist the necessity of realising the supernatural dignity attaching to him—a task in which he was not at all successful. A word with regard to accessorial details. It is certainly recorded that the Archangel brought down a chain from heaven to bind the Serpent; and in a work of sculpture commemorative of the event, some reference might properly be made to it, as being by no means unimportant; but, at the same time, we could have wished that the said chain had not been made quite so much of, and in such hard angular outline as Mr. Stephens employed; that it had been, at most, faintly indicated as encompassing the prostrate Evil Spirit, and not held up in triumph, in the hand of the Archangel. All such efforts at perfectionising petty details are unworthy of art, and betray a want of confidence in its higher resources. The "Cain," by Jehotte, was a spirited attempt, in plaster, after the school of Michel

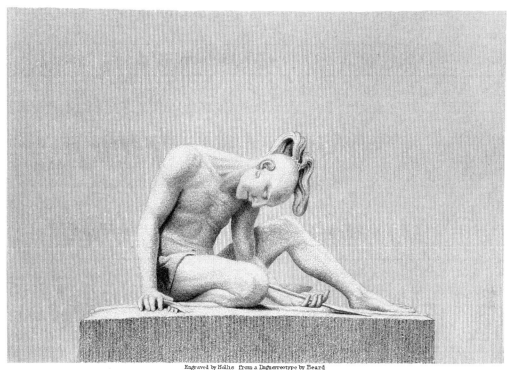

Engraved by Hollis from a Daguerreotype by Beard

THE WOUNDED INDIAN,

FROM THE ORIGINAL BY STEPHENSON OF BOSTON, UNITED STATES

Engraved by Hollis from a Daguerreotype by Beard

A DEER STALKER.

FROM THE ORIGINAL BY E. B. STEPHENS.

Engraved by Hollis, from a Daguerreotype by Beard.

THE ARCHANGEL MICHAEL HAVING SUBDUED SATAN

MILTON

FROM THE ORIGINAL BY LOUGH

Engraved by Hollis, from a Daguerreotype by Beard.

SATAN VANQUISHED BY THE ARCHANGEL.

FROM THE ORIGINAL BY STEPHENS

Engraved by G Greatbach from a Drawing by W Tomlinson

MALACHITE DOORS

Engraved by G Greatbach from a Drawing by W Tomlinson

MALACHITE VASES

Angelo,—but crudely wrought out. The catalogue stated that the first murderer was supposed to be exclaiming, " My punishment is greater than I can bear ;" but, for this, the attitude was inappropriate. It would have suited better for the first impulse of horror on seeing the dead body of his brother. We shall resume our remarks on the sculpture of the Great Exhibition at a future opportunity.

CHAPTER XX.

FOREIGN AND COLONIAL DEPARTMENTS—*continued.*

RUSSIA—GOLD, SILVER, AND PRECIOUS STONES—RAW MATERIALS—MALACHITE DOORS, ETC.— WORKS OF ART—MANUFACTURES, ETC.—SPAIN—RICH PLATE—TOLEDO BLADES—FURNITURE —MINERAL PRODUCE, ETC. ETC.

THIS immense empire, occupying nearly one-seventh of the terrestrial part of the globe, and one twenty-seventh of its entire surface, was represented at the Exhibition by specimens of her chief agricultural and mineral produce, as well as by the productions of her looms and workshops. The magnificent candelabra placed at the entrance of their principal department, and the splendid profusion of diamonds, rubies, emeralds, pearls, and turquoises therein exhibited, attested to the wealth and showy magnificence of the Imperial Autocrat, the Emperor of all the Russias. In no country in Europe is there so large a quantity of jewels used as in Russia. The imperial family never travel without an abundant supply of them, to distribute among those whom they deem worthy of their favour. It was not, however, in these gauds and trinkets that the mighty empire of Russia was chiefly represented at the Great Exhibition, but in her vases, her doors of malachite, her specimens of gold, platinum, and iron, the produce of her mines ; in the skins, furs, leather, bristles, and tallow, the produce of her numerous herds of cattle ; and, above all, in the varied specimens of corn, flax, hemp, &c., the productions of her vast and wide-spreading plains. We shall offer a few remarks as we proceed on various points connected with these raw materials, but we will first describe that portion of the Russian exhibition which was exclusively devoted to the display of the most rare and costly articles, destined for those alone whose wealth enabled them to set no limit to the indulgence of their tastes.

By the pillars at the entrance of this *sanctum sanctorum* of wealth and splendour, stood the two great candelabra we have already alluded to. They were from the manufactory of Krumbigel, of Moscow, and spoke well for the taste and resources of the " frozen Muscovite." They were of richly-gilt bronze, each ten feet in height, and made for fifteen lights, and were valued at £500 a-piece. Looking from the centre aisle into the compartment, the most striking object was the folding doors of malachite, thirteen feet high, panelled and ornamented in gilt bronze. Our readers have probably made acquaintance with malachite as a precious stone, in brooches, jewel-boxes, and other small articles of ornament, but never dreamt of seeing it worked up into a pair of drawing-room doors. The effect was exceedingly beautiful; the brilliant green of the malachite, with its curled waviness, like the pattern of watered silk, and its perfectly polished surface, was heightened by the dead and burnished gold of the panellings and ornaments, and set one imagining in what sort of fairy palace, and with what other furnishing and decoration the room must be fitted to satisfy those who had made their entrance by such precious doors. They were valued at £6,000. The large vases on either side of the compartment were also, pedestals and all, in malachite like the doors, ornamented in gilt bronze, and were valued at from £1,500 to £3,000 a-piece; and to show that a whole suite of apartments might be decked out in the same bright precious stone, there stood to the left, and not far from the doors, a mantelpiece, in Louis Quatorze style, before it ran quite wild in confusion of ornamental form; the fender, hearth, fire-back, and grate, in bronze gilt and burnished gold; the mantelpiece in beautifully-shaded malachite, with just enough of ornament for contrast; and on either side of this splendid fire-place were a table and chair of the same material. The chairs were valued at £120 each, the tables at £400. In the next compartment the malachite (carbonate of copper), was exhibited in the strange-shaped rough lumps in which it comes from the mine, and in every stage of preparation. It is found in the copper-mines of Siberia and the Ural Mountains, and has lately been met with in equally large pieces, and of not less beauty, in the Burra Burra mines, in Australia. That in the Exhibition was from the mines of Prince Demidoff. The manufacture of articles of malachite is in itself a work of art; and, smooth as the surface seems, it is made up of a multitude of variously-shaped little pieces carefully selected to produce particular patterns, and which in their fitting require the greatest exactitude. In the doors there might have been some 20,000 or 30,000 pieces imbedded in cement, made of the malachite itself. The doors were of wood covered with copper, the malachite being about a quarter of an inch thick. The vases were of three-quarter inch cast iron, and the malachite in the same way inlaid. Nor was this the only precious stone made to serve such large uses in this Russian compartment; there were also upon the left-hand side, near the great candelabrum, three real jasper vases, one of them three feet six inches in height, which excited the admiration of those most skilled in such matters, by the exquisite cutting of its border of leaves, which, as the process is not explained, they have come to the conclusion must have been done by mounting the diamond, the only mineral of sufficient hardness to cut agate, in some specially contrived machine. The value of this vase was not stated, but the cost of the workmanship alone exceeded £700, and the vase could certainly not be under £2,000. These vases were the property of the emperor, and were made at his own manufactory at Katrinburg. The great vase in the centre front was in porcelain, from the imperial manufactory at St. Petersburgh, and was valued at £2,500.

To the left and right in front were jewels valued at £40,000, and which were exhibited by M. Bolin and M. Kammerer, both crown jewellers at St. Petersburgh. Nothing could exceed their richness and splendour. The plate, which was on another table at the right, and comprised a great variety of articles, was entirely from the workshop of M. Sizikoff, of Moscow, one candelabrum shown by whom contained two cwt. of silver, and set forth an incident memorable in Russian history. The Duke de Merti, Grand Duke of Muscovy, in a fierce battle with the Tartars, in 1380, fell severely wounded by a blow on the head with a hammer, a main weapon of warfare with the Tartars at that time. The duke, surrounded by his staff of knights in armour, lay under a fir-tree, faint, and, to all appearance, dying, when a soldier of his army galloped up and announced the battle won—the duke revived and recovered. The candelabrum represented the fir-tree and the above incident. On the same side of the compartment was an ebony cabinet, designed by Baron Clott, one of the first artists in the Russian empire. On the top was a bunch of grapes, in amethyst, so modelled that, as the light fell upon them, they seemed to show the very juice of the real fruit of the mountain ash in coral. In the background were seen specimens of inlaying in wood for floors; a Warwick vase, in hammered iron, from Warsaw; a curious carpet, very bright in its colours and effect, made in squares of squirrel-skin, surrounded each by a border of needlework; and near this stood a cabinet, made by M. Yanebs, of St. Petersburgh, in light wood, with porcelain medallions, from the imperial manufactory, valued at £500, and a second porcelain vase of azure and gold, from the same works.

Almost all the articles exhibited in this Northern Bay were the produce of a system, almost universal among the monarchies of Europe, of carrying on royal or national manufactories, as a matter of luxury and as an example of taste. Such in France are the national manufactories of Gobelins tapestry, of Beauvais carpets, and Sèvres china; in Prussia, of iron-casting and porcelain; in Saxony, of porcelain; and in Tuscany, of mosaic in *pietra dura*. To several of these establishments, particularly in Russia, and in the Gobelins establishment in France, schools for instruction in drawing and painting, as applied to manufactures, are attached for the benefit and the due training of workmen. In England, it is with difficulty that money is obtained for schools of design; but although we wisely rely on private enterprise for manufacturing excellence, it would pay us to devote more money to cultivate taste.

On leaving the splendid department dedicated to luxury and the fine arts, we found in the small avenue to the north some more real and utilitarian specimens of Russian industry, in a set of very handsome carriages, of a peculiar national form. These were the Russian drosky, equally available on wheels, or in the winter on runners, and the favourite carriage of Russian gentlemen. They were on four wheels, very low, with a strong iron forked perch, and a double body, the first of which either held one or two persons abreast. There were specimens of both kinds. The other merely held a seat for the driver, who sits close upon his horse or horses; when a pair are used, the correct thing is for a shaft-horse to trot, while the second, harnessed to an outrigger, gambols at a canter beside him. They were very stylish, and the workmanship deserved unqualified praise, except in the shafts, which were heavy and clumsy. The leather splash-boards round the wheels were particularly well arranged; no stitching appeared, and they looked like pieces of solid japan; the lining and the varnishing were equally well finished. If the wood was sound and well seasoned, they were not dear at the price set upon them—£47. A set of harness in the large room was also of a fashion peculiar to Russia. It is difficult to explain, to those who have never seen them in use, the arrangement of a great birchwood bow, which is an indispensable ornament of Russian harness, and from which bells are suspended over the horse's neck.

The staples which constitute the export trade of Russia were exhibited in great variety; one part of the walls was hung with leather, including choice specimens of the "Russia" dear to book collectors. Amongst the boots and shoes were a pair of dress-boots, made of the thinnest and best calf leather we ever remember to have seen. It was as soft and flexible as kid, but stronger. We were informed that the material is much used in Russia for full dress boots. If it can be delivered here at a reasonable price, a large demand is certain. On the same counter as the leather were a number of stockings, shoes, and other articles made of felt by the Russian peasantry. A very curious manufacture, indeed, well worth the examination of the trade. Each article seemed felted separately, and made solid yet soft. On the opposite table were basins, jugs, cups, helmets of the same material japanned inside and out. They were light, tough, and not to be broken. A wash-hand jug and basin were rather dear (17s.), but they would be famous articles for sea voyages. Gutta percha has been tried for that purpose, but it melts in tropical climates.

A trophy of sheafs of seed-bearing agricultural produce, very elegantly arranged, containing every kind of wheat, barley, oats, rye, buckwheat, flax, hemp, peas, and beans, grown in the Russian dominions, occupied the centre of a counter, round which were arranged in bowls the seed and flour of these articles. Among them our cooks may find it worth while to try a small kind of dried pea for winter use, in soups, of a very sweet taste. On the walls around were specimens of the famous Russian hemps, raw and manufactured, with canvass, and ropes, and twine, which, with grain and tallow, have been too well known to our merchants for this last hundred years to need further notice. The dried provisions included *caviare*, dried sturgeon, isinglass, a substance resembling isinglass made up in the shape of a rude whip, which is obtained from a fish called the *Vesiga*, and used in Russia to make pies. But, perhaps, the article most likely to become a new staple of commerce, was the *glaze*, then imported, as we were informed, for the first time. This article, so much used in this country for making sausages and soups, in clubs, hotels, and great houses, is obtained in Russia by boiling down the flesh of horned cattle, which, on the plains of the interior, are only valuable for their hides and tallow. Anything that can be made out of concentrated meat or glaze is so much additional profit. But it is an operation which requires care—a little burning will spoil the whole boiling. Liebig gives directions for the operation in his last work: as commonly conducted, the product affords very little nourishment.

The specimens of iron and copper, in ore and in a manufactured state, were numerous. The iron, some of which was of a very fine quality, is a matter of interest to us, because Russia, in conjunction with Spain and Sweden, supplied most of the iron consumed in this country for more than one hundred years, between the time that the timber for charcoal in Surrey, Sussex, Kent, Staffordshire, and Worcestershire, was exhausted; and the successful application of coal to smelting iron, by Abraham Darby, at the Colebrook Dale Works, in 1713, and the application of the use of blowing cylinders, instead of bellows, at the Carron Works, set up by Smeaton in 1760. Our connexion with the Russian iron is of very ancient date. In 1569 the English obtained, by treaty, the right of seeking for and smelting iron ore, on condition that they should teach the Russians the art of smelting this metal, and pay, on the exportation of every pound, one halfpenny. Every branch of mining received great development under Peter the Great, who seems to have neglected no branch of material prosperity. It was under his reign and direct patronage that the Demidoff family rose to importance as miners, and obtained the property which has rendered them ever since one of the wealthiest families in Europe. Up to 1784, Great Britain imported a continually increasing quantity of iron from Russia, which in that year amounted to 40,000 tons; after that period, in consequence of improvements in machinery for smelting by coal, the importation gradually declined to about 5,000 tons in 1805, and continued at that figure up to 1837, and, probably, is about the same now, being all of one quality in the trade, called C. C. N. D. old sable iron, which is used for the manufacture of steel.

The fire-arms and white-arms exhibited had all been made at one of the four crown manufactories, where the work is done, under the inspection of government officers, by serfs of the crown. The oldest manufactory is at Tula, where, besides muskets and side-arms, the iron-work of horse harness, iron bedsteads, files, chains, &c., are made. This establishment was burnt in 1834, according to the rumour of the day, by the workmen, who hoped to get rid of the forced labour imposed on them by the ceaseless wars of the emperor in Turkey, Persia, and the Caucasus. Under the Russian royal factory system, increased work does not give increased wages. But the Tula establishment was rebuilt.

In the North Gallery, the emperor exhibited, with other furs, a black cloak made from the neck of the silver fox, which he valued at £3,500; this valuation brought out a letter from Mr. Nicholay, the well-known furrier, who offered to make a finer cloak for £1,000, and explained that black and silver fox skins, so much valued in Russia, and so little used here, are chiefly imported into London from the territories of the Hudson's Bay Company, and then purchased up for the express purpose of "being smuggled as occasion may offer." What a commentary on the Russian protective system! In the back of the same case as the furs, were two splendid specimens of twilled shawls, by a Cossack woman, from white goats' hair, of wonderful fineness. One of these shawls was the property of the empress, and justly valued at the price of Brussels lace. Russian manufactures are for the most part inferior and dear; while mineral, vegetable, and animal produce could be supplied in unlimited quantities, at a profit, if roads were made and facilities given to trade. But Russia is essentially a military country, prepared to take advantage of events, and probably the emperor considers that a large trade might produce inconveniently pacific tendencies in his own land-owning nobles.

We will now, by a special privilege granted to every one who visited the Palace of Wonders, of rapid transition even from the far east to the remote west, pass at once to a different region of the globe; and leaving the numerous tribes, civilized or barbarous, of the wide extended empire, enter upon the territories of the most Christian king—the country so celebrated for love and war—the land of song, and of the chivalrous hidalgo; and more than all, the land wherein the incomparable knight of La Mancha, and his no less incomparable squire, pursued their romantic adventures.

The intelligent visitor to the Spanish court in the Crystal Palace could hardly glance over its scant collection without some regretful reflections on the mutability of human greatness, and the liability to decadence in all great and powerful states. When he thinks that the comparatively unimportant objects that were there arranged, "few and far between," and which only served to reveal the nakedness of the land, were all that could be sent forth by the people who overthrew the great and gallant Moors, who colonized America, who received into their laps all the gold of Mexico, and all the silver of Peru, who equipped the world-famed armada, happily without success, to "fright this isle from its propriety;" the country of Ferdinand and Isabella, the kingdom of Charles V., the birthplace of the Cid and of Gonsalvo de Cordova, and the foster-land of Columbus,—how cheap must he not hold the result of mere military glory, and the gains of conquest and rapine, as compared with the honest profits of legitimate commerce, and the development of the industrial energies, as exemplified in the career of our own happy land. Yet there is hope for Spain. Nature, always young, is as bountiful to that country as when she fed the legions of imperial Rome, or tempted the invasion of the Saracens,—or when, at a later period, the invader himself, hanging up his sword and buckler, and betaking himself to the arts of peace, converted the whole surface of the country into one vast garden, glowing with the orange and the grape, and decorated its cities with those light and graceful arabesques which have made the Alhambra one of the architectural wonders of the world. The wheat of Spain is as fine, her olives are as plentiful and well-flavoured, her timber is as abundant and valuable, as when she victualled vast fleets for discovery or for conquest, or built those leviathans of the deep which gave Ferrol the foremost place among the naval arsenals of Europe. What is better still, her men have not, in the main, deteriorated. Protracted political convulsions, always demoralizing, may have lowered the standard of patriotic feeling and of manly energy in her large cities, where also the strong infusion of Jewish blood has, no doubt, had its effect in making avarice take the place of nationality; but her rural peasantry, her mountaineers, and her muleteers, are the same brown manly fellows as ever, living frugally, walking proudly, and ready at any moment to play over again the guerilla game of the Peninsular war, and to teach the invaders that the spirit of old Gothic Spain is "not dead, but sleepeth," and as dangerous when aroused as at any former period of her history.

Foremost in the Spanish Court stood the silver-gilt tabernacle from Madrid, a gorgeous specimen of ecclesiastical plate, showing the direction in which Peninsular art received its greatest stimulus. The world-famous blades of Toledo also held a conspicuous place in the proud display of their vaunted armoury. There were several specimens of the black lace of the country, in robes and veils, with which Byron was so enchanted, when worn "by an Andalusian girl going to mass," and some gold and silver stuffs used in the sacerdotal costumes of her innumerable priests. In the more substantial manufactures there were specimens of coarse woollen cloth, but not so many nor so good as one might have expected in a country where the most voluminous of cloaks is an almost universal article of costume. But we believe the fact to be that the best Spanish cloaks are made of French or English cloths; indeed we know that in our own woollen districts there are particular descriptions made expressly for the Spanish and Italian markets. The priests of both countries affect a certain tinge of "blue black" in their ordinary costume, and our English manufacturers, with an expansive liberality that does them infinite credit, contrive to hit their reverences' taste to a shade. The only specimens of metal work in addition to the arms which came from Spain, were a few ornamental iron bedsteads, which were certainly very creditable specimens of Spanish workmanship, and might have taken their place beside some of the best articles of the kind made in this country. Another class of Spanish artificial productions that remains to be noticed was the inlaid cabinet work, of which the *piece de resistance* was the octagonal table sent by Perez of Barcelona. As a monument of patient industry it was certainly wonderful, containing, as we are told, three million of pieces, worked up into a design of which the most prominent feature was the shield with the arms of England in the centre. The general effect hardly justified the labour bestowed in the construction, the decoration being so minute as to require a powerful magnifying glass to show off its beauties. There were some other specimens of furniture, but they do not require any special notice. The centre of the court was devoted to a large case containing specimens of the minerals and cereals of Spain, in both of which that country is superlatively rich, and in describing which we can hardly do better than quote M. Ramon de la Sagra, whose "*Notes sur les Produits Espagnols*," enter very fully into the subject. The writer commences by complaining that " Les échantillons envoyés par les diffferentes contrées de l'Espagne et ses colonies à l'exposition de Londres, ne peuvent donner qu'une faible idée de ses richesses naturelles," and affirms that, with the exception of some choice mineral specimens, the articles exhibited were insignificant and ill chosen. He instances the wonderful quicksilver mines of Almaden, of which the specimen sent over " semble plutôt faite pour la boîte d'un élève, que pour donner une idée approximative de ses merveilleuses galeries." The writer also complains that the exhibitors wanted variety in their specimens, and that they gave more importance to metallic minerals than to combustibles, in which the mineral wealth of Spain is most prominently developed. M. Ramon, in his classification, first calls attention to the vast beds of coal, which he states are to be found in the Asturias and various other parts of the kingdom, and gives tables of the expense at which the article can be delivered at Santander and other places on the coast. But it is to be regretted that his calculations are made in Spanish weights and Spanish money, and would, therefore, hardly be capable of comparison by the general English reader. He hopes for a glorious future for this trade when the railroads of Alar and Santander, and of Madrid and Valladolid, shall be opened to public traffic. Sulphur, he states, abounds in Murcia and in Salamanca; and that the recently-introduced article of commerce, asphalte, has been discovered in large quantities in the province of Loria, and is now worked by a company. Of the salts to be found in Spain, M. Ramon gives a long catalogue, and proceeds to the metals, in which he very properly gives the first place to iron, the most useful. Leon, he says, abounds with this metal of first necessity, where also is to be found kaolin, that indispensable ingredient in ceramic manufactures. Abundant mines exist also in Alava and Guipuscoa, and specimens of their produce were to be seen in the gallery of the Crystal Palace, in the shape of two pieces of cannon manufactured by the Carlists, in the village of Onate, in the year 1837. The riches of Spain in lead are, according to our author, really surprising, there being hardly a province in which it may not be found in abundance. Copper, zinc, and tin, antimony, nickel, and cobalt, are also among the mineral treasures of Spain; and, lastly, gold, which is beginning to be sought for in the beds of various rivers.

CHAPTER XXI.

INDUSTRY AIDED BY SCIENCE—ARTIFICIAL LIGHT—PHOTOGRAPHY—DAGUERREOTYPES—CELES-
TIAL OBJECTS—THE MOON—FALLS OF NIAGARA—APPLICATION TO METEOROLOGICAL SCIENCE
—ROYAL OBSERVATORY—COLOURED DAGUERREOTYPES.

WHEN, according to the ancient Greek fable, Prometheus drew down fire from heaven to inspire with the breath of life the image he had formed, the writer of that myth little imagined to what purposes the application of light from the all-vivifying rays of the sun would, in future ages, be employed in the world of science and of art—purposes which impart a vivifying principle and activity to operations which the utmost labour and ingenuity of man could in no other way accomplish. For the following remarks, which we have selected from some papers which appeared in one of our leading journals, we are indebted to the learned pen of the philosophic Dr. Lardner, and which we shall forthwith, without further apology, submit to the consideration of our readers.

And, first, with respect to artificial light.—Marvellous are the uses, says the learned Doctor, to which science has rendered heat subservient; those which have been obtained from light by the combination of the researches of the mechanical philosopher have not been less striking. Ready-made flame is fabricated in vast establishments, on an enormous scale, and transmitted in subterranean pipes through the streets and into the buildings and dwelling-houses, where, after the close of the natural day, an artificial day is thus created, guiding us in the pursuit of business or of pleasure, and adding to the sum of life by rendering hours pleasant and useful, which must, in the absence of artificial light, have been lost in torpor, or in sleep. It is supplied according to individual wants, in measured quantity, and at every door an automaton is stationed, by which a faithful register is kept of the quantity delivered from hour to hour. Flame, which is in most cases the source of artificial light, is gas rendered white hot. The gas, such as is prepared for the purposes of illumination, contains, in the latent state, the heat which, in the process of combustion, renders it incandescent. The moment combustion commences, the gas entering into combination with the oxygen, which is one of the constituents of the atmosphere, the heat which was till then latent becomes sensible, and affecting the gas itself while combining with the oxygen, renders it *white-hot*. Lamps in which artificial light is produced by means of a liquid combustible, may be reduced to two classes: one in which the liquid is drawn to the wick by capillary attraction, and the other in which it is propelled by mechanic agency. It is evident that in the former the distance of the reservoir from the wick must be more limited than in the latter.   Hence we find that the mechanical lamps, known as Carcels and Modera-tors, are more elegant in their form than those which, depending on capillary action, have oil vessels of greater or less magnitude immediately under the flame, and which therefore cannot be sinumbral.   Of the capillary lamps, in which oil or fatty liquids are burnt, the most simple is that called the solar lamp; but by far the most brilliant in its illuminating power is one of recent introduction, called the camphine-lamp.

Of the mechanical lamps exhibited, especially in the foreign department, the most efficient and the most elegant in its form was the Carcel lamp.   The more scientific expedients for the production of artificial light depend, in general, on imparting such an intense heat to a solid body as to render it vividly incandescent, without, however, liquefying it or causing its combustion.   The expedient of this class which is best known is the oxy-hydrogen light, by which the microscope and lanterns for dissolving views, exhibited in the Polytechnic Institution, are illuminated, and which were found in various improved forms in the Exhibition.   We refer more particularly to an apparatus improved by the Reverend Mr. Beechy, and exhibited by Messrs. Abraham and Co., Liverpool.

The apparatus for the production of the electric light, which is still more intense than the oxy-hydrogen light, and produced under conditions which present greater probability of being ultimately adapted to economical uses, were exhibited in different forms by Messrs. Deleuil and Co., and by Messrs. Duboscq, of Paris.   This light is of the most intense splendour,—so much so, that it cannot be looked at without protecting the eye with coloured glasses.   The colour and quality of the light is similar to that of the sun, as is proved by the fact, that when it is analysed by the prism it gives the same component parts.   It is only just here to state, that the merit of the first application of the electric light to the microscope, and to the general application of optical phe-nomena, is due to M. Leon Foucault, who has lately obtained a world-wide celebrity by his beautiful experimental test of the rotation of the earth.

PHOTOGRAPHY.

It resulted, from scientific researches on the properties of solar light, that certain metallic preparations were affected in a peculiar manner by being exposed to various degrees of light and shade. This hint was not lost. An individual, whose name has since become memorable, M. Daguerre, thought that as engraving consisted of nothing but the repre-sentation of objects by means of incisions on a metallic plate, corresponding to the lights and shadows of the objects represented, and as these same lights and shades were shown, by the discoveries of science, to produce on metals specific effects, in the exact proportion of their intensities, there could be no reason why the objects to be represented should not be made to *engrave themselves* on plates properly prepared! Hence arose the beautiful art now become so universally useful, and called after its inventor, *Daguerreotype.*

The object of which it is desired to produce a representation, is placed before an optical instrument, with which every one is familiar as the camera-obscura.   An exact representation of it, on a scale reduced in any required proportion, is thus formed upon a plate of ground-glass, so that it may be viewed by the operator, who can thus adjust the instrument in such a manner as to obtain an exact picture of it.   If it be desired to make a portrait, the effect of the posture of the sitter can thus be seen, and the most favourable position ascertained before the process is commenced.

When the light is favourable, four or five seconds are sufficient to produce the desired effect by the processes which have been hitherto generally adopted.   According as it is less intense, the necessary time may be greater but should never exceed a minute.   One of the defects of Daguerreotype, as applied to portraiture, arises from the impossibility of bringing the entire person of the sitter at once into focus. To render this possible, it would be necessary that every part of the person should be at precisely the same distance from the lens of the camera, a condition which obviously cannot be fulfilled. It happens, consequently, that those parts which are nearest to the lens, as may be particularly remarked with respect to the hands, will be represented on a scale a little greater than those which are most distant; and if the instrument be adjusted so as to bring the nearer into very exact focus, the more distant will be proportionably out of focus. These defects cannot be removed, but they may be so much mitigated as to be imperceptible. By using larger lenses the camera can be placed at a considerable distance from the sitter, without inconveniently diminishing the size of the picture. By this expedient the difference between the distances of different points of the sitter from the lens will bear so small a proportion to the whole distance, that the amount of distortion arising from the cause just mentioned may be rendered almost imperceptible. Large lenses, however, when good in quality, are expensive, and it is only the more extensively-employed practitioners in this business that can afford to employ them.

The discovery of this beautiful application of the chemical properties of light is of very recent date. Efforts to fix illuminated images by means of the chemical agency of light, were made by Wedgwood and Davy as early as 1802, but without success, no preparation being discovered sufficiently sensitive to be affected by the subdued light of the camera. Sir H. Davy obtained a faint impression of the illuminated image produced in a solar microscope; but being unacquainted with any method of suspending the further action of light on the picture, no permanently perfect effect resulted, and the subject was laid aside. In the fourteen years which elapsed between 1814 and 1828, the labours of M. Daguerre and M. Niepce were directed to the solution of the problem. In 1827, a memoir was presented by the latter to the Royal Society, accompanied by several specimens of *heliographs,—sun-drawn* pictures. These, which are still extant, show that M. Niepce was acquainted with a method of forming pictures, by which the lights and shadows are represented as in nature; and when so formed, of rendering the picture proof against the further effects of light. M. Niepce, however, having concealed his processes, describing only the results, the society could not, according to its rules, admit his memoir into the Transactions. The surfaces upon which he produced his pictures were those of glass, copper plated with silver, and well polished tin. Those upon which M. Daguerre produced his first pictures, were paper impregnated with nitrate of silver. About six months before the disclosure of the processes of Daguerre and Niepce, Mr. Fox Talbot read before the Royal Society a memoir, in which he explained his photographic researches, and showed the manner in which he produced upon paper, rendered sensitive by chemical preparation, photographic pictures.

The vast number of beautiful sun-drawn pictures, on various sorts of surfaces, which were presented in the Exhibition, demonstrate how great and how rapid has been the progress of the art from the date of its invention. These results are invariably denominated either from the name of their inventor or discoverer, as daguerreotype and talbotype, or from the chemical principle by which the surface destined to receive the picture is rendered sensitive to light, as cyanotype, chrysotype, chromotype. Pictures produced by the photographic processes are of two kinds: first, positive pictures, in which the lights and shadows correspond with those of the object represented; and second, negative pictures, in which the lights and shadows are reversed; the lights being represented by shadows, and the shadows by lights. In the talbotype process, as it is sometimes called, the picture produced in the camera is usually negative. This picture being laid upon another paper, coated with chloride of silver, and then exposed in sunshine, a positive picture, corresponding exactly with the negative one, is obtained. Mr. Samuel Butler, of Peterborough, obtained a council medal for a beautiful series of photographic pictures obtained by this process, called photographic printing. The pictures represented scenes in and near Peterborough and Bury St. Edmunds. The application of glass to photography has lately occupied many experimentalists, and more especially Sir J. Herschel. The surface of the glass is *albumenised* by a coating of a solution of the iodine of potassium and the white of egg. This having been carefully dried, is washed with a solution of the gallo nitrate of silver, previously to being placed in the camera, by which it is rendered highly sensitive to light. Messrs. Ross and Thompson obtained a council medal for this improvement. Among the numerous uses to which this invention is applicable, examples were presented in the Exhibition of its power in delineating, with incontestable accuracy, the lineaments of celestial objects. Thus, photographic images of the sun and moon were exhibited; also images of the solar spectrum, produced by a prism on surfaces prepared with iodide and bromo-iodide of silver. The application of this process to produce permanent pictures of astronomical phenomena, so transitory in their appearance as to render any direct and accurate observation of them difficult or impracticable, such, for example, as certain appearances in the solar eclipses, would be highly advantageous. Among the most interesting objects presented, were daguerreotypes of the clouds, taken in boisterous weather, forming an instructive study, not only for the meteorologist, but the artist. In photography, the American department was peculiarly rich; and it is but just to state, that many important improvements in the details of photographic processes have been supplied by the skill and unwearied experimental research of our transatlantic cousins. Mr. J. Whipple, of Boston, exhibited several remarkable daguerreotypes, among which one of the moon was especially remarkable. In this picture, taken by means of a large equatoreal, the lineaments of the lunar surface were very beautifully displayed. Mr. Bond, another American, exhibited at one of the late meetings of the association, several daguerreotypes of the moon, taken with the twenty-three feet equatoreal of the Cambridge University (United States) Observatory. Mr. Bond, however, stated, that although very steady, the instrument was not sufficiently so to give pictures with very high powers. Sir David Brewster stated, that if daguerreotypes of similar magnitude had been taken on transparent sheets of gelatine paper, and so placed before a telescope as to subtend an angle of half a degree, they would assume the same appearance as the moon itself. Mr. J. H. Whitehurst, of Baltimore, exhibited some beautiful daguerreotypes of the Falls of Niagara. The cloud of white spray which rises from the base of the fall, and the white sheets of foam on the water, contrasted with the trees and the surrounding scenery, produced a remarkable effect. It is generally imagined that the motion of the water and of the spray would render a distinct picture by daguerreotype impracticable. In practice, however, this is not found to be attended with any injurious effect upon the result.

One of the most striking, and we may add, unlooked for uses of the photographic art, is its application to the constructing of a self-registering apparatus for meteorological phenomena, an invention of Mr. Charles Brooke, of London, who has been most deservedly rewarded for it by the council medal. It is known to all who take an interest in physical science, that the most important laws which prevail in atmospherical and terrestrial phenomena, are intimately related to the horary and diurnal variations of the barometer, thermometer, hygrometer, the declination-needle, dipping-needle, and, in fine, to the changes which continually affect all those delicate and sensitive instruments, which the skill and genius of scientific men have contrived, to indicate the succession of meteorological phenomena manifested around us. To obtain a perfect record of the indications of these several instruments, it would be necessary that an observer should be stationed at each of them continually, night and day, in all seasons, to note down their changes, which are continual, and sometimes sudden, such as cannot be foreseen or anticipated. These changes, moreover, are in some cases so rapid and fleeting, as to be incapable of exact estimation or measurement, even by the most vigilant and practised observers. The object of the invention of Mr. Brooke is, to make the phenomena keep a constant and unerring *record of themselves* in photographic writing. Without attempting a detailed description of this very beautiful automatic apparatus, which, besides, could not be made intelligible without several complicated drawings, the general principle by which its indications are made, may be briefly and clearly explained. A pencil of light brought to a focus by spherical or cylindrical lenses, or reflectors, is so governed, that its point or focus has motion identical with, or bearing a known proportion to, the motion of part of the instrument which affords the indications to be registered. Thus, if the instrument be a magnetic needle, the axis of the lens or speculum is made to coincide with, or make a known and constant angle with the needle, and therefore, to participate in its movements. The focus of the pencil, refracted or reflected, receives a corresponding motion. If it be a column of mercury, as in the case of a barometer or thermometer, the direction of the pencil of light is varied, either by means of a float, which rises and falls with the mercurial column, or by transmitting the light through the tube, so as to produce the shadow of the column, in which case the movement of the shadow will be registered. The focus of the luminous pencil is made to fall upon a sheet of photographic paper; and if both it and the paper were stationary, a spot would be produced upon the paper at the place where the focus falls upon it. If, owing to the variation of the instrument, whose indications are to be recorded, the focus of the luminous paper moves, a line will be traced on the photographic paper, the length of which will bear a known relation to the variation of the instrument. Thus, if it be a magnetic needle, a variation of one degree east or west in its direction, may impart a motion of an inch right or left to the focus of the luminous pencil, and a line of corresponding length would be traced upon the photographic paper. But by this means nothing would be recorded, except the extreme variation of the needle, in a given time. An observer would still be necessary, and nothing would be accomplished more than is already attained by the self-registering thermometers, which show the maximum and minimum temperatures indicated during a given interval. The apparatus is, however, rendered perfect by rolling the photographic paper on a cylinder, which is moved by clock-work, so that a known length of the paper moves under the focus of the luminous pencil in a given time. When the focus of the pencil is stationary, a straight line is traced on the paper, in a direction at right angles to the motion of the paper, and therefore parallel to the axis of the cylinder; but when the focus moves, as usually happens, to the right and left alternately, an undulating curve is traced upon the paper, the distances of the points of which, from a known base line (also traced upon the paper,) show not only the particular minute and second at which each change took place, but the actual state of the instrument at that moment. In this way, the heights of the barometer and thermometer, the variations of the declination and dipping needles, the directions of the wind-vane, and, in fine, the indications of all other meteorological instruments, are faithfully and continually registered from minute to minute, and from hour to hour, by night and by day, in summer and winter, and in all positions which it may be necessary to give the instrument of observation, whether on the summits of lofty towers or mountains, in the caves of the observatory, or in the workings of mines, hundreds or thousands of feet above or below the common surface, in the absence, and independent of any other care or interference on the part of an observer save that which is necessary from time to time to supply this ever-wakeful and ever-active scribe with a fresh supply of paper. An apparatus, constructed in this manner, has been adopted for registering the meteorological indications of the instruments at the Royal Observatory at Greenwich, with the greatest advantage. Since its introduction, the staff of observers has been reduced in number, and the fatiguing process of nocturnal observation has been altogether superseded. Specimens of the registers obtained by this apparatus were exhibited in the Crystal Palace, including a lithographic fac-simile of one day's work of all the instruments.

There is no question connected with photography which the public regards with so much interest, as that which refers to the possibility or probability of producing sun-drawn pictures of objects in their natural colours. The fact which has been established, from a variety of experiments, that the rays by which photographic pictures are produced, are rays of *dark light*, and are distinct from colorific rays, are certainly unfavourable, *primâ facie*, to this expectation. Nevertheless, it is certain that within the last two years Sir John Herschel succeeded in drawing a coloured picture of the prismatic spectrum; and, in a recent letter addressed by him to Professor Hunt, he affirms that he had specimens of coloured pictures of the spectrum, in light colours upon a dark ground; and adds, at present he is not prepared to say that this will prove an available process for coloured photographs, *though it brings the hope nearer*. Professor Hunt himself says, that he has obtained beautiful coloured pictures of the spectrum upon daguerreotype iodidated tablets, on which the colours had peculiar softness and brilliancy. M. Edmund Bequerel is stated to have obtained, recently, bright impressions in colours. Mr. Hill, of New York, affirms that he has obtained more than fifty pictures from nature, in all the tints of natural colouration. The process by which this is said to have been effected is not disclosed, but is said to be a modification of daguerreotype, one material, however, altogether new, having been introduced. It is said that the process will be made public so soon as the manipulatory details have been perfected.

Although our limits exclude us from entering into the details of some other wondrous facts, which the untiring researches of scientific men have disclosed in this department of physics, we must not omit to mention that M. Moser, of Konigsberg, has shown that light constantly emanates from all bodies, even *in complete darkness*, and that when placed near each other, they receive upon their surfaces reciprocally *pictures* of each other. These photographic pictures, however, are invisible, and continue to be so until they are developed by the application of certain vapours, such as that of water, mercury, iodine, &c. These marvellous discoveries of M. Moser have been fully confirmed by other more recent enquirers. Attempts have been recently made, with more or less success, to remove the metallic or *leaden* hue, which has been found disagreeable in daguerreotype portraits. This is effected by colouring them, by means of dry colours rubbed into the incisions made by the action of the light. These coloured daguerreotypes, though more open to objection on artistical grounds, are, nevertheless, decidedly popular, when judiciously executed. Artists, and especially miniature painters, are naturally opposed to daguerreotypes. The *artist* can soften down defects, and present the sitter under the most favourable aspect. The *sun*, however, is no flatterer, and gives the lineaments as they exist, with the most inexorable fidelity, and the most cruel precision. Nevertheless, it is known that some of the most eminent portrait-painters, those whose productions have raised them above petty feelings, do avail themselves of the aid of daguerreotypes, where well-executed representations of that kind are attainable, and they see in this no more degradation of their art, than a sculptor finds in using a *cast* of the subject which his chisel is about to reproduce.

CHAPTER XXII.

ORNAMENTAL SILVER—ITS EXTRAORDINARY PROFUSION—FRENCH AND ENGLISH ARTISTS—
VARIETY OF SPECIMENS DESCRIBED—VINDICATION OF ENGLISH TASTE, ETC. ETC.

FAR down in the depths of Laxey Glen, in the Isle of Man, and overshadowed by the mountain of Snaefell, are some of the most valuable lead mines in the United Kingdom. Here, amid the green glory of nature, and with the solitude and stillness engendered by the constant contemplation of mountain scenery, clinging around them like a second nature, men work in bringing the ore from the bowels of the dark earth. This lead ore contains a large per centage of silver, which is extracted from the baser metal by a peculiar process, and specimens of which silver were to be found in the Exhibition. Other masses of silver ore, from Ireland, Cornwall, and countries far over sea, were also shown. A large proportion of the silver of commerce is obtained from the ores of other metals, and from these therefore proceeded the rich display of plate which was to be seen in various parts of the Exhibition.

The brilliant array of wrought, chiselled, and embossed silver-work collected throughout the principal compartments of the Great Exhibition, seemed to indicate that this noble art has been shorn of none of its pristine lustre, since the days when kings and princes, popes and cardinals, were sole patrons of the handicraftsman. Precisely three centuries have elapsed since the art of chiselling silver was at its zenith. On looking round and seeing the prodigious number and beauty of the works exhibited, one almost fancied that the many hammers which beat in such unison at the command of Cellini in the " Petit Nesle," had never ceased to resound on the banks of the Seine. England, on her side, strove with the wondrous aid of science to keep up the illusion, particularly by the dazzling brightness with which she invests the precious metals. In both England and France were found tacit acknowledgments of the eminent fitness of the Renaissance style of workmanship over all others, especially the classical, which is just at present under a complete ban. If we inquire further into the possible cause from which has arisen the present taste for all that appertains to the sixteenth century, we find that, as has ever been the case, the minor arts are influenced by the prevalent taste in architecture; as it is a fundamental principle of ornamentation that the component parts which serve to adorn any structure, even its furniture, should necessarily partake somewhat of its character. To Mr. Chenavard, patronised by the late Duke of Orleans, and an able architect, the French ascribe the honour of driving them out of the classical slough in which Gallic art was so long imbedded. The British silversmith, on the contrary, has seldom allowed himself to be influenced by the fluctuations of fashion, but has steadily, perhaps too steadily, adhered to time-honoured traditions and old sculptural forms. We fancy we recognise the hand of Flaxman even to this day, with its pure but somewhat quaker-like conceptions. One cannot be too thankful that the animal and vegetable kingdom should have been the only source of inspiration; or it is difficult to conceive all the vagaries and waste of metal which the straight lines of our perpendicular architecture and its Flamboyant traceries might have led us to. But if timidity has hitherto been the besetting sin, there is at present rather an opposite tendency, which is evinced in the somewhat audacious rejection of all wholesome rule. Silver is expanded over large surfaces, and made to branch in large chandeliers which would have made the old artificers stare at the lavish expenditure of the precious metal. We believe it is no exaggeration to say that the compartment of Messrs. Hunt and Roskell, late Storr and Mortimer, alone contained no less than three tons' weight of silver.

It was almost a relief to turn from the precious stones, whose intrinsic value escapes mental evaluation, to the more tangible merits of human workmanship. Contrasted with the bright and finished groups in silver, two works, executed by A. Vechte, in mingled iron and silver, stood out prominently by their subdued tones. The first was a shield, which, though unfinished, promised to be a most exquisite piece of embossed workmanship. It represented Shakspere, Milton, and Newton, surrounded by their embodied conceptions. The style of the figures was a singular medley of Raphael and Buonarroti's designs; that is, rather calling to mind the conceptions of the great Italians than closely adhering to them. The same might be said of the " Vase of Etruscan form," also executed by the same artist, and representing Jupiter hurling thunder at the Titanic host. The anatomy was worked out in a manner which would bear extension on the largest scale. Vases, salvers, and centre ornaments, presentation cups, &c., filled up the remaining portion. Messrs. R. and S. Garrard shone in bellicose groups, executed mainly in entire relief by the able designer, Mr. Cotterill, who identified himself with bull fights, boar hunts, and hunting meetings. Ever full of spirit, his groups were sometimes marred by a want of finesse in detail-work. Mr. Cotterill was too much at the mercy of the polisher; we need only point at the otherwise pleasant performance of the rider entrapping the wild horse by the lasso. A perforated chandelier attracted as much notice by its size and polish as the " Brassey testimonial" by its massive effect. In the assembled company of engineers whose portraits were here gracefully collected together, we fancied we saw the heroes of speed, which had its tardy counterpart in the progresses of Elizabeth, who was evidently a favourite with the silversmith. There were two effigies of her; the first had been somewhat modernized by B. Marochetti, for Mrs. Hancock, who had other meritorious productions on view. The next, of somewhat exorbitant dimensions for silver, had been worked under the direction of Mr. Morel, from the great seal of the time. The way in which the minutiæ of dress had been worked showed how far embossed work may go. Those who were curious in technical peculiarities might notice with satisfaction that there was no trace of subsequent soldering, her majesty being daintily fitted, as beseemed her precious person, on the barb or state horse. Her weight was considerably above a thousand ounces. Mr. Morel also exhibited a centre-piece of Children Playing with a Panther, which displayed all the fancy of Poussin in the juvenile attendants of Bacchus. The frosted imitation of the flesh texture was novel and pleasing. Caps of agate and lapis-lazuli of unusual dimensions, and convivial weapons, showed combined taste and art. As defenders of the powers of electro-metallurgy, Messrs. Elkington and Mason, of course, reigned supreme. It is well known that in the ordinary methods of electro-plating it is usual to construct a plated article as far as possible from plated sheet metal, while the edges and ornamental parts are completed by soldering thereto parts either stamped in plated metal or in silver. By this method of manufacture the design must necessarily be limited, being confined to such ornamental forms as could be produced by stamping or otherwise fashioning sheets of metal. The pernicious process of gilding by an amalgam of mercury and gold is superseded by the voltaic reduction of gold; and the voltaic precipitation is effected with far greater economy than the mercurial process. Messrs. Elkington and Co., though their patent has received wide extension by the grant of licences even to French firms, maintained their supremacy, and sorely puzzled their imitators by the great brilliancy of their gold and silver work. But it may be doubted whether the merits of the voltaic precipitation of metals are not more conspicuous in the larger scope afforded in its application to sculpture. In this respect it is to be regretted that fitter models than the lively Cupids of Fiamingo or the dull effigies lately applied to the houses of parliament, were not selected to inaugurate the processes of electro-bronzing. In the

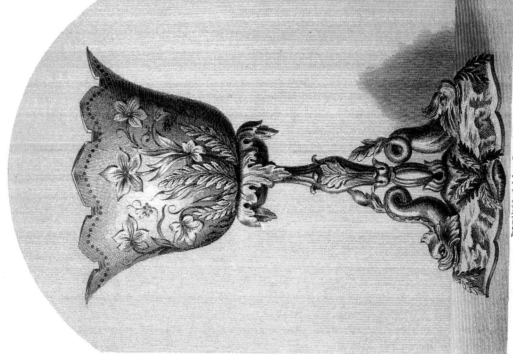

SILVER ICE DISH

BY DODD.

Engraved by G Greatbach, from a Drawing by H Mason

FLOWER VASE

BY JOHANN GASSER VIENNA

Engraved by G Greatbach, from a Drawing by H Mason

nave was a horse's head executed life-size by electro-deposit; it was from the hand of Marochetti, and interesting by the variation of its tone. It has always been an acknowledged fact in electro-metallurgy that the cost of the reduction of iron far more than counterbalanced the original cheapness of the raw material: whether this was the case in the instance we have cited we had no means of ascertaining. The East Indians, who laid bare the gorgeous splendours of the kingdom of Oude, displayed in the inlaid gold of their tents, crowns, and horse trappings, all that barbaric splendour which charms the eye by the natural and choice harmony with which colours are blended, regardless alike of the inroads of science on one hand, or calculations of novelty on the other. The sceptre and the fly-flap, as well as other accessories which filled their tent, showed that a spirit somewhat akin to that of the ancient Assyrians, is still abroad among these Indians. The transition from these vestiges of primitive splendour to the nicer discrimination of the present day is rather an abrupt one, but the same may be said of every stride taken in the Great Palace.

It is singular to find our neighbours, the French, doing their utmost to extinguish the brightness of the metals which the English handicraftsman does his utmost to preserve. It is well known that not only a certain dulness of tone is the natural consequence of the continual hammering and oiling of the silver necessary to bring it to a completion; but, not content with this, it has been the fashion, for the last year or two, of oxidising most part of the silver-work, which thereby acquires prematurely the sober and dusky veil which time has cast over all the brilliant sleights of hand bequeathed to us by the artists of the sixteenth century. Greater durability and a more permanent defence against the inroads of time, are also said to be secured by the present process. The system adopted consists in plunging the groups into acids, whence they emerge with their present sombre hue. Mr. Durand's " *Théière à grande réception*" was the greatest compliment ever yet paid to England's favourite beverage. It consisted of seventeen pieces, which combined chiselling, gilding, niello, and even oxidising. Though Diane de Poitiers had made way for an allegorical figure of Charity and her Children, the whole work smacked of the gusto prevalent in the reign of Francois I., in the imitation of the Florentine architecture and its incrustation of small figures. The whole design, and its adaptation to its purpose, was exceedingly ingenious, and was, we believe, originally designed by Klagman. The Louis XV. style, which the French now designate as " *rocaille*," was splendidly represented. Mr. Durand exhibited a table-ornament of assembled cupids, with decorations in this style, which showed how far a skilful hand can reconcile one to the wildest vagaries of fancy. The firm of Rudolphi made oxidising their specialty, and seemed bent on proving that the process is equally well adapted for the largest or minutest proportions. They exhibited a circular table, or " *gueridon*," ornamented with cupids and slender leaves at the base, the top part consisting of an inverted shield, with the embossed head of Medusa. There was also a salver with one of those nymphs Jean Goujon has made us familiar with. M. Odiot made the purpose of his ornamental work at once plain by chiselling fish, flesh, or fruit, with perfect freedom. decking his richly worked specimens.

Messrs. Smith and Nicholson exhibited a centre-piece representing a group of Arab merchants halting beneath the spreading leaves of one of those noble palm-trees, which affords them protection from the rays of their burning sun, and re-invigorates them by its refreshing shade. They were equipped in the usual travelling costume of Arabia, and were supposed to be in the midst of an oasis in the desert, watered by a solitary spring. The singular mode of life pursued by these nomadic tribes is forced upon them by the very nature of the country in which their lot is cast, and which necessarily imparts to the character and countenance an apparent solemnity not inconsistent with the perils they so frequently encounter in crossing vast scenes of sandy desolation. The camel, the "ship of the desert," as he is poetically termed, was looking round upon his rider as if desirous he should dismount, so that he should be free to pick the herbage and enjoy the repose which the situation affords. As a whole the performance was full of character, and the disposition of the group was as picturesque as its execution was chaste and expressive.

The next subject we have to notice was of a very different kind. It was so essentially English that it was impossible to mistake the costume for that of any other country. It was an exquisite performance, coming home to the heart in all its fulness, and awakening associations with which every English reader is acquainted. It was an embodiment of the humour of Addison in the scene of Sir Roger de Coverley with the Gypsies. The good old knight was in the attitude of hearing his fortune told through the dubious light of palmistry, whilst the dark-eyed daughter of the East was wiling her way into his heart, and breaking down every barrier of prejudice that might arise to prevent the natural generosity of Sir Roger from displaying itself in a sum sufficient to reward her cabalistic knowledge. The spirit of the scene enabled us to fancy even her gradually experiencing emotions of kindness towards the knight, whom everybody esteemed, and for whom the inmates of his household felt the tenderest regard. The figure in the background, leaning upon the horse, was intended to represent Addison himself, who was evidently taking that brief interest in the scene which enabled him to realize it in a future Spectator. Messrs. Angell, of the Strand, were the exhibitors of this fine centre-piece. On the left foreground stood a sideboard bottle in the antique style, ornamented with Gothic oak leaves. This idea was suggested by the skins used in Spain for carrying wine down the mountains. The height of the object was twenty-four inches, and it was capable of containing eleven quarts. It was silver gilt, and made entirely out of one piece of metal. On the right we had a handsome claret jug, of a richly chased wine pattern. It was exhibited by Messrs. Lambert and Rawlings. We next noticed a magnificent ewer or race cup, from the establishment of Messrs. Garrard, of the Haymarket. It represented a group of Sioux Indians hunting the bison in one of the North American prairies. This was a work which deserved something more than a passing notice. Its original was run for at the Doncaster races, and the present was manufactured expressly for the Exhibition. In originality of conception, spirit of design, and elaborateness of finish, we think it will bear comparison with any production of the same class submitted for examination. The kindled rage of the infuriated bison, tossing his head as if to gore the horse and bring his foe to the ground, was striking and life-like, and, artistically speaking, formed an exquisite base to the column of the uplifted horse; whose position carried the eye freely to the top of the ewer. The strained attitude of the steed, too, was excellent, and the precision which was intended to be conveyed in directing the lance of the rider, was exemplified in the position he maintained as he seemed to rivet himself to his seat. On the other side was another Indian in the act of discharging an arrow.

Messrs. Gass, of Regent-street, exhibited a brilliant collection of elaborate workmanship, among which was a dessert service of an entirely novel character, consisting of four pieces, each representing different species of aquatic plants, modelled from water-plants growing in Kew Gardens, the leaves forming dishes. One of the pieces represented the beautiful and graceful *nymphæa thermalis*, or Hungarian water-lily, in flower, springing from rock-work, on which were several rock plants. The second was the rich *nymphæ rubrea*, or red water-lily of the East Indies. The third was modelled after the *calladium*, and the fourth after the *dillirea speciosa*. Mr. Emmanuel, of Hanover-square, exhibited a splendid silver *pendule*, surmounted by a figure of Apollo driving the chariot of the

THE HOURS CLOCK

Engraved by G Greatbach from a Drawing by T H Wilson.

DESIGNED BY JOHN BELL. — MANUFACTURED BY MESSRS ELKINGTON.

SILVER GROUP — SIR ROGER DE COVERLEY AND THE GYPSIES.

Engraved by G Greatbach from a Drawing by T H Wilson.

BY J ANGELL

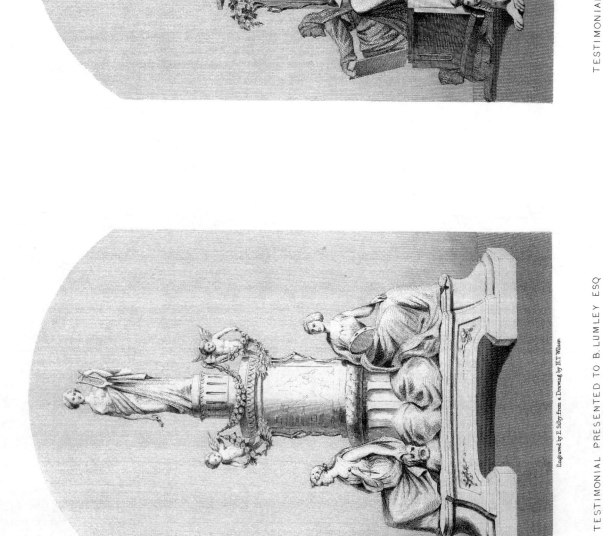

TESTIMONIAL PRESENTED TO SIR M. MONTEFIORE.

Engraved by E. Silby from a Drawing by H T Wilson.

TESTIMONIAL PRESENTED TO B. LUMLEY ESQ

Engraved by E. Silby from a Drawing by H T Wilson.

MANUFACTURED BY HUNT & ROSKILL

Sun, drawn by four horses, and supported by the Four Seasons. In the frieze were represented the Four Winds, and in the front of the dial the figure of Time recumbent; the whole designed and modelled by Woodington. Messrs. Hunt and Roskell, as we have before observed, made a grand and magnificent show. Their collection was worthy a palace, and was a source of great attraction in the central south gallery, where works in gold and silver of enormous value were deposited. There was placed the testimonial in silver, designed by Sir George Hayter, and modelled under the direction of Mr. E. H. Baily, R.A., presented a short time since to Sir Moses Montefiore, by members of the Jewish persuasion, as a mark of respect for his exertions on behalf of the persecuted Jews of Damascus. The group consisted of sphinxes—indicative of the captivity of Israel in Egypt—with a figure of Moses supporting the tables of the law, and of Ezra reading a scroll, upon which was inscribed the 22nd verse of the 8th chapter of his book. There were also two Jews of Damascus, one loaded with chains, and the other released, overshadowed by the vine and the fig-tree. The group on the summit was a representation of David rescuing the lamb from the jaws of the lion. In the *bassi rilievi* were pourtrayed,—the Israelites crossing the Red Sea, and the destruction of Pharaoh's host, the landing of Sir Moses and Lady Montefiore at Alexandria; Sir Moses obtaining the firman from the Sultan; the persecuted Jews of Damascus returning thanks for their deliverance; and the thanksgiving in the synagogue by Sir Moses on his return. Under the latter was inscribed the 124th Psalm. This firm has long been celebrated for the production of exquisite works of art known as race-plate; and in their stand was exhibited the Emperor of Russia's Ascot prize for the year 1847. It was an elaborately-chased vase, representing in the base and upper part, " Peter the Great receiving the swords of the Swedish generals after the battle of Pultowa, and an event which occurred shortly previous to his death :—Being near Cronstadt, he saw a boat full of men and officers upset by the violence of the waves. He ordered instant assistance, which being ineffectual, he then seized a small boat, waded through the surf, and succeeded in rescuing the sufferers, though it brought on the disease which terminated his life a week afterwards." On the base were relievi of the palaces of Peterhoff and Smolenski.

Notwithstanding the inroads which the electro-metallurgic art has made upon the old-established manufacture of plating, this method has, nevertheless, partizans, who insist on its special advantages over the new process. Mr. John Gray, of Billiter-square, exhibited a series of articles illustrative of the old method of plating, commencing with the ingot and terminating in the finished article. The ingot, as used in the old manufacture, is composed of copper alloyed with other metal, so as to impart to it the necessary toughness and rigidity. The plate of silver is tied upon its polished surface with wire, and the combined metals are then heated in a furnace. When the temperature is raised to a certain point, their union takes place, and the ingot is then submitted to the processes of manufacture. An ingot of copper previous to this process, with the plate of silver tied upon it with wire, was shown by this gentleman. The next articles in the series were ingots of copper and white metal, after the silver plate has been united to them by an elevation of temperature only, and without the intervention of solder or any other substance. The next article was the sheet of plated metal, which is obtained by submitting the plated ingot to the rolling process. A table dish, made from the rolled metal, was the next in the series, with the silver mountings laid upon it, but not yet soldered. The steel dyes in which the silver mountings are struck, together with the mountings produced by them, were also exhibited; in fine, the table dish was exhibited in its finished state, as well as a specimen of a salver produced by the manufacturer as above described.

Among the productions of " *La Belle France,*" we must not omit to notice those of

Froment, of Meurice, which, taken altogether, formed one of the most attractive features in the Exhibition. His gorgeous silver centre-piece, representing the Four Seasons, obtained, as it well deserved, the great medal. Numerous other evidences of his taste, skill, and high perception of art, were to be seen in the case appropriated to his works. An agate cup, of extraordinary beauty of form and skilful workmanship, we particularly admired, the frame and stand being gold and silver, gracefully twisted in the form of a vine.

Although in these and other exquisite productions of our continental neighbours, we fully appreciate their excellent invention and taste, still it must be allowed that British workers in precious metals have laboured successfully to place themselves in dignified contrast with their foreign rivals; and to vindicate themselves from the vulgar charge that they lack the taste necessary for the perfection of objects in precious metals designed for use. Our British exhibitors in plate, one hundred and twenty-eight in number, represented very fairly the manufacturing excellence of England in this department of industry; and their specimens, apart from their excellence as manufactures, included not a few curious and attractive objects. The collective value of this section it was hardly possible to estimate, but it must have been enormous. There were some fine specimens of chasing, which, before we conclude our present chapter, we shall endeavour to describe. The most conspicuous among them was a figure of "Death on the Pale Horse," after the well-known design by West. The silver on this figure was stated to be no more than $\frac{1}{34}$nd part of an inch in thickness. This specimen was contributed by Mr. T. Woodbridge, of Holloway. Messrs. Elkington and Mason exhibited a splendid display of electro-plated candelabra, tazzas, vases, table ware, &c.; and in the collection of Messrs. Martin, Basket, and Martin, of Cheltenham, we noticed a handsome model of a Great Western steam-engine, and a highly wrought inkstand, called the Milton inkstand. Bracelets, guards, chatelaines, tea and coffee services, flower-stands, &c., were to be seen in almost endless variety A fine vase in silver, after a marble antique, in the Capitoline Museum, was exhibited by Messrs. Payne and Sons, of Bath; and amid the brilliant collection were found a silver tea-pot, coffee-pot, and tea-kettle, weighing together only 140 grains. As a curious subject for chasing, Messrs. Connell's cup, carved with designs from scenes at Donnybrook Fair, may be remarked; and the registered brooches, from the mineral products of Ireland, were interesting specimens of dawning industry. Effective specimens of industrial skill and taste were exhibited in some finely-chased silver mountings for a highland dress, richly studded with carbuncles, and exhibited by an Edinburgh firm. Passing by brilliant specimens of electro-plated articles, exhibited by Messrs. Wilkinson and Co., of Birmingham, and others, and plate in all its varieties—forks, spoons, fish-knives, candlesticks, Etruscan jugs, taper-stands, &c., we came to a solid silver table-top, 55 inches in diameter, weighing nearly 900 ounces, and manufactured for the Governor of Aleppo, by Mr. Collis, of Birmingham. Passing from this gorgeous and costly specimen of the silver-smith's skill, the next object which claimed particular notice, was an epergne and sculptured silver candelabra, weighing about 750 ounces, and designed by V. Nicholson. This fine specimen of British taste and skill was the production of a Sheffield firm, Messrs. Dixon and Sons. Passing on, rapidly surveying the bright collections of tea-urns, tureens, claret jugs, communion plate, candlesticks, coolers, plated articles with silver mountings, venison dishes, rams' heads mounted as cigar cases, snuff boxes, &c., dirks, purses, ornaments of highland regiments, imitations of or-molu, we came to a fine embossed and chased salver representing Aurora, or the Hours, after Guido, surrounded with a border after the Tredacna shell. This brought us to a gorgeously mounted meerschaum pipe, exhibited by the celebrated Inderwick, of Leicester-square. Not far from this luxurious tobacco bowl, sentimental young ladies in dense clusters might have been found admiring ingenious patterns, worked in hair by Mr. Cleal, of Poland-street, Oxford-street, while not far distant, thoughtful people of a "certain age," examined with painful attention, Mr. Mortimer's mechanism for rectifying irregularities in the growth of teeth. This class included also some ingenious specimens of imitation Cameos; but the admirers of brilliants clustered eagerly about Mr. Hope's casket, containing a blue diamond, weighing 177 grains, mounted as a medallion, surrounded by brilliants, "and supposed, from its size and colour, to be unique."

The dessert service, exhibited by Messrs. Gass, of Regent-street, we have already noticed. This firm also exhibited a dazzling silvered jewelled dessert service, in the Elizabethan style, and a bracelet, set with brilliants and carbuncles, and including portraits of the Queen and the Prince of Wales, after Thornburn, executed in niello, and engraved by J. J. Crew; also a silver gauntlet niello bracelet, designed by Maclise. In oxidised silver the English exhibited some fine specimens—among these the statuettes of Phillips, Brothers, of Cockspur-street, were particularly noticed. The progress of a lump of metal through its various stages till it is perfected in the shape of a bracelet, was illustrated by Messrs. Wheeler, of Bartlett's-buildings, Holborn. Rambling on in the vicinity of cases of gorgeous works in the precious metals, we came to a curious gold watch, invented by S. Boreham, to beat seconds and to strike at the minute. This watch attracted considerable attention, and was certainly a curiosity as a specimen of minute clock-work. Other attractions led us in various directions, and it would be impossible to carry a notice of the glittering display to any length. First, we were attracted by a fine drawing-room clock, designed by C. Grant, with subjects by G. Abbott. This composition was inclosed in an electrotyped case, and stood upon a base and pedestal of turquoise blue glass. Then we paused to notice a child's mug, upon which Wilkie's "Blind Man's Buff" was finely chased. Next our attention was attracted by the royal arms of England since the Conquest, engraved upon various metals. Then came the splendid cups, caskets, tazzas, centre-pieces, candelabras, vases, etc., exhibited by Messrs. Hunt and Roskell; then a tea-tray, illustrative of the purposes of the Exhibition, finely engraved by Donalds; then, in melancholy mood, we paused over the last work of Wagner, of Paris, a silver rose-water dish, exhibited by Mr. Forrest, of the Strand; then we endeavoured to picture to ourselves the delight of Staunton before the gorgeous chessmen, exhibited by Eady, of Clerkenwell; and then we could not but notice the candelabrum, given as a testimonial to Mr. Macready. Designs in every variety appeared to be here assembled, from the rigid Elizabethan style to the familiar and homely illustrations of Donnybrook fair. Here was a chased shield, representing the battle of Alexander and Darius; further on a salver, illustrating the labours of Hercules. Messrs. Armitage and Horsley's "Spirit of Religion," had been adapted to the dimensions of a silver tablet for a Bible binding; while the national pride had been fed with the Shakspere Cup, already described, chased with subjects from Lear, Julius Cæsar, Othello, the Tempest, Macbeth, and Hamlet. *Ohe jam satis !* we imagine our readers will be tempted to exclaim. We shall, therefore, conclude our remarks on the present subject, and commence a fresh chapter.

CHAPTER XXIII.

LETTERS OF M. JOHN LEMOINNE—LETTER I.—FOREIGN IMPRESSIONS—BRITISH AMENITY—
VAST BUSTLE—OMNIBUSES—SUNDAY VISIT—FINE CLIMATE OF ENGLAND—INVALIDS—HER
MAJESTY—VARIETY OF NATIONS.

WE shall now pause awhile in our own retrospective survey of the glories and the
wonders of the Fairy Palace, and present our readers with the *naïve* remarks of a lively
and talented French writer on the all-engrossing topic of the World's Fair, which evince
in a remarkable manner, the admirable spirit of kindliness and good feeling that has
already resulted from the amicable admixture of all nations in a cause devoted entirely
to peace, order, good-will, and mutual benefit and improvement; a cause of which the
effects will, we doubt not, continue to extend themselves to the extremest points of
social civilization.

LETTER I.

London, June, 1851.

If I remember rightly, it is Jean Jacques Rousseau who affirmed that he would
rather be accounted a man of paradoxes than a man of prejudices; I hold the contrary
opinion.   There are amateurs of paradoxes, who come to London *not* to go and see the
Exhibition.   I was so prejudiced as to go there on my arrival, and was still more
prejudiced, in common with many others, by being overwhelmed with admiration at the
marvellous spectacle.   This sentiment is universal.   I hear it on all sides, and in all
languages.   There is no spirit so critical or sceptical as not to bend before this vast
display.   Independently of the difficulties opposed to the mere execution of the enterprise, there was a certain feeling of hesitation in the public mind as to its result.   The
effect of its opening was regarded with a certain misgiving, and the first month produced a degree of disappointment among the Londoners.   The hotels were scarcely fuller
than usual.   The lodging houses exhibited their melancholy bills, and the innumerable
preparations made to receive the whole world, seemed as though they had been made in
vain.   So much had been said in anticipation of the millions about to pour into the
great metropolis from the first day, that vast numbers were alarmed rather than attracted,
and paused to hear the result of the opening before venturing to come.   It had been
imagined throughout Europe, that it would be impossible to move in the streets; that
persons would be compelled to sleep in the open air,—not a very agreeable anticipation,
considering the opinion generally entertained of the climate and atmosphere.   It soon
appeared, however, that these were exaggerations.   By degrees our fears were removed,
and when it was discovered that everything went on in the most quiet and regular
manner possible, the visitors commenced their journey; and now, from the shores of the
most distant seas, numberless caravans come to plant their tents around this great mart
of the universe.   It is like the movement of an ocean, one wave following another.
The tide has been slow, because its point of departure was distant; but once in motion,
it will not cease.   This pacific invasion of all nations has changed the aspect of London.
In this immense city, which has no barriers, still less fortifications, and which is an
aggregation of small towns and villages which have grown into one another, and have at
length coalesced, and formed the great metropolis, the presence of foreigners is, in
general, rarely observable.   At present, however, one's ears never cease to be struck with
all dialects, known and unknown.   From the Chinese, true and false, to the serfs of

Russia, all races are represented, and are walking about in all costumes, to say nothing of the beards and moustaches, which here in England are still a foreign garbment.

The English have on this occasion abandoned their usual habits. In very truth, I think they are becoming social and familiar. They have always been polite and hospitable to those who bring proper introductions to them, but now one actually meets some who enter into conversation without such preliminary condition. Decidedly, British manners are altered. This exceptional conduct arises, however, from an excellent sentiment,—the English are now offering hospitality to the whole world, and they pique themselves on receiving it graciously. They are desirous, too, that the highest idea should be formed of their national grandeur, and they question you with evident solicitude on the impression produced by the inspection of the Exhibition. This impression, it must be admitted, is very grand. You feel it even before you reach the Crystal Palace. As on a journey you recognise the approach to a great city by the perpetually increasing number of persons you encounter on the road, so in the movement which is accelerated and increased on the road to the Exhibition, you recognise the approach to a great centre of attraction. I here notice only the simple impressions of the spectator or the tourist, but I can easily conceive the effect which the sight of Piccadilly, Hyde Park, and that great road which leads to the Crystal Palace, must produce on strangers. It is an inconceivable bustle, which defies all description. The uninitiated traveller is absolutely bewildered. The passing and repassing of horses and carriages seem like the crossing of several trains on a railway. It is indeed a *mêlée*, which, when seen for the first time, leads one to fear that the result will be collision, and a general upset. We are quite surprised to see nothing overthrown, nothing broken, and that all these carriages make their way out from one another, as if they were of gutta percha. The multiplication of omnibuses, especially, seems fabulous. They may be counted by hundreds in a quarter of an hour. The best method of seeing in this country, and at the same time the most democratic, is to mount the top of an omnibus. From thence you have a view of the whole route, and this astonishing palace of glass may be seen long before reaching it.

Nothing can be more striking than the first view of the transept. Facing you is a large tree, which has been placed, as it were, under a bell, like a plant. Advancing, you make the tour of this immense dome, amidst verdure and flowers, the murmur of waters, and encounter at the other extremity two other large trees, likewise enclosed in this prodigious glass case. Imagine, now, 50,000 men, women, and children, walking about in this vast green-house, without the least tumult or disorder. On the days on which the price of admission is one shilling, about 70,000 persons sometimes visit it. There are two days on which the price is higher; on Friday half-a-crown is paid, and on Saturday five shillings. Saturday is the fashionable day, and as the palace is not closed until seven o'clock, Albion may be seen from four to six in all the *éclat* of her beauty. The shilling days are not less curious. These are the days for country people, who arrive in their rustic dresses, with their wives, their children, and provisions. The railways bring them to London at reduced fares, and at the station they take large waggons, which bring them to the Exhibition. Caravans full of them are thus encountered in the streets. Whole parishes sometimes come, headed by their clergymen. The colonels of regiments send their soldiers, and the admirals their sailors. Not less worthy of observation are the hundreds of charity children, in their blue dress with yellow stockings, that are frequently met, marching in rank and file. About two or three o'clock every one eats, and takes his luncheon. There are several buffets, where there are all kinds of fearful pastry, and horrible creams that would be ices. The prices are fixed by the committee, and marked up. No wine, beer, or spirits are allowed, but of course there is tea.   There are, besides, interspersed in the palace, several fountains of filtered water, ornamented with small drinking cups, at the disposal of the promenaders. Saturday morning, until twelve o'clock, is reserved for the infirm and the invalids, who are drawn in small carriages, and of these there are a great number.

I have seen the Exhibition also under an aspect which is not void of picturesque,— I have seen it on a Sunday.   I should have thought this undertaking impracticable, for here the earth is not permitted to turn on its axis on Sundays, whatever Foucault may think proper to assert.   I did, however, succeed in entering, thanks to patronage which I will not betray.   Silence reigned around; the very clocks were still; I believe there was but one going.   The statues, enveloped in wrappers, resembled ghosts, and the most precious articles were also covered up.   I was particularly struck at the sight of a policeman, quietly occupied with his Prayer-book, whom our desecration of the Sabbath must have somewhat scandalised.   Sixty years were required for building St. Peter's, at Rome.   The new Houses of Parliament, at London, were commenced fifteen years ago, and are not yet finished.   The Palace of the Exhibition was begun and finished in three months.   Will it live like the roses, only for a season?   This is the question of the moment.   For poetic imaginations, there would be a certain charm in the destruction of this magical work, which would only, as it were, have appeared on the stage as a passing scene.   Cleopatra, indeed, caused the most costly pearl in the world to be dissolved in a cup, and gratified herself by drinking a million at a draught. Why may not a great nation indulge in caprices such as that of Cleopatra?

One of the greatest and rarest curiosities that England presents at this moment to foreigners, who come to see the Exhibition, is decidedly the sun.   I am not speaking of the famous *Mountain of Light*, but the veritable sun in the sky, which diffuses light and heat.   For some days London has had a factitious air of Naples.   Piccadilly and Regent-street are as scorching as Santa Lucia and the Chiaja.   There is, however, this difference, that in Italy the streets are deserted during the whole day, and that here the movement of the population is never for one moment suspended.   Some tourists, who have come with the idea that the sun is never to be seen in London, and that people walk about with torches in mid-day, feel actual disappointment in being able to dis- tinguish the dome of St. Paul's.   Some there are, indeed, who wish to falsify the proverb, " *Solem quis dicere falsum*," and who are quite ready to believe that the English have invented some process to warm their climate for this particular occasion.   And why not? These Englishmen are so vain, and they have invented so many machines!   You may easily imagine that, in such weather, the Crystal Palace somewhat resembles a hot-house. One spends one's time in looking for seats as near as possible to the fountains and basons of filtered water, and in eating those eternal creams, which are something like iced pomatum.

It is more in vogue than ever to go on Saturday morning.   I have before said that the forenoons of Saturday are reserved for invalids, who are admitted in their wheeled chairs, in which they are drawn about.   There are many real invalids, but there are also some false ones, who, so soon as they have obtained admission, like Sixtus Quintus, get rid of their crutches, a circumstance which gives the Crystal Palace a certain likeness to the Court of Miracles.   On Saturdays, one meets regularly her Majesty and suite, and then the organs play spontaneously, " God save the Queen."   In this country, all instruments play this air; in the same way as everything is called " Waterloo,"—the streets, the bridges, the omnibuses, the paletots, the boots.   Not to be behindhand with the public in politeness, let us leave the queen peaceably to her promenade, and let us continue ours.   It is a mere promenade of curiosity, only a little tortuous, that I ask permission to make.   If we would proceed regularly, it would be difficult.   We should

SILVER VASE.

MEURICE PARIS

Engraved by G Greatbach from a Daguerreotype.

THE TRIUMPH OF THE ARTS AND SCIENCES.

BY ELKINGTON.

Engraved by G Greatbach from a Daguerreotype.

lose ourselves. The police office is every day encumbered with objects that have been lost, from umbrellas to children. Yesterday, the policemen collected, along with sticks and parasols, half-a-dozen little girls, who had arrived by a " pleasure train." Happily, they were ticketed and numbered as bales of goods, and were marked from " Bristol." After having received lunch, they were taken back to the sheep-fold.

England, as you are aware, reserved half the Crystal Palace for the exhibition of its own products—all the left-hand, on entering by the principal door. This is comprised under the name of the United Kingdom. Nothing can better represent " *penitus toto divisos orbe Britannos.*" With England, Scotland, and Ireland, there are India, Jersey, Guernsey, the Ionian Islands, Africa, Malta, Canada, Nova Scotia, New Zealand, the Bermudas, the Bahamas, Trinidad, Ceylon. The United States of America no longer belong to the mother country. They walk alone, having attained their majority : they are at the extremity of the other nave. On the right side are all the nations who have flocked together to this great rendezvous. France is placed amidst Turkey, Egypt, Italy, Spain, Portugal, China, Switzerland, and the Brazils. To the name of France has been added that of Algiers, a sign that they do not endeavour, as heretofore, to contest our conquest, and that they now regard it as a " *fait accompli.*" The middle of the great nave is occupied by objects of art, disposed with much skill and effect. On the first *coup-d'œil* of this avenue, which is one-third of a mile in length, one may form a philosophic idea of the genius of the different nations who figure at the Exhibition. Thus, while the foreign nave is filled with *objects of art*, properly speaking, the English is principally occupied by *objects of utility*. As I cannot write a catalogue, I pass over the statues and the organs. The capital work of sculpture in this gallery is the *Amazon*, by Kiss, of Berlin. It is an Amazon, who strikes with her javelin a tiger, which has fastened on the neck of her horse, and is a masterly performance. Something less severe, but more pleasing, is the *Greek Slave*, by an American sculptor. It is not, perhaps, an *ideal* type, but is a copy of an admirable figure. The young slave is placed in a niche, in velvet, on a turning joint, and must be a little giddy by the end of the day.

After indulging, contrary to her custom, in a work of art, America exhibits another work, which characterizes her much better. It is an enormous supply of articles in *caouchouc!* It is difficult to conceive anything more ugly, but possibly it is useful. I presume the United States were desirous, by this frightful edifice of india-rubber, to symbolize themselves, and typify the development to which they are destined. Beside this are two of those poor Indians (*Iowas,*) whom we formerly saw at Paris, and with whom I remembered to have breakfasted. I still remember their air of profound sorrow, which betrayed their nostalgia, and the delight which they exhibited when in a large garden. There is something cruel and ostentatious in the exhibition of these two poor red-skins. It is nothing but a trophy. They are the slaves chained to the car of the conqueror ; they are the shadow of the old races that the victorious and implacable civilization of the West crushes in its progress. The American exhibition is crowned, at the extremity of the nave, by an immense organ, the pipes of which are ornamented in such a manner, that they resemble great penny trumpets or gigantic sugar-sticks. From American to English art the transition is easy. Both are of the same character, generally prosaic. I should except a very graceful group in marble, representing Venus and Cupid, by Davies; but the rest of the objects which fill the English nave are composed, in general, of works in which the useful is more prominent than the agreeable. We now have before us a trophy, not in caouchouc, but in silk. It is the exhibition of home-made manufactures, at least so called ; but wherever you find very beautiful silks, they probably are from Lyons. After this you see another trophy, in Canadian timber, surmounted by a skiff then another in Sheffield cutlery, consisting of pen-

2 Q

knives with five or six hundred blades, two hundred and fifty pair of scissors of every kind, one of the triumphs of England.   Then enormous glasses; then light-houses and improved telescopes; then a trophy in furs, exhibited by the Hudson's Bay Company; then models of every kind.

After this excursion in the nave of the Crystal Palace, let us go, if you please, to see the adoration of the relics. On the right, and nearly at the entrance of the foreign nave, you observe a crowd, curious and eager, flocking about a great parrot-cage with gilded bars.   Within that is placed on a cushion the *Koh-i-Noor*.   This diamond supplies, in the history of Central Asia, the place of the golden fleece, and has occasioned more than one bloody war.   It ultimately came into the hands of Runjeet Singh, and when, after his death, England annexed his kingdom to its Indian possessions, the "Mountain of Light" was sent to London.   It is now, if not the most curious, at least the most attractive article in the Exhibition.   It weighs 186 carats.   As to its value, it is necessarily nominal; it may be worth two millions, or nothing.   To ordinary eyes it is nothing more than an egg-shaped lump of glass.   They may show us what they please, and call it Koh-i-Noor.   On ordinary days, that is, the shilling days, it is exposed in its great cage, ornamented with a policeman, and they rely on the sun to cause it to sparkle; but on the Friday and Saturday it puts on its best dress; it is arrayed in a tent of red cloth, and the interior is supplied with a dozen little jets of gas, which throw their light on the god of the temple.   Unhappily, the Koh-i-Noor does not sparkle even then.   Thus the most curious thing is not the divinity, but the worshippers.   I have seen a pretty considerable number of relics adored, from the *Bambino* in wood of the *Ara cœli* at Rome, to the blood of St. Januarius at Naples.   The adoration of the *Mountain of Light* is quite of the same character.   One places one's-self in the file to go in at one side of the niche, looks at the golden calf protected by the impassable policeman, and goes out on the other side.   If the organs should chance to play at the same moment, the illusion is complete.   There is another thing, also, which has the same effect.   It is a fountain of Eau de Cologne of Maria Farina.   This is also guarded by a policeman, who takes quietly your handkerchief, passes it across the *jet d'eau*, and returns it perfumed.   The Koh-i-Noor is well secured; it is placed on a machine which causes it, on the slightest touch, to enter an iron box.   It is thus put to bed every evening, and does not get up till towards noon.   The procession of the faithful then commences, and only finishes at seven o'clock.

We shall here, for the present, take leave of our lively and intelligent correspondent, with the intention, however, of renewing our acquaintance with him at a fitting opportunity.

CHAPTER XXIV.

THE POTTER'S ART—STAFFORDSHIRE POTTERIES—SEVRES PORCELAIN—DRESDEN PORCELAIN—
MEISSEN PORCELAIN—VIENNA PORCELAIN—ENGLISH PORCELAIN—STATUARY PORCELAIN—
VARIOUS SPECIMENS OF STATUARY PORCELAIN—ORNAMENTAL PORCELAIN—NEW USES OF
PORCELAIN.

WE shall again, in this chapter, occasionally avail ourselves of the assistance of our learned friend, Dr. Lardner, and present our readers with the substance of a portion of his lucubrations respecting "THE POTTER'S ART," as connected with the Great Exhibition.

No department of the great museum of industrial products presented to the attention of the intelligent visitor, attraction stronger and more peculiar than that which was devoted to the ceramic manufactures, including porcelain in all its varieties, Oriental and European, earthenware, stoneware, flintware, faïence, delft, ironstoneware, terra-cotta, bricks, tiles, and in general every form of baked earth used in the arts and sciences. In no branch of the useful arts do the ultimate results differ so immeasurably from the original materials as in this. What can more powerfully excite our wonder and admiration at the value which labour and art can confer on the basest materials, than to reflect that the beautiful portraits in Sèvres porcelain of the Queen and Prince Albert, after Winterhalter, and the magnificent vases which were seen both in the British and foreign collections, are composed of nothing more than so many lumps of a whitish clay, and a collection of the rusts (oxides) of certain metals, all beyond this being the work of art? Another circumstance which conferred peculiar interest on this section of the Exhibition was the extraordinary rivalry which it developed among different countries, and the unequal conditions under which British industry entered into this competition. Seven imperial and royal establishments for the manufacture of porcelain, supported by state subsidies, and encouraged by state patronage, sent their choicest productions to be displayed beside those of the unpatronised, unsubsidised enterprise of Staffordshire and Worcestershire. Thus we had, in the French department, a magnificent collection of the finest pieces of porcelain from the National (late Royal) manufactory of Sèvres. A similar collection was sent from the celebrated Royal porcelain manufactory of Berlin, and the Imperial porcelain manufactory of Vienna also sent a rich collection of its productions. Besides these, the Royal manufactories of porcelain at Copenhagen and Nymphenburg, near Munich; and, in fine, the Imperial porcelain works of St. Petersburgh, severally unfurnished their museums, and transferred their richest treasures to the Crystal Palace.

The fabrication of ornamental porcelain in these several national establishments is conducted irrespectively of commercial profit. If any expedient for the improvement of the art be proposed to the British manufacturer, he must necessarily consider the probable cost of trying it, and the probable loss in case of its failure. These considerations are, however, disregarded in establishments supported by the state, and every expedient for the improvement of the art, presenting the slightest probability of a successful result, is tried. All that is most eminent in science, in each of the countries above-mentioned, is brought to bear upon the improvement of the ceramic art. Besides pecuniary emolument, personal honours and rewards are lavished on all who contribute to its advancement. Thus, we find at the head of each of these establishments, as well as at the head of each of their departments respectively, individuals who have attained the greatest eminence in those sciences which are more immediately connected with this branch of manufacture, and personal honours and distinctions, such as orders of knighthood, decorations, crosses, &c., lavished upon them as a farther stimulus to exertion. The antiquity of the ceramic art renders it an object of special interest. Everybody is familiar with the allusions to the potter's wheel in the Old Testament, and indications of the prevalence of the manufacture at an early epoch in the history of the human race are abundantly confirmed by the annals of Oriental nations, and by the material evidence of vases of baked earth which have been found in ancient tombs, and which are preserved in the national collections.

Among the objects exhibited in the Chinese department was included a complete collection of the various materials employed at the great porcelain works of Kiang Tiht'Chin, as it was named in the catalogue; otherwise, according to better authorities, King Te Tching. This collection consisted of specimens of the plastic clay of which the

Chinese porcelain is formed, and of the various colouring matters with which it is decorated. The place from which these specimens were sent is the seat of a very ancient manufactory of porcelain. Father Entrecolles, a French missionary, resided there in the beginning of the last century, and he states in his letters, that there were in operation at this place, in 1712, not less than 3,000 ovens, which gave the town, during the night, the aspect of a vast furnace with a multitude of chimneys. It is impossible, in reading his description, not to be reminded of the appearance of certain parts of Staffordshire at night. Ancient pottery, in his time, was in great demand in China, and extremely dear. Many vessels of great antiquity were obtained from tombs and other ruins. Vases were said to have been discovered of the times of the Emperors Yao and Chun, who flourished above two thousand years before the Christian era. In the ancient tombs at Thebes also several vases of Chinese origin were found, which, by their inscriptions, appeared to have been fabricated eighteen centuries before Christ. The fine porcelain, however, was not known before the year 900, A.D. In Europe the first collection of fine porcelain was imported in the year 1518, by the Portuguese, and for 200 years after that period Europe derived its entire supply of that article of luxury from China. About the middle of the seventeenth century, a small factory for the manufacture of pottery was established at Burslem, in Staffordshire, which, in the year 1690, owed considerable improvements to the Messrs. Elers, who had immigrated there from Holland, and to their exertions may be ascribed the origin of the celebrated Staffordshire Potteries, now an absolute hive of industry, employing 70,000 operatives. It is there we find the splendid establishments of Messrs. Copeland, Minton, Wedgwood, Alcock, Pratt, and others, whose productions enriched the gallery of the northern transept of the Exhibition. Among amateurs in porcelain there prevails a notion, that the art of fabricating the tender porcelain of Sèvres has been lost, and that, since it is impossible to reproduce the articles, they must necessarily have a high value in the market. This is, however, erroneous. All the materials and processes for the fabrication of this description of artificial porcelain are preserved at Sèvres, and the manufacture can be re-established whenever it is desirous to do so. Indeed, we are informed at this moment that the administration entertains an intention of recommencing the fabrication of this description of porcelain for articles of ornament, such as vases, pictures, &c., the imperfections incidental to it not affecting such objects. All the Sèvres porcelain sent to the Exhibition was of the kind called *hard*, that being the only description fabricated for the last fifty years. The portraits of the Queen and Prince Albert, in the great aisle of the Crystal Palace, are fine specimens of the largest porcelain painting which has been produced at Sèvres. These portraits, after Winterhalter, were executed by command of Louis Philippe, and presented to the Queen. They were commenced before the revolution of February, but not finished till afterwards. Louis Philippe claimed them as his private property, and they were surrendered to him by the Republican Government; but the portrait of Prince Albert had met with an accident by which it was broken. Louis Philippe desired to have another made, but the Queen would not hear of this expense being incurred, and the fracture being repaired at Sèvres, the portraits were sent to England, and delivered to her Majesty. The portrait of her Majesty was by Ducluzeau, and that of Prince Albert by Bezanget.

Among the most splendid collection of paintings and vases exhibited by the National manufactory of Sèvres, the most valuable and most worthy of attention and examination, were the following :—The picture of the Virgin, known as the *Vierge au Voile*, by Madame Ducluzeau, copied after Raffaelle in the Louvre. The porcelain was of the same size as the original, and was valued at £1,000. Another, after Tintoretto, by Madame Ducluzeau, at £880. A flower subject, 40 inches high, by M. Jacober, £800. A large cup,

Victoria

Portrait of Her Majesty on Sevres China by A. Duduzeau.

Exhibited in the Great Exhibition by the French Government.

Engraved by D. Pound, from a Daguerreotype

Engraved by D Pound from a Daguerreotype

Albert

Portrait of H. R. H. Prince Albert on Sevres China by A. Ducluzeau.
Exhibited in the Great Exhibition by the French Government.

THE LONDON PRINTING AND PUBLISHING COMPANY

POKAL OR DRINKING CUP

ROYAL PORCELAIN MANUFACTORY AT DRESDEN

Engraved by G.Greatbach, from a Drawing by T.H.Wilson.

POKAL OR DRINKING CUP

ROYAL PORCELAIN MANUFACTORY AT MUNICH.

Engraved by G.Greatbach, from a Drawing by T.H.Wilson

Engraved by G.Greatbach. from a Daguerreotype

GROUP OF DRESDEN CHINA,

EXHIBITED IN THE SAXON DEPARTMENT

Engraved by G.Greatbach from a Daguerreotype

GROUP OF DRESDEN CHINA,

EXHIBITED IN THE SAXON DEPARTMENT.

GROUP OF SEVRES CHINA

IN THE FRENCH DEPARTMENT

VASES FROM THE SEVRES PORCELAIN WORKS, FRANCE.

45 inches diameter and 34 inches high, porcelain biscuit; the three principal figures upon the cup represented Industry in the fields and the workshop, and Education; the three corresponding medallions represented Ceres, Vulcan, and Minerva; around the foot of the cup were grouped three figures representing the Fates. Several vases of rich design and elaborate execution; a pair, in particular, with landscapes representing the Seasons, valued at £216. Various cups, also of splendid workmanship, after Benvenuto, Cellini, and others. The style of the Dresden porcelain is familiar to all amateurs, and, whatever difference of opinion may prevail as to its taste, there can be none as to the admirable excellence of its execution. All who have visited the collection at Dresden, will be familiar with the series of animals, represented on a scale approaching to the natural size, including bears, rhinoceroses, vultures, peacocks, &c., made for the grand staircase which conducts to the electoral library. These were fabricated as early as 1730. At a later period, when the manufacture had undergone improvements, large ornamental pieces of porcelain were made, such as the slabs of consoles and tables, some of which measure from 45 to 50 inches by 25, and are richly decorated with flowers.

Among the objects exhibited, the most conspicuous were two magnificent vases, one after a design by Semper, decorated with painted medallions and gilding, and another ornamented with painted figures and flowers after Watteau. The frame of a mirror, richly decorated with coloured flowers in relief and girandoles, was also much admired. The grotesque figures and groups of Dresden porcelain have always been admired for their execution, if not for their style. The costumes are especially admirable, and the representation of fine work, such as lace, truly wonderful. Some specimens of this were seen in the Exhibition. One of the grotesque pieces which obtained most celebrity, and was familiar to all amateurs, was the famous tailor of the Count de Bruhl, a figure whch was remarkable for the difficulty of its execution, owing to the numerous accessories it included. The figure of the tailor was represented riding on a goat surrounded with all the implements and appendages of his trade, and was about 20 inches in height. A beautiful specimen of flowers was also exhibited, consisting of a *camellia japonica*, with leaves and white flowers in porcelain, in a gilt pot, on a stand of white and gold porcelain. This article was priced at £90.

The Royal manufactory at Meissen exhibited two vases of light blue, with portraits of the Queen and Prince Albert, adorned with escutcheons filled with flowers and rich gilding; a girl playing on a guitar, with laces; a fluteplayer; an *étagere* with girandoles in flowers in relief; a picture of a lacemaker, after Slingeslandt, price 50 guineas; a picture of a Ganymede, after Thorwaldson; and statuary porcelain. Besides the ornamental porcelain exhibited by the Royal manufactory, two collections of painting on China after classical pictures, were exhibited by the well-known artists of Dresden, Bucker and Walther. The former exhibited eleven paintings, in gilt frames, from Corregio, Carlo Dolce, Titian, Murillo, Gessi, Guido, Raffaelle, &c.; also eighteen paintings of larger size, including specimens from Ruysdael, Claude Lorraine, &c. The latter also exhibited a variety of subjects.

The Imperial porcelain manufactory of Vienna was established in the year 1744. One of the foremen of Meissen, named Stobzel, had deserted from that establishment about the year 1718, and escaped to Vienna, where, aided by a Belgian, named Pasquier, and favoured by a privilege, or a sort of monopoly for twenty-five years, granted to him by the Emperor Charles VI., he established, in 1720, a small porcelain manufactory. Not, however, having sufficient capital to carry it on, it declined, and was finally purchased by the Empress Maria Theresa, in 1744, and erected into a Royal manufactory. It was, in like manner, by means of information brought by deserters and runaways from factory to factory, that the fabrication of porcelain came to be established successively

2 R

in the Royal manufactories of Louisberg, near Stuttgard, at Berlin, Copenhagen, Brunswick, and St. Petersburgh.

The first English porcelain was manufactured at Bow and Chelsea, the paste being composed of a mixture of sand from Alum Bay, in the Isle of Wight, with a plastic clay and powdered flint glass; this was covered with a leaden glaze. This manufactory had considerable success. In 1748, the manufactory was transferred to Derby; and in 1751, Dr. Wale established at Worcester a manufacture of tender porcelain, called the "Worcester Porcelain Company," which still exists, though in other hands. If the British manufacturer have not attained the high excellence in the ornamental department of the manufacture of porcelain, and cannot produce paintings after the great masters, enamelled on large slabs of porcelain, to rival those of Sèvres and Meissen, he has proved by the late Exhibition, that the day is not far distant when even those productions may be executed in Staffordshire, and that meanwhile, he has outstripped altogether, all rivals in the production of articles fitted for the common use, not only of the middle, but of the most affluent classes, at a price which sets all foreign competition at complete defiance. We must not omit, in recording these advances in ornamental pottery, to make honourable mention of the name of Josiah Wedgewood, who introduced into the Staffordshire potteries all the improvements of science, and the elegance of art, both with respect to form and material; and the effect of his exertions has been, that the wares of that district are not only brought into general use in England, to the exclusion of all foreign manufactures of the same kind, but English earthenware is sought for and celebrated all over the world, and nowhere more than in those places where foreign porcelain has been previously in use.

Many eminent foreigners have borne testimony of this, especially M. Faujas de St. Fond, who says:—"The excellent workmanship of English porcelain, its solidity, the advantage which it possesses of sustaining the action of fire, its fine glaze, impenetrable to acids, the beauty and convenience of its form, and the cheapness of its price, have given rise to a commerce so active and universal, that the traveller from Paris to St. Petersburgh, from Amsterdam to the farthest part of Sweden, or from Dunkirk to the extremity of the south of France, is served at every inn with English ware. Spain, Portugal, and Italy are supplied with it, and vessels are loaded with it for both the Indies, and the continent of America." One of the branches of the manufacture of porcelain, in which British industry and art has of late years had the start of the Continent, is statuary porcelain. This has been lately introduced by the Staffordshire manufacturers, and numerous specimens of it were seen in the Exhibition. The Duchess of Sutherland, to whose munificent patronage the local manufacture of Staffordshire is so greatly indebted, was one of the first to perceive the capabilities of this material, and to encourage its extension and use. Gibson, the sculptor, having his attention attracted to it by her Grace, admitted that it was the next best material to marble, and was desirous to see some of his own works reproduced in it. By permission of the Council of the Royal Academy, a reduced copy of his "Narcissus" was accordingly made at the manufactory of Alderman Copeland.

The process of producing this imitation of sculpture is extremely interesting. Since its first introduction it has undergone great changes and improvements; it is now composed of one homogeneous mass of statuary porcelain, whereas at first a thin superficial coating was laid over a coarser material, which produced a far inferior article than the present mode. The process, however, is much more difficult and liable to fracture, in consequence of the great contraction it undergoes in the oven. The linear contraction in the process of baking is about one-fourth; a figure four feet high, on coming out of the oven, being only three feet. The actual contraction of bulk corresponding to this linear contraction is more than one-half. When a figure or a group is to be cast, a considerable number of separate moulds are required, each separate part of the figure or group being separately and independently cast. Sometimes as many as fifty moulds are required for a single group. The cast taken from each of these moulds is first retouched, the seams produced by the junctions of the mould being cleaned off by scraping with a knife. The several parts are then united,—a difficult process, and requiring the most consummate dexterity in the operator. The parts are united by applying slips to the surfaces in contact, but the clay being in this state extremely tender and friable, the weight of the projecting parts would be more than the cement used in joining them is capable of resisting. After being well dried in the air, the figure is placed on "saggers," a name given to the props which are placed under every part, so that the whole is well and evenly sustained.

The difficulties attending this fabrication may be imagined by following the several stages through which the article passes before the baking is completed. Assuming the height of the object to be 24 inches, the shrinkage in leaving the mould, before exposure to heat, will be an inch and-a-half. After the several parts, which, as we have just stated, are moulded separately, and are separately subject to a like shrinkage, have been put together, and the seams produced by their junction cleaned off by the "figure-maker," the article is thoroughly dried in the air without exposure to heat. This process is necessary, because the quantity of moisture incorporated in this state is such that the expansion occasioned by exposure to an elevated temperature would produce fracture. In this process of air-drying, a further linear shrinkage of an inch and-a-half takes place; so that, before being placed in the oven, the linear dimensions, from 24 inches are reduced to 21. And, lastly, when it is "fired" in the bisque oven, it is contracted to 18 inches. In the entire process, therefore, it loses one-fourth of its linear dimensions, and consequently nearly one-half of its actual cubical bulk. The consummate skill, however, that is brought to bear upon this beautiful manufacture is such, that not the slightest defect of form or outline is to be discovered. Nothing, indeed, could be finer than many of the groups that were exhibited; such, for example, as the Ino and Bacchus, after Foley; or the Narcissus and Venus, after Gibson. Indeed the objects exhibited in this department were so numerous that it is difficult to specify such as were most worthy of notice. The figure of Sappho, three feet high, from the original marble of Theed, was entitled to attention, were it only for its extraordinary magnitude, a circumstance which greatly enhanced the difficulties and hazards of its execution. The original statue is the property of Prince Albert. The following were also worthy of examination:— The Indian Girl and the Nubian, by Cumberworth; the Prodigal's Return, and Rebecca, by Theed; a Venus by Gibson; a bust of Juno from the antique; a Goat-herd by Hyatt; Sabrina, by Marshall; Innocence, by Foley; and Narcissus, by Gibson; Godiva, by M'Bride, executed for the Art Union of Liverpool; an equestrian statuette of Emanuel Phillibert, Duke of Savoy, by the Baron Marochetti; her Royal Highness the Princess Alice as Spring, the Princess Royal as Summer, the Prince Alfred as Autumn, and the Prince of Wales as Winter, from the original models by Mrs. Thorneycroft, executed for her Majesty. It was impossible to contemplate this collection of imitation of statuary without being impressed with an idea of its utility in disseminating copies of the great works of ancient and modern art to an extent hitherto unknown, with a fidelity, too, as to colour and texture, unattainable by any other process.

The British department of the Exhibition was extremely rich in ornamental porcelain. A dessert service was exhibited by Messrs. Minton and Co., original in its design, and novel in its principal features of ornamentation. The combination of statuary porcelain, which is the hard species, with the coloured and gilded porcelain, which is the tender species was here attempted, and gilding on the statuary porcelain was also successfully accomplished. The turquoise ground on this service was scarcely inferior to that of the old Sèvres, and it is capable of resisting the strongest vegetable and most of the mineral acids. It consisted of 116 pieces, the most remarkable of which were two flower-stands with figures representing the Four Seasons, two wine coolers, with hunting groups, and two oval baskets, with oriental figures. Several of the pieces were supported by figures with fanciful designs, and the plates, 72 in number, were perforated and richly ornamented. This service was purchased by Her Majesty, to be presented, it was said, to the Emperor of Austria. Many articles in statuary porcelain were purchased by Her Majesty in the Exhibition. Among others were the equestrian figures of the Amazon, after Faichères, and Theseus, Flora, and Temperance, from bronzes in the collection of the Duchess of Sutherland, and Love restraining Wrath, an original group.

The Parnassus Vase was another striking example of the combination of statuary with painted porcelain, the *bas-relief* illustrating Apollo and the Muses. Several vases in the Copeland collection were very beautiful and of novel design, in coloured enamel, with imitation of pearls and gems, inlaid in gold. A large copy of the Warwick vase was also well worthy of attention. One remarkable feature in the collection of porcelain exhibited by British industry, was the various and unexpected uses to which it had been applied—uses which will doubtless be more and more extended and various, as the art progresses. An example of this was presented in a chimney-piece of statuary porcelain by Messrs. Minton, an extremely advantageous application of the material, not being liable to stains from smoke, or other causes, to which marble is subject. There were also porcelain panels, plateaux, and slabs for the covings of fire-places, tops of consoles, toilet and chess tables, panels of doors, and window shutters. We observed panels executed by order of Prince Albert for Osborne House; furniture panels and toilet table, with porcelain slab, and porcelain panels in the door and drawers, painted with wreaths of japonica on a rustic trellis, for the Duchess of Sutherland.

A large variety of slabs for wash-stands and tables of every description were exhibited, displaying the admirable qualities of this durable material, which is capable of any style of decoration, easily kept clean, and in no ways affected either by the action of soap or acids. In Pugin's mediæval court were exhibited specimens of porcelain tiles, slabs, and other objects illustrative of the variety of purposes to which this material may be applied, and the variety of ornamentation of which it is susceptible.

In the basement were exhibited by Minton and Co., two of the largest terra-cotta vases ever made in this country in plastic material; they were modelled by the Baron Marochetti. There were also two enormous garden pots in stoneware, with medallions in statuary porcelain, after the classic Thorwaldson, the first sculptor of his day, representing the Four Seasons, and the four stages of human life. These attracted great attention. Specimens of encaustic Venetian, and other ornamental tiles for flooring, were also exhibited. This branch of earthenware manufacture has recently acquired great importance; a large quantity is annually exported. The palace of the Sultan at Constantinople is paved with these porcelain tiles, as are also the House of Lords, Osborne House, and St. George's Hall, Liverpool; and they are getting into general use in churches, private houses, and conservatories, being equally durable as marble, less liable to stains, and capable of being decorated. The largest piece of pottery ever produced in a single piece, was a figure of Galatea, seven feet high. We understand that attempts are being made, and with likelihood of success, to execute it in statuary porcelain. Before we conclude our observations on the subject of "Pottery," we will take a glance at the estimated value of this branch of our manufactures, and see to what an extent the simple material of "clay" is rendered productive by the addition of human ingenuity and labour. At the potteries alone the value of the earthenware annually produced is about £1,700,000; and that of the manufactures of Worcester, Derby, and other parts of the country, about £750,000; making a total annual value of £2,450,000.

We shall now close our remarks on this beautiful and important branch of artistic manufacture, and in a fresh chapter, renew our acquaintance with our agreeable French correspondent.

CHAPTER XXV.

SECOND LETTER OF M. J. LEMOINNE: INCREASING TIDE OF VISITORS—ELECTRIC TELEGRAPH— THE TWO SOSIAS, OR THE TRUE AND THE FALSE KOH-I-NOOR—THE GREAT MASS OF COAL, THE REAL DIAMOND—ENGLISH JEWELLERY—FRENCH SILKS—SEVRES AND THE GOBELINS— RUSSIAN DISPLAY—THE ZOLLVEREIN—A HINT TO TAILORS. THIRD LETTER: FRENCH COM- PLACENCY—PARISIAN BELLES—ENGLISH MACHINERY—ENGLISH INDUSTRY AND FRENCH TASTE—FRENCH FREEDOM AND ENGLISH ORDER—AMERICA—PRODUCTIONS IN INDIA-RUBBER AND CAOUCHOUC—FASHIONS—CARRIAGES—GO A-HEAD—APOSTROPHE TO THE FAR WEST.

LET us continue our ramble among the curiosities of the Exhibition. We go to the Crystal Palace on a common day, Monday, for example, at ten o'clock, when you will see the arrivals of the country folk and the schools. Four-horse coaches, such as were used before the establishment of railways, carrying four inside and about twenty outside passengers, are again brought into requisition for this occasion. From these elevated vehicles descend multitudes of females in very gay toilettes. Being safely landed, they leisurely arrange their dresses, and readjust that prodigious development which betrays the use of "crinoline." It is much to be regretted that, in this instance, the efforts or art should not be better directed than in spoiling nature. After these arrive large waggons, with a series of seats, bringing the young folks from the boarding or charity schools. I could never have conceived that so many living beings could be packed into so small a space without being suffocated. Out they come, fifty at a time, and when you imagine the vehicle has delivered all its load, out pours a new batch; in sooth, this beats Robert Houdin.

But let us enter. One of the principal advantages of the Crystal Palace is the great number of avenues; there is no necessity of twice treading the same ground. If, by chance, you have left your carriage at one of the extremities, and you find yourself at another, don't be uneasy, you have at command a rapid and intelligent slave, more prompt than any footman. In passing along the galleries, you may have perceived several little boys twelve or fourteen years old. These are the keys which govern the wires of the electric telegraph. In a moment you may have your carriage called from one end of the building and sent to any entrance you may desire. The telegraph is, moreover, at your service for communication with all the principal railway stations, and thence with all the principal towns in the kingdom. From the Exhibition you may send any mes- sages you please to Dover, Bristol, Edinburgh—everywhere. The tariff is 1s. for twenty words, increasing, of course, in proportion to the distance. A despatch of twenty words sent to York or Edinburgh costs 8s. 6d. In addition to this, you may write your letters at the Exhibition, and in the transept you will find a branch post-office.

We will not now stop at the Koh-i-Noor, which is still offered to the worship of the faithful. A very good imitation of this jewel, in pure crystal, has just been made. The original and the imitation resemble each other as closely as two drops of the clearest

2 s

water. The two Sosias were not more like. It is said that the Koh-i-Noor is only half its original size, the other half being in its native country, where it has been found in the possession of an honest " proletaire," who made use of it as a flint to strike a light. This anecdote, which was related the other day at a meeting of *savans,* appears to me full of philosophy. I am no less interested by a drawing which represents coalheavers contemplating the huge block of coal which decorates one of the entrances to the Exhibition, and exclaiming, " This is the real diamond !" It is, in truth, the real diamond of England ; and, after all, it seems that the other itself is but a species of coal. Never mind, however, all the philosophy in the world will not prevent the diamond being the loadstone of the fair sex. Wherever the ladies obstruct the circulation, and crowd one on the other, you may be sure there are jewels exhibited. It is the hardest service of the poor policeman, who dares not behave rudely to the fairer half of the creation, and who, from time to time, exclaims, in a voice somewhat severe, sometimes in despondency, " Pass on, ladies—pass on." I have told you that wherever there were jewels you would be sure to find a policeman ; he is the body-guard of the diamonds and pearls. There is one stationed near the blue diamond, for there is a blue diamond, as there must be, somewhere, a white blackbird. This curiosity forms part of the collection of Mr. Hope, and has no marketable value, being unique. M. Bapst, of Paris, has also a phenomenon of this kind, the black diamond. Mr. Hope shows, also, as an amateur, the largest known pearl in the world, which is in shape like a small pear. In valuables of this kind the Indian exhibition is unrivalled. It contains the Durria-i-Noor, or Sea of Light, a large diamond, estimated at £320,000 ; a girdle of superb emeralds, and necklaces of two hundred fine pearls, surpassing all that have heretofore been seen in Europe ; a costume of an Indian prince, with two epaulettes in fine pearls ; thrones and palanquins in ivory ; saddles, mounted with diamonds, rubies, and emeralds ; and sandals ornamented with precious stones. There are also some *chefs-d'œuvre* of human industry, a collection of shawls, scarfs, and carpets of incomparable richness and beauty. Whole days may be spent in inspecting this division. It is a dangerous place for the rich—they may ruin themselves there. We should walk through it with the consciousness of an empty purse, and then there would be freedom from temptation. This East is still the country of the Arabian Nights, the region of Aladdin and the Wonderful Lamp.

The English jewellery is very beautiful, although it cannot, I think, be properly said to be English, since it is principally the production of foreign workmen. The great superiority in this division of English manufacture is found in the plate, and that description of ornaments which consists in silver vases and statuettes. These latter are, in England, peculiarly national. *Testimonials* are much in vogue here. They are given as racing and hunting cups, for speeches in parliament, the construction of a railway, or the building of a bridge. They are family furniture, the ornaments of the sideboard and the table ; they are a species of art and manufacture developed by the taste for horses, and the habit of horse exercise, hunting, and what is called *sport.* It is in works of taste that France excels, and in this category may be classed the silks and lace. The Lyons manufacturers have made a collective exhibition ; they have glass cases containing the choicest articles, and which are thus, of their kind, somewhat like the Tribune of Florence, or the " Salon Carre" in the Louvre, a collection of *chefs-d'œuvre.* This comparison is induced by the magnificence of the design and of the colours ; they are real pictures ; and there are some silks in imitation of Chinese, which may be compared to beautiful landscapes. But here are Sevres and the Gobelins ! Here we are incontestably masters. This division is a little kingdom, of which no nation can dispute with us the sovereignty. Crowds of foreigners congregate here to admire and purchase our productions, and almost everything here has been long since sold.

Russia also has a sumptuous display. It would be necessary to build a palace expressly for the enormous doors and vast vases in malachite which fill this division. They are a little heavy, but still truly magnificent. Prince Demidoff exhibits pieces of malachite and gold from his mines. But here are again some policemen on guard; there must be some jewels. In fact, Russia exhibits the most beautiful diamond ornaments, very delicately mounted, and a jewel-case in black marble, with bunches of grapes in amethyst, and cherries in coral. In general there is, in this Russian division, a certain air of grandeur and rude luxury—riches, as it were, fresh wrested from nature, and torn from the bowels of the earth.

Let us give our eyes a little repose, by going to see the stuffed animals in the department of the Zollverein; they are among the most amusing and "spirituel" objects of the Exhibition. There is a series of scenes in caricature imitation of life, in which small animals are introduced with a most ludicrous fidelity. There is a rabbit-hunt by weasels; a fox who seduces an innocent little cat; a party of little animals drinking tea; others who are seated at the piano and singing; and several other scenes, in which the perfect imitation prevents them from being caricatures. I prefer this imitation of animals to that of man, such as may be seen in the English division under the form of a mannikin. This is an Apollo Belvidere in mechanism, for the use of tailors, that may be lengthened or shortened at pleasure. It seems that the anatomy of this movable doll is very curious, and contains about 7,000 pieces. Whilst we are on the subject of tailors, I would direct your attention to the waterproof paletots, to which they have given the name of *piuma*, and which are so light, that they may be put in a small case, and carried in the pocket. I really think they might be enclosed in a cigar-case. As a contrast to this, go and look at the immense sheet of paper exhibited in the English nave, and which is not less than 2,500 yards long. When we imagine that this endless paper may, perhaps, be filled with the prosaic effusion of some dull writer, we begin to feel some scruples, and find it necessary to allay the apprehensions of our readers, and close this letter.

LETTER III.

A Frenchman may, I think, look at the Crystal Palace with pride. In this festival of nations, in this pacific and glorious competition of human industry, France stands pre-eminent in the products of art, taste, and imagination. To her, as to her daughters, is accorded, in all times and in every clime, the palm of grace and elegance. We are told that when the fairies, in the dispensation of beauty, distributed their gifts to the women of the various nations of the world, they gave to one regularity of feature, to another symmetry of form, to this the lustre of the eye or the luxurious richness of the hair, to that the complexion of the lily and the rose, but that it happened that in this distribution, the fair one of France, or rather the "Parisienne," was overlooked. The other daughters of the earth, to repair the injustice of chance, and to afford consolation to their sister, deprived themselves for her sake of a part of their attributes, and each plucked from her crown or her girdle a flower, wherewith to form for the neglected fair a bouquet. Thus the "Parisienne," instead of one gift, participated in all, and of these varying fragments she formed that inimitable and indefinable whole which bears her name. Like to this, it would seem, is the character of the products of France; the industry of France is now, as ever, that of art. Look at her silks, her carpets, her porcelain, her jewellery; they are the work of the veritable artist, and their taste is always superior to their material. It may aptly be said that France produces the flowers, and England bears the fruits of civilization.

The department where England shines in all her splendour, is that of machinery. It is indicated by its deep and heavy murmur, like the distant roar of the torrent. There the ebullition of the steam-boiler, the cataract of the centrifugal pump, the groan of the press, and the whirl of the spindle, combine in acknowledging the supremacy of science. Fire, air, water, steam, electricity, are all exerting their agency, and may, without much figure of speech, be said to be monsters of nature chained to the triumphal car of the human will, and venting their impotent rage in groans and imprecations. Beware how you approach them in their fury. Extend to them but a finger, they will seize the hand, and powerless in their grasp, you will become a victim to your imprudence. When unenlightened by practical science, as I confess myself to be, we are perhaps more forcibly struck by the mysterious grandeur of this spectacle. Here thousands of threads, little sticks, and bits of steel, are engaged in incomprehensible warfare, and resemble so many demons under the influence of some occult power. A few delicate hands, the slight finger of a woman or child, can regulate and direct these myriads of movements. Machinery gradually supplies the place of handicraft, and we may venture to foresee an epoch at which man will have no occupation, and may sit beside it, viewing its occupations with folded arms. And one may say with the poet :—" Thou art black but comely, O city of man! Thou hast a soul, the fatal and glorious creation of our hands. Thy thousand intelligent arms leave us to inaction ; and man is left with nought to do but to think, and inebriate himself with thinking till death."

There is in the Exhibition one thing which particularly attracted my attention, albeit though modestly placed in a retired position,—a small glass case, containing copies of the Bible in all languages, with this motto, " *Multæ terricolis linguæ, cœlestibus una.*" This collection of Bibles forcibly exhibits the ardent propagandism of the English, one of the grandest and finest aspects in which this nation can be viewed. With steam and the Bible, the English traverse the globe. One of the great results of the Exhibition will be, that all nations will improve by means of mutual example and comparison. If the English give us lessons in industry, they may, on their part, learn from us to assign to art, properly speaking, a higher position. Taste is perfected in proportion as the level of equality ascends ; inferior products are no longer in demand, superfluities have become necessaries, and the beautiful is as requisite as the good. I have always thought, that if the English are not real artists, the reason is to be found in their indisposition to lose their time. Works of imagination are the offspring of repose and leisure. The poetic spirit is naturally free and spontaneous, and will not endure coercion. There are some people who seek all means of killing time. The English, on the contrary, seek all means of saving it. It is sometimes fatiguing. You must be always on the alert ; even the double knock of the postman, which warns you from the other end of the street not to keep him waiting, at last irritates you. This is a country in which it is impossible to be otherwise than punctual. And then everything in it is so well regulated. After observing that people walking in the same direction keep the same side of the foot-path,—after observing the policeman, so well dressed, and so perfectly buttoned, walking before houses which resemble each other exactly, one feels occasionally the imperious necessity of irregularity.   *   *   *

Let us turn to America; it is there we shall find works of art ! The Americans have invented, for instance, a piano which plays violin; 'tis original, and economical to boot —it saves one man's time; it is one artist the less in the republic, and Plato was opposed to having any. The anticipations of the Americans were more "grandiose" than their display. They complained that they had not had sufficient space assigned to them ; a concession was made of as much as they desired, and it was comparatively empty. To conceal the nakedness of their walls, they sent quantities of india-rubber. They exhibited gigantic boots in caouchouc—really seven-league boots—fitting emblems of Jonathan, who, when he walks a step, necessarily makes the stride of a giant. They were seized with a mania, too, for exhibiting ladies' bonnets! 'Tis true, gentle reader; yes, actually, fashions from America! Now, what the "fashions" of England are to "the modes" of France, the "just the thing" of America is to the fashions of England. Carriages form another curious specimen of American exhibition. There is one so light, it may be moved with the finger; you may imagine it to be made of paper, and the wheels have not the breadth of a quarter of an inch. It reminds me of the bailiff of Fœrrette, whose legs were so thin, that Talleyrand called him the most courageous man in the world for venturing to stand. With this break-neck affair, the American traverses space like an arrow. It is not idly he takes for device "Go ahead!" He is ever going, and he will go further still. A model is exhibited in this division of the large steamboats which descend the rivers of the New World, carrying whole houses, in which you may hire apartments! * * * * *

Oh, America! America! with thy *"far west,"*—thy prairies without limit,—thy forests, compared with which ours are but as clusters of trees,—thy rivers, near which ours would diminish to brooks,—thy lakes, vast as our seas,—thy cataracts and abysses —America! with thy growing industry, with thy indomitable spirit of enterprise, and the superb and insolent daring of thy children —oh! there is in thee, in thy new race, and thine adolescence of nature, something which attracts as the sun, as the future and the mysterious! From the over-populated shores of the Old World, what thousands of desires are directed to thee, thou land boundless and free! I picture thee, America, opening thine arms to the hungry, the outcast, the hopeless, and the wretched of all nations, and exclaiming—Come ye! Come ye! I have space for ye—I have land and sea, woods and rivers! I have iron and lead! I have work, I have bread, I have air, and ye may breathe! I have gold, and ye may be enriched! Cast off your shoes, shake off the dust of the Old World; come and refresh yourselves in the living waters of nature! *"Ad nos, ad salutarem undam, venite, populi."*——

Such are the remarks of our lively Gallic neighbour; strongly tinctured with nationality, but not the less valuable on that account; indeed rather more so, for what an interesting volume might have been formed of the various aspects under which the Crystal Palace and its contents were viewed by individuals of the countries that contributed to its treasures, could their impressions, as they wandered through its different departments, have been preserved by any process of mental daguerreotype, in all their genuineness and originality! In what opposite lights should we find the same objects regarded by inhabitants of opposite latitudes! Those who pant under the equator would cast an eye of indifference upon the furs of Russia and North America, however they might admire the "webs of woven air" produced by the Arachne like fingers of Hindoo women; nor can we imagine the gallant Captain Ommaney, the Arctic voyager, and his Esquimaux attendant, envying the silken robes of the Orientals, glittering with gold and silver, though we may allow the possibility of their fixing their attention on the yarns and the woollens, the doe-skins and gutta perchas, all the impervious and impermeable articles, in short, that bid defiance to St. Swithin and Cape Horn. Certainly,

> "The turban'd Turk, with his alcoran,
> And the stately Don, with his whiskers on,"

would view very differently the same things; the Roman from the banks of the Tiber, the Croat from those of the Drave, the Hindoo from those of the Ganges, the Fleming from Brabant, the Walloon from Luxembourg and Hainault, the Prussian from Westphalia and the Rhenish provinces, the Swiss from his snow-capped mountains, the Austrian from a hundred regions, the hydra-headed Russians, the Swedes, the Danes, the bearded Poles, the smug Chinese, our brother Jonathan; all, in short, of the vast family of the human race that sent their representatives to us at the call of peace and science, and brotherly love, must have seen the objects around them according to their own national tastes, habits, and associations. Then, again, in those national peculiarities how many individual peculiarities must also exist! What two persons ever think exactly alike, or are equally interested by any one object whatsoever! The sculptor gazes with delight upon the "storied urn, or animated bust," whilst he scarcely glances at the ponderous iron masses that represent the wonders of machinery; and the engineer turns away from the breathing marble, to contemplate utility and strength in a rougher material, and luxuriates in images of power and steam.

The philosopher exclaims, with Diogenes, "How many things are here that I do not want!"—the poor man, "how many things that I wish I could have!"—the rich one, "how many things that I have already! how many more that I will have!" The military man handles the blades of Toledo, the sabres of Damascus, the Highland dirk and claymore, the guns, pistols, and rifles—single and double barrelled, self-priming, self-loading, revolving. The lover of peace turns to the pruning-hooks, the ploughs, the spades, the hoes, and the garden-rollers. The philanthropist looks round for suggestions that may benefit the human race; the missionary for the means of evangelizing it, casting a longing eye towards the Holy Bible in its hundred and fifty different languages. Those who "go down to the sea in ships," examine the models of vessels, and life-boats, light-houses, harbours, and breakwaters—but the ladies are all unanimous in their raptures with the treasures of dress and decoration expressly framed for the heightening of their attractions, and consequent extension of the empire of their charms.

What a variety of thoughts, sentiments, comparisons, and calculations, must have passed through the minds of the motley crowd that daily congregated under that crystal canopy! numerous as the motes in the sunbeam, rapid as the movements of the gnat-fly's wings—which wings, be it known to you, gentle reader, have been ingeniously ascertained to flap at the rate of fifteen thousand times per second. The Crystal Palace, with all its wonders, could never have produced a wonder like that little insect, even had it stood for a million of years.

CHAPTER XXVI.

THE APPLICATION OF SCIENCE TO THE PURPOSES OF HUMANITY—SMITH'S YIELDING BREAK-WATER—NATURE'S SIMPLE BARRIER, THE TRUMPET-MOUTHED WEED—HINTS ON PHILAN-THROPY AND ECONOMY—LOCOMOTIVES—THE VILLAGE OF REDRUTH—THE LORD OF THE ISLES—THE CORNWALL—THE LIVERPOOL, ETC. ETC.

"Paulo majora canamus," was the exclamation of the Mantuan bard, when he meditated a loftier theme than his bucolic muse was accustomed to inspire. "Paulò majora canamus," we repeat, as, somewhat reluctantly, we confess, we turn from the flowery fields of poesy, the beautiful and graceful forms, in ever-changing variety, that art, with lavish hand, so profusely scattered through the various mazes of the Crystal Palace, "to please and sate the curious taste." But we feel we should not be doing justice to our subject, were we to confine our lucubrations solely to what relates to the gratification of taste, however pure and refined that taste may be. Other objects there were within those memorable walls, which tended to excite even loftier emotions than could be awakened by the proudest display of imitative art. Science unfolded her wonders before the astonished gaze of the bewildered spectator; her gigantic powers, and almost illimitable resources, were exemplified in innumerable inventions, in the subjugation of the elements of air, water, and fire, and in the adaptation of a vast variety of means, which even the Marquis of Worcester, in his celebrated *Century of Inventions*, never dreamed of, to advance the well-being and prosperity of mankind.

It has been judiciously remarked by an able writer, that "the influence which machinery is destined to exert over the fortunes of mankind, is but little understood even by the most enlightened amongst us; and though the day has past—or is quickly passing—when the operative looked with gloomy jealousy on the introduction of every new mechanical invention, as being likely to deprive him of a portion of his hard-earned bread; though the majority of thinking men have long ago come to the conclusion that steam and iron ought to, and eventually will, do the positive labour of the world—the lifting, carrying, driving, and toiling—yet we have not altogether overcome our prejudice to whirring wheels and hissing boilers. If it be a good thing to get rid of some of these narrow notions; if it be well to put off, not for a time, but for ever, something more of those popular feelings and nationalities which see danger in the increase of mechanical contrivances; if we discover in the march of education, a surer and a better road to greatness than we have been accustomed to travel—a road less dusty with the evidences of manual labour, and less crowded with old-world prejudices and exclusive ideas; if we recognise the upward tendency which machinery has in the world—then is the peaceable reunion of the nations in Hyde Park a glorious thing to contemplate, and the iron and wood of giant enginery a sort of triumph of which this little island of ours may well be proud" It is, however, when the resources of science are more particularly directed to the purpose of benefiting mankind; when her efforts are guided by the promptings of humanity, that they especially recommend themselves to our attention. And it is under this aspect that we propose, in our present chapter, to consider the subject.

On proceeding to the western end of the edifice, in the central nave, the visitor found himself surrounded by an infinity of models, and all the leviathan appliances of marine engineering. Bridges, harbours, docks, breakwaters, lighthouses, &c. &c., were on every side contending for superiority. And first and foremost among them was the Breakwater of Mr. William Henry Smith, civil engineer, applying most happily to mechanical action, one of the most beautiful, and, we may add, if rightly understood, instructive principles in nature, namely, the *yielding* one. A principle, indeed, the efficacy of which nature herself has beautifully illustrated in various situations on the coast of Africa, where, with the trumpet-mouthed weed of the Cape of Good Hope, the *Laminaria buxinalis*, growing to the height of twenty or thirty feet, she has formed an imperishable breakwater, which, alternately yielding to and opposing the force of the waves, serves as a complete barrier to their destructive fury; and likewise on our own canals and river-banks, where the pliant resistance of common reeds and bulrushes is found to be more effectual in protecting them from being undermined and washed away, than walls of solid masonry, exemplifying the sagacity of the old Scottish motto, "You may bend me, but you cannot break me." The ingenious inventor of this most admirable means of promoting the security of commerce, and the protection of human life, affords in his own character an encouraging illustration of his own scientific principles. To the conflicting opinions and interested oppositions with which he, like all men of original genius, has had to contend, one anxious year after another, in the commencement of his career, he knew how to bend; but he defied the power of any, or all of these opinions and oppositions, jointly or separately, to break his spirit of determination to go through with an object, which he felt to be as valuable to the interests of humanity as to his own, personally considered. For ten years he bowed before the waves of prejudice and interested opposition—opposition even from those high quarters which ought to have been the first to uphold his efforts, and, like Antæus, rose with renewed strength after every hostile attack. What lover of science, what philanthropist, but must sympathize in such enduring, such noble perseverance, and wish it all the success it deserves? It only remains with us to describe the principle on which the plan is founded. The harbour is formed of a series of independent frames or gratings, each about fifty feet long, and rising from the bed of the sea about ten feet above high water mark; each, though separated, forming a continuous line, and being free to play beneath the roadway, which is, by a very simple means, rendered immoveable above. The frames are secured at the bottom of each extremity to pile-heads, and by braces with counterbalance weights and screw piles, or other holdfasts attached. As waves in succession strike, and, according to their size and force, drive forward the framework, the weights are uplifted. The greater the elevation of the weights, the greater is the resistance of the frame to the waves. But all is equable; no jerk or shock is suffered; for while the impetus of each wave exists, the frame still yields to it. After the wave has become disseminated through the gratings, the weights in turn prevail, and sinking, draw back the frame, again to yield before and subdue each wave in succession; for as there are no two hills without a valley, so there are no two waves without an interval; and as every separate wave in a gale can only impel even a solid drifting body ten feet, it stands to reason that this open frame can never be driven that distance; and even were it so, at ten feet the strain on the iron braces or other part of the fabric, would be only one-twelfth of what they can bear, for the elasticity may be produced to any length or degree. In all except actually stormy weather, the braces are sufficient to act as tension rods, and keep it perfectly taut and quiescent; thus altogether avoiding the wear and tear to which the cables of lightships are subject, owing to the gravity of the counterbalance weights, which then rest upon the bottom. The moment any strain or pressure comes upon the frame-work, about one-tenth of its force must always press downwards, instead of having an upward tendency, as in all structures, giving rise to the term, uptearing gales. Exclusively, therefore, of the elasticity of the braces, it is stronger than piling, depending merely upon the water-tight nature or tenacity of the bottom. The framing being open, with a greater or less space beneath, admits of a free tidal current and scour of the sea; and thus avoids bars and deposits, so invariable with stone structures, when the littoral currents are suspended. The durability of prepared timber in sea-water is very great; that of wrought iron is an historical fact. In the event of the bottom deepening or filling up, or the harbour otherwise requiring improvement, the structure can, by the facilities afforded by the well-known screw pile, be readily fixed from the surface at any depth, or raised, lowered, or removed.

The principle of Mr. Smith's Lighthouse and Asylum is the same as that of the breakwater; the yield, even in a gale of wind, will be almost imperceptible, like the springing of the trunk of a tree. There is no other way of erecting a lighthouse in deep water, or in bad and quicksand bottoms, as a safe and permanent structure. Lightships have therefore been employed at a considerable expense, with a number of men as a crew, sufficient to manage them when they go adrift. In case of accident, there is not the loss of the lightship and crew alone to be apprehended, but possibly of vessels in the same gale, misled by not seeing their accustomed beacons, and often in hazy weather from missing their lights, as nothing but a lighthouse will admit of the requisite size, height and power. This Lighthouse presents the greatest strength of wrought iron in the direction of the strain, that is the line of tension, and the minimum of surface resistance to the wind, draft, and blow of the wave. The Lighthouse as well as the Break-water is thus not only applicable to every situation, but it is at the same time applicable with great economy and ample strength. The system has met with the medals and approbation of all the scientific boards and societies before whom it has been discussed, as well as the concurrent favourable notices of all the morning papers, and most of the scientific and general press; and in no one instance have such discussions and reviews, shown otherwise than the great beauty and economy of the principle. Indeed, one great point in this invention is its cheapness; in fact, a single year's interest of the cost of the breakwater at Plymouth would be amply sufficient for the construction of a harbour on the plan proposed by Mr. Smith. This, moreover, is a quality which would enable its advantages to be extended to all parts of our coasts; and the time may not be far distant when the storm-tossed mariner shall no longer look with dread upon the shores of his own native land, which having long desired to revisit, now too frequently greet him only to be his grave.

We offer no apology for dwelling upon this subject at some length, since, to a country like England, surrounded on all sides by the waves, commanding the commerce of the world, and boasting herself of her unconquered navy, there is scarcely a question pregnant with such important consequences as that of the best and simplest means of overcoming the impetuous and disastrous power of the ocean on our coasts, and affording harbours of refuge for the storm-tossed vessel. Every year adds a long list of shipwrecks, with an appalling sacrifice of human life, the greater portion of which could have been prevented had there existed harbours of refuge in sufficient number on our coasts. Many have been the plans proposed, and the experiments tried, to accomplish this desirable end, but, as yet, in every case failure to a greater or less degree has resulted. Some have endeavoured to breast the roaring billow with a perpendicular wall, after nature's pattern on the rocky coasts, while others would use the more persuasive resis-tance of a gentle slope, or incline, suggested by the beach of sand, or shingle. To imitate either, however, is a matter of no small difficulty, and is attended with enormous labour and expense, added to which, should the position chosen fail to effect its purpose properly, the huge mass of materials thrown together *must* remain, to the injury, if not the complete destruction, of the part it was intended to improve.

We will now take our leave of Mr. Smith, and pursue our investigations among the important discoveries that human genius has achieved for the service of mankind. The genius of Great Britain is peculiarly mechanical, and the steam-engine and the loom divide between them the glory of her industrial triumphs; for, to relieve the sons of labour from their severest toil, and to substitute iron and steam for bone and muscle, is the peculiar office of machinery. Stand we in the department devoted to machines in motion. Do the immense collection of contrivances to lighten toil convey no moral— the interesting objects there shown read us no lesson? " In the Crystal Palace we discover," says an eloquent writer, " how mechanism is extending her dominion over the whole empire of labour; how she rises in textile fabrics to the manufacture of the most delicate and intricate lace; how from wood she aspires to fashion iron into the most exact proportions; how, with steam as her handmaid, she works the printing-press and navigates the ocean, and outruns the swiftest animal in her course. Turn into the agri-cultural implement department, and we find everything now done by machinery. By it the farmer not only sows and reaps, but he manures and hoes. By it he threshes out and grinds his corn, and prepares the food for his cattle. He can even drain by machinery, and it is difficult now to find a branch of his business into which it does not largely enter. In our manufactures the mechanical genius of the country reigns supreme. Those beau-tiful fabrics are nearly all the evidences of its power. Soft goods and hardware are

2 U

equally indebted to it, and in its presence the unaided efforts of handicraftsmen appear small and insignificant indeed. It travels everywhere, and invades every compartment, even that of the fine arts, in the court dedicated to which some of the most conspicuous contributions are specimens of printing in oil, and attempts to reproduce by mechanical means the sentiment and inspiration of the painter."

But let us turn to another phase of the subject. A few years since—so few indeed as to come within the recollection of most living fathers—and the stage-coach was the swiftest vehicle we possessed; *now*, the locomotive carries its hundreds of passengers at the rate of sixty miles an hour. Is there not cause for gratulation in this fact? Our fathers were content to travel from London to Liverpool in twenty-four hours, and thought they had achieved wonders; we go the same distance in a fourth of the time, and grumble at the tedious length of the journey. It is not our province to speak of the rise and progress of the railway system—other pens have been busy with that theme; but it may not be out of place to contrast the present with the past, in drawing the attention of our readers to the locomotives that were gathered together in the north-west angle. From generalities to particulars is an easy descent. Here we had a picture of the LORD OF THE ISLES, one of the largest class of locomotive engines, a leviathan of the first class. This, it will be remembered, was one of the ordinary class of engines constructed by the Great Western Company since 1847. It is capable of taking a passenger train of 120 tons, at an average speed of sixty miles an hour upon easy gradients. The evaporation of the boiler, when in full work, is equal to 1,000-horse power. The weight of the engine, in working order, is 35 tons, which does not include the tender, which, under similar circumstances, weighs 17 tons 13 cwts. The diameter of cylinder, 18 inches; length of stroke, 24 inches; diameter of driving-wheel, 8 feet; and the maximum pressure of steam, 120 lbs. The stately proportions of this engine were seen to great advantage in the Crystal Palace, and, contrasted with the light locomotives of Messrs. Adams and England, seemed quite a giant of power and capability. To see this engine, however, in its full glory, the spectator should be at its side when it stops, after a heavy run at express speed—when the furnace is too white with heat for the naked eye to look upon without pain, and the steam, blowing off like thunder, shakes the very ground. One of these engines was nicknamed by the men, "The Emperor of Russia," on account of its extraordinary appetite for oil and tallow. In order to distribute the weight more equally over the rails, it will be observed that the engine alone has eight wheels. The cylinders were laid horizontally under the front end of the boiler, and could in this case be very conveniently inspected, together with the rest of the working parts, by going down into the pit provided for that purpose under the engine.

It may, perhaps, serve to amuse our readers, if we describe at length the peculiarities of this giant example of the travelling propensities of modern Englishmen. One dark night, in the year 1784, the venerable clergyman of Redruth was taking an evening walk in a long and lonely lane leading to his church, when his ears were suddenly assailed by a most unearthly noise, and, to his horror, he beheld approaching him, at a furious speed, an indescribable creature of legs, arms, and wheels, whose body seemed glowing with internal fire, and whose rapid gasps for breath appeared to denote some deadly struggle within. His cries for help brought to his assistance a gentleman of the name of Murdoch, who, no doubt to his infinite relief, explained to him that this terrific apparition, which he had taken for the Evil One himself, was a runaway locomotive, which he, Mr. Murdoch, the inventor and proprietor, had incautiously allowed to escape from its leading strings. In this way was the FIRST LOCOMOTIVE, which was ultimately to exercise so important an influence on the progress of civilization, introduced into the world; but the world was not yet prepared to receive it, and for nearly twenty years nothing was done towards the practical application of Mr. Murdoch's idea. It was not until the year 1804, that Messrs. Trevithick and Vivian, of Camborne, near Redruth, patented and constructed the first actually useful locomotive.

An extraordinary misconception for a long period obstructed the use of locomotives. It was gravely alleged that the wheels would turn round without the engine advancing; and this notion having once got abroad, people would hardly be persuaded to the contrary, even when they saw it with their own eyes. Much money and ingenuity were expended in making steam walking machines, in which legs and feet pushed the engine along. It was not till 1814, when the truly illustrious George Stephenson constructed a locomotive for the Killingworth Colliery, that all these crude ideas were swept away, and from that time we may date the introduction of the locomotive system. From that date to 1823, when the Liverpool and Manchester Railway was projected, Mr. Stephenson and others spent large sums of money in improving the details of the engine; so that on the opening of that railway, a very excellent performance was at once attained, and the benefits of the railway system began to be appreciated. The great superiority of the engines used on this line over that just described, arose from the use of a boiler containing a number of tubes or small flues, through which the flame passed, and which generated steam much more rapidly than the former boiler with a large single tube through it.

The specimens of the light locomotive carriage exhibited by Messrs. Adams and England, while possessing all the advantages which experience and skill have worked out in the heavy engines, are not more than one-third of the weight and half the cost. Mr. Adams' plan consists in combining the engine and carriage in one, so that there is no superfluous weight; the stoker can act as guard and take the tickets. The boiler is a cylinder full of tubes placed vertically; but this plan, in subsequent engines, has been given up in favour of the ordinary horizontal construction, as shown in the locomotive carriage in the Exhibition. Mr. England, on the other hand, combines the engine and tender only in one frame, thus adapting it to carriages of the ordinary description. Both these plans have been satisfactorily tested in practice, and bear out the views of the projectors, carrying a moderate load at a high speed, with a small consumption of fuel, and a diminished destruction of the permanent way. In addition to these, we had specimens from numerous other eminent engineers. Mr. Trevithick, of the London and North Western Company, sent his express engine, the "Cornwall," in which the boiler is placed very low, and the driving wheels are obtained of large size, by allowing the shaft on which they are fixed to pass through the boiler. Mr. Crampton's patent narrow-gauge engine "Liverpool," is said to be the most powerful engine in the world, being equal to 1140-horse power. The peculiarity of this engine consists in the position of the axle of the driving wheels, which is placed behind the fire-box. Mr. Fairbairn, of Manchester; Messrs. Wilson, of Leeds; and Messrs. Kitson, Thompson, and Hewitson, of the same town, exhibited specimens of the combined engine and tender variety, or "tank engines," as they are technically termed. We must not omit a very beautiful specimen of the first class engine by Messrs. Hawthorn and Co, of Newcastle. The visitor might assure himself, in dwelling on this collection of firesteeds, that in this respect at least his country has no competitor to fear. A traveller tells, with pardonable exultation, how comforted and at home he felt at an Italian railway station by seeing on the name-plate of the engine the familiar words, "Sharp, Roberts, and Co., Atlas Works, Manchester," and hearing a genuine English "All right!" given, before the train was allowed to move from the platform.

CHAPTER XXVII.

SCULPTURE *continued.*—FLORENCE.

COMPARISON BETWEEN MARBLE AND BRONZE—GOLD AND SILVER—A PEEP INTO THE MAIN
AVENUE—THE BAVARIAN LION—KING AND QUEEN OF BOHEMIA—THE EAGLE SLAYER—GROUP
OF QUEEN MARGARET AND HER SON—SAPPHO—WAR OF THE TITANS, BY VECHTE—MAGNIFI-
CENT SHIELD BY THE SAME—SPLENDID OVALS—CHANGARNIER'S SWORD—CONVERSION OF
ST. HUBERT—DANCING FAWN—GROUP OF FRENCH BRONZES—PRINCE OF WALES'S SHIELD—
DIFFICULTIES OF THE ART—BENVENUTO, CELLINI, ETC. ETC.

In our former remarks on the Plastic Art, it was chiefly towards productions in marble
that we directed the attention of our readers. We have still, for the field is by no
means exhausted, many rare specimens of the same class to hold up to observation, but
for the present we shall, for a while, quit the "breathing marble," and proceed to
examine the no less imposing display of talent that was manifested in the Great Exhibition, in bronze, that imperishable material which, defying all the rigour of the
elements, and the rude hand of time, has preserved to us such abundant proof of the
talent and genius of former ages, in so many parts of the civilized world, and more
especially on the classic shores of gifted Italy.   In Florence, for example, we can scarcely
stir a step without feeling ourselves accompanied by the shade of some illustrious one
among the dead. The presence of Michael Angelo seems to haunt us as we wander
among the battlemented palaces, and rare old Benvenuto comes athwart our "mind's
eye" as we visit the precincts made glorious by his art. John of Bologna points to his
living form of the Messenger of Jove; and the sculptured gates of the renowned
Baptistry recall to us the times when wars were waged for their possession, and which
still, in undiminished excellence, invite the admiration of the stranger as models of
perfection in art.

Before entering upon any individual examination of the objects we have selected for
description in our present chapter, we shall lay before our readers a few judicious
remarks by an eminent lecturer on the sculptor's art, as exemplified in the different
materials in marble, metal, or bronze. "The peculiar refinements of form and texture
which fall within the especial province of the sculptor to carry to their highest pitch of
perfection, he constantly heightens by availing himself of the effect on the senses of
the simultaneous contrast of form. Thus he exaggerates the roughness of the hair, and
the coarse texture of every object coming in contact with his flesh, in order to give
to it the exquisite smoothness of nature; he introduces straight lines, equally balanced
folds, and angular breaks into his draperies, in order to bring out the tender sweeping
curves of the outlines of the limbs he so gracefully disposes. His is, of a truth, the
happy art which begins by collecting all that is most sweet and fresh, and then by one
additional touch, one further artful contrast, he 'throws a perfume on the violet.' In
sculpture, as in every other of the decorative arts, changing circumstances bring ever-
changing conventionalities; and, as supreme arbiters over the propriety of one and all,
still preside our original great principles—*variety, fitness, simplicity,* and *contrast.*

" In turning to those departments of practical art into which Sculpture enters as a
predominant ingredient, metal-work first presents itself to our notice. Nothing can be
more apparent than the variety of properties and qualities of the several metals, nothing
more consistent than to prescribe a different mode of treatment to each.. Sculpture in
metal, partly on account of the much greater ductility and tenacity of the material, and
partly on account of its peculiar colour and power of reflecting light, can rarely,

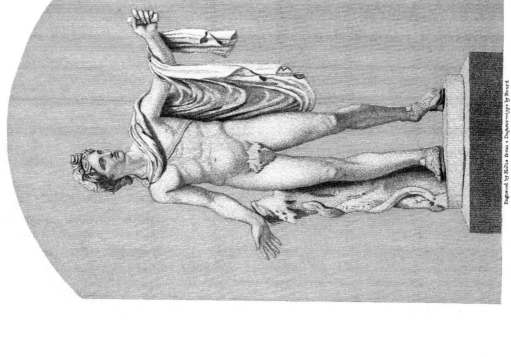

APOLLO BELVEDERE.

FROM THE ORIGINAL OF D. BRUCCIANI

Engraved by Hollis from a Daguerreotype by Beard.

THE EAGLE SLAYER.

SPECIMEN OF IRON CASTING BY THE COALBROOK DALE COMPANY.

DESIGNED BY J. BELL.

Engraved by Hollis from a Daguerreotype by Beard.

TO THE GALLERI

GREAT EXHIBITION, MAIN AVENUE,

LOOKING WEST.

Engraved by T. Hollis, from a Daguerreotype by Mayall.

however highly its degree of finish may be carried, be mistaken for that which it professes to imitate. Hence it arises that elaborate execution of details may, and indeed should, be carried in metal to the most minute perfection. Works in gold or silver should, as a general rule (except in instances where an overpowering display of wealth is intended, in which case art does not much signify), be confined to small dimensions, and those relatively correspondent to the associations of idea connected with the rarity and value of each. It was from inattention to these conditions that many of the largest pieces of plate in the Exhibition failed to interest us, and that the eye dwelt with much greater complacency upon the smaller than upon the larger objects." Among the exhibitors of specimens of gold work, Messrs. Morel, Watherston and Brogden, and Froment Meurice, held the most distinguished place in point of excellence and appropriateness of design; among those who contributed silver work, Messrs. Hunt and Roskell, Wagner, Froment Meurice, Lebrun, Rudolphi, Garrard, Morel, &c.

We will now proceed to examine some of the chief specimens in bronze and metal that in various parts of the building attracted the observation of the curious visitor. Of the group of the Amazon attacked by a Tiger, we have already made honourable mention. In our daguerreotype of the Main Avenue, looking west, our readers will find in the immediate foreground its fac-simile in miniature, as it stood on its rocky base, surrounded by so many sculptured forms of grace and loveliness, and backed by its long perspective, while the busy moving crowd of delighted spectators are represented thronging about each favourite object of attraction. Next in size and importance, about the middle of the nave, stood, open-mouthed on his pedestal, the Bavarian Lion, of colossal proportions, measuring 15 feet in length, by 9 in height, belonging, as we are told, to a group of four intended to be attached to a car, destined to adorn the triumphal arch at Munich. It is after the design of Halbig. It appeared in the same state as when it left the founders, being raw-cast in bronze, and, together with another of the group or "team" referred to, was cast at the same time out of one furnace, showing the possibility of executing casts in one piece of almost any weight and size. "It was exhibited also as a specimen of the new method of the founder to preserve the pure natural colour of the cast, without being obliged to use the chisel." This extensive production will long be remembered by all frequenters of the Crystal Palace, as the veritable "lion" of the Great Exhibition. For the lion itself, apart from the mechanical difficulties which have been overcome in the casting, it is, after all, but a so-so affair, as lions go with us. We have many a lion of pure British metal before whom this foreign monster of the forest—coming all the way from Munich—is not fit to wag his tail. The noble beast at the top of Northumberland House, for instance, and another, of minor growth, which stands, or stood, at the corner of Berners-street, are old familiar friends whom we would match against the world.

Near to his lionship two noble figures in bronze reared their stately forms—Libûsa, Queen of the Bohemians, anno 700; and George of Padiebrad, a king of the same people; the latter in armour, with chain-mail shirt and fur-lined cloak. These statues were modelled by Schwanthaler, and cast by Müller, of Munich, the artist of the famous Lion. Separating them was a fine group of a Boy and Swan in bronze, by Th. Kalide, of Berlin, and the property of his majesty the king of Prussia. Close at hand was an admirable work of art in a large font surrounded with semi-nude sculptures representing domestic scenes, children playing, &c., by Professor F. Dräke, of Berlin.

The Eagle Slayer, designed by John Bell, and cast in bronze by the Coalbrookdale Company, attracted much attention from its grand and imposing character Two statuettes also, designed by the same hand, and executed in bronze by Messrs. Messenger and Sons, of Birmingham, were exceedingly admired. The first of these formed a

2 x

most interesting group, representing Queen Margaret and her son interceding with the robbers after the disastrous battle of Hexham. She was presenting her infant boy to the daring robber, with the words, "My friend, to your care I commit the safety of your king's son;" and it is pleasant to recollect that poetical justice resulted from so romantic an incident; the fierce man of blood was touched by her appeal, and not only defended the queen and her son from further insult, but concealed them in the forest till they were enabled to escape to Flanders. Of a truth, nobility of mind is not confined to the wearers of court dresses. The second of these statuettes, a figure of Sappho, was also exceedingly graceful and imaginative. Neither by any means second to them in elegance or beauty, was Foley's much admired "Boy at the Stream," executed in bronze by Hatfield.

We will now, however, turn to our Gallic neighbours, and it is with equal delight and admiration that we do so. Among the numerous competitors for fame, who stood nobly forward in this department of art, first and foremost we place M. Vechte, whose rare talent was eminently displayed in the magnificent vase representing the War of the Titans against Jupiter, which, for its elegance, spirit, and pure classic taste, was truly unrivalled, and worthy of the most renowned master-pieces of antiquity. On the summit of the vase, seated on the wings of the imperial bird, the Thunderer, with frowning and awful aspect, was launching his destructive and irresistible bolt upon the heads of the rebellious crew, who, in their senseless fury " piling Pelion upon Ossa," were endeavouring to scale the celestial seats. At the base were lying, in the agonies of death, several of the bodies of the discomfited host. The drawing of the figures in this noble performance was equally correct and powerful, and altogether the whole composition breathed the true spirit of poetry and Homeric fire. By the same master-hand we also noticed an unfinished shield, worthy of the arm of the great Pelides himself, divided into various compartments, full of poetic fancy and graceful design. France also had to boast of a number of admirable designs from the hands of Collas, Barbedienne, Vittoz, Matifat, Susse, and other excellent artists; some of them, indeed, produced works of such rare, beautiful, and minute details, as, in the words of our great poet, *mutatis mutandis,*

"Would have made *Cellini* stare and gasp."

We more particularly allude to two oval designs representing, in high and most intricate relief, military and gorgeous processions in some old Norman town, whose antique roofs and gable-ends aptly designate the locality of the scene. Among a variety of smaller articles, the sword of the redoubtable Changarnier, with which we suppose he intended to lay waste our peaceful shores, lay quietly sleeping in its scabbard, and gave us full leisure to examine its rich and elaborate workmanship. But the pride of all weapons was a superb *couteau de chasse*, or hunting-knife, which reminded us of the old stag and boar-hunts of the *ancien regime*, so charmingly illustrated in the time of Louis Quatorze by Vander Meulen. This magnificent knife was composed from the legend of St. Hubert, of Albert Durer celebrity. The figure, in *ronde bosse*, surrounded by the hounds, formed the handle. The mouth of the sheath was ornamented with a large bas-relief, representing the moment when the hunt was interrupted by the vision of St. Hubert; that is, the apparition of the cross on the stag's head. The rich ornamentation and figures were first composed and modelled in wax, then sculptured in plaster, and finally moulded in metal and chiselled. The blade was of the finest steel, forged with steel hammers, and the moulding creased or hollowed by the hand with a graver. This work, which was from the studio of Marrel Frères, was thus eulogized by the jury in their report :—"The jury would further mention a very beautiful silver hunting-knife,

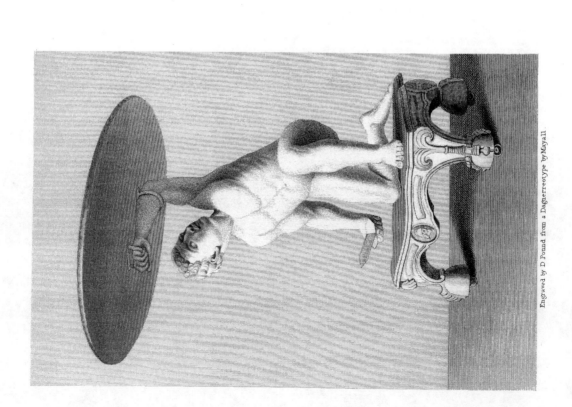

THE DANCING FAUN

Engraved by D Pound from a Daguerreotype by Mayall

FROM THE ORIGINAL OF LEQUESNE.

GLADIATORIAL TABLE

Engraved by D Pound from a Daguerreotype by Mayall

FROM THE ORIGINAL OF J.FLETCHER, OF CORK.

the hilt of which represents St. Hubert standing within a niche; the cross is ornamented with a fox at bay, defending itself against several dogs. Upon the chape of the sheath is a handsome bas-relief, representing the conversion of St. Hubert, and lower down is a hunting trophy. The execution of this hunting-knife leaves nothing to be desired."

M. Lequesne exhibited a Dancing Faun, which, for spirit and motion, was well deserving of praise. This subject has always been a favourite one both with painters and sculptors, and excited a good deal of attention. We shall lastly notice a remarkable group of French bronzes, taken from the contributions of MM. Vittoz and Matifat, both of which manufacturers also contributed various artistic ornaments, clocks, chandeliers, cups, lustres, vases, and different articles of *virtu*. The male figure of this group represented Benvenuto Cellini, the celebrated sculptor, and would seem to have been designed with a view to associate the grand with the beautiful. The attitude was not without spirit, whilst the expression of the countenance would seem to be that of a noble character conscious of the inherent power of his own genius. The vase he carried in his arm was, no doubt, intended to emblemize the profession he so successfully pursued. Cellini, as our readers are aware, was an eminent sculptor, jeweller, and goldsmith, contemporary with Michael Angelo and Julio Romano, and was employed by popes, kings, and other princely patrons of science and art, in the time of Leo X. and Charles V. His productions are exquisite in design and execution. He lived to a considerable age, and his life almost to the last was a series of adventures, persecutions, and misfortunes. He wrote the history of his own life, which has been well translated by Roscoe. The column and fountain in the same group were the productions of Matifat; the former was intended as a gas candelabrum, and the latter for a garden ornament. They were both beautiful specimens of art of that mixed kind, which aims at combining the fanciful with the useful. The female figure was one of those classic productions so frequently to be found emanating from the prolific ideality of our Gallic neighbours, possessing the usual pure and graceful outline which characterizes the *beautiful* in sculpture; it was not, however, of that *dignified* beauty which marks so many of the productions of the ancients, but rather of that subordinate kind, known as the *attractive* among the various styles. Altogether, this group may be said to have exhibited a useful combination of the artistic and the utilitarian—an end of no small importance in these iron times.

We must not omit to notice a complimentary tribute from the King of Prussia to his Royal Highness the Prince of Wales,—a splendid shield, presented in commemoration of the baptism of the infant Prince, for whom his Majesty acted as sponsor. The pictorial embellishments of the shield were designed by Doctor Peter Von Cornelius, and the architectural ornaments by Counsellor Stüller. The execution of the goldsmith's work, enamel, &c., was performed by M. G. Hossauer; the modelling by M. A. Fischer; the chasing by M. A. Mertens; and the lapidary work by M. Calandrelli. In the centre of the shield was a head of our Saviour. The middle compartment, surrounded by a double line of ornamental work, was divided by a cross into four smaller compartments, which contained emblematic representations of the two Sacraments, Baptism and the Lord's Supper, with their Old Testament types—the opening of the rocky fountain by Moses, and the fall of manna. At the extremities of the arms of the cross were represented the Evangelists, noting down what they have seen and heard in the Gospels, which are to communicate to all futurity the plan of man's salvation. On the extreme points of the arabesques that rose above the Evangelists were representations of Faith, Hope, Charity, and Christian Righteousness. Around the entire centre stood the Twelve Apostles. Peter was seen under Faith, represented in the arabesque; on the right and left of him were Philip and Andrew; under Hope was James; on either side were Bartholomew and Simon; John was placed beneath the figure of Charity; on either side were James the younger and Thomas; under Righteousness was Paul; on the right and left were Matthew and Judas Thaddeus, going forth into the world to propagate the kingdom of the Redeemer. The relievo which surrounded the edge of the shield represented the Betrayal, the redeeming Atonement of Christ, and his Resurrection. Another portion represented our Lord's triumphant Entry into Jerusalem; a third portion the Descent of the Holy Ghost, the Preaching of the Gospel, and the Formation of the Church. The fourth compartment contained an allegorical representation of the Birth of the Prince of Wales, and of the Visit of the King of Prussia, accompanied by Baron Humboldt, General Von Natzmer, and the Count Von Stolberg, welcomed by his Royal Highness Prince Albert and the Duke of Wellington: a Knight of St. George being represented on the beach, standing on the Dragon. The shield has been denominated the Buckler of Faith. The inscription on the shield ran thus:—

"FRIDERICUS GULIELMUS REX BORUSSORUM,
ALBERTO EDUARDO, PRINCIPI WALLIÆ,
IN MEMORIAM DIEI BAPT. XXV. JAN. A. MDCCCXLII."

Before we conclude our present chapter, it may not be uninteresting to our readers to be made acquainted with some of the difficulties that occasionally beset an artist in the prosecution of his labours. We will therefore give in Benvenuto Cellini's own words, his account of the casting of his celebrated Perseus, which we have already alluded to. "As I had been particularly successful in casting my Medusa," says Cellini, "I made a model of my Perseus in wax, and flattered myself that I should have the same success in casting the latter in bronze, as I had had with the former. Upon its appearing to such advantage, and looking so beautiful in wax, the duke, whether somebody put it into his head, or whether it was a notion of his own, as he came to my house oftener than usual, once took occasion to say to me, 'Benvenuto, this statue cannot be cast in bronze; it is not in the power of your art to compass it.'" Our gifted Florentine was naturally annoyed at this remark, and endeavoured to convince the duke that the affair, in spite of its exceeding difficulty, (which all those having any knowledge of the art, and who have seen the noble figure where it stands, before the ducal palace at Florence, must readily admit,) was not beyond his skill; but the self-opinionated prince refused to listen to him, and sceptically shaking his head, left the artist to his own inventions. But Benvenuto, whose courage always rose in proportion to the obstacles he had to encounter, after his vexation at losing his royal patronage had subsided, set about the work with a cheerful and undaunted spirit. "I still flattered myself," says he, "that if I could but finish my statue of Perseus, all my labours would be converted to delight, and meet with a glorious and happy reward. Thus, having recovered my vigour of mind, I, with the utmost strength of body and of purse (though, indeed, I had but little money left), began to purchase several loads of pine-wood from the pine-grove of the Serristori, hard by Mont Lupo; and whilst I was waiting for it, I covered my Perseus with the earth which I had prepared several months beforehand, that it might have its proper seasoning. After I had made its coat of earth, covered it well, and bound it properly with irons, I began by means of a slow fire to draw off the wax, which melted away by many vent-holes—for the more of these are made the better the moulds are filled—and when I had entirely stripped off the wax, I made a sort of fence round my Perseus, that is, round the mould above-mentioned, of bricks, piling them one upon another, and leaving several vacuities for the fire to exhale at. I next began to put on the wood, and kept a constant fire for two days and two nights, till the wax being quite off, and the mould well baked, I began to dig a hole to bury my mould in, and observed all those fine methods of proceeding which are prescribed by our art. When I had completely dug my hole, I took my mould, and by means of levers and strong cables directed it with care, and suspended it a cubit above the level of the furnace, so that it hung exactly in the middle of the hole. I then let it gently down to the very bottom of the furnace, and placed it with all the care and exactness I possibly could. After I had finished this part of my task, I began to make a covering of the very earth I had taken off, and in proportion as I raised the earth I made vents for it, which are a sort of tubes of baked earth, generally used for conduits, and other things of a similar nature. As soon as I saw that I had placed it properly, and that this manner of covering it, by putting on these small tubes in their proper places, was likely to answer, as also that my journeymen thoroughly understood my plan, which was very different from that of all other masters, and I was sure that I could depend upon them, I turned my thoughts to the furnace. I had caused it to be filled with several pieces of brass and bronze, and heaped them one upon another, in the manner taught us by our art, taking particular care to leave a passage for the flames, that the metal might the sooner assume its colour and dissolve into a fluid. Thus I, with great alacrity, excited my men to lay on the pine-wood, which, because of the oiliness of the resinous matter that oozes from the pine-tree, and that my furnace was admirably well made, burned at such a rate, that I was continually obliged to run to and fro, which greatly fatigued me. I, however, bore the hardship; but, to add to my misfortune, the shop took fire, and we were all very much afraid that the roof would fall in and crush us; from another quarter, that is, the garden, the sky poured in so much rain and wind that it cooled my furnace.

"Thus did I continue to struggle with these cross accidents for several hours, and exerted myself to such a degree, that my constitution, though robust, could no longer bear such severe hardship, and I was suddenly attacked by a most violent intermitting fever; in short, I was so ill that I found myself under a necessity of lying down upon my bed. This gave me great concern, but it was unavoidable. I thereupon addressed myself to my assistants, who were about ten in number, consisting of masters who melted bronze, helpers, men from the country, and the journeymen that worked in the shop, among whom was Bernardino Manellini di Mugello, who had lived with me several years. After having recommended it to them all to take proper care of my business, I said to Bernardino, 'My friend, be careful to observe the method which I have shown you, and use all possible expedition, for the metal will soon be ready. You cannot mistake; these two worthy men will quickly make the tubes; with two such directors you can certainly contrive to pour out the hot metal, and I have no doubt my mould will be filled completely. I at present find myself extremely ill, and really believe that in a few hours this severe disorder will put an end to my life.' Thus I left them in great sorrow, and went to bed."

His fever, meanwhile, continued to increase, he could get no rest, his faithful house-keeper endeavoured in vain to console him, and in the midst of all this affliction a man suddenly entered the room, like him who

> " Waked Priam, in the dead of night,
> And would have told him half his Troy was burned."

"This man," to resume Cellini's own language, "who in his person appeared to be as crooked as the letter S, began to express himself in these terms, with a tone of voice as dismal and melancholy as those who exhort and pray with persons who are going to be executed: 'Alas! poor Benvenuto, your work is spoiled, and the misfortune admits of no remedy.' No sooner," continues our poor artist, "had I heard the words uttered by this messenger of evil, but I cried out so loud that my voice might be heard to the skies, and got out of bed." Dressing himself with all possible speed, and bestowing sundry cuffs and kicks on his surrounding attendants, he hastens to his workmen, who, one and all, confirm the evil report of the messenger. "Whereupon," continues the excited and irascible Benvenuto, "I turned round in such a passion, and seemed so bent on mischief, that they all cried out to me, 'Give your orders, and we will all second you in whatever you command; we will assist you as long as we have breath in our bodies.' These kind and affectionate words they uttered, as I firmly believe, in a persuasion that I was upon the point of expiring."

Rallying all his energies, increased no doubt by his fever, he now bent his ardent mind to the work. Fresh wood was procured, old dry oak in abundance was heaped upon the furnace, so that the concreted metal again began to brighten and glitter; where the wind and rain entered a screen was constructed, and, encouraged by the example of their master, all his hands obeyed him with such zeal and alacrity, that every man did work enough for three. "Then," says he, to continue the spirited narrative, "I caused a mass of pewter, weighing about sixty pounds, to be thrown upon the metal in the furnace, which, with the other helps, as the brisk wood fire, and stirring it sometimes with iron, and sometimes with long poles, soon became completely dissolved. Finding that I had effected what seemed as difficult as to raise the dead, I recovered my vigour to such a degree, that I no longer perceived whether I had any fever, nor had I the least apprehension of death." But the climax had not yet arrived. "Suddenly a loud noise was heard, and a glittering of fire flashed before our eyes, as if it had been the darting of a thunderbolt. Upon the appearance of this phenomenon, terror seized on all present, and on none more than myself. This tremendous noise being over, we began to stare at each other, and perceived that the cover of the furnace had burst and flown off, so that the bronze began to run. I immediately caused the mouths of my mould to be opened, but finding that the metal did not run with its usual velocity, and apprehending that the cause of it was that the quality of the metal was consumed by the violence of the fire, I ordered all my dishes and porringers, which were in number about two hundred, to be placed one by one before my tubes, and part of them to be thrown into the furnace, so that all present perceiving that my bronze was completely dissolved, and that my mould was filling, with joy and alacrity assisted and obeyed me." Filled with gratitude and thankfulness at the success of his work, and with a piety that throws an additional lustre on his character, the first impulse of our hero, for he is worthy of the appellation, was to throw himself on his knees in the presence of all his workmen, and return thanks to Almighty God for his success. After which, his fever having completely left him, he ate and drank with a good appetite, and returned joyful and in good health to his bed. The duke, on learning the issue of the affair, received him in the most gracious manner, and took him into high favour, although his enemies endeavoured to persuade him that it was owing to infernal agency that success had been obtained, since he had compassed that which was not, according to their views, in the power of art to effect.

Of the antiquity of the art of working in metal, and producing graven images, we have early testimony in Scripture. Profane writers also make mention of early specimens of the same species of sculpture. Herodotus visited Babylon while it was in a state of tolerable preservation, and in describing the temple of Jupiter Belus, he says, "In a chapel which stands below, within the temple, is a large image of gold, representing Jupiter sitting upon a throne of gold, by a table of the same metal;" he alludes also to another statue of solid gold, twelve cubits high, which, he says, was not seen by him but described to him by the Chaldeans. According to Diodorus Siculus, the weight of the statues and decorations in and about the temple amounted to five thousand talents in gold; and their value has been estimated at about one hundred million of dollars. The vessels and ornaments are supposed to have been those which Nebuchadnezzar had brought to Babylon from Jerusalem; for he is said to have dedicated in this temple the spoils of that expedition. Semiramis, the wife of Ninus, finished the stupendous walls of Babylon, which were reckoned among the seven wonders of the world, and her palace is celebrated by historians for the emblematical sculptures with which the walls were covered, and for the colossal statues of bronze and gold of Jupiter Belus, of Nimrod, and of herself, with her principal warriors and officers of state.

CHAPTER XXVIII.

CONTRIBUTIONS FROM THE HIGHLANDS.

GENERAL CHARACTER OF THE COUNTRY—MR. MACDOUGALL—THE HIGHLAND STALL—TARTAN PLAIDS—HIGHLAND BONNETS—WOOLLEN HOSE—HIGHLAND SHOES—HIGHLAND ORNAMENTS AND PRECIOUS STONES—DIRKS AND QUAIGHS—DEER HORNS—DEER STALKING—CLOTH AND GLOVES FROM ST. KILDA.

WHEN we take into consideration the state of the rude and thinly scattered population of the northern extremity of our island, and reflect upon the toil they have to undergo to win from an ungrateful soil their scanty means of subsistence; when we look upon their barren mountains, their pathless moors, their lonely isles, "placed far amid the melancholy main," devoid in many instances of either "herb, tree, fruit, or flower"— when we bring before our imagination the forlorn and desolate nature of their country, so beautifully summed up by Collins, when, speaking of those sterile districts, he says—

"Nor ever vernal bee is heard to murmur there,"

when we see all this, and acknowledge the poverty of the neglected highlander, and his utter destitution of all the means and appliances which more fortunate England so abundantly enjoys, we are not surprised that he contributed so little towards the national display, but rather wonder that out of so slender and inappropriate means he should have been able to furnish the respectable quota, his stall, for he did not claim the honour of a department—in the Crystal Palace—presented before the eyes of the gratified spectators.

With the exception of the home manufacture of a few coarse articles of attire, the industry of the Celt is confined to the rude and insufficient tillage bestowed upon his "croft" of stunted oats or barley; or, if he be located near the sea, to a clumsy and inefficient system of fishery, carried on without proper boats or tackle, and seldom or never succeeding in rearing really bold or skilful mariners. The Celt, indeed, seldom makes anything but at most a freshwater sailor. He is accustomed to set at nought the wildest wintry storms on the high hillside, searching with his faithful "colleys" for the sheep smothering in the snow-drift, but the sea always daunts him. If anything can induce him to change his landward habits for a time, and fairly take to the brine, it is the herring; and those wondrous shoals of dainty fishes luckily come upon the coast during the summer and early autumnal season, when the weather is settled, and the harvest moon round and bright. Destitute then, in a great measure, of that pushing energy, and hard and keen spirit of industry and enterprise which have made England and the south of Scotland what they are, the poor highlanders of the north and west have very seldom any leaders or teachers who might pioneer the way to a better and a busier state of things. Capitalists pass them over, and their own lairds and native dignitaries are very much the same stuff as themselves. Good, hospitable, easy-going gentlemen, tolerably well skilled in black cattle and Cheviot wedders; hunters and fishers, to a man; great upholders of the bagpipes, and great connoisseurs of whiskey; they are still not the race of magnates who are the best suited to promote the true interests of the poor people among whom they dwell. They have been accustomed for ages to think of the poverty and idleness about them as the normal and natural state of things, and the poor cottar entertains precisely the same views. He has had nobody to put other ideas in his head. A little oatmeal, a herring in the season, a few potatoes, perhaps a little dairy produce, particularly goat's or ewe milk, and he is abundantly satisfied. His hut is chimneyless, sometimes windowless—a mere hovel of piled-up turf, with a smouldering peat fire in the centre, over which hangs the one pot which performs all culinary operations, and round which are tolerably sure to be stretched a ring of shaggy colleys; but leave him this—leave him his native atmosphere of peat smoke, and he is ready cheerfully to rough out any of its incidental hardships as the merest matter of course. In these respects the Scotch Celt is very much akin to his Irish brother. Both of them appear lazy; rather, however, because they have been brought up in idleness, than because they have any natural horror of work. Connemara and the Isle of Mull both get capitally ahead when the muscles and sinews they send forth are used in conjunction with those of England and Lowland Scotland. Donald and Pat trot cheerfully in the team, and pull with the rest of their compeers; but leave them together with a couple of spades and a couple of wheelbarrows, and short and scanty will be the day's work achieved. A main point of difference between the two races, or rather the two branches of the same race, is the sober and serious-mindedness of the Scot, and his invincible respect for the sacredness of human life. No one ever heard of a highland evicting landlord or his agent being shot from behind a hedge. The Irishman always cries out when he is hurt, and in a score of ways lets the world know his grievances; sometimes, indeed, he proclaims them through musket-barrels. Not so the Scotch highlander. In no part of the west of Scotland have the people suffered more than in some of the poorer islands of the Hebrides. There have been comparatively as many evictions, as many "fires quenched upon the hearth," in the wild islands and portions of the mainland of the west, as in Cork, or Roscommon, or Tipperary; but not one-tenth so much noise has been made about them. There has been no tumult, no agrarian outrages, no private and cowardly assassinations. The people have died or gone away to America, and made no sign. Highland grievances are scarcely ever heard of, but they are not one whit behind the woes and the wrongs of Ireland in number or intensity.

Life in the highlands, then, so far as national industry is concerned, is little better than passive vegetation. The yearly irruption of English tourists and sportsmen into the country furnishes, no doubt, a certain amount of employment, and distributes an important sum of money. The energies of no inconsiderable portion of the population are called into action as guides, boatmen, game-keepers, and the whole tribe of rural supernumeraries, who hang upon the skirts of a pleasure and sporting-seeking community who come abroad to spend money and amuse themselves. But the facilities thus afforded for labour can hardly be said to amount to a national industry. The working season extends only over three or four months, with, generally speaking, unnaturally exaggerated prices paid for the services performed. Holiday work, indeed, as it is rare and uncertain, ordinarily releases exceptional prices, a fact of which the population of watering-places, and bathing-places, for example, are amply aware. In the highlands, then, the people are destitute of the faculty which carves out profitable employment for itself. They are energetic to the utmost as sportsmen, lazy to a degree as labourers; just, in fact, because sporting in some shape or other is the labour to which they have been taught to consider themselves devoted. Above the class of the peasantry there is as little enterprise or desire for change as lower down; the only social revolution favoured by the lairds being the removal, either to the south or across the Atlantic, of as many poor and half-starved "crofters" as possible, in order that their vacant patches of land may be flung together into huge expanses of grazing ground for lowland sheep farmers. Under these circumstances, we repeat, we hardly expected to have seen the highlands represented in the Crystal Palace at all; and we probably should not have been so agreeably disappointed as we were, had it not been for the manful and single-handed exertions of one singularly enterprising, active, and indefatigable tradesman of Inverness. The name of this individual, Mr. Macdougall, has now attained something like a European reputation as a dealer in all textile and other productions manufactured in, or characteristic of, the highlands. From Inverness, the capital of the highlands, and the centre, judicial and commercial, of a large district of interesting country, it was to be expected that a comparatively large and characteristic collection—illustrative, not indeed, of a commercial industry—but of those domestic pursuits and household works which every people, however rude, must in some degree practise—would be sent. Nothing of the kind however. The enlightened Invernessians declined to form any local committee, or to take the slightest trouble about the matter; and Mr. Macdougall, after in vain trying to inspire his townsmen with a spark of his own spirit and energy, was actually obliged to put himself in communication with a committee formed in the small and rising little town of Elgin, in order to have the means of forwarding to the Crystal Palace a collection of highland manufactured stuffs, in the original production of which he himself had no mean share. In the gallery above China stood the stall which alone represented the industrial condition of the Scottish highlands. We shall select a few of the objects exhibited, and string them together by a slight thread of personal highland reminiscences and remarks.

The various tartans of the clans naturally formed a conspicuous object among the textile stuffs exhibited. The several checks were stated to have been arranged upon the very highest authority; for, be it known to our readers, there are formidable differences of opinion among the authorities relative to the exact and orthodox plan and colour of the checks of more than one tartan. You shall have a couple of fiery highland antiquarians disputing the shade of a red, or the proper breadth of a stripe of green, as if the fate of the world rested upon the issue. But if you wish to see both gentlemen roused to the pitch of the most appalling indignation, hint Dr. Johnson's theory, that the origin of tartan was rags, and that the different colours are counterfeit presentments of the variously hued shreds and patches with which the Doctor maintained that his highland friends used to clothe themselves. Recent investigations, we believe, however, give a higher antiquity to the tartan than it is generally believed to possess. Down to the reign of the sixth James, tartan is now said to have been a common wear, both in the lowlands and highlands; and recent discoveries in ancient costume seem to prove that a chequered species of garment, woven of many colours, was a favourite with a large body of semi-civilized men, the ancient stuffs disappearing from the more busy and changeful parts of the world, but still lingering in such nooks and corners as the until recently almost inaccessible highland hills. The Scotch lowlanders never seem, however, to have worn the kilt. At one time, no doubt, the kilt and plaid were simply one piece of cloth, folded at once over the shoulders and the loins. The separation of the whole into two distinct garments was a decided improvement, as the plaid for mountain countries, and for the use of a pedestrian, is one of the handiest garments which can be conceived. He can use it as a scarf, or a cloak, or a hood; rolled up and disposed round the body, it offers no impediment to walking; in wet and stormy weather the wearer can wrap at least half a dozen folds around his person, from the throat to the thighs; while, however the cloth may be disposed, the effect is almost uniformly picturesque. At the present day, the gorgeous clan colours formerly worn in the highlands are very generally superseded by the dull uniform grey of the shepherd plaid, a species of stuff which Lord Brougham has fairly immortalized. Everybody who has seen his lordship for the last fifteen years or so, has seen the famous black and white trowsers in which he delights. The fact as to these monotonously succeeding garments, we believe, from good authority, to be this: when Lord Brougham, then holder of the Great Seal, was in Inverness,—when, indeed, he made the celebrated declaration at a public meeting, that he would write to the King by that night's post, he purchased from Mr. Macdougall cloth for no less than forty pairs of shepherd tartan trowsers, and in this ample supply he has been going on ever since. The tendency of greyish stuff, however, to take the place of the ancient clan colours, would not have been less marked had Lord Brougham never worn anything but broad-cloth. The simple web of uniform hue is more easily produced than the kaleidoscopic coat of many colours, and, in case of damage, is more easily and effectively repaired. It was, however, the mean sumptuary law, passed in 1747 by the legislature, which gave the death-blow to the tartan, the kilt, and the plaid. Upon the people being permitted, in 1782, to return to the garb of the Gael, the general use and wont of the country was found to have worked out for itself another channel; and the philabeg is now, to all intents and purposes, a fancy costume. In Mr. Macdougall's stall, all the adjuncts of this dress were shown, constructed after the most orthodox fashion. There were several bonnets characteristic of the highlands, all neat, small, and fitting close to the head. The dreadful monstrosity of ostrich feathers, which our unhappy highland regiments are obliged to wear as head-gear, and which look exactly as if the men had adorned themselves with the spoils of an undertaker's warehouse, have nothing to do with the original highland bonnet, and we should be glad to see them scouted from the army. Slaves as we are, in some way, to the tyranny of all sorts of abominable hats, there is nothing worse in Britain than the heavy cylinder of feathers worn by the highland regiments. How much smarter all the men would look, each with a neat Glengarry bonnet, light and warm; jaunty and gay when worn with a cock over the front of the head, and cosey and comfortable if pulled over the ears, and made to do duty for a nightcap. The broad blue bonnet is essentially lowland, as its common Scotch name, the "Tam O'Shanter," testifies; but the mountain head-gear is infinitely the smartest and the most picturesque. There was a good show of hose, mostly woollen, in the stall, and in a great measure knitted by hand. These coverings for the feet, strong, elastic, firm of fabric, yet fleecy and warm, are capitally adapted for hard pedestrian work upon the mountain side, preventing the skin from being chafed, and absorbing and removing the perspiration from the limb. The hose, according to old use and wont, are always manufactured on a pattern larger and simpler than ordinary tartans, but, of course, harmonizing with the general colour of the dress which they are intended to complete.

Some interesting specimens of the old brogue were shown. The wondrous peculiarity to an English eye in the highland school of shoe-making, is that the upper leathers are pierced with rows and arches of holes arranged in fanciful combinations, and interspersed with little scolloped and jagged edges of leather, designed to ornament the shoe. "Well now, if I ever saw the like of that—making holes in their shoes to let the wet come through! they must never be without colds in the head," was the purport of a not unnatural remark we heard made, in different words, more than once while examining Mr. Macdougall's stall. But the speaker was not aware that wet feet is a bugbear unknown in the highlands. Shoes without holes may do capitally well for the *pavé* or the turnpike, but transfer the scene of operations to a mossy hill-side or a wild ravine, down which scores of tiny brooks come foaming to join the torrent at the bottom, and the wearer will shortly find that no holes are no protection against the water getting in, but a great hindrance to its getting out, and so will go hobbling along with an uncomfortable quantity of fluid splashing between his toes; while his brogued guide, on every dry bit of ground, squirts the superfluous moisture about with every step. Shoes intended for hard work among the heather are peculiarly made, in being double-toed. One or two strongly and firmly made specimens were exhibited. The stem of the heather plant is very rough, and nearly as hard as wire, so that the toes of the sportsman's shoes who forces his way amongst it, are speedily, unless they be thus doubly armed, reduced to a pitiful condition of thinness and whiteness. In these brogue-shoes, the nails which fortify the soles, are driven in diagonal lines across, the arrangement giving a surer footing to the wearer, when scrambling among slippery rocks, or making his way amid the green and slimy pebbles of a highland burn, with the fierce stream shaking him on his legs; for highland sporting, and especially highland fishing, requires that the adept shall be no more afraid of water than a kelpie or a merman. Mr. Briggs goes out a-fishing in the quiet southern streams with a pair of patent waterproof india-rubber goloshes, to keep his precious feet dry; but if he adventures on a foaming, rattling highland river, and essays the noble salmon instead of the contemptible pike, he must make up his mind to many a plunge, waist deep or deeper, in the stream, if he have the luck not to flounder over the slippery stones, and get carried off altogether by a current running like a mill-sluice down into the next deep swirling pool.

The highland ornaments displayed were few, but in correct taste, and of the orthodox old fashion. The principle of the ancient brooch, used either as an ornament, or for fastening the drapery of the plaid, is a very simple one. A number of silver spokes, springing more or less up from a circular rim, support a cairngorm pebble in the centre. Sometimes a set of small pins rise from the circumference of the ornament, each topped by a small cairngorm, arranged like moons around the centre stone. The cairngorm is indeed the national precious, or, at all events, ornamental, stone of Scotland: specimens are not uncommon of as bright a sparkle and as pure a crystalline splendour as are to be found in emeralds. The search amongst the wildest Grampian hills for these beautiful rock crystals, has lately, we learn, been prosecuted with uncommon enterprise and perseverance, and a deposit of splintered and disintegrated rock has been discovered, in which abundant pebbles have been found, formed in six-sided prisms, terminated by six-sided pyramids, extending from one inch to six or eight in length. Some of these lumps have weighed as much as ten pounds, and they have been discovered of several colours. Mr. Macdougall furnished his stall with some remarkable specimens, of a dark port wine hue, fully six inches in length, and we should think double as many in circumference. The pyramidal tops had been wrought, and exhibited a lustrous polish. These stones, we believe, were part of the produce of the labours of a party of upwards of forty people, who a couple of years ago proceeded from various parts of the highlands, in a regular caravan, to the remote district in which the mineral wealth lies thickest, pitched their tents or erected bothies on the heath, and after a search extending over several weeks, returned to their homes loaded with the rough crystals of the hills. The remaining accoutrements of the highland dress were shown in specimens of the dirk, to be worn by the side; the *skean dhu*, or "black knife," frequently carried in the garter; the naked blade resting against the leg, and which was used by the highland sportsmen to cut the throat of the wounded deer, and afterwards, in all probability, to carve and help the smoking haunch; the powder-horn, generally set jauntily off with cairngorm and silver mountings, and hung by a silver chain, although we suspect that in most of these little matters, a smirking spirit of small dandyism has encroached upon the veritable simplicity of the garb of old Gael.   A whiskey flask was seldom, however, left out of the list of the mountaineer's equipments.   We observed that the present fashion of disposing of the mountain dew for a day's trudge among the hills, is to place it in a miniature barrel, very much like that carried by Continental *vivandières*, and certainly, to our minds, neither elegant nor likely to be convenient. The spirit, however, thus provided for, you imbibe by means of the *quaigh*, or wooden drinking-cup, a handy little vessel, neatly scooped out of a block of hard wood, and sometimes carved with taste and ingenuity round the rim.   The quaigh is occasionally made very ornamental, and we have seen them with very large and brilliant cairngorms let in at the bottom.   The contents of an ordinary sized quaigh must be equal to at least two wine glasses and-a-half; but hardy and strong-headed Donald will fill it to the brim with whiskey, perhaps eleven over proof, and turn it coolly over without a muscle wincing, or a pulse beating the faster for the exploit.   In some of the more unfrequented parts of the country about the highland line, where these wooden implements of festivity have found their way without bringing their Gaelic names along with them, we have heard a quaigh called a *tass*, the word being one of many hundreds of corrupted French expressions, which still live in old-fashioned neighbourhoods, to demonstrate the ancient social, as well as political alliance of Scotland and France against our "auld enemies of England."   Above the stall, and forming a central top ornament, was a magnificent red deer's head, with no less than fourteen tynes or branches to his horns—an uncommon quantity, "a stag of ten" being generally reckoned to have a very liberal allowance of antlers.   Beneath this was ranged a curious collection of very coarsely woven and peculiarly tinted stuffs, expressly intended for the use of the deer-stalker, and dyed so as to resemble the most common patches of hue which prevail upon the dun mountain-side.   Englishmen, who form their notion of deer from the delicate little creatures, no bigger than goats, but as graceful as Italian greyhounds, which gambol upon the smooth shaven turf and the woodland vistas of our parks, have little idea of the fierce, powerful, majestic, and thoroughly savage animal known as the red deer.   It is but seldom that the ordinary traveller in the highlands gets a glimpse of him.   He must be sought for in his own haunts—in the wildest, most rugged, and inaccessible recesses of the hills—and his vigilance must be evaded by the most careful and experienced manœuvring.   The red deer has an eye like an eagle's, and a nose like a bloodhound's, or even more delicate still, as a human being passing him to windward a mile off, communicates a subtle taint to the keen air, which his moist and quivering nostrils—a perfect ball of acute nerves—catch in a moment, and which is almost certain to produce a rapid flight, the animal running perhaps a dozen of miles ere it couches down again into the heather and fern.   At some seasons, however, the red deer shows no such timidity or instinctive desire to take refuge in flight.   Unwary wanderers in the hills have been suddenly startled at finding themselves confronted in a moment with a magnificent stag, who, emerging from his cover, stands, all save his gleaming eyes and dilated nostrils, as rigid as a stag of bronze, gazing in grim silence upon the profaners of his temple of the wilderness.   Occasionally we have heard of large herds of deer, the hinds led by their magnificently antlered lords and masters, surrounding the astonished wayfarer, and after gazing for an uncomfortable number of very long minutes at the intruder, as if giving him to understand, by the silence and solemnity of the ceremony, the dreadful sacrilege of which he had been guilty in penetrating their enchanted domains—in an instant, upon a toss of the head of the ancient leader of the herd, leaping round, and in a moment disappearing in the cover of the surrounding copse. The reader can conceive the difference between these thoroughly wild creatures of the wilderness, as perfectly savage in their nature, as when the boar and the Caledonian bull were their compeers in the waste, and the half-tamed roes, which form picturesque groups in English parks; or the carted stag—Nelson or Billy—which is turned out of a waggon and chased like a hare across stubble and clover fields. All other game may be shot, but the red deer must be stalked. You walk coolly over the stubbles or over the heath, and bid the luncheon be ready by one o'clock, under such a tree or at the side of such a spring, and there you empty your bag and count the partridges or grouse, as the case may be. Not so with the red deer; you start rifle in hand and telescope slung across your back, upon an indeterminate expedition, perhaps of days; you walk as many miles over moss and moor, up vast sloping mountain sides, or down wild and rugged mountain ravines, as would suffice for many a tolerable pedestrian in the south over a turnpike road; you examine, hour after hour, with the glass the great dun slope of the opposite side of the glen. Then perhaps you have to make half-a-score miles circuit to " wind" the game, or to get to a ford in a deep river, or a ferry over a narrow loch. Then, approaching the slumbering herd, perhaps you have to crawl a mile or so upon all-fours, painfully dragging your rifle with you, and hardly daring to breathe, far less to speak; or you have to wade, waist-deep, double the distance down some roaring stream, or up it, which is worse; and after all it may chance, after fifteen good hours' work of walking, running, climbing, creeping, crawling, and wading, that some unexplained alarm is taken, and that, in thorough anguish of heart, you see the coveted antlers still beyond rifle reach, moving gaily off above the cover. No help for it—dash yourself down among the heather, execrate the whole race of stags, deers, roes, hinds, and does, but bid Donald prepare the "braxy" and the kebbuck; unsling your flask or little "anchor" of mountain dew; make your supper (it will be sure to be a good one); speculate with the faithful gillie about the likely whereabouts of the herd to-morrow, and then, rolling yourself from head to foot in as many folds of the tartan plaid as the web will admit of, fix your eyes for a space upon the dark mountain tops cutting rounded or peaked slices out of the clear blue sky, all twinkling with stars, and bidding bold defiance to a distinct chilliness in the atmosphere, nay, perchance, even to a touch of early frost, go soundly to sleep amid the deer's-foot and the bracken, to be on foot next morning before the dew-drops, lit by the sun, are gemming with diamonds the purple of the heather.

The proper style of costume for this class of sporting is peculiar. It is essential that it be very strong, very light, warm and fleecy; not too easily soiled; and that the colour or the prevailing colour harmonize with the most frequent shades of clustered vegetation upon the mountain side. All these essentials were fulfilled by the specimens of fabrics exhibited in the highland stall, and all these fabrics were manufactured from the native productions of the hills—the wool, in some cases, undyed, the coat of the black-faced highland sheep; the tinctures in other cases applied to it, extracted from highland herbs, barks, and mosses, so as to impart to the stuff the exact hue of the original plant or lichen; the thread spun upon the distaff by old highland crones and buxom highland lasses; the warp and the woof crossed by means of a hand-loom of the oldest fashion; the entire work, indeed, done in the hills from the productions of the hills, and by the natives of the hills. The cloth thus produced is well worthy of attention, from its stoutness, elasticity, evenness of fabric, and honesty of manufacture. You certainly might be looked at askance were you to sport the stuff in Regent-street or the Boulevards; but for the hill, the loch, and the moor, it is the *beau ideal* of

3 A

apparel. The cloth was shown of several colours, each produced by a native dye: some of these dyes have been long known in the highlands; others were new, particularly one from a species of moss locally called "crotach," and the colouring matter extracted from deer's-foot, one of the most beautiful herbs of the North. Clad, then, in such garments, the sportsman has the best chance of escaping the vigilant eye of the red deer, which may range over the hill-side without being able to separate him from the heather or the lichen in which he may be lying. The cloth, is of course, excellent for sporting and country purposes in general as well as for deer-stalking; and as such we should be glad to see its use made a fashion by English sportsmen on their annual visit to the moors. Handloom weaving of coarse stuff is certainly not a very exalted or economically profitable industry for a country. But, at all events, it is better than no industry at all; and it may be very well combined with the small agricultural operations to which the greater number of the weavers devote a portion of their time. We shall rejoice, then, to hear that the manufacture of home-made sporting stuffs flourishes in the North, convinced that it will bring along with it useful habits of industry, of course accompanied by the produce of industry to many a humble highland home. Mr. Macdougall has been attempting, not only to get up new native dyes, but new native materials for cloths. He exhibited two stuffs which were great curiosities in their way. One was a cloth made out of the down of the bog cotton, and the other a fabric manufactured from the fur of the white or alpine hare. Both of these products, however, may be considered of a fancy nature, as it is out of the question that the raw material should ever be supplied in sufficient abundance to make its spinning and weaving a regular means of employment. Knitting is another species of textile industry which is being extensively introduced in the north by the proprietor of the late highland stall, and also, we believe, by Mrs. Mackenzie, of Gairloch, who takes measures for the transmission of the domestic labours with the knitting-needle of the people over a vast district of the north-westerly coast to Glasgow, where the stuffs, admirably warm, fleecy, and honestly made, command good prices. Mr. Macdougall has 600 or 700 women employed in the production of similar articles, and copious specimens were exhibited in his stall. The fleecy hosiery of the Shetland Islands, entirely wrought by the hand, has long enjoyed a very well-merited pre-eminence, and is known as an article of commerce. The manufacture now appears likely to spread to the mainland, and the knitting-needle, in company with the hand-loom, will, no doubt, be found capable of materially increasing the scanty comforts of many a smoky bothy. One very rough piece of woollen was stated to be from St. Kilda, the furthest from the shore of the British subsidiary isles, and to have been worked in a rude machine constructed in the island; and some mits and warm gloves were shown, which also came from that locality.

Altogether, then, the highland stall was, to a great extent, satisfactory. It presented us with favourable specimens of certain infant local industries, and afforded samples not only of new materials of textile manufacture, but of new ways of combining and colouring them. We could have wished for a collection of highland agricultural and fishing implements, and of specimens of the ordinary furniture of the bothies, to show the low and degraded condition in which, as regards physical comfort, the people are living; but, in the absence throughout the North of that public spirit which, in other districts of the island, is so strong, we can only so far congratulate ourselves, that a single individual came forward to exhibit at least one phase of the industrial highlands, composed, indeed, almost wholly of infant efforts at production, but which were so excellent of their kind, and so promising for the future, that we can only hope that an extensive and extending demand will reward the efforts of the promoter, and the labours of these work-people of the far north, in their new and experimental career.

CHAPTER XXIX.

FOREIGN AND COLONIAL DEPARTMENTS—*continued.*

TURKEY—BRASS LAMPS—MANGALS OR BRAZIERS—BASINS, EWERS, AND SHERBET CUPS, CAMP
EQUIPAGE— BEADS—WATER-PIPES—COSTLY SPOONS—GOLD EMBROIDERED SHIRT—MOLDAVIAN
SLEDGE—FIRE-ARMS, SILKS, ETC. ETC.—VARIOUS ARTICLES FROM TUNIS.

THE contributions from Turkey were exhibited in a bay at the north-east angle of the
transept, where by their gorgeous variety of bright colours and embroidery, they
produced a very striking effect in the general *coup-d'œil* on entering the building.
Apart altogether from its intrinsic worth, is, moreover, the interest naturally attaching to
the industry and productions of an empire the condition of which must always be
regarded by the Englishman as of vital importance. Turkey justly looks to Great
Britain as one of the foremost, the sincerest, and the most potent of her allies and
friends; while Great Britain cannot feel indifferent to all that illustrates the internal
condition of an empire that fills up so much of the vast space intervening between our
Indian dominions and the central countries of Europe—an empire which includes within
her territory the mouths of the Euphrates and the shores of the Persian Gulf on the one
hand, and on the other divides with Austria the kingdom of Croatia.

In many of the products of Turkish industry we distinctly recognise a close analogy
to what the ancients have left behind us of their domestic manners; much of the
ancient forms found by the Moslems in the countries which they conquered have been
left with little alteration. Of this no one can doubt who paid attention to the
collection in question, from the brass lamp with its scissors, pincers, and bodkin, still
used in many parts of Italy, to the arabesque plaster moulding and other slightly altered
traditions of the world, of which the excavations of Pompeii have given us such interesting glimpses. But it is not the conquerors of the empire of the East that entwine
themselves with our modern sympathies. Gibbon, with all his rhetorical splendour,
illumines, but does not vivify the Amrus, the Saladins, and the Amuraths. Uhland,
in one of his most exquisite sonnets ("Kaiser und Dichter") contrasts the duration of the
conquests of princes and bards; and all must agree with him, who visited this collection, and think less of those who trod over great monarchies than of those who
depicted the manners and superstitions of the Orientals. Not one in a hundred of those
who visited these interesting collections, remembers that three centuries ago all Europe
quaked with terror at the name of the Grand Turk, and that Solyman the Magnificent
was an even more powerful sovereign than Charles V.; but all remember, and none
ever will forget, the heroes and heroines of the "Arabian Nights Entertainments."
The Ottoman empire is now an essential part of the "grand tour;" and, therefore,
many who paced the Crystal Palace may have had comparatively little new to see in
the Turkish department; but these few form, after all, an insignificant portion of the
hundreds of thousands who have never seen either the Black Sea or the White Sea,
the desert, or the palm grove; but are, nevertheless, familiar with the sayings and doings
of the guarded city of Bagdad, from the street porter with his weary burthen, to the
caliph himself, attended by Jaifar the Barmecide and the redoubtable Mesroua-el-Siaf.
It is, therefore, the latter portion of our fellow-countrymen that we invite to accompany
us in a tour through the objects that appeared on the tables and in the stalls contributed
by all parts of the Ottoman empire.

Prominent in the centre of the tables stood a large machine of glittering brass and of
elegant form, which looked like a huge tea-urn. This was a mangal or brazier, for

charcoal, with which apartments are heated in winter.   People in England may abuse
our climate as they choose, but they may rest assured that in many respects it is not easy
to find a better, for we are neither roasted in summer, nor frozen in winter; and at
Christmas time recommend us to the sun of Wall's-End or Newcastle-upon-Tyne, which
blazes in every snugly carpeted English parlour, in preference to the charcoal of the
most elegant mangal that ever was constructed.   The mangal stands in the centre of the
room, and a coverlet being thrown over it, the ladies of the harem sit around it in a circle,
and thus warm themselves in a manner not the most healthy or improving to the
complexion.   Beside the mangals were the basins and ewers, such as are used for washing
before and after food—the servant holding the former in his left hand, while the water
is poured out with his right.   Here, too, were sherbet cups, the Bohemian practice of
gilding stained glass having been originally borrowed from the East; and we need
scarcely say that the European offspring excels by a long way the Oriental parent.   But
those shown at the Exhibition were creditable to the manufactory of Ingekyoi.   It is
climate that suggests the quality of diluents; and while the North is cunning in the
distillation of strong liquors, the South is equally remarkable for the ingenuity with
which cooling drinks are compounded, from the choice lemonade and orgeat, to the
delicious chopped-ice sherbet with the orange flower flavour.   Let it not be supposed
that it is only in idleness and in the arts of pleasing that the ladies of the East pass their
time; here, to be sure, were ingenious cosmetic boxes, with various compartments
for the different dyes used in adornment: they are equally skilled in the useful and
domestic arts, and the ladies of the highest rank are acquainted with the art of preparing
such drinks.   In that of preparing fruits they even excel our own housewives, and a
very large mother-of-pearl frame for embroidery reminds us that the most beautiful
dresses of the wealthier classes are the product not of the professed milliner, but of the
domestic hareem.

The military character of the Turks was sufficiently recognisable in the collection;
many objects showed them to be essentially a nation that mounts much on horse-back,
lives much under tents, and has adapted its habits to military locomotion.   It would
take too much space to enumerate the articles illustrative of this part of our subject:
their camp dishes fitting into each other and easily portable, their lanterns that shut
up and open out like magic, and many other articles, showed that with the Orientals
there is not, as with the Europeans, that broad line of distinction between the habits of
residence and the habits of locomotion that exists in the West.   It is not merely the
aboriginal and nomade habits that account for this; there is a political reason: the
constant fear of the great dignitaries of the empire acquiring a formidable local influence,
causes a perpetual circle of recalls and nominations in order to maintain in efficiency the
functions of the central government; this produces a great deal of movement from one
end of the empire to the other on the part of those dignitaries, military and civil,
who in the Ottoman empire stand in the place of a hereditary aristocracy.   Thus,
whatever is portable, whether diamonds, carpets, or shawls, is prized; hence, too, the
expensive velvet, and gold embroidery bestowed on their saddles.   And instead of such
ponderous fixtures as the European writing desk, the pianoforte, and the organ, there is
the diminutive cocoa-nut, or brass inkstand and pens for the hours of business; or for
the hours of diversion there is the light reed *nay* or flute, the lute, or the violin, of the
most primitive construction, such as one sees in the productions of the very early Italian
painters.   But we are getting into a tangled web of philosophy, instead of proceeding
with our catalogue *raisonné* of the different objects.   An examination of the collection
of beads repaid trouble—the habit of passing beads through the fingers being as inveterate
with many Turks as the perpetual wood-whittling of a Kentucky man; we have even

known an individual who weaned himself from this practice, and who yet never met another person with beads without being unable to resist the old temptation, and beg for them to pass through his fingers.

Fezes from Tunis and Egypt there were in abundance, and also plenty of stuffs for wrapping round them hanging in various parts of the collection, from simple cotton to fine shawl; but we saw no regularly wound and made up turban, such as is worn in the East, although we observed a not uninteresting substitute in one of stone or plaster, such as usually adorn the cemeteries of the Turks. The water-pipes were uncommonly beautiful; we mean those in which Bagdad timback is smoked through snake-formed tubes, and which, from the noise produced by the passage of the air through the water is commonly called the hubble-bubble. In those vases and in the snakes were found a skilful attention to effects of colour; and if we pass to other objects, such as dresses, shawls, scarfs, girdles, we may remark that the suitableness of very bright and contrasted colours to these warmer climates, springs from the semi-obscurity of apartments partially darkened to exclude the heat and light of the sun. It was the Venetians that most fully understood this phase of the beautiful. Hence, in consequence of the limpid depth of his shadows, the boldest colours of Paul Veronese never shock us, which is certainly more than can be said of Rubens, with all his genius and facility; and this peculiar quality of the Venetian school could never be attained by northern painters living in climates where every effort is made to get as much of the sun as possible, nor by any set of men whose eyes are not educated to the effect of brilliant colours in every variety of sombre shadow. From tracing the connexion of Venice with the manufactures of the Levant, so frequently introduced into the Venetian pictures, the observation of the relation of the Levant to the arts of Italy cannot be considered as a *baroque* transition, and those who took an interest in the old pottery of Faenza might remark the prevalence of that Faenza-like green and yellow in the rude pottery of Tunis.

Such observations are made for the many who paid their shilling, and not for the season-ticket holders, who have lounged up and down the Levant, and may have made such remarks for themselves; but even to the *homme blasé*, in relation to Oriental life, there was much to fix attention. A jar of dates is a jar of dates, but certainly a common jar of Barbary dates has not the same interest for us as one from Medina, grown under the aëronautical sarcophagus of the prophet himself. One jar of curdled milk is like another; but when we know that the one before us is that of an African ostrich, it ceases to be common milk. "Would you like to give a guinea for one of those spoons?" said a friend who conducted us through this portion of the Exhibition. "We should be very sorry." "Well, there is one that you cannot have for less than £30 sterling." We saw that it was not of tortoise-shell nor of ivory, but something of excessively fine texture, between the two, and learned that it was a beak of the spoonbill heron, a bird now so rare that it promises to become at no distant date as extinct as the *Megatherium* or the *Ichthyosaurus*. Even the specimens of ingenuity degenerating into the *baroque* were not without interest: here was a wooden chain, each link perfect without a joining, and cut out of one piece of wood, a piece of laborious handicraft. On seeing a shirt almost stiff with gold lace, we were reminded of the quaint pages of Southey's *Doctor*, who on reading of some man who had a shirt of gold and a shirt of silver-thread, declared his preference for the perhaps unkingly but more comfortable nether garment of Flanders linen. And much as we have praised the Turkish aptitude for the portable, it was scarcely without a smile that we passed the odd combination of a chibouque and the crutch of an invalid.

But it was not merely the gratification of a fastidious curiosity that rendered a visit to the Turkish collection attractive; it was in fact the best and most interesting lesson in physical and commercial geography, in relation to so large a part of the world, that has hitherto been offered in this metropolis. Turkey has neither the scattered colonies, such as the British empire, nor has she the vast extent of territory possessed by Russia; but no state in the world is, to use a German phrase, so many-sided, or presents such contrasts of productions and manners in consequence of the diversities of her nations and climates; and her vast contiguous territory is rather ruled by Turks than quickly settled by them, for they are rather the conquerors than the colonists of the wide territories stretching from the Caucasus to Algeria, from the Adriatic to the Persian Gulf. Most travellers dilate very largely on the vices and corruptions of the Turkish administration of the various departments of government; but it cannot be denied, that although the march of government is less regular than in Europe, the state itself is without the burthen of a national debt; that the internal taxation, although somewhat arbitrary in application, is, upon the whole, very light. The principal cause of this is the very large revenue which she derives from a scale of customs duties fixed upon solely with a view to revenue, and not adapted to produce an artificial scarcity favourable to the few who have to sell a particular commodity, and injurious to the general interests.

We usually associate the Ottoman dominions with heat rather than with cold; but there was exhibited an elegant sledge from Jassy, the capital of Moldavia, which showed not only the love of luxury in the boyars of that principality, but reminded us that Russian vicinity has imprinted Russian manners on a part of the Ottoman empire, which, from its level plains and severe winter, in no way belongs to the East as sung by the Byrons, Goëthes, and Moores, and which, if it has not the azure skies of summer climes, has, throughout the length and breadth of its territory, the thick rich alluvial soil which makes the plains of the north of the Black Sea a granary of all Europe, and procures for the boyars of those principalities incomes far exceeding those of the average of the impoverished *noblesse* of the continent of Europe. We therefore see that the manufactures of those parts spring from their economical circumstances; they have neither silks nor velvets, but their wax-lights, and other modifications of native productions, surprise by their cheapness.

On crossing, in imagination, the Danube into Turkey in Europe, we found in this exposition comparatively little to remind us that Ternovo, a city of Bulgaria, was, at the end of last century, one of the most active manufacturing towns in Europe. But in Turkey much the same phenomenon is to be found as in India—the immensity of British capital and machinery has swallowed up the smaller industries, as the large fishes eat the small, and the two thousand looms of Ternovo have fallen down to a mere remnant. The Turkish Exposition was, therefore, less remarkable for its manufactures than for those articles in which patient and ingenious handicraft was exercised upon manufactures, such as the embroidery of female articles of dress; among which we may specify gold upon a light-blue ground, silk of various colours worked upon white muslin, and the winter dresses, remarkable for their elegance, the best combination of which was black silk upon a chocolate ground. In Albania, that land of mountain warfare, it were vain to expect the results of either capital or machinery. The turbulent character of the population was brought to observation by the excessive elaborateness of their rifles and pistols, which are as much an object with a wealthy Albanian as a horse to an Arab, or a carriage and a box at the French theatre to the boyar of the principalities. In the vast plains of Roumelia, we observed signs of a climate more genial than that of the principalities, and of a population less turbulent than that of Albania. The sight of the cotton and tobacco of Macedonia was pleasantly relieved by the fragant odour of otto of roses from Kasanlik. The heavy articles of export were not so much from the capital itself as from Salonika, Smyrna, and other ports. The capital is the receptacle of a large mass of British, French, and Austrian manufactures, annually exported to Turkey, but it is at these other ports that vessels seek their return cargoes. As a place of manufacture, Constantinople itself is a sort of Paris to the eastern world, and productive rather of the diversified objects of luxuriant convenience adapted to eastern usages than of articles of first necessity, which recommend themselves by cheapness and general use. For instance, the cymbals of our military bands were originally introduced from the East, which is shown by the habit of the cymbal players in various European armies still wearing an oriental costume; and we were amused on seeing an English inscription, rudely engraved on a pair, which runs as follows :—"This sort of zieh was invented by Mr. Kevork, A.D. 1730; and the present has been manufactured by his grandson's grandson, Mr. Kirkov, A.D. 1851.—Psamatia, Constantinople."

After contemplating the very neat model of a Bosphorus kaïk, and having taken our readers across the marvellous and beautiful river of salt-water, flowing between its umbrageous banks to the Sea of Marmora, let us occupy ourselves with the Asiatic portion of the Ottoman contributions, which is still more highly favoured by climate, richer in classical associations, not less remarkable for natural capabilities, having mineral and agricultural wealth—much of it, alas, too dormant considering its advantages!—being bordered with most excellent ports from Trebizond and Samsoun round to Marmorice, and other ports on her southern coast, which everywhere present themselves to facilitate communication. Here was the copper of the mines of Tokat; here was the excellent sword cutlery of Adana; here was the wealth of the waters of the Archipelago, the sponge torn up from the depths of the Mediterranean by the boldness and ingenuity of the diver, with the still adhering oyster; here was the large black wheat of Konich, the ancient capital of Turkish power, long before the sons of Orchan became the terror of Europe; and here, too, were those large and excellent Turkey carpets, which stand their ground so successfully against the skill and capital of our own Kidderminster.

Let us now make haste to cross the Taurus, and get into Syria, which has much to interest both in the way of natural productions and manufactures. Latakia exhibited tobacco, beyond all comparison the best either of the New or the Old World; for no American tobacco is in delicacy of flavour equal to that grown in the mountains between Tripoli and this place. The silks of Mount Lebanon and of Broussa, in Asia Minor, were also put together, and were well worthy of an examination. The silk of Syria has been until lately unsuited for exportation to England, in consequence of its being long reel; but, latterly, by the exertions of M. Portalis, a French merchant in Beyrout, and of the active and ingenious Messrs. Barker, of Aleppo, sons of our late well-known Consul-general in Egypt, manufactories, with improved machinery, have been established by the former firm in Mount Lebanon, and by the latter gentlemen at Suedia, near the mouths of the Orontes, with such results as to leave no doubt of the advantages likely to accrue from an extension of British capital in this direction. On passing from the coast to the interior, the great cities of Damascus and Aleppo arrested our attention by their manufactures of mixed silk, cotton, and gold thread, equally remarkable for their richness, their elegance, and their substantial strength, being universally used for the holiday dresses of the inhabitants of those countries; the ingenuity and machinery of France and England having produced no successful imitation, these native manufactures, along with those of silk sashes for turbans and girdles at Tripoli (Syria), still continue to vegetate, although certainly in a decayed condition. Of other manufactures, the saddle from Damascus was characteristic of the country, but did not give a favourable idea of the ingenuity of the Damascenes. What a European most prizes is their excellent preserved fruit, the whole territory that surrounds the town being one vast orchard, intersected by the seven-armed Barrada; while the principal art and handicraft of the place—which is that of mosaic pavements, the beauty of which strikes all strangers —is not of a nature offering capability of being shown in an Exhibition such as we are describing.   As for Arabia—that waterless land of stones, sand, camels, and starved shrubs—so lacking in corn, wine, and oil—so contrasting to Egypt with her flesh-pots, and fertile rather in rhymes and metaphysics than in the good things of this world—it certainly had very little to show; but, as a natural production, the coffee of Mocha was not to be despised.

In a department of the building near the south end of the transept were to be found the Tunisian contributions to the Exhibition, guarded by persons whose attire instantly recalled many a tale of Turkish or Corsair life, and almost rendered one dubious as to the reality of a scene in which such mentally and traditionally fearful individuals were playing the part of competitors in the peaceful arts.   When a few glances had reassured the spectator, and he had time rapidly to draw a favourable comparison between the present and the still recent past, he might begin to examine some of the objects presented to his view. In a glass-case of huge dimensions were to be seen an assemblage of curious articles of dress, all heaped together in not unpicturesque confusion.   Conspicuous amongst them were several riding-hats, circular in form, not very unlike a parasol, minus the handle, and of a girth which put to shame the broadest brimmed straws seen in this country in the hottest summer; the materials of which they were composed were feathers, figured satin, &c.   In the same case was a lady's dress of figured satin, of smock fashion, the breast decorated with rich gilt embroidery.   A gentleman's cloak was similarly adorned, and some striped figured bed-hangings also invited inspection.   In ledges round this case were contained various ornaments for female use, consisting chiefly of gold and silver bracelets and necklaces, and of what, for want of a better term, we must call silver anklets—these last being silver ornaments for feminine ankles, yet of so massive a description, that it would be difficult for the uninitiated to conceive how they could be worn, except indeed in a state of complete repose.   The little boxes which bordered the case contained also handkerchiefs and neckerchiefs, slippers, gilt pouches or wallets, and other slight articles of personal application.   The steed of the wealthy inhabitant of northern Africa has often been pourtrayed as the object of lavish adornment; and of this kind of display the people of Tunis afforded some interesting specimens.   The most prominent equestrian article exhibited was a gorgeously gilt saddle, so large as to form what are commonly described as the trappings of the animal, as well as a seat for the rider.   This article had an extremly rich appearance.   The decorative work, if it did not appear particularly delicate on a minute inspection, produced a dazzling effect at a short distance.   The back portion of the seat rose perpendicularly in front; a pistol holster was attached to either side of the fore part of the saddle, and the stirrups, of highly polished brass, were shaped like a shovel or flat scale.   Every provision was made for the safety and ease of the rider.   There was another saddle of blue velvet, destined for female use, richly embossed and gilt, having polished silver spurs.   Amongst the personal attire there was one article which, though small, deserves a brief notice.   It was a cap of ordinary Turkish fashion, but of very rich materials, designed to be worn by either male or female in the juvenile period of life; it had depending from it a rich sweep of gold fringe terminated or fastened at the extremity with small circular ornaments. Amongst a mass of objects on one side of the department were morocco boots and slippers, in great variety and abundance; knives in cases, straw hats of vast circumference; and baskets of dates in such numbers as to justify a suspicion that they were brought by the exhibitors for use as well as display.   There was also a lofty wooden gate, having two folds and several panels, the latter laced with bamboo.   The productions of the country were deposited in glass jars.   They were of a very miscellaneous character, comprising pomegranates, almonds, raisins, corn, butter, and many other equally familiar and equally useful articles.

CHAPTER XXX.

STAINED AND PAINTED GLASS—*continued.*

GENERAL RULES TO BE OBSERVED—COMPARISON OF DIFFERENT STYLES—ANCIENT AND MODERN WORKS—ERRORS IN MODERN IMITATORS—LARGE PAINTED WINDOW BY BERTINI OF MILAN, "DANTE AND HIS THOUGHTS"—CAPRONNIER OF BRUSSELS.

OF the glass paintings, displayed in the Exhibition, there were some whose subject was a picture, a pattern, an heraldic device, or an intermixture of these three; and some of the pictures, and of the pattern glass paintings, appeared to have been designed and executed in a particular style of their own. The various works thus presented so many different points for consideration as to render it impossible to lay down any one general rule for deciding on their pretensions; but by stating as concisely as we can the principles by which we have been guided in making the following observations, an opportunity is afforded of ascertaining their correctness or incorrectness; and the exhibitors may be enabled to draw their own conclusions as to the opinions which we entertain of the merits of their works.

It is hardly necessary to observe that glass painting must be judged by a different standard from that which is applied to other kinds of painting. The material employed imposes upon the artist an obedience to certain conditions in the design and execution of the work. His object should be, not to produce the best possible picture, but the best brilliant and transparent picture. Among the excellences which are equally essential to a good glass painting, and to an oil or fresco painting, may be mentioned,—a design which is pleasing in itself, and which is composed with reference to the effect sought to be produced at the distance from which it is intended to be viewed, correct drawing (which includes the course of the shadows as well as the outlines), and harmony of colour. But such a composition must be chosen, and such a mode of colouring must be adopted, as are calculated, among other things, to display to the best advantage the brilliancy and transparency of the material, and to accord best with the mechanical construction of glass painting, which, unless it is of very moderate dimensions, must necessarily consist of several pieces of glass, connected together with lead or other metal, and supported with iron bars. As a general rule, the best, because the most effective, composition for a glass painting (not being a mere pattern), is a single figure, or a group consisting of foreground figures, with either a landscape, an architectural, or a plain coloured background; the landscape, if any, being treated as a mere accessory to the group. And the mode of execution, which appears to display to the best advantage the brilliancy and transparency of the material, is, where the colouring is chiefly produced by means of glass coloured in the manufacture; where the shadows are transparent, but have hard and sharp edges; and, above all, where a large proportion of the lights are left clear and unencumbered with enamel paint.

Of the correctness of this view, so far as it relates to the sort of composition, and to the mode of colouring best suited for a glass window, we have less doubt, since nearly all the exhibitors have acted consistently with it; but we also find that our opinion of hard-edged shadows and clear lights is opposed to the practice of nearly all the exhibitors, including those most distinguished by their works. To their authority we can only oppose that of the glass painters of the first half of the sixteenth century, when, owing to the similarity of the material, the conditions of glass painting very closely resembled the conditions of modern glass painting; and we would invite a comparison of such works, as for instance, the window of the chapel of the Miraculous Sacrament, on the north side of the choir of St. Gudule's Cathedral, Brussels, and the two transept windows of that cathedral, with the windows of Gouda Church, Holland, and of Amsterdam Cathedral, both which are of the last half of the sixteenth century, with any of the works now exhibited; and if it appears that the Brussels and Lichfield windows are more brilliant, more glass-like, and (allowance being made for modern improvements in drawing) as pictorially effective as any of the other works to which we have referred, then we are justified in considering that the limit to which the obscuration of the glass may be carried was reached at the end of the first half of the sixteenth century, and, consequently, in regarding the works of that period as standards of true glass painting by which other works of similar nature may be judged. The question, however, must ever be matter of opinion, and must ultimately resolve itself into a question of taste, which can only be determined by actually making the comparison suggested, and inspecting the windows themselves. In estimating, then, the merits of a glass painting, we have to consider, first, to what extent the conditions of the art have been observed; secondly, its artistic merit as a picture or painting. According to these principles, a work in which the composition and drawing are indifferent, but which displays vivid and powerful colouring, or is brilliant in effect, is preferable, as a glass painting, to one which is dark and dull, but in which the drawing and composition are good. Of this we have a striking example in the ante-chapel of New College, Oxford. Sir Joshua Reynolds' window, with all its excellencies of drawing and composition, is not to be compared in effect with the rude windows of Wykeham's time that surround it. Still, though a due regard to the conditions of the art is of such preponderating weight in the merits of a glass painting, other artistic qualities, as has been said before, are not to be overlooked; and, consequently, of two glass paintings in which the conditions of the art have been equally observed or equally violated, that is to preferred which displays the highest merit in composition, drawing, and other qualities of a good picture.

But besides the two points of view just mentioned, in which a glass painting is to be considered, it is necessary, in order to estimate the quality of a work professing to be executed in imitation of any ancient style, to judge of it with reference to the standard which its author has himself chosen. To condemn it, on the one hand, if it falls short of the model which it professes to follow, and fails in the effect which it professes to produce; and, on the other hand, perhaps to make some allowance for peculiarities which would be objected to as faults, if they were not excused by the necessity of adhering to some characteristic feature of the adopted style. On examining an original specimen of any ancient style of glass painting, we cannot fail to be struck with the general harmony of its features. Not only does a strict consistency exist between the character of the figures and of the ornamental details, but these agree with the nature of the design and mode of execution, which again seem to be adopted and formed with reference to the nature and quality of the material used. The changes effected in process of time in the composition and texture of the glass appear to have involved, in the opinion of the ancient artists, corresponding changes in the very condition of glass painting.

In all the glass paintings of earlier date than the last quarter of the fourteenth century —until which period the material commonly in use was not over clear, substantial in appearance, or intense in colour—the articles seem to have relied for effect principally on the richness and depth of the colouring. In these works the means of representation may be said to have been reduced almost to the lowest degree. Even the picture glass paintings are little else than exceedingly powerful and brilliant mosaics. The figures are hardly distinguishable from each other, nor from the back-ground of the composition, otherwise than by their outlines and local colouring. The style of the painting is simple, bold, and forcible, as if the artists apprehended that softness of finish and nice gradations of light and shade would be useless and ineffective, and deemed those qualities to be alike incompatible with the simplicity of the composition, the positive character of the colouring, and the general brilliancy of the work. The drawing is effected by thick black outlines, which always strengthen and sometimes even supply the place of broader shadows, and these shadows, when compared with those of later times, are weak, and are in great measure lost in the depth of the local colouring; which circumstance, however, renders their hardness the less perceptible. The same style of execution is extended to patterns as well as to pictures. The design is traced on the glass with firm and strong outlines; and it is hardly necessary to remark—for this is observable in every original work—that the harmony in form and character between the figures and the ornamental details, proclaims them to be the production of the same hand, and the conception of the same mind. In all subsequent glass paintings, until the revival of the more ancient styles, which took place about twenty-five years ago, we may observe that in proportion as the glass became more pellucid, more flimsy in substance and appearance, and less powerful and intense in colour, a less mosaic and an increased pictorial effect was aimed at. The weakness of the individual colours was in a great measure compensated by their employment in larger masses, by judicious contrasts, and by harmonious arrangement. Their depth was increased by means of broader and more powerful shadowing, and a certain degree of richness was imparted by the more liberal use of diaper patterns and other minute embellishments. The drawing became more delicate, nicely graduated and highly-wrought shadows were to a great extent substituted for stiff black outlines, and in many instances considerable attention was paid to perspective and to atmospheric effects. In short, it would seem that the artists considered that the more refined nature of the material demanded as well as favoured a more refined pictorial treatment, and sought to compensate for its comparative thinness and weakness by the introduction of beauties of another description. The new system, it is true, was not fully developed until the middle of the sixteenth century; but its commencement may be easily traced as far back as the end of the fourteenth, by which time the principal change in the nature of the material had taken place.

Many persons, and among them some whose opinions are entitled to consideration, differ from the opinion that the material used previous to 1380 has not hitherto been successfully imitated; but on a point of so much importance we are bound to retain our opinion until convinced of its fallacy. That there is a visible difference in the appearance of modern glass and of that belonging to these early periods is admitted; but it is attempted to be accounted for by the supposition that it is solely due to the effect of age and exposure to the weather, and that the ancient glass, when first put up, must have appeared as weak and flimsy as our own. But as it is evident, on breaking a piece of ancient glass, that the effect of antiquity is confined to its surface, the above supposition is destroyed by the observation, that modern glass whose surfaces have, by artificial means, been reduced as nearly as possible to the same condition as that of the old glass, fails, nevertheless, in its resemblance to the old. One of the most favourable examples of the closeness to which imitation of the thirteenth century glass can be carried by splashing the glass with enamel brown and other expedients, is afforded by a window recently put up in Mans Cathedral (the third clerestory window from the west on the south side of the choir). We are unable to say by whom it was painted. But although the design, owing to the breadth of its colouring, is favourable to modern glass, the deception is decidedly incomplete. Equally unsuccessful are the admirable restorations of the earlier thirteenth century windows in some of the apsidal chapels of Bourges Cathedral, executed, we believe, by M. Lusson. The modern glass may here be easily distinguished from the old by its want of crispness and its thinness, although it has been obscured in imitation of the effect produced by age and long exposure to the atmosphere. We are strongly impressed with the opinion, that the difference in effect between such ancient and modern glass does not depend on the state of the surface, but on the composition of the material; and this opinion has been much strengthened by the result of some chemical experiments recently made, by which the very great difference in the composition of modern glass, and that of glass of the thirteenth century, is clearly demonstrated. Assuming the truth of the foregoing observations, it is obvious how important a bearing they have on modern imitations of the ancient style of glass painting. Those of the periods earlier than the last quarter of the fourth century having to be worked out in a mode of execution adapted to, and formed with reference to, a material very different from that of the present day, and therefore labouring under a disadvantage which hardly any skill or ingenuity can overcome; whilst, on the other hand, the glass of the present day resembling that of the fourteenth, or still more closely that of the sixteenth century, there is proportionably less difficulty, as far as material is concerned, in the way of the successful execution of works in the style of these periods.

The defects which appear to us to prevail the most generally are—First, the misapplication of the materials, so that works which would have possessed merits as enamel paintings on china or any other opaque body, are, as glass paintings, weak in colour and deficient in transparency. The ill effect of thus confounding the principles of painting on an opaque surface with principles of painting upon a transparent body, like glass, are strikingly exemplified by observing, in the works of this description in the Exhibition, the difficulties the artist has had to contend with in the management of his material, notwithstanding the dexterity of his handling. The vividness of effect produced is barely superior to that of an oil painting, and in tone, transparency of shadow, and general harmony, the glass is very inferior to a painting in oil. The metallic framework which, in every well-contrived glass painting, is conducive to the good effect of the work, is here an eyesore, imparting to those outlines which it follows a harshness which does not accord with the elaborate softness which many of our modern artists have adopted in lieu of the severer style of their predecessors.

Secondly. Non-adherence to the style, which has been selected by an artist for imitation in any particular work. For instance, we have sometimes found associated together, in the same glass painting, borders in the style of the fourteenth century, canopies of the fifteenth, and figures of the sixteenth. In others, though the ornamentation is drawn and executed in the style of an early period, the figures are either wholly in the style of a later one, or else accord with the ornamentation only in the drawing or composition; the elaborate softness of their execution having been borrowed from a considerably later period. Others, in which the drawing, mode of execution, and composition of an early period are scrupulously observed, both in the figures and ornamental details, are executed in a material, which, owing to its greater pellucidness, is essentially different from that in use at the period chosen for imitation; so that sometimes the different portions of the design itself are incongruous; sometimes the design is of such a character as to be unsuitable to the nature of the material in which it is worked; and we may add that the various attempts which have been made to imitate the richness and depth of the ancient material, by coating the glass with enamel paint, have produced no other effect than that of depriving it of its brilliancy, and consequently the glass paintings,

STAINED GLASS WINDOW

THE LIFE OF ST PETER

BY J. A. GIBBS, NEWCASTLE.

Engraved by G Greatbach from a Daguerreotype.

PAINTED WINDOW REPRESENTING DANTE AND SOME OF HIS IDEAS.

BY G. BERTINI MILAN.

Engraved by G Greatbach from a Daguerreotype

in which this expedient has been resorted to, of one of their chief and distinguishing merits These observations apply, in our opinion, very generally to the modern style of imitating ancient glass paintings. Improvement in the style of drawing, and many other beauties, were to be met with in the objects exhibited in Hyde Park, but these beauties were too often neutralised by the defects to which we have ventured to allude. The works were not original compositions, nor were they correct copies of the various styles which they professed to imitate.

Bertini, of Milan. " Dante and his thoughts."—In point of size, harmony of design, and beauty of drawing, this window was certainly entitled to claim a first-rate place; nor was there any work in the Exhibition, which, taken as a whole, was so superior to it as a glass painting, as to prevent its merit as a work of art preponderating. Its defect was certainly the want of general brilliancy. Except in the Queen's glory, in letters of the inscription over Dante's head, in the shields below, and the wreath surrounding his name (all which were true specimens of glass painting), and in the border of the windows, there were no sharp clear lights; and although pot-metal or flashed glass was used in places, as in Dante's robe, in the steps of the seat, in the sky to Domenico and Francisco, and in the robe of the figure in No. 4, it had been reduced to the same opacity as that of the enamel colouring employed in other parts of the window. The subjects taken from the infernal regions, Nos. 1, 2, 3, 4, were scarcely fitted for a glass painting, which is not suited for dark effects. The whole work was executed with so much softness, and was so highly finished, that the metallic fastenings had a harsh effect, and formed black lines, which did not harmonize with the delicacy of the painting: and though in general they were concealed with wonderful skill, yet they appeared in places, and riveted the attention the more the window was looked at. It may seem presumptuous thus to criticise one of the best works of the day; but the admiration which we felt for it, has led us to compare it more rigidly with the windows at Brussels, and to arrive at the conclusion that it would suffer by comparison in point of general effect, though it would doubtless be superior to them in artistic refinement and drawing. Compared, however, with the more modern works, it appeared to advantage; for the quantity of white light introduced in the upper part of the design, in the Madonna, and in the tracery above, the angels, the crockets, and above all, in the ornamental bands or fillets which served at once to connect together and to frame the different subjects, imparted to the window a silvery or glass-like effect, which none of the others possessed, and which completely rescued the work from the imputation of being like a fresco painting. The execution of the crockets and of the foliaged ornaments round the shield was quite perfect; but perhaps the greatest display of skill is the manner in which Dante's head was made to stand free from the chair's back. The representation of one of the ladies' silk dresses and of the lining of Dante's cloak was a wonderful achievement in painted glass, and perhaps could not be accomplished in a work in which clear lights were considered indispensable. In conclusion, we have only further to observe, that the defects which we have ventured to notice are those which prevail very generally in the works of the present day; but the beauties exhibited by M. Bertini in this production greatly preponderate, and are his own.

Capronnier, J. B., Brussels.—The conditions of the art of glass painting appeared to have been complied with, on the whole, in this work more fully than in any other of equal or superior size in the Exhibition: for not only was the drawing good, the composition simple, and calculated for distinctness of effect at a distance, but the angular character of the draperies, and the fineness and decision of the entire execution, were admirably suited to the nature of painted glass. The style principally followed was that of the first half of the sixteenth century. The absence of clear light, and over-painting of the head of the principal figure, were to be regretted as deviations from what we consider to be a correct observance of the style adopted. Still it is impossible to refuse to this composition a first-rate place.

CHAPTER XXXI.

EDINBURGH REVIEW—LETTERS FROM M. BLANQUI—FIRST IMPRESSIONS — CLASSIFICATION— WEALTH OF ENGLAND—MR. PAXTON—INAUGURAL DAY, ETC. ETC.—LETTER II., GRANDEUR OF THE EXHIBITION—ENGLISH HOSPITALITY — REFRESHMENTS—FRENCH DISPLAY — ENGLISH MACHINERY—BOHEMIAN GLASS, ETC. ETC.

WITH a prescient glance, savouring of vaticination, an able writer in the *Edinburgh Review*, descanting on the great theme of the day, the topic of all hearths, the chosen subject of Fame—after detailing the enormous extent of labour and research, the unheard-of expenditure of materials employed in the composition and printing of the mighty catalogue, whose myriads of copies flowed in so vast a stream through all parts of the civilized world,—gives promise of future still more elaborate works on the inexhaustible treasures of the Great Exhibition.

With the fact before our eyes, exclaims our writer, that the average number of volumes in ten of the largest libraries of the world* exceeds but by one half the volumes thus pushed into circulation, we cannot feel much surprise that this catalogue should, like Aaron's rod, have swallowed up the whole literary activity of the last twelve months, and that the ordinary book trade of the country should have been almost altogether suspended. Nor should it be forgotten that much of the knowledge and information—forming the staple of the book trade in ordinary times—has been forced into new and unaccustomed channels by the necessity for its rapid dissemination within the limited period of the illustrations remaining accessible. In almost all of our leading political journals the new facts of science and art, dressed up with all the attractiveness of news, were related in a form that admitted of easy modification in their statement, and discussion in their bearing. That this lull is but the prelude to animated gales we feel confident. The past few months have been a period of patient suspense or critical examination. We have had the things themselves before us. A knowledge of their qualities must precede any theoretic analysis. It is also a most important fact, which seems to have been little regarded, that the leading scientific minds of Europe have been hitherto in a measure bound to silence and secrecy, from being included in the lists of the juries. But let this seal be once removed—let the critical reports of thirty sections, and at least one hundred and twenty sub-sections— giving the history of what has been, and is, and guesses at what ought and will be in every department of knowledge—and we have little doubt that a goodly array of commentaries, theories, systems, in the old established form of full developed tomes— besides all the lighter skirmishing of pamphlets—will soon make their appearance. It is scarcely too much to predict that for every three lines in this catalogue (the average length of a description) we shall soon see at least one or two works issue from the press,

---

* Number of volumes in Bibliothèque du Roi, at Paris, 650,000; Munich, 500,000; Copenhagen, 400,000; St. Petersburgh, 400,000; Berlin, 320,000; Vienna, 300,000; British Museum, 270,000; Dresden, 250,000; Milan, 200,000; Gottingen, 200,000; Bodleian, 160,000; Trinity College, Dublin, 100,000.

either questioning or discussing the merits there claimed, or the abstract principles involved in their statement. The wrongs, hardships, and injustice which have been hitherto tamely endured, by all whose contributions have been placed by the jurors in any other than the highest category of merit, will find a vent when these violations of all truth and reason become known. To this prediction might have been added, with equal certainty, the foretelling of the appearance of a variety of works, on which all the industry and talent of our best artists would be employed to illustrate and perpetuate the recollection of the Great Wonder of the Age. Our spirited and liberal publishers have done their best to ensure a high station for the present work among the numerous competitors with which it is surrounded, and we trust, from the success and the praise it has already met with, as well as from our anticipations for the future, he will be able to exclaim with the poet—

" Opus exegi ære perennius."

Foremost among those writers, who rushed to the literary field to bear testimony to the grandeur and excellence of our magnificent Exhibition, were the French, who, with their usual generous and chivalrous feeling, accorded their full meed of praise to a rival nation. We have already noticed the observations of M. le Moinne, and now turn to those of M. Blanqui, a member of the Institute of France, which, from time to time, we propose to lay before our readers, and which we hope will equally serve for their instruction and gratification.

LETTER I.

The first impression created upon the mind of the spectator on beholding this magnificent structure, erected with almost miraculous rapidity, is that of marvel at its grandeur, simplicity, and elegance. All the proportions are maintained with consummate art, and with mathematical precision. The horizontal measure of 24 English feet was taken as the unit of the building, every horizontal dimension of which is either a certain number of times or divisions of 24 feet. For instance, were it required to elevate any part, two pieces of 24 feet were placed one on the other, and thus a height of 48 feet was obtained; and in the same manner a height of 72 feet is reached by the addition of another piece of 24 feet. The same as to length or breadth, which is always a multiple of 24. The result has been the formation of a symmetrical palace, constructed of pieces of cast-iron of equal length, fastened together with iron bolts, and nearly all cast after the same pattern, or, as we should say in political economy, of the same standard. Should it be found necessary some day to pull down this edifice, it may be taken to pieces, and rebuilt elsewhere without any change. The building consists of an immense nave, transversely intersected by a shorter one, called the transept, of a height sufficient to enclose trees of venerable growth in perfect preservation, producing a most charming effect. An upper gallery, approached by numerous and commodious staircases, runs along the whole of the building. From this point I was enabled fully to enjoy the magnificent spectacle of the opening ceremony, at which there were present more than 20,000 persons, most of whom were arrayed in the most elegant attire. The English papers will not fail to give you the details of this splendid solemnity, to the *éclat* of which our organs and organists greatly contributed. It was truly a noble and most imposing spectacle.

Previous to entering upon my feeble labours with regard to this great Exhibition, I must give you a general outline of the manner in which the different nations are classed in the respective places allotted to them. England has retained for herself half of the ground—the entire of the western part of the Crystal Palace; and it must be acknowledged that she has so well filled it that she cannot be blamed for having appropriated to herself the lion's share. The space in the eastern side is divided—it must be confessed somewhat unequally—among all the other nations, and in this portion France bears the palm. The transept is like the equator of this industrial world. China, Tunis, Brazil, Persia, Arabia, Turkey, and Egypt, are grouped near to it like a kind of torrid zone. Conspicuous among the colder regions stands Switzerland, whose exhibitors have distinguished themselves by their promptitude, and the happy arrangement of their contributions. There they are united like the children of one family, with exquisite taste and the most pleasing harmony. Be assured they will create an impression. Spain, and even Portugal, Italy and its different states, have sent products, doubtless insufficient to exhibit their agricultural and manufacturing position ; but these second-rate states have contributed works of art or raw materials of a somewhat original character.

France was really not ready, and a few hours before the opening, a crowd of exhibitors, in their shirt-sleeves, might be seen hurriedly arranging their most beautiful wares. As regards taste, art, and elegance, nothing was wanting ; and I may say that the general impression was, that France was pre-eminent in its artistic superiority over all other nations. If I might venture to hazard an expression without wounding any one, I would add, that all the products, from whatever part they have come, have a common and provincial apppearance, when compared with those of France. The French articles alone bear that stamp of elegance which is due to the talent of our designers, and to the incomparable skill of our artists. To execute anything to equal them, other nations must deprive us of these, and, unfortunately, the revolution of February has lost us more than one. The United States, which occupy the eastern extremity of the large nave, and whose Eagle, with outstretched wings, soars over the whole Exhibition, have sent mostly raw materials, and few manufactures. It is said that they have sulked, and it would be unjust to judge of their industrial power from the specimens—moreover very remarkable—which they have exhibited. Austria and the Zollverein of Germany are the nations which, together with Belgium, occupy the most distinguished rank after France.

Austria exhibits products sufficiently remarkable to astonish the most competent judges, and those best acquainted with the country, from having made it their especial study. Russia is still behindhand ; but it is generally understood that the contributions from that country, impatiently looked for, will manifest a progress not less astonishing than that of Austria. That which struck at the first glance the most practised judges, were the truly novel and curious raw materials from India, Australia, and the American colonies; among the contributions of England, the carriages, the machinery, and above all, the chemical products, which are admirable—prodigious; in Austria the glass-works, shawls, and carved work ; in Belgium, the lace and fire-arms ; in Switzerland, the muslins and ribbons; in France, the works in precious metals of Oudiot, the bronzes, the shawls, the carpets, the cloths, and the woven goods of Alsace. When you cast your eye upon this panorama of the industrial world, your attention is so much divided that the sense aches at it. But, be assured, that from henceforward the English have inaugurated a new era. The whole world will receive a lesson in that country, where the peaceful struggle of nations is proceeding with so much *éclat*.

In order to draw as much instruction as possible from this inexhaustible field of study, it behoves us to omit nothing essential. Everything here is so different from what we are accustomed to see, and all has succeeded so well, that we may find plenty of matter of useful information, if we will lay aside, for the nonce, our national pride. Thus, first, to speak only of the idea itself, the mere enunciation of it was sufficient to excite the enthusiasm of all the leading men of this country. They assembled; they calculated the cost of an immense edifice, worthy of the undertaking; they appealed to the most distinguished architectural talent of all countries; and when it became necessary to find the requisite pecuniary resources, the Bank of England opened its treasures, upon the sole condition of obtaining security for the sums it might advance. Immediately the highest and wealthiest of the land hastened to co-operate in this great national work, by offering the guarantee of their fortunes. Noblemen came forward, some to become security for £8,000, some for £20,000, others for £40,000 pounds. One private individual is said to have subscribed to the guarantee fund for £50,000. Whilst this significant proof of the confidence of the wealth of England was given, the subscribers for the season-tickets added their guarantee to that of their munificent countrymen, who so spiritedly had come forward to carry out this grand project, which originated in France, but, like many others, with such barren results for our country. It is now almost placed beyond doubt that the undertaking will not only be most advantageous to England, but that there will be a large pecuniary surplus. Mr. Paxton, the able designer of the Crystal Palace, itself unquestionably the most wonderful specimen of English industry, on the opening day headed the royal procession. It was at the express desire of Prince Albert that this public honour was paid to the architect who had erected a marvel to enshrine so many other marvels. Thus England, after bringing to an auspicious termination the project of an universal Exhibition, did not forget worthily to honour those who so much contributed to its success. Could there be a more popular sight, I would ask, than that of this humble architect, this builder of hot-houses, walking at the head of the royal procession of the Queen of England on such a day? The interior order of arrangement of the building is also beyond all praise. The nations are arranged in order, according to the importance of their contributions, and are distinguished from each other, either by having the names or the flags of their respective countries displayed over their compartments. The approach to all the stalls is perfectly easy, the circulation everywhere free and commodious. The articles are exhibited in classes—machinery, carriages, and woven goods, of the same kind, being pretty generally placed together. Each nation has had perfect liberty to fit up and arrange, according to its own peculiar taste and fancy, the bays and glass cases for the display of its goods. Hence a diversity has resulted, not less interesting than the goods themselves, and which, in a somewhat original fashion, represents the characteristics of the various nations enlisted in peaceful struggle. England, which, as I have said before, has appropriated to itself one-half of the entire space, had to provide, besides, the best means of insuring the comfort of the visitors, and the embellishments which should make the great building worthy of its destination. These results have been most happily achieved by the distribution in the middle of the principal nave of all the large casts or pieces of sculpture contributed by Prussia, France, and Belgium, but particularly Prussia. At intervals several gushing fountains, one of which is a magnificent crystal one, spread freshness and animation over this vast space, through which reverberate the sounds of three organs erected in the most original and picturesque fashion. Lastly, some venerable trees, preserved as a kind of scale by the aid of which the height of the immense fabric may be measured without effort, add the charm of their rapid vegetation to this graceful and imposing *ensemble*. Such is, in its simple grandeur, the general aspect of the Exhibition of all Nations. On the inaugural day there were upwards of 25,000 persons present, and yet the extremes of the building appeared like a desert. The hum of these thousands of voices was hardly to be distinguished, and was really lost in this aërial fabric, from which an azure glimmer, like that of the firmament, was shed upon the multitude, producing a most singular and unexpected effect. Nothing, also, can be more striking than this buzzing of so many different languages and the chequered array of the many gro-tesque costumes of all these foreigners.

Each nation occupies an unequal space at the universal Exhibition; and it is but just to remark, that several among them—foremost of which is our own—are only represented in a very imperfect manner. It is evident that the North Americans have only sent to this great gathering some indifferent goods, and they have had to give up to neighbouring exhibitors a portion of the space which was useless to them. A few ploughs, some canoes, some very inferior maps; such is the actual stock of the North American portion of the Exhibition; but every one acquainted with the industrial skill and laborious energy of that great people must admit that its productive powers are not represented by these few sorry specimens. Spain has furnished little beyond raw materials, some wool, a few silks, and scarcely any woven goods. Catalonia, the last haunt of the pro-tectionists of that country, has not exhibited anything. It feared, not without reason, being crushed by the comparison of its wretched cotton cloths with those of the whole world, and being called to account by the Spanish people for the tribute which it levies upon them, almost without profit to itself. But the experience will not be the less decisive; and, by allowing judgment to go by default, the ashamed protectionists will not be the less condemned—some for their impotence, as in the case of Spain, others in consequence of their inferiority, denied by themselves, and from motives of cupidity, as in France. At every turn in this Exhibition the truth strikes every one. Only look at the Sheffield cutlery! what admirable variety! what richness! what amazing cheapness! as the English say, with pride and with reason. And we have also reason to say— "When our manufacturers shall have iron and steel at more reasonable prices, they will manufacture equally well." But our iron-masters will not have it thus. Look, again, at the English carriage department, exhibiting such variety, richness, and elegance; yet the importation of carriages is prohibited in France, and France is thereby deprived of the means of comparison and imitation, which would greatly benefit the coachmakers them-selves. And so to the end of the chapter. We shall demonstrate, beyond the shadow of doubt, that there would be no want of superiority in our manufactures from the day when France, exempted from the tribute which is levied upon her under the guise of protection, shall, in the plenitude of her liberty, exert herself without undergoing or imposing the yoke of restriction.

This fact is especially striking on examining the Swiss department of the Exhibition. Switzerland occupies in the building a limited space. It is a land of free trade, mountainous, and without facility of communication, and, nevertheless, it has acquired a very distinguished rank in European industry. It is really wonderful to see the elegance of its Bâsle and Zurich ribbons, its embroidered muslins, its taffetas, and its velvets, worthy to vie with the school of Lyons, whence, doubtless, they derive their origin. Austria, although it leaves much to be desired on the score of taste, even in its Bohemian glass, and although exhibiting a great want of design in its exquisitely-carved furniture, still merits an honourable place by the side of the Zollverein and of Russia, which seem to exhibit more life and progress.

I will not at this stage venture to hazard a premature judgment. It is only after an attentive and comparative study of all these innumerable products, that it will be possible to attempt expressing a serious and profound opinion on so many *chefs-d'œuvre*, and on the relative value of each country. Suffice it to say, that, as regards France, our manu-facturers of Lyons, of Mulhouse, of Tarare, and of Roubaix, had scarcely commenced the arrangement of their goods, notwithstanding the zeal and diligence of the commis-sioner-general, M. Sallandronze, whose attention and courtesy are above all praise. It certainly was not his fault that goods left at Dunkirk, or at the railway station at Paris, were not displayed sooner. But we shall have lost nothing by waiting; and I dare to assert that, in spite of numerous gaps, the French exhibition will ever be what it ever has been in our own country, as elsewhere, unique for good taste, gracefulness, and elegance in every department.

LETTER II.

Before giving any definite opinion upon the ultimate results of the Exhibition, I shall have much to say with regard to it as a whole, its grandeur seeming to increase the more minutely it is examined. The observer is, as it were, carried away by magic from country to country, from east to west, from iron to cotton, from silk to wool, from machines to manufactures, from implements to produce. You wander to and fro, your eyes perpetually dazzled by a kind of mirage, scarcely being able to cast even a glance at the visitors from all countries of the world, who are, nevertheless, not the least curious articles of the Exhibition; for, if there is a vast quantity of goods in all the galleries, there is also a crowd of Englishmen, of Germans, of Frenchmen, of Turks, of Italians, of Spaniards, of Indians, whose motley costumes deserve the attention which is still withheld from them, in consequence of its being diverted in a thousand directions by the all-powerful fascination produced by the magnificent spectacle of so many *chefs-d'œuvres* of human industry. I cannot too strongly recommend to my fellow-countrymen to come and visit this marvellous Exhibition at all hazards. They may be assured that, during the course of their lives, they will not look upon its like again. But, first, we must warn them against the spirit of depreciation which has distorted the truth in several of the French papers. It is not true, as it has been unscrupulously asserted, that no exhibitor has been admitted without paying three guineas for a season ticket; all exhibitors, on the contrary, have free admission on presenting a ticket issued at the office of the commissary-general. Neither is it true that apartments are enormously dear; they are not let higher than usual, and they are not all occupied. All classes in this country manifest eagerness to show hospitality to strangers. To whatever rank they may belong—for here there is rank—strangers are sure to find, among their equals in position, friendliness and cordiality. There is nothing talked about but friendly soirées. To commence with the scientific. The president of the Royal Society is this month to give three routs to the *savans* of all nations. Lord Granville has thrown open his mansion, and the queen will give several balls. All the corporations are making preparations worthily to entertain their guests. The lord mayor is to give a splendid entertainment at Guildhall, to the principal manufacturers who have contributed to the success of the great undertaking. Were I at liberty to quote names, besides those of official persons, I could furnish you with a really curious list of the most eminent men in various walks, who have deemed it a duty to do the honours of their country to the entire world summoned to this great federation. But, above all, those whom I would desire to see arrive in crowds at the Universal Exposition, are the French artisans. Our great manufacturing towns and manufacturers cannot make too great sacrifices to send over the largest possible number. A special agency should have been established in London, with the view of facilitating to them the study of those questions which interest them most, and to initiate them into those marvels of art, the bare sight of which elevates the mind above our miserable pothouse politics. French workmen stir abroad too seldom, and even then rarely beyond France. In coming to London they would, with very little effort and at a trifling expense, make the tour of the world—they would learn more in a week's visit to London than ever they learned— excuse me saying so—in clubs, when clubs were in existence.

It is here, in fact, that we must come to learn what industrial trophies the spirit of order and the genius of man, bent to industrial discipline, can achieve. Only think that this immense Crystal Palace has been cast, piecemeal, and put together in less than six months; cast is literally the word, for there was not so much as one piece of glass and iron of the myriads of pieces which compose it, in existence in the month of September last. And when within its precincts even now we observe the admirable order which reigns throughout, when we behold thousands of labourers assembled in silence in small groups at meal times, under the direction of their foreman, with an almost military discipline, afterwards leaving through the small exit-doors, without confusion or hindrance to the public, we can better understand this wisely-regulated power, master of itself, which forms so striking a contrast to what we behold in our country. Permit me to add some details which, I think, will not be without interest to the visitors from our country, and which may, perhaps, induce others to come to this great gathering. The arrangements for the disposal of the space have been so well made throughout the whole of the building, that even on the most crowded days there has never been the slightest obstruction. Sixty thousand persons can walk about with ease, and at the same time without being in the least incommoded. A large number of easy seats are distributed along the entire length of the galleries for those who are fatigued. Three large refreshment-rooms, where everything is sold at moderate prices, according to a tariff conspicuously displayed, afford visitors the opportunity of spending the whole day in the building without being obliged to leave to take their meals. The price of an immense catalogue, by the aid of which anything may be found with the greatest facility, is limited to one shilling.

Nevertheless, our countrymen do not as yet arrive in large numbers, and notwithstanding the activity which they display, the French expositors are still behindhand, without a pretext for excuse like Russia, whose goods were detained by the ice of the Baltic. As these magnificent goods are opened to the view, and are displayed in the places allotted to them, the influx of visitors commences. Already the English ladies may be seen gazing with rapt admiration at our gallery of shawls, at the jewellery of Froment Meurice, or the works in precious metal of Odiot. What will it be when Lyons and Mulhouse will have displayed their unrivalled productions? Our cabinet-makers of the Faubourg St. Antoine have been greeted with a general burst of admiration. They alone, up to the present moment, are completely established in the gallery which has been apportioned to them, and their works immeasurably surpass anything that has hitherto been attempted in this branch. Oh, matchless workmen! why do you not make more furniture and fewer revolutions. That great branch of English industry, machinery, is now also beginning to work. You know that the English have conceived the happy idea of erecting outside the building a steam-engine, conveying by means of subterranean pipes the motive power throughout the building. It has been so cold during the last few days that the steam, being condensed on its way, did not reach its destination; but since it has, a vast number of spinning, weaving, and other machines, may be seen at work side by side, directed by workmen in the costumes of their countries and calling. One of our men who had the charge of a spinning machine, having the other day tied a broken thread, "Bravo, Frenchman!" exclaimed a number of voices, and overwhelmed him with applause. Everywhere the principals exhibit their machinery to the public with the utmost readiness. Pumps, of which there are several, of novel and powerful effects, throw out veritable cataracts. It is in this department that the English shine and are pre-eminent above all other nations. Their immense display of machinery resembles an artillery park. There are engines for steamers, of 700 horse-power, of incomparable perfection; gigantic eight-wheeled locomotives of novel construction, Crampton's patent, said to be capable of running seventy-two miles an hour with perfect ease. Their hydraulic presses surpass all proportions hitherto known. They have exhibited the one used in raising the Britannia Tubular-bridge, that vast tube suspended in the air through which runs a railway, and under which a ship of the line can pass at full sail. Besides these huge specimens of engineering art, there are on all sides hundreds of small machines, executing before the public the most ingenious tricks, from the manufacture of knife-handles to that of letter envelopes. In the different processes employed by the English, it is easy for an attentive observer to discover the distinctive character of the nation in point of political economy. They work particularly by means of their capital, and in everything they have recourse to mechanical means. Their Crystal Palace is composed of three or four different models of cast-metal, of which they have worked off some hundred thousand of copies, of which they might, in case of demand, immediately publish five or six editions. Their printed calicoes, which are not equal to ours in taste, surpass them in cheapness, thanks to their mechanical power, which enables them to produce millions of pieces, and thus almost reduces to nothing their general expenses. The bold reform which they have made in their tariff and navigation laws has been an actual increase in the wages of their workmen, the interests of whom the government takes to heart, and for whom it acts more efficaciously than our government, without a perpetually heaping of stale and fulsome compliments upon them. But it is, above all, in the lower qualities of the raw materials that the English shine. This department of the Exhibition will be visited with care by reflecting minds, who know the real source of national wealth, and where an enlightened people should go in search of it. The English Exhibition offers in this respect a spectacle worthy of the liveliest interest. They have exhibited with a proud simplicity, the most varied samples of their subterranean produce. Among these may be enumerated, within and even outside of the building, enormous masses of coal from all their mines, with small models of the works of the mineralogic sections, and all the accessories of this curious industry. They have likewise exhibited specimens of all their building-stone, their slates, their chalks, their plasters and their mill-stones. Their iron, coal, lead, tin, and copper mines, are represented by the richest collection of minerals, in every stage of preparation and on an immense scale. Everything is explained by drawings, models, tools, forges, and furnaces, and the whole is worked by little figures similar to children's toys.

It is evident that few of the English producers have failed to answer the summons to the general gathering, and the more carefully the great gallery is visited—that is to say, half of the entire space occupied by the English—the more one is struck with the display of power and riches of this great people. The struggle, in fact, is only between them and us. Belgium and Germany, no doubt, deserve particular attention; but the real competition is between France and England. All the other nations will only, in this strife for the palm, play the part of supernumeraries. They themselves admit the inimitable superiority of the two great industrial powers of our time. It by no means follows that therefore the efforts of Austria, Russia, the Zollverein, and even of Switzerland, can be spoken lightly of; but all these united would be unable, for the present at least, to enter the lists with the two first manufacturing nations of Europe. It is by studying in detail the respective merits of all the people invited to concur in this great assemblage of nations, that we shall be able to award to each the degree of merit to which it is entitled. Saxony, for instance, has sent topographical maps of such rare perfection, that, in point of engraving, they immeasurably outstrip the most wonderful things of the kind that have been attempted by France, England, or even the ordnance of Austria, so justly renowned in Europe. There is a map of the environs of Dresden, which is a real *chef-d'œuvre* of its kind, and well worthy the attention of our officers. The advancement of more than one art may be judged of by such specimens, which honour the nation capable of producing them. The glass work of Bohemia has upheld its old reputation, which our protectionist manufacturers have not dared to compete against. But protection, gentlemen, has had its day, and ere long, like feudalism, it will only be an insolence of the past.

We shall at length penetrate the mysteries of the cost price system, and we shall know what tribute France pays to a few manufacturers who have hitherto levied a downright poor-rate upon her. Those who have refused to exhibit have impliedly acknowledged the futility and uselessness of the protective system. They feared the exposure in all its nakedness of a system which henceforth can have no other possible result than that of raising the price of things, and condemning France to dearth, whilst everywhere else nations labour to achieve cheapness. After international exhibitions, prohibition will become simply an absurdity. Is it to make us suffer the torments of Tantalus that we have been summoned to this grand spectacle? What! we shall not be able to receive at our domestic hearth a wadded sheepskin, a knife, a razor, a glass tumbler, a cast-metal chimney-piece, merely because there happen to be in France a few private individuals who imagine it to be to their interest that these things should be prohibited!

No, no; this scandalous state of things cannot last long. France, I hope, will soon be tired of the reign of ignorant declaimers, and will profit by the unmistakable lessons which spring from the spectacle before our eyes. When the whole world shall know that the Almighty, and the genius of man, His noblest work, have created throughout the earth the elements of well-being by means of labour, and that a little commercial freedom would suffice to diffuse these blessings, it will no longer be possible to maintain the restrictions which lower us to the rank of nations still in their swaddling-clothes. All that we behold here cannot be a mere theatrical representation, calculated to amuse idlers, but a decisive inquest, at the issue of which the old Chinese brick-wall of the insulation of nations shall crumble away under the public scorn.

CHAPTER XXXII.

THE FINE ARTS COURT—ARMITAGE'S SYBIL OF PEACE—WOOD WHITTLING, ETC.—AMBER—ITALIAN PAPER—WINSOR AND NEWTON—ROBERTSON, ROWNEY, AND MILLER—BAXTER, AND KRONHEIM—ENAMELS BY ESSEX—WOOD CARVINGS—MECHI'S FARM—TESSERAN AND ENCAUSTIC TILES—LITHOGRAPHS—WYON'S SEALS—PRINCE ALBERT'S MODEL LODGING HOUSES FOR FAMILIES.

IF, according to the philosophic axiom, "things are known by their opposites," then the pretentious title given to this portion of the Great Exhibition, of THE FINE ARTS COURT, was most wise and judicious, aptly illustrating the truth of the oft-repeated line of the poet, "Lucus a non lucendi." Every one more or less deeply versed in the cheerful subject of criminal statistics, has seen those strange foreign maps, in which the different degrees of moral culpability of a whole nation are rendered visible at a glance. Thus while some departments are made to assume an unenviable hue of black, others appear on the contrary quite fair, with of course numberless shades between, denoting clearly the average depravity of these provinces. If an industrial map of this description had been made out of the contents of the Great Exhibition, we know of no compartment which would have come out of a more unmitigated black than the Fine Arts Court. It is quite incredible what an agglomeration of artistic delinquencies were there offered to mortal vision, thinly scattered with perhaps a dozen works of real merit and sterling character. Foremost amongst the latter we would place Mr. Armitage's " Sybil of Peace," whose attitude and expression seemed to indicate a doubtful sense of the honour or possibility of mixing in such company. Her glances seemed less directed to the smouldering implements of war at her feet, than at the dubious carvings, would-be new inventions, and the thousand knick-knacks, which would just have passed muster in some provincial museum. Perhaps one of the most deplorable symptoms to be met with in the Fine Arts Court was the boast of self-tuition; and the egregious complacency with which this was announced, not to claim leniency for such efforts, but as it were calling for superior admiration at the results. Every man who could whittle at wood, who could handle card-board with a pen-knife, or design with a hot poker, at once fancied himself a prodigy; cork, elder-pith, bog-wood, and leather, were made to alternate in the abominable mimicry of nature.

Before noticing more particularly the few good specimens of decorative manufacture, the raw materials of art collected here and elsewhere call for notice. At one of the nave entrances of the Zollverein department was an unpretending little box, containing, besides numerous fragmentary specimens of amber, different solutions of this material, which have attracted the attention of the artistic community. In three small glass vials might be seen that problem to the ancients, the " magisterium succini"—a solution of amber, by means of alcohol or volatile oils. The " succinic acid" was here in a state as clear as it has hitherto been turbid. An ample account of this vehicle is to be found in Sir Charles Eastlake's able work. Merely indicating the subjects to those more immediately concerned therein, and pointing to the numerous specimens of amber, rough or ready, dug out of pits, or washed on the shores of the Baltic, we pass on. Whilst every one must easily comprehend that Dantzic must always have the command of the amber trade, owing to natural or antediluvian laws, which cause the material to be blown on its coast, it becomes just as difficult to understand why in Italy the manufacture of paper has remained stationary. Strange as it may seem, the drawing paper still in use is now made at the same place, and we believe by the descendants of the same firm which furnished Italy's greatest draughtsmen with materials; the watermark clearly indicating Fabriano, between Ancona and Perugia. While thus seemingly digressing, we now arrive at the driven point. Both the northern amber-varnish and the southern paper are allowed to be the best for their several purposes; and yet neither are to be had, except of course in the gross. Neither were to be found, for instance, in Winsor and Newton's splendidly got up case of artistic materials, in the gallery allotted to the chemical compounds. Here might be found in tempting array every vehicle from poppy to mastic, from copal to linseed, but no label pointed to the mixture exhibited by a Dantzic apothecary. Messrs. Winsor and Newton, of Rathbone-place, exhibited cobalts and cochineals, chromes and cinnabars, emeralds and ochres, canvasses and panels, brushes and badger tools, which even a Gerard Dow or a Mieris would in vain have called for. In the Fine Arts Court, Messrs. Robertson, Rowney, and Miller, erected stands of artistic manufacture. Whilst Messrs. Robertson had successfully solved the problem of blending copal and varnish into what is known as their medium, Mr. Miller had taken out a patent for having rendered colours vitrifiable, and in consequence more durable. Silica is the name of the substance, which is employed alike in oil and water colour. While, however, bearing ungrudging witness to the decided superiority manifested in the method of preparing and grinding colours, it is impossible not to perceive the glaring errors into which that very perfection may have led us; and it is not going too far to assert, that all the schemes for producing paintings by mechanical processes, have ended in the utter discomfiture of the system.

Messrs. Baxter and Khronheim can never be conceived to be even art's journeymen, as long as they imitate painting so abominably. Blocks, in the heads of these gentlemen, assume all the virtues of brains. If Mr. Baxter crams an incredible number of tones into a very limited space, Mr. Kronheim, on the other hand, offers some compensation, negativing his scale of harmony as far as possible. Both are supremely painful for two reasons—first, because they annihilate all sense of form and light and shade; secondly, because the colours as put on are essentially false and inharmonious. This statement of plain fact is only warrantable by the strange infatuation with which these paintings are held up as miracles of power and invention; they are as paltry in power as others by hand are the reverse. Nevertheless, as inducements to a more general love and study of art, they may be useful, inasmuch as to the uncultivated eye the display of crude and gaudy effects of colour, are more attractive than the sober and chaste realities of truth and nature. As a contrast to these puerilities, we need scarcely point to the enamels of Essex, in which surprising fidelity in reproduction is united to imperishable execution. Though Mr. Carrick does not lay much stress on intrinsic durability, it is but too evident that the relatives of those he has delineated on white marble, in preference to the usual ivory, will be anxious to combat with care, the effects of time on the too-fleeting colours. Other miniatures of royal ceremonies may possibly in time acquire that interest with which their execution as yet fails to invest them. By far the pleasantest features of this compartment were the wood-carvings executed by Wallis and Rogers. We shall, however, be brief in our notice of these objects, as we have already devoted a chapter to the subject in an earlier portion of this work. The first of these gentlemen, perhaps, followed a little too closely on the heels of Grinling Gibbons, in the way of composition, though perhaps he is superior in other respects. Mr. Rogers appeared to have nursed his reputation in his Cradle,—a most dainty and delicate piece of workmanship: he must, however, be on his guard against his finikin tendencies: the lime-tree and boxwood, doubtless, invite detail, but the British oak is not to be tickled with penknives. Larger tools were evidently employed on the Kenilworth buffet, exhibited by Cooke and Sons, of Warwick. It is massively constructed, and not over-elaborated with figures, and these skilfully executed; nevertheless, a more decidedly Elizabethan character would have been desirable. There was Elizabeth in one of her progresses; there were courtiers and poets; and, more conspicuous still, dancing bears. Though sometimes, it is said, still to be met with on occasions of festivity, this animal has hitherto been confined, as a decorative member, to Bernese monuments. Pleasant associations, however, and difficulties vanquished, served to render the piece of furniture unusually interesting. The same could scarcely be said of the Irish bog-yew carving, which was made the medium of compositions of " Harpers in Tara Hall," Cormac and Brian Borohme. It is difficult to decide whether these, or the Edinburgh pier-table carvings, bid more defiance to an invisible foe than to the commonest rules of design. In comparison with these, the rough carpentry of the Victoria shiphead almost elicited admiration. One could fancy this figure already mounted on the prow of a vessel, and steering clear of the obstacles of an over-crowded harbour. The spectator might well wish to follow her example. Here to the right we fell foul of a three-decker, 120 guns; to be sure, its substance was only cork, but cork of as inferior a description as the handicraft bestowed upon it. Turning away from this, and a little way off, you came in collision with the Dundee Anglo-Saxon arch, which manifestly bore off the palm of ugliness, only equalled by its originality. It would require the whole vocabulary of tracery to distinguish one after the other five orders superinduced. It would seem as if the architect was anxious to collect all the fragments of Saxon architecture into one composition, just as another gentleman thought fit to gather the valuable morsels of the shattered Portland Vase.

THE ROYAL CRADLE

CARVED BY ROGERS

END VIEW OF THE ROYAL CRADLE,

Flying from the frigid "Altar of Minerva" by Pidgley, one found pleasant shelter in Mr. Mechi's farm close by. While occupied with this charming model of rural agriculture, the eye was insensibly attracted to certain azure combinations, tesseræ and encaustic tiles; at once the mental vision wandered from the precincts of Tiptree Hall to the Hall of the Lateran.

The lithographic ventures, as might have been expected, were highly creditable to us in the several branches of landscape, architecture, and their components. But it is lamentable to reflect that not the slightest hope was held out of mitigating that pictorial nuisance, the vast annual influx of foreign studies of heads and figures. Admirable as are the productions of Hullmandel and Walton, whose prints from Cattermole are only next best to originals: also the works of Haghe and D. Roberts, printed by Day and Son, &c., these either cannot or will not compete with Lemercier, Jullien, and Company. The fact is, that peculiar branch to which attention is more particularly directed on the continent, is with us entirely left to ticket embellishers. To the man through whose agency the world is made acquainted with certain incomparable pickles and pomade, soap and salad oil, &c. (samples of which illuminated proclamations were most unaccountably found in the Fine Arts Court), to him, as the supreme arbiter of taste, was left the care of producing the most refined subjects. The consequence obviously served to deter the skilful artist from encountering his rough treatment. The seals executed by Wyon need no recommendation of ours. That proposed as a prize medal for the Great Exhibition promised to be a handsome reward, as well as a token of superiority.

With these remarks, which we regret we cannot render more commendatory, we now dismiss the Fine Arts Court, and to refresh our readers by a complete change of scene and subject, invite them to a stroll outside the Crystal Palace, where, at the side of the drive, a little west of the barracks, stands a small block of neat, cheerful-looking, newly erected houses. These were the philanthropic work of the Prince Consort, who, in the midst of the splendid attractions of a court, and the pursuits of science and art in their higher branches, did not disdain to give a careful consideration to the condition of the hardworking artisan, in the humbler fields of industry. It was an intervention which was much wanted, which humanity had loudly called out for in vain, as all know who have inspected the abodes of the industrious and poorer classes, not only in the crowded city, but in the rural village; for neglect for the sufferings of others, and a niggardly denial of the essentials of health, cleanliness, and comfort, have been equally manifested in the town and provincial districts throughout the country. This has long been a crying evil, but too long only heard as the wail of the lowly and defenceless, and dependent classes, which found no way into the ears, much less into the hearts of those who should have heard their complaints, and solaced their rugged course of life by all means reasonably within their power It was not until half-a-dozen years ago that the sanitary condition of the poorer classes was forced upon the attention of the legislature and the government, as a matter worthy of public consideration; and the pleadings of the humane and the warnings of the wise having been fearfully supported and confirmed by that providential scourge, the cholera, a board of health was appointed with certain powers, which have already been put in course of carrying into operation in nearly two hundred populous districts, with already very important and salutary results. The disclosures made by the inspectors appointed by this board, as to the wretched home accommodation of the poorer classes, which existed as a rule, with scarcely any exception, throughout the kingdom; the utter want of drainage, of water supply, of the ordinary precautions for the means of personal cleanliness, and the denial of the breath of life, through a wholesale and almost wilful neglect of ventilation, were such as to startle many even of those inhabitants of the very towns in which these flagrant evils existed.

The consequences upon the health of communities were also shown to be most serious, excessive mortality existing in some places to the extent of being *two* and *three-fold* what, with ordinary sanitary precaution, it might fairly be expected to be; two and three-fold what it actually was in some other districts more happily circumstanced. Added to this, the charge upon the public purse in the cases of sickness, of widows and orphans left to burthen the parish, of labour lost by temporary incapacity during illness; and a case was made out which convinced all cool and dispassionate individuals that it was the wealthy who had a direct pecuniary interest in the health of the poor; and that as regarded health itself, they were not altogether exempt from participation in the sufferings of their fellows—the parting breath of the dying pauper not unfrequently poisoning the atmosphere of his richer neighbour. Upon this subject, also, contemporaneously with the inspections of the board of health, the correspondents of some of the morning papers—more particularly the *Morning Chronicle*—lent their useful aid, and brought in a vast mass of corroborative evidence, thus giving increased publicity to facts already too well established in professional and official quarters. The journal last mentioned states, in a recent article :—" A couple of years ago our correspondents in the metropolitan, agricultural, and manufacturing districts, painted a succession of the most melancholy pictures of the wretched and degrading tenements in which the poor are lodged, both in town and country—in London alleys and manufacturing suburbs, and in rural lanes. The dens of lodging-houses in the great towns—the cellars and garrets where thousands of unhappy creatures are penned, sometimes three and four in a bed, and very often without distinction of sex—have been amply described in letters pourtraying the east end of London and the huge and swarming towns of Lancashire; while the hovels and dilapidated cottages which stud the agricultural districts, particularly in the south and west of England, have been sketched in colours just as dismal. Turning back to our files of a couple of seasons ago, we find column after column, and letter after letter, devoted to the exposition of the miserable, the worse than savage condition of the dwelling accommodation of a great portion of the peasantry of England. We read again and again of cottages crumbling into ruins—the cold wind blowing in at every chink and cranny—the rain sopping the mud flooring—the dunghill overflowing and sending its fœtid juice in streams across the threshold. We read of bed-rooms immediately beneath the putrid and leaking thatch—of bed-rooms in which a whole family, father, mother, adult and infant children, young men and young women, all slept together like so many pigs in a sty; of cottage accommodation, in fact, which made us wonder how there was any natural decency and feeling, or human restraint of behaviour left amidst a great proportion of our rural population. In many parts of England it is perfectly clear that the people are not better, perhaps they are worse lodged, than they were under the Plantagenets and the Tudors. No dwelling can by possibility be worse than a ricketty cottage, open to every wind of heaven, admitting rain through the roof and wall, a dunghill piled before the door, and men and women, children and parents, lying down to sleep together on ragged mattresses and straw in the same fœtid, unventilated room. Indeed we suspect that in many cases the condition of our rural population is even worse than it was in the days of the most despotic of our early Norman kings, because a greater proportional amount of rent is squeezed out for accommodation in nowise better than that possessed by the ' villains' and the ' varlets' of the good old times. Rents have risen, in fact, while cottages have not improved; and, worse even than that, as our agricultural correspondents have proved, population has in many districts increased enormously, and cottages not at all. It is to be earnestly hoped that a change in this respect is now at hand, nay, that it has already begun. The conveniently arranged and substantially constructed model cottages in

Hyde-park, to say nothing of the model lodging-houses in various parts of London, prove that good houses can now be erected as cheaply as bad ones, and that the building of such dwellings may be made to form at once one of the safest, most profitable, and most philanthropic means of investing money. Those who would be inclined to sneer at the juxtaposition of philanthropy and profit in the same sentence, know very little of human motive. Men naturally like to get as much for their capital as they can— society would not hold together unless such were the case; and men also—the monetary advantages being equal—just as naturally prefer realising these advantages through supplying the means of comfort and contributing to the well-being, rather than through a bare and insufficient ministering to the actual physical requirements of their fellow-creatures. The new houses erected in Hyde-park are calculated to pay seven per cent. on the outlay—a very handsome return—and they are calculated, at the same time, to rear a population brought up in decent household comforts, adapted alike to their physical and moral well-being."

The model house in Hyde-park consists of four dwellings, compactly put together— two on the ground, two on the first floor; the latter attained by an outside staircase, which gives a feature of architectural beauty to the elevation. Each dwelling (they are all *fac-similes*) contains a general sitting-room and kitchen, entered by a lobby (an essential requisite), two small bed-rooms for the male and female branches of the family, a large bed-room for the parents and the younger children, a scullery, and a decent water-closet. The whole of the rooms are full of cupboards and such conveniences, the building is fire-proof, there being no particle of wood in the whole structure; water is laid on; a passage to a general dust-hole communicates with all the sculleries; the kitchen ranges are models of economical neatness; ventilation has been carefully attended to on the most scientific principles; the walls are built of a peculiar species of hollow bricks, which are cheaper than the old ones, and have another most important requisite, that of deadening sound—and altogether the cottages are models of the most ingenious compactness and simple comfort.

CHAPTER XXXIII.

COMPREHENSIVE NATURE OF THE GREAT EXHIBITION—WALKING STICKS—PILGRIMS' STAVES— SWORD, DIRK, AND SPEAR STICKS—ALPENSTOCKS—FERULAS—BAMBOO AND ORIENTAL STICKS —STAVES OF OFFICE AND SCEPTRE STAVES—EARLY ENGLISH STAVES—STICKS OF THE TIME OF QUEEN ANNE—CLOUDED CANES, ETC.—GROTESQUE STICKS—PROCESS OF THE MANUFACTURE OF STICKS—CONTRIBUTIONS FROM DIFFERENT COUNTRIES.

ONE of the distinguishing characteristics of the Great Exhibition was its vast comprehensiveness. Nothing was too stupendous, too rare, or too costly for its acquisition; nothing too minute or apparently too insignificant for its consideration. Every possible invention and appliance for the service of man found a place within its all embracing limits; every realization of human genius, every effort of human industry might be contemplated therein, from the most consummate elaboration of the profoundest intellect, to the simplest contrivance of uneducated thought. The philosopher and the savage stood side by side; the accomplished artist and the rude boor alike were free to choose, "a local habitation," and might each with equal advantage, hope to acquire "a name;" from the wondrous calculating machine, down to the simplest toy, there was "ample space and verge enough" to display whatever might be deemed worthy of public attention. All therefore might find abundant matter for wonder and delight.

We were led into these reflections after contemplating one of those great masterpieces of human genius with which the Crystal Palace abounded, by casually wandering into a department wherein was arranged every possible form, shape, and variety of "walking sticks;" yes, gentle reader, we repeat, of every specimen and description of walking-sticks, from the plain and unadorned shepherd's staff, to that of gold and ivory, fit for the hand of royalty itself. We shall select for the amusement and gratification of our readers, a few remarks, on this apparently insignificant subject, from the "Juries' Reports." "Whensoever," they observe, "the heroic period may be supposed to have existed, the staff, as employed for the support of old age, was then well known, since it is referred to in the enigma, put forth by the Sphynx, and solved by Œdipus." "There is a Being," said the questioner, "which has four feet, and it has also three feet, with only one voice; but its feet vary, and when it has the most it is the weakest." "This is man," was the hero's answer, "who when he is an infant, crawls upon his hands and knees; when he is a man, he walks uprightly, and when he is old he totters with a stick." The use of the staff for support in walking appears to be so natural and inartificial as not to require any illustration; and yet the Pilgrim's staff of the middle ages, and the *Alpenstock* of the present time, have a certain amount of historical interest. The *Bourdon*, or Pilgrim's staff, was a strong and stout stick, apparently about five feet in length, armed at the lower end with an iron spike, and intended to supply a support and balance to the body, when the traveller was climbing up slippery paths, or steep acclivities. About a foot from the top of the staff was generally found a large protuberance, either artificially or naturally formed around the staff, on which the pilgrim's hand securely rested, without danger of sliding downwards. The lower part of the staff was altogether solid, but the upper joint was a hollow tube, capable of containing small articles, like a long hollow box. It is probable that these articles were originally reliques of saints, or the "signs," as those emblematical figures were usually termed, which were commonly sold at the shrines to which pilgrims travelled, as proofs that they had really visited those sacred parts. In the latter ages of pilgrimage, however, this part of the staff was sometimes converted into some kind of pipe or musical instrument, such as sticks have frequently contained in modern times. Above the tube, the staff was surmounted by a small hollow globe, and it was also furnished near the top, on the outside, with a kind of crook, for the purpose of safely sustaining a gourd-bottle of water. After the pilgrim had completed his votive journey, and returned from Palestine, he commonly brought with him a branch of palm, fastened into the top of his staff, as a proof of his travel into Palestine or Egypt. It is, however, unquestionable that the pilgrim's staff frequently became the receptacle of secular articles. It is recorded by Holinshed, that in the hollow part of a pilgrim's staff the first head of saffron, afterwards so successfully cultivated at Saffron Walden, was secretly brought over from Greece, at a period when it was death to take the living plant out of the country. The silkworm also found its way to Europe in the hollow of a pilgrim's staff. So late also as the time of Cervantes, certain Spanish pilgrims existed, who had collected upwards of an hundred crowns in alms, which, being changed into gold, they concealed in the hollow of their staves, or the patches of their clothing. It seems to be a natural observation in this place, that the ancient contrivance of making a repository in the hollow of a walking-stick, is not yet obsolete. In the Great Exhibition, Dr. Gray, of Perth, displayed a medical walking staff, containing a variety of instruments and medicines; and the same principle has also been frequently employed for the portable conveyance of telescopes, and other important articles.

Several varieties of sticks were also exhibited, inclosing in them swords, dirks, and spring-spears: the principle of the construction of the sticks last-mentioned being, that they required a heavy blow to be given with the armed end before the strong spring could be overcome which held back the spear-head. Sword-sticks, and dagger or tuck-sticks, are of a more recent period; but this kind of weapon walking-staves is not of later invention than the last century, though that which contained fire-arms existed in the early part of the reign of Henry VIII. The *Alpenstock* is another ordinary walking staff requiring to be noticed, of modern use, though of great antiquity. It is a stout pole of about six feet in length, provided with an iron spike at the lower end, and surmounted with a chamois' horn as an ornament. It is almost indispensable in mountain journeys, and may be procured for two francs throughout Switzerland. Another order of walking-sticks comprises those light wands to which the name is now exclusively attributed; and these also are descended from a time of considerable antiquity. The stem of the giant-fennel, the *Ferula* of Pliny, is the chief progenitor of this family, and he derives the origin of the name of the plant either from *fero*, from the stock being employed in walking, or from *ferio*, because schoolmasters used it for striking boys on the hand. It would seem as if the latter interpretation had become established at an early period, since Martial terms the ferula *sceptrum pedagogorum*; and even down to the present day the word popularly conveys no other meaning. The tough lightness of the fennel-wood rendered it especially fitted for a support to aged persons, while the imposing length of the staff gave an air of importance to those who carried it. Hence it became the prototype of those lighter wands, which have continued as a sign of seniority or gentility to the present time.

In oriental countries the substitute of the ferula was naturally some kind of native reed; and the employment of such a plant as a support, and also as an emblem of Egypt, is noticed, in probably a proverbial form, by the Assyrian general Rabshakeh, in his speech to the servants of Hezekiah, in the eighth century, B.C. "Now, behold," says he, "thou trustest upon the staff of this bruised reed, even upon Egypt; on which if a man lean, it will go into his hand and pierce it."—2 *Kings*, xviii. 21. The supposition that the ferula was supplied by some local plant, must be also equally true concerning other regions, and especially in those in which the bamboo was indigenous. This was probably the first kind of the cane tube introduced into Europe, since the word *cane*, in all its original forms, appears intended to express a hollow tube or channel, for which purpose the bamboo is still extensively and constantly employed. Although the generic name of cane has long since supplanted all others for ordinary walking-sticks, yet at different periods they have been made of a great variety of materials. A slight glance may be taken at some of the substances employed, and some of the peculiarities of the common walking-sticks of other times. In the Egyptian sculptures, persons of importance or official rank are represented walking with tall slender staves, having the lotus-flower on the top. Several ancient specimens of these sticks have been discovered in Egypt, made of cherry-wood and other substances, measuring from three to four feet in length, some being surmounted by a small knob, or a flower, and others having a curved projection standing out on one side, like the tusk of a boar, as if it had been intended for the hand to rest upon. At a very early period of the sacred history, the distinctive character of the staff carried by an individual, is indicated from his immediate recognition simply by the production of it with his signet and his bracelets—*Genesis*, xxxviii. 18—25. Homer has commemorated the "sceptre-bearing princes" of the Greeks, and especially the sceptre-staff of Achilles, adorned with golden studs: "I will swear a great oath," says the hero, "even by this sceptre, which shall never again bear leaves or shoots, nor bud again from the time it left its trunk upon the mountains, when the axe stripped it of all its leaves and bark." These sceptres, although they were indisputably the insignia of rank and authority, were also evidently the usual walking-sticks of persons of the highest class. Agamemnon, it is stated, never went forth without bearing with him his paternal staff of royalty.

In the portraits of many of the noble personages of English history, painted in the sixteenth century, may be seen instances of the richness of the superior walking-sticks carried at that period, when they appear to have been tall, stout, and mounted and adorned with gold. In 1531 a cane-staff and a stone-bow were brought as a present to Henry VIII., by a certain fletcher, or arrow-maker, whom the king rewarded with forty shillings. Some far more curious instances of canes belonging to the same sovereign are, however, described in the manuscript inventory of the contents of the royal palace at Greenwich, in the following entries:—"A cane garnished with sylver and gilte, with Astronomie upon it. A cane garnished with golde, having a perfume in the toppe; under that a diall, with a pair of twitchers, and a pair of compasses of golde; and a foot-rule of golde, a knife and a file of golde, with a whetstone tipped with golde." From the middle of the seventeenth century, walking-sticks appear to have increased in luxury, both in regard of the mountings, and also of the materials of which they were manufactured, the improvements being derived principally from France. In the early part of the following century, the most fashionable sorts were made of certain fine marbles and agates, exhibiting either a splendid variety of colour, or a rich semi-opaque plain tint, which was most expressively described by the English term "clouded." These wands were made of the most slender proportions, both on account of their specific gravity and the quality of the persons by whom they were to be carried; and they were often richly mounted with silver, gold, amber, or precious stones. Such were the "clouded canes" of the age of Pope and Gay, which were frequently so greatly valued, as to be preserved in cases of shagreen or sheaths of leather. Every reader of the *Rape of the Lock* will remember—

> " Sir Plume, of amber snuff-box justly vain,
> And the nice conduct of a clouded cane,"

as well as Gay's commemoration of the same kind of walking-stick in *The Van*—

> " Here clouded canes, 'midst heaps of toys are found,
> And inlaid tweezer-cases strew the ground."

The most curious account of the walking-sticks of this period, is, however, contained in the *Tatler*, No. 103, written by Addison and Steele, and published on Thursday the 6th of November, 1709. In that paper, Isaac Bickerstaff represents himself as issuing licences and regulations for the beaux of the time, as to the carrying of " canes, perspective glasses, orange-flower waters, and the like ornaments of life." The first part of the essay is intended to ridicule and abolish the prevailing absurd, though fashionable practices connected with walking-sticks; hence the respective parties were licensed to carry them, provided they did not walk with them under the arm, nor brandish them in the air, nor hang them on a button. One of the petitioners desires permission to retain his cane, because it had become as indispensable to him " as any other of his limbs," and because "the knocking of it on his shoe, leaning one leg upon it, or whistling upon it with his mouth, are such great reliefs to him in conversation, that he does not know how he could be good company without it." The cane of this person being produced, it is described to be " very curiously clouded, with a transparent amber head, and a blue riband to hang it on his wrist!" In the second half of the last century, there was one peculiar form of walking-stick prevailing, which was generally used by females advanced in life. The sticks referred to were between five and six feet in height, taper and slender in substance, turned over at the upper end, in the manner of a shepherd's crook, and twisted throughout the whole extent of the wand. The materials were either wood, ivory, or whalebone, mounted with silver or gold, and sometimes they were formed entirely of a clear pale green glass. The length of the most fashionable walking-stick of this period, is noticed in a number of *The London Chronicle*, published in 1762, wherein the writer says, "Do not some of us strut about with walking-sticks as long as hickory poles, or else with a yard of varnished cane, scraped taper, and bound at one end with waxed thread, and the other tipped with a neat ivory head, as big as a silver penny." Towards the close of the eighteenth century, two peculiar forms of walking-sticks were commonly carried by the most gay of the young men of the period, one being a very short and strong bamboo-cane, bent over at the top, and the other a stout knotted stick, in which the grotesque natural growth of the wood was frequently regarded as its greatest excellence.

Another kind of walking-sticks comprises those grotesque staves, which have been devised or adopted by individual fancy or eccentricity. It is possible that this peculiar humour may be of considerable antiquity, since the knotted walking-staff and wallet were the distinctive attributes of the Greek and Roman philosophers, and especially of the cynics. The chief peculiarity of this class of staves, however, consists in an ingenious adaptation of the excrescences of the wood of which they were made, into grotesque human heads and faces, of which the Exhibition contained many curious and remarkable instances. The old English form of these staves may perhaps be referred to the baubles carried by the fools and jesters, who were retained by sovereigns and noblemen of the sixteenth and seventeenth centuries. The jester's bauble consisted of a short stout staff, surmounted by the carved figure of a puppet or a fool's head; and the modern practice of carrying sticks decorated with humorous faces appears to have existed early in the eighteenth century. About 1730, *The Universal Spectator* states, that at the court end of the town, instead of swords, many polite young gentlemen "carry large oak sticks, with great heads and ugly faces carved thereon." Perhaps some of the most remarkable instances of these carved sticks ever exhibited, were those executed and carried about by James Robertson, of Kincraigie, otherwise called "the daft highland laird," of whom Kay published an etching in 1784. In the latter part of his life he adopted the amusement of carving, for which he had some talent, and sculptured in wood the effigies of such persons as attracted his imagination, whether friends or enemies; the latter, however, being executed in caricature. These small figures he mounted on the upper end of a walking-stick, sometimes one above another; and as it was reported that he produced a new one every day, he was commonly accosted with the inquiry, "wha hae ye up the day, laird?" to which he would readily answer by naming the individual, and the reason for selecting him.

It might be supposed that the manufacture of walking-sticks could not form a large branch of commerce, and yet a vast quantity and great variety of materials are annually consumed in it. There is scarcely a grass or a tree of sufficient elasticity or strength, which has not at times furnished the material for a staff or walking-stick. The stick-maker, however, gives a decided preference to some few kinds out of the almost infinite variety offered to him by Nature. Amongst European woods, the blackthorn, the crab, especially the warted-crab, the maple, the ash, the oak, especially the young, or sapling oak, the beech, the orange tree, the cherry tree, the furze bush, the cork tree, and the Spanish reed (a grass called *Arundo donax*), are those principally used; and these woods are most generally cut towards the latter end of autumn, especially when it is wished to preserve the bark. The West Indies furnish a copious supply of the most approved materials for walking-sticks, in supple jacks (vine stems,) pimentos, cabbage stalks, orange and lemon-tree sticks, and the coffee shrub and Indian briars. Numberless canes, the product of climbing palms and gigantic grasses, are also largely used by the stick-maker. The principal of these are the following:—ratans, dragons, and Penang lawyers, which are the stems of a species of calamus, or climbing-palm, and are obtained from India, Singapore, Java, and China; white and black bamboos, fluted bamboos, wamgees, jambees, and dog-head canes, which are the stems of various species of bambusa or grasses, attaining a height of from fifty to sixty feet, and are exported from China; ground ratans, large ground ratans, malaccas, and dragons from Singapore. There are also the bamboo and jungle-bamboo, imported from Calcutta; and lastly, canes from Manilla. It must not be supposed that these various materials in the unwrought state, present an appearance at all resembling the finished sticks. Indeed, the copious examples in the north-east gallery, fully confirmed this statement; but the truth is much more strongly impressed on the mind, after an inspection of the immense ware-houses of Mr. B. Meyers, who contributed them. Those repositories appear, at first sight, to contain stores of little value above that of fire-wood; yet many thousands of pounds have thus to be locked up for a time, in order that the various woods may become properly seasoned. It is only, indeed, after having passed about twenty times through the hand, that even the commonest walking-stick assumes a saleable appearance: the better descriptions require more operations. The principal processes of this manufacture deserve to be described.

1. *Peeling off the bark*.—From most of the forest-woods, the bark has to be removed before the separated boughs can be made into polished sticks; but in some cases it is left on. One of the most difficult articles to manipulate is the warted-crab, the excrescences of which are produced by an abnormal growth of the tree, resulting from the puncture of an insect. As a halfpenny is the payment for peeling one of the most complicated kind, it will be readily concluded that there must be some simple means of facilitating this operation; and, accordingly, the sticks are boiled for a couple of hours; the bark then yields to the incision of the finger nail, and may be stripped off without difficulty.

2. *Forming the crook and straightening the stick*.—Few limbs of trees, or even canes, are sufficiently straight, in their natural condition, to answer the purpose of a walking-stick, and very few present those conformations which can be readily fashioned into handles; hence the necessity for these two operations, which claim our admiration for their ingenious simplicity. The handle is formed by softening the wood or cane in hot *damp* sand, when it becomes pliable and non-elastic, and readily assumes and retains any curvature or bend that may be given to it. Minute attention, however, is required with regard to the temperature for each description of wood; hence the precise degree which is proper for each can only be learned by long experience; and in some cases, where a new variety of material is imported, some experimenting becomes necessary. The straightening is performed in a similar manner, excepting that the previous softening is effected in *dry* sand, heated on an iron plate, that is, in the ordinary sand-bath. When the stick has become sufficiently pliable, it is inserted into a deep notch cut in the edge of a strong plank, and is strained first in one direction and then in another, until it has become straight. The stick, when softened, takes any form, much as a piece of red-hot iron would do. The straightening-plank is three inches thick, about six feet long, and one foot wide, and is inclined away from the workman at an angle of about thirty degrees from the perpendicular, it being firmly secured to the floor at the lower end.

3. *Fashioning the stick*.—In this operation some sticks are wrought to assume a twisted or spiral form, and others the knotted appearance of a bamboo or whangee; these characteristics are imparted chiefly by rasping and filing. Heads or hoofs of

various animals very commonly adorn stick heads, and grotesque human heads frequently display proofs of considerable skill and surprising humour in the artisans employed. Examples of this latter description were exhibited in Class xxix., by most of the German and Austrian exhibitors.

4. *Staining.*—After straightening or carving, the sticks are in many instances brought to a very smooth surface, by means of emery or glass-paper, and finished off with fish-skin; and they are then, previously to the varnishing, made to asssume so many different hues by means of dyes, that the uninitiated would conclude that each was a perfectly distinct variety. The surface is sometimes likewise charred, and the charred portions scraped off partially here and there, so as to produce a very ornamental appearance. Sticks are also embellished with lithographic transfers, but not in England, as hand-labour is too expensive. Malacca canes, when not sufficiently long between the joints to form a straight stick, are made to appear continuous, by reducing the larger part to correspond to the smaller, and tapering it gradually from the point of juncture. It then becomes necessary to colour that portion which has been reduced in size, and this is done with so much skill, that the stained and natural surfaces are not distinguishable.

Hitherto, mention has been chiefly made of sticks of vegetable origin. Of such as are made of animal substances may be instanced whalebone, tortoise-shell, ram's horn, rhinoceros' horn and hide, as commonly employed for sticks; and occasionally the real bone of the whale, the spine of the shark, the horn of the narwhal, and ivory. The horns of animals, under particular treatment with heat, and by mechanical appliances, are drawn out into long cylinders; and tortoise-shell raspings are easily conglomerated by heat and pressure, and in the soft state formed into elongated rods, applicable to the manufacture of sticks. The hide of the rhinoceros forms a very transparent horn-like substance, and is very elastic and tough. The feet of fawns, which are frequently used for stick-handles, are made to retain the required form by merely baking them. Ivory, horn, and bone, are also largely used for stick and umbrella handles, and give, in their preparation for these purposes, employment to a considerable number of workmen.

Before proceeding with the review of the contributions of the several nations, attention is claimed to the fact that London, Hamburgh, Berlin, and Vienna, are the chief seats of the manufacture under consideration, and that by a curious coincidence the principal makers in three of those cities bear the name of Meyer or Meyers. Two of them, namely those residing in London and Hamburgh, were present by their works in the Great Exhibition, but the third of Vienna, did not exhibit. The manufacture of sticks in England is in an exceedingly flourishing condition. The principal London maker alone sells annually above 500,000 sticks of various descriptions. The specimens exhibited by English manufacturers comprised many instances of the employment of walking sticks for containing various implements alluded to in the introductory matter. Besides which, were to be found a walking stick which served the purpose of a miniature wine cellar and larder; one which contained a voltaic battery which continually subjects the owner to an electric current; one to contain guide maps, and two or three others convertible into seats, umbrellas, and other instruments. The British colonies exhibited a vast variety of specimens. From Western Africa was a stick, or rather staff of honour usually carried before the African chiefs. The Indian courts displayed their accustomed profusion of gold, ivory, and ornamental work in every variety of decorated sticks sent by various rajahs, besides many beautiful articles that were purchased by the Company expressly for exhibition. The island of St. Vincent sent its supple-jacks; while Van Diemen's Land chiefly confined its contributions to specimens of sticks made with the hard portion of the bone of the whale, with heads carved out of the whale's tooth.

France, as usual, exhibited her wonted elegance. The chief specimens sent from this country consisted of articles made of elongated ram's horn, and conglomerated tortoise-shell. In 1847 there were in Paris one hundred and sixty-five manufacturers of walking sticks, and riding and driving whips, employing nine hundred and sixty-two workpeople, who produced goods valued at £140,320. About nine-tenths of these articles are exported. The most important display of walking-sticks was, however, unquestionably that in the Hamburgh department, contributed by H. C. Meyer, jun., who it appears is the most extensive stick-maker in the world. His collection contained about five hundred varieties, comprising most of the known materials. The Austrian collection was also very extensive, and exceedingly good in point of workmanship. Belgium offered a small but neat display, as did also the Grand Duchy of Hesse, and Wurtemburg. Sardinia and Tuscany were also represented, as well as Switzerland, and Prussia; a few specimens of stick manufacture being supplied by each of these countries. China was more magnificent, contributing curiously carved bamboos, elaborate sceptres, and other ingeniously wrought specimens, exceedingly rare and interesting. But it is in the raw material that the commerce of the country is more particularly represented, large quantities of which are annually exported. From Canton alone 1,200,000 sticks of various kinds were exported in 1846, consisting chiefly of different kinds of canes and bamboos, but comprising also laurel-sticks, stems of the tea-plant, and the root of the fig-tree of the Pagodas.

The United States were represented by one solitary contributor, who exhibited a gold-headed walking-stick, made from the curled hickory. We shall conclude with remarking, that though the Jury, with the impartiality which marked all their proceedings, allowed that whalebone sticks are made cheaper and better in Germany, and that the continental makers were more proficient in making sticks from the hide of the rhinoceros, they pronounced England unrivalled with regard to the chased, gilt, and silver handles, and that its ferules and metal works, generally, were unsurpassed. Five prize medals were given, one being to Mr. Meyers, of Crutched-friars, and honourable mention made of three other candidates for fame in this apparently trifling, but really important department.

CHAPTER XXXIV.

THE FAN—ITS HIGH ANTIQUITY—ITS VARIOUS USES, MILITARY, AGRICULTURAL, AND DOMESTIC—
USED IN ANCIENT GREECE AND ROME—ITALIAN FANS—GENERAL USE OF THE FAN IN ENGLAND
IN THE LAST CENTURY—CHINESE FANS—FRENCH FANS—FANS FROM THE BRITISH COLONIES
—EGYPTIAN FANS—SPANISH FANS, ETC. ETC.

As in our preceding chapter we have dwelt at some length upon that most important addition to the toilet of the beau, videlicet, the cane or walking-stick, so we feel ourselves called upon to devote a few pages to the description of a no less important appendage to that of the belle, in whose hands, as Addison playfully remarks, the Fan has perhaps achieved as many victories as the sword. We shall hasten therefore, to present to our fair readers, for their especial gratification, a full account of

" That graceful toy, whose waving play
With gentle gales relieves the sultry day."

In short, to exhibit before their delighted vision, the gay and wondrous variety that, in various parts of the Crystal Palace, the simple manufacture of the fan called forth from every quarter of the civilized globe. A display so bright and alluring, that we could almost fancy that Queensbury's favourite bard had penned his celebrated description in anticipation of it—

> "The Fan shall flutter in all female hands,
> And various fashions learn from various lands.
> For this shall elephants their ivory shed;
> And polished sticks the waving engine spread;
> His clouded mail the tortoise shall resign,
> And round the rivet pearly circles shine.
> On this shall Indians all their art employ,
> And with bright colours stain the gaudy toy,
> Their paint shall here in wildest fancies flow,
> Their dress, their customs, their religions show:
> So shall the British Fair their minds improve,
> And on the Fan to distant climates rove."—*Gay.*

We shall now again take the liberty of turning to the pages of the "Juries' Reports," and select from their learned lucubrations, with all due acknowledgment, our materials for the present chapter. "Upwards of three thousand years ago," observes our classical investigator, "the artist of ancient Egypt painted the fan on the walls of the tombs at Thebes. There the Pharaoh sits surrounded by his fan-bearers, each in his due rank; and there is seen an investiture of a fan-bearer, which realises the description in Genesis of the honours paid by Pharaoh to Joseph. The office of fan-bearer must have been honourable, and the insignia of office were long, slender, vividly-coloured fans on variegated or twisted handles. In war the same officers acted as generals, using their fans as standards; and in peace they assisted in the temple, and waved their variegated fans, both to produce a cooling breeze, and to guard the sacred offerings from the contamination of noxious insects. The fan is mentioned by Euripides, and its origin from "barbarous countries;" its use in Greece was similar to that in Egypt, but its forms were far more beautiful. The wings of a bird joined laterally and attached to a slender handle, formed the simple yet graceful fan of the Priest of Isis, when Isis became a Grecian deity; but it had not this form alone, for the Greek vases of Sir William Hamilton show that feathers of different lengths were taken and spread out somewhat in the form of a semicircle, but pointed at the top; a thread connected the feathers at the base, and another near their summit, and the fan thus made was fixed in a handle. This fan, the precise type of the state-fan of India and China of the present day, was waved by a female slave.

The fan, according to Virgil and Apuleius, was sacred to Bacchus, and the "*mystica Vannus Jacchi*" was carried in procession in the feast of that deity, as well as in the Eleusinian Mysteries. Its appellations multiplied, though its office remained the same, and it was termed indifferently "Flabellum," or "Muscarium." The modern Greek church is careful to place a fan in the hands of its deacons, to guard the officiating priest and the elements from desecration. The Roman ladies certainly enjoyed the luxury of the fan, which, gorgeous with peacock's feathers, or delicate with the tinted plumes of the ostrich, could not yet be folded, and rendered the services of an attendant necessary.

In the works of the middle ages references are made to the two forms of the fan: to that employed in winnowing the grain, and that used in the service of the church, alternately to court the breeze or wave away the flies, till we hear of the fan as brought to France by Catherine de Medicis, when it was no longer stiff and unyielding, but light and pliable. In the early part of the seventeenth century, it was so constructed that it could be folded in the manner of those used in the present day. Formed of paper and perfumed leather, it became the delight of the French court; and attracting the attention of artists, fans, in the luxurious reigns of Louis XIV. and Louis XV. (in the latter under the name of " Pompadours") shone with gilding and gems, and at length glowed with the pictures of Boucher and Watteau, until at length no toilet was esteemed complete without a fan, the cost of which was frequently in those days as high as from £12 to £15 sterling.   In Italy, on the contrary, in the early part of the seventeenth century, even painted fans were of a very moderate price, and of universal use. " The first fans," says Coryat, in his *Travels in* 1608, "that I saw in Italy, I did observe in this space between Pizighiton and Cremona; but afterwards I observed them common in most places where I travelled.   These fans both men and women of the country do carry to cool themselves with in the time of heat by often fanning of their faces.   Most of them are very elegant and pretty things.   For whereas the frame consisteth of a painted piece of paper and a little wooden handle, the paper which is fastened into the tops is on both sides most curiously adorned with excellent pictures, either of amorous things, having some witty Italian verses or fine emblems written under them, or of some notable Italian city, with a brief description thereof added thereto.   These fans are of a mean price, for a man may buy one of the fairest of them for so much money as countervaileth an English groat."   England must have been a great buyer of fans in the last century, as a lady of that period would have felt as awkward without her fan as a gentleman without his sword.   Indeed Addison makes the comparison, and in the *Spectator* he describes an academy where the use of the fan is taught. " In the flutter of the fan," he observes, "there is the angry flutter, the modest flutter, the timorous flutter, the confused flutter, the merry flutter, and the amorous flutter."   He says, " I have seen a fan so very angry, that it would have been dangerous for the absent lover who provoked it to have come within the wind of it."   Gay, again, gives the fan as a present from Venus to a despairing lover, in order to soften his mistress, and describes in verse the hint which the peacock's tail presents for its construction.

CHINA.

In fan-making the Chinese and French are the great rivals, and may be said to monopolise the supply of the whole world.   In the lacquered fans the superiority of the natives of China is fully admitted.   They are unrivalled, especially when price is taken into consideration, in the sculpturing and piercing of the wood, bone, ivory, or mother-of-pearl framework.   Even their commonest fans are remarkable for boldness and originality of design, brilliancy of colouring, sharpness of drawing, and solidity and correctness of workmanship.   The manufacture of fans is carried on almost exclusively at Canton, Soutchou, Hangtchou, and Nankin.   The fans of ivory and bone and of feathers, are made exclusively for exportation to Europe or America; those used by the Chinese are of bamboo polished or japanned, and covered with paper.   They are sold at from 10*d.* to 14*s.* 6*d.* per dozen, according to the quality of the frame and the design of the leaf.   The examples which were in the Great Exhibition did not, however, come direct from any Chinese maker, but were contributed by three English exhibitors, viz. Messrs. C. T. Braine, J. Daniell, and Hewett and Co.   The examples exhibited comprised fans of painted and embroidered feathers; a feather-fan painted with silver outlines, representing groups of Chinese figures, the feathers being alternately blue and white; an ivory fan elaborately carved and pierced, and, considering the amount of work, very cheap, its price being only 20*s.*   There were also several very common paper-fans, ornamented either with rude delineations of landscapes, or besprinkled with gold-spangle.

FRANCE.

Fan-making has arrived at a high degree of perfection in France, and presents a remarkable instance of the subdivision of labour, as may be gleaned from the statement that about twenty different operations, performed by as many pairs of hands, are necessary to the production of a fan which sells for less than one halfpenny; and that these various processes are not all carried on in a single manufactory, but, on the contrary, form four distinct branches of trade, directed by masters employing the various artisans, who, for the most part, work at their own homes, and who are frequently assisted by their wives and children. A fan consists of the frame of solid material, called a "*pied,*" which is composed of the inner ribs, or "*brins,*" and the two outer ribs, or "*panaches,*" and likewise of the flexible leaf, or "*feuille.*" The frame is made of wood, bone, ivory, tortoise-shell, or mother-of-pearl. The first operation is performed by sawing the material into the required form for the inner and outer ribs. These ribs then pass into the hands of another workman, who shapes them with a file, and they are then taken up successively by the polisher, the piercer, the sculptor, the gilder, and the workman who fixes on them the spangles and pins of gold, silver, and steel. The frame is now sent to the manufactory which furnishes the necessary drawings for the series of operations, where it is riveted, the rivet being frequently ornamented with a precious stone. The leaf, or feuille, is sometimes single, but more often double, and it is usually made of paper lined with silk or calico, but also of parchment, lamb's skin, satin, and silk gauze. The richer kinds of feuilles are painted in water-colours on vellum, by artists known as *feuillistes;* and the highest and most expensive class by artists of celebrity, since Boucher and Watteau, Camille Roqueplan, Gavari, Clement Boulanger, and Dupré, have affixed their signatures to fans which they have decorated. The devices on the more ordinary descriptions of fans are printed from copperplates, and coloured by hand, and the most common sorts are ornamented by the process of chromo-lithography. The feuille is folded in a mould of strong paper, and is then mounted on the frame and glued to the prolongations, or "*bouts*" of the inner ribs. The feuille of the best fans is after this painted on the edge with gold size, and gilt with leaf-gold; but the feuille of the common fans is printed in Dutch metal previous to its being cemented on the frame. The decorator now ornaments the frame with gold or coloured ornaments, and the fan lastly passes into the hands of the overlooker, who attaches the tassels, and selects the proper sized sheath, into which she places it. The frame, or "*pied,*" is made in the parishes of Andeville, the Deluge, Boisière, Corbeil-Cerf, and St. Geneviève. In the district situated between Méru and Beauvais, in the department of the Oise, 2,000 workpeople, men, women, and children, are employed in the fan-trade. The woods used are the beam-tree, the plum-tree, ebony, sandal, and the lime-tree. The dexterity and sureness of hand of the peasant workman are said to be quite wonderful. Considering his want of knowledge of the principles of drawing, his facility in engraving, sculpturing, and gilding, is certainly remarkable. The piercing is performed by means of minute saws, which the workman makes for himself with pieces of watch-spring. A remarkable piece of saw-piercing, in the shape of a mother-of-pearl fan, was exhibited in the French Section, No. 149; it contained no less than 1,600 holes in the square inch. This *tour-de-force* was the production of one of these peasant artisans, named Désiré Henry. The printing, the colouring, and the mounting of the feuille, and the final embellishment of the fan, are usually performed at Paris, under the direction of the fanmaker, called, *par excellence*, "Eventailliste," though he has really but little to do with the manufacture of the fan, and must be regarded rather as the collector into one focus, and arranger of the produce of others; yet his labours are not the less essential. The mounting of the feuille, its ornamentation with feathers, and final decoration, are the operations usually performed by a small number of work-people in his own establishment; besides which he furnishes the drawings to the peasant in the Oise; for the framework to suit the constant changes in fashion, he instructs his feuilliste as to

3 K

the style of ornament; he groups together the frames and feuilles; and, finally, he overlooks the whole, to see that the workmanship has been well executed. Except the mountings of the feuille, and the final adorning of the fan, the other operations are usually performed by workmen at their own houses. The number of fan-makers, or *Eventaillistes*, in Paris, in 1827, was 15, who employed 1,010 workpeople (344 men, 500 women, and 166 children), and sold about £40,420 worth of fans. According to the *Statisque sur l'Industrie à Paris*, drawn up by our colleagues, M. Natalis Rondot and M. Say, it appears that in 1847 there were 122 fan-makers, comprising chamber-masters as mounters, feuillistes, painters, and colourers. The value of the fans made was £110,000. These masters employed 575 workpeople (262 men, 264 women, 29 youths, and 20 girls.) The workmen, on the average, earn 3s. and the women 1s. 8d. per day. The men were, for the most part, copperplate engravers and printers, litho-graphic draughtsmen and printers, painters, colourers, and overlookers. Thus in twenty years it appears that the produce in fans had increased in value nearly threefold, whilst the number of workpeople had diminished to one-half. This change is to be attributed to the employment of machinery, especially of the fly-press in stamping out and embos-sing the ribs, and the extensive employment of chromo-lithography, an art not practised at the former period. By these means the French have been enabled greatly to increase their exports by the production of cheap fans, to compete with those made by the Chinese. P. Duvelleroy exhibited some small fans, the price of which was as low as 5d. per dozen.

The collection of fans in the French department was most complete, and contained several specially decorated in honour of the Exhibition, and of her Majesty and Prince Albert. Among these the "Royal Fan," by Duvelleroy, attracted general admiration. It comprised a pleasing group of the whole of the royal family, with a rich emblazonment of the arms of England. Besides these and others painted by first-rate artists, it also comprised most of the descriptions manufactured for exportation, and which possessed distinctive characters, according to the market for which they were destined. For instance, some displayed great differences in the length of the ribs and the portion of the circle occupied by the fan when open; other fans, intended for Turkey and Morocco, were composed entirely of feathers, and, in conformity with the Mohammedan doctrine, no living object was painted on them. The principal foreign market for fans made in France are the South American States. In the decoration of such fans as were intended for Buenos Ayres, blue and green were carefully omitted, these colours having political significance, and being prohibited from use on pain of death. All the exhibitors were of the class called "*Eventaillistes*," as none of the manufacturers of the department of l'Oise sent their productions.

BRITISH COLONIES.

The colonial dependencies of Great Britain contributed many examples of fans, some of which were interesting on account of their simplicity, whilst, on the other hand, those from India presented most striking proofs of the luxurious splendour of the Indian princes. There were, for example, two fans contributed by H. H. the RAJAH of KOTA, one with an ivory handle, the other with a gold handle; but as the names of the various manufacturers were unfortunately not ascertainable at the time the Jury examined these specimens, no prizes were awarded in their favour. The Indian fan differs from that of Europe and China in not closing, and likewise in its form, and it is usually kept in motion by an attendant. Beside the fans affixed to central handles, all of which were most gorgeously enriched with embroidery and jewels, there were exhibited others resembling a curtain suspended from a silver rod, which is held horizontally by the attendant, and waved backwards and forwards over the head of the wealthy Hindoo:

J.Mason.   G. Greatbach.

THE ROYAL FAN.

BY P. DUVELLEROY PARIS.

J.Mason.   G. Greatbach.

FRENCH FAN

BY P DUVELLEROY PARIS.

and there was also the circular standard-fan; the handle being a silver staff, crooked at the top, to which the fan is attached on the opposite side to the crook. The attendant stands by the side of his master, and placing the end against his foot, inclines it away from his body, and slowly swings it to and fro. There was also a beautiful peacock-feather fan from Assam, and a fan, or *punkah*, composed of China beads and pearls, and made in the city of Delhi. The most simple, however, were those made of the entire or the divided leaf of the *Borassus flabelliformis*, manufactured at Calcutta, and commonly used both by natives and Europeans. The other examples comprised a punkah made of khuskhus grass (*Andropogon muricatus*) which, when wetted, emits a fragrant perfume; fans made of sandal-wood, from Calcutta; a fan made of bamboo, from Moorshedabad, and several of a similar description, from other parts of India; and lastly, from Bengal, large hand-fans, made of the palmyra-leaf. The inspection of these beautiful productions of Indian workmen, naturally suggested the idea that their skill and remarkable taste might be turned to profitable account, if directed to the production of fans suitable to the European and American markets. *Nova Scotia* sent an example of a very simple Indian fan. From *Trinidad*, Lord Harris, the governor, sent examples of fans for ladies. And from *Western Africa*, Mr. R. Jameson, of Liverpool, exhibited several fans from the banks of the Niger, one of which was made of a species of grass. A few specimens were exhibited in the collection from Egypt, to which much interest was attached, as coming from a country in which, possibly, the fan was first devised.

SPAIN.

There were two exhibitors of fans in the Spanish Court, one of whom contributed painted, and also printed "Feuilles" and the other both feuilles and complete fans, some of which were copies from French models. The examples, although they bore no comparison in point of taste or execution with the splendid fans from France, were good of their kind; and it would appear that the attention of their exhibitors had been directed rather to the manufacture for an article of general sale, than to the production of works of art. But it is remarkable, that no finer specimens should have been sent from a country, in which the use of fans is so prevalent, that they are commonly offered for sale outside the arena of the bull-fights, and other places of amusement. The fans in the Tunisian Court were ten in number, and in some cases ornamented with rich embroidery. From Turkey, the only specimen was an embroidered fan, made at Constantinople. Wurtemberg contributed several bone and ivory fans, reasonable in price, but very inferior to the ivory fans exhibited by the French makers. The number of exhibitors of fans was twenty-three; of these two received a prize medal, and one obtained honourable mention.

M. Duvelleroy and M. Felix, both of Paris, were the holders of the prize medals; the former for a display of fans, ornamented with artistic paintings, and remarkable for the beauty of the inlaying and the pierced ivory and mother-of-pearl frames. The most elegant fan in this collection was one painted by Roqueplan; the ribs were of richly-pierced, and sculptured, mother-of-pearl, inlaid with gold; it was valued at £40. Besides the above, others intended for foreign markets were exhibited, the prices of which varied from 5d. to 40s. per dozen. M. Felix obtained his for a collection of fans, for the most part copies of the best examples of ancient fans: these were such remarkably beautiful specimens of vellum-painting, that they fully entitled this manufacturer to the award, and were moreover the richest of any exhibited.

CHAPTER XXXV.

BOOKBINDING—BRITISH WORKMANSHIP—REMNANT AND EDMONDS, BARRITT AND CO., WRIGHT,
MACOMIE AND CO., EVANS, BATTEN, ORR AND CO., LEIGHTON, CHURTON, LEWIS, TARRANT,
RIVIERE, WESTLEY, ROGERS, ETC. ETC.—FOREIGN BOOKBINDERS—M. GRUEL, NIEDREE, MAME
AND CO., HANICQ, LEISTLER, ETC. ETC.—STATIONERY—VARIOUS CONTRIBUTORS—GREAT BRITAIN
— FRANCE—SWITZERLAND—BELGIUM—ETC. ETC.

THE various specimens of bookbinding exhibited both on the British and foreign side,
afforded evidence that an animated struggle is going on for pre-eminence in the
ornamentation of the outer parts of books; and many ingenious and gaudy devices
are the result. But upon the whole, we cannot approve of the taste which lavishes
so much upon the externals of our literature; it is neither in harmony with the calm
spirit of intelligence which should preside over the hours of study, nor, to speak upon
decorative points, do we think that so much laboured and far-fetched vanity, improves the
appearance of the shelves of the library. Besides, where the exterior is so much cared
for and attended to, it frequently happens that the interior is but slightly regarded.
Pope, in one of his moral essays, has presented us with an amusing account of a book
collector of this description, in Lord Timon:—

> " His study! with what authors is it stored?
> In books, not authors, curious is my lord;
> To all their dated backs he turns you round;
> These Aldus printed, those Du Suël has bound!
> Lo, some are vellum, and the rest as good,
> For all his lordship knows, but they are wood."

Waiving, however, further discussion, let us proceed to examine some of the numerous
specimens that were exhibited for public admiration; and, first, we will enter the British
department, in which Remnant and Edmonds contributed a good selection of bindings,
including Owen Jones's stamped leather covers, and a pleasing specimen or two of
"classic" books in calf. Barritt and Co. next showed the wonders of their workshop.
Their huge bibles, with the sunk panels, gilt metal ornaments, and profuse embellishment, cannot please any one with good taste. Wright, of Noel-street, sent a copy
of "Sylvestre," in morocco, very finely tooled; and "Das Niebelungen Lied," in white
vellum, inlaid with lines of orange and purple leathers, making a tasteful pattern. Let
us here, once for all, protest against the absurdity of decorating the edges of books with
pictures. Macomie and Co. contributed a large bible, bound in morocco, with a bronze
ornament running round the side; another bible, in buhl-work, and a "Boccacio," in
white vellum, inlaid with colour. Mr. Macomie seems fond of the raised panels, a style
we cannot admire. Evans, of Berwick-street, "the inventor of English illuminated
binding," as he calls himself, filled a case with examples of this wonderful art, and of
the "Victorian" style of binding. Here we had a copy of one of the book covers in the
British Museum, very well executed in coloured leathers: the rest was mere "fancy
stationers' work." Batten, of Clapham, had a case containing some richly-tooled bindings
for the "Song of the Bell," "Moore's Melodies," and a "Shakspeare;" but Gothic
church windows are not fit ornaments for the bookbinder's use, even on bibles and
prayer-books. Orr and Co. showed books published and bound by them: some of them
with good gilt ornaments. Josiah Westley had a case chiefly filled with publishers'
bindings, that are certainly a great advance in style on the productions of even two
years since. Binns and Goodwin, of Bath, showed one specimen elaborate enough, but

SPECIMEN OF BOOK BINDING IN METAL.

BY LEIGHTON & SON.

Engraved by G. Greatbach from a Drawing by H. Mason.

SPECIMEN OF BOOK BINDING.

BY LEIGHTON & SON

Engraved by G. Greatbach from a Drawing by H. Mason.

not to be praised beyond the execution; and then we come to the large show made by Leighton, of Brewer-street. There was a great deal of pretence about this case, which we cannot say was particularly well carried out. In one compartment we noticed manuscript copies of old printing and old engravings marvellously executed, and there were some unostentatious examples of excellent binding; but who will admire the decorations of a bible, which, because it is called "King William's Bible," mixes up things sacred with things profane, and has the clasps formed of cables and anchors "in *honour* of the Sailor King?" Who cares to see "Burnet on Colour," with a painter's palette on the side—mind, not a conventional ornament, but the verisimilitude of a palette. dabs of colour and all? Then there was "Rasselas," bound in oriental stripes; but this was so richly and well done, that we will not quarrel with it; we protest, however, against such barbarous wit in "binding," such clumsy punning, as "Bacon's works" in hog-skin! Nor can we admire Vernit's "Life of Napoleon," bound in tri-coloured morocco, the edges diapered with bees ascending and *fleur-de-lis* reversed, "typifying the rise of Napoleon and the fall of the Bourbons." Thomson's Seasons," in somewhat better taste, was illustrated with the twelve signs of the Zodiac; and "Horatius" and "Macaulay's Lays" appeared in classically ornamented calf.

There were also some books with painting on the side on sunk panels—good enough as far as the painting is concerned—but is it not a poor idea thus to ornament a binding? But if Messrs. Leighton's conceits are somewhat absurd (their workmanship is excellent), what shall we say to Mr. Churton, who is blessed with "a plan for ornamenting books by era or subject?" A work on railways has what is meant to be a tunnel, elaborately worked on the side with gold lines. The Pirate and Three Cutters is decorated with cable ornament; and Shakspeare with an Elizabethan architectural scroll. Surely these puerilities can hardly find patrons. Mrs. Lewis had a case of well-bound books—one on heraldry, appropriately enough ornamented with small coats of arms at the corners; Cundall and Addy showed some examples of the morocco bindings of Mr. Hayday (who, unfortunately, did not himself exhibit), and an elaborate pierced metal cover, executed by Burtt and Sons, for choice examples of art workmanship. The design of this ornament—copied from an old Venetian binding of the seventeenth century—is very beautiful. Leighton and Son next exhibited some clever designs for bindings by Luke Limner; two bibles very creditably bound, and an elaborate cover for a small bible in stamped gilt metal. One of the best and most honest-looking bindings in the show was contributed by Mr. Tarrant, a copy of Sir Thomas Lawrence's works in orange-coloured morocco, richly gilt, and with a little inlaying of other leathers. Clarke, of Frith-street, showed a variety of good, substantial volumes, in the old "tree-marbled" calf, and regular library bindings—his green and purple stainings were more curious than admirable. Mr. Bridden and Mr. Wiseman, from Cambridge, each exhibited large bibles, elaborate and creditable: and our Scotch friends sent us a bible bound in white morocco, inlaid with coloured roses, and ornamented in the centre with a gilt fountain and flowers! From other specimens from the north country we are only able to gather that good taste has not yet been introduced to the Scotch bookbinders. Mr. Parker, of Oxford, sent a case hardly commensurate with his reputation. Mr. Riviere, of Great Queen-street, had, perhaps, the choicest collection of all. He contributed but four books, and all were excellently well bound. Spenser's Works, in morocco, elegantly tooled with lines, somewhat in the Grolier style, among which the letters V. R. are just traceable. A Common Prayer, in morocco, of an old style; Virgil, in white vellum, rather too much inlaid with colours; and a good example of "tree-marbled" calf. Bone and Son had a case containing some of the best designs for cloth bindings, well carried out in all their detail. Westley and Co. had a large display; among some very good cloth and morocco examples, we found a huge bible, ornamented on the inside of the cover (which was shown to the spectator) with a Gothic church window, elaborated with a profusion of detail, all tending to prove what excellent workmen, but what wretched artists, in this instance, Messrs. Westley have employed. In the Fine Arts Court was a bible, contributed by Messrs. Nisbet, but bound by Mr. Hayday, each side exquisitely ornamented with a richly carved panel, in boxwood, designed by Harry Rogers, and carved by his father, Mr. W. G. Rogers. This was the only binding worthy of great admiration contributed by English exhibitors.

We will now take our readers to the Foreign side, and enter the division appropriated for the reception of the contributions of the French bookbinders. M. Gruel has the first claim on our attention, for his two large volumes bound in morocco, inlaid with coloured leathers, forming very bold and good designs; and for a missal in velvet, richly ornamented with gilt metal and jewels. But of still "more attractive metal" were some smaller books of "Hours," one in carved ebony, one in velvet covered with a tracery of ivory, another in bright velvet, with a beautiful design in carved boxwood. Two or three other volumes claimed admiration, in Russia and velvet, slightly ornamented with metal hinges and clasps of exceedingly graceful ecclesiastical design, very different from the ill-formed and heavy Gothic patterns to be found on our English bibles. In the adjoining case M. Niedrée exhibited the perfection of workmanship in delicate gilding. There were two tiny volumes of this collection that might challenge the world for their superior. M. Niedrée seems to prefer spending his chief talent on the inside of his covers; and on one of these little volumes especially there was the most exquisite design most ably executed. For honest bookbinding, without the factitious aid of metal-work, carving, or inlaying, M. Niedrée clearly, in our opinion, bears the palm; and a refined taste would, perhaps, be better pleased with this little show of volumes, than with all the glories of their more magnificent-looking brethren. M. Simier sent a "Don Quixote" bound in light calf, with a good ornamental design darkened upon it, and as a centre the celebrated windmill; and a "Molière" decorated with a Grolier pattern: his other specimens were not to be praised. Mame and Co., the great publishers, of Tours, exhibited a variety of cloth and morocco bindings, which we are sorry we cannot commend. In general the ornamentation was gaudy and ill-designed. Parisian taste does not seem to extend much through the French provinces.

In the Northern Gallery, over the courts appropriated to Belgium, M. Hanicq, of Mechlin, exhibited a trophy, as it were, of liturgies in various languages and all sizes, some of them illustrated and illuminated, and nearly all bound in a showy way with stamped metal corners, clasps, and ornaments. The first impression promised something worthy of praise, but we were sorry to find that a closer inspection dispelled the illusion. In the room in which MM. Leistler, of Vienna, displayed their beautiful bookcases, there were some marvellous examples of Austrian work by Habenicht and Girardet.

Commencing at the left-hand side of the Gothic bookcase, we first admired a folio volume, bound in blue velvet, ornamented with silver tracery of a rich Gothic design. In the centre was a figure of Christ, and at the four corners was the symbol of the Evangelists—an angel, a lion, a bull, and an eagle—all in silver. The next was an album, likewise in blue velvet, ornamented with gilt metal and tracery of ebony (beautiful in design); the centre was a bronze medallion, set round with a string of pearls. The third was a large volume in green morocco, inlaid with red and buff leather, ornamented with gilt metal-work, enclosing ten medallions, painted like bas-reliefs, in metal. Next came a large and beautiful book, entitled "Landschaften," bound in purple velvet, exquisitely ornamented with pierced ivory of most elaborate pattern. Then there was a volume of "National Music," covered with metal-work and carved ivory. In the centre were the arms of Austria; and, surrounding them, fourteen little oil-paintings, mostly of rural costume, descriptive, we imagine, of the national songs. Next was a book in morocco, inlaid with ivory and a light blue enamel, beautifully ornamented with gold; and, behind it, a volume bound in tortoise-shell, with gilt and silver ornaments of Gothic design, and three female allegorical figures in metal. These books claim admiration for the elaborate and costly ornament upon them. They were, with the Gothic bookcase that held them, a present from the Emperor of Austria to her Majesty. We have our doubts, however, as to whether all the credit is due to Vienna; (with respect to sculpture, we have already seen how Austria has laid claim to the genius of Italy, as if it were her own;) more especially as some plain morocco books in the same case did not exhibit the same amount of taste or excellence of workmanship. Among the minor volumes we noticed a peculiarity not unpleasing; the titles of the books were lettered in raised metal letters, chased or burnished on the surface.

Let us not, however, be dazzled with all this show—"Splendour in the binding of books," observes an able writer in the Juries' reports, " is a taste which dates back from remote times. The rarity of manuscripts, and the ornaments of every kind with which they were enriched, rendered them so precious, that they were exhibited upon desks for the purpose of gratifying the sight and the pride of their possessors. Seneca said of them, 'Plerisque libri non studiorum instrumenta sunt, ad ædum ornamenta.' But if these rich bindings, some beautiful models of which still exist in public libraries, were suitable before or soon after the invention of printing, when books were almost as scarce as manuscripts, they are an anachronism, when we are compelled to heap them so closely in our libraries. These magnificent covers, executed for the greater part by jewellers, who enriched them with reliefs in gold, silver, steel, and ivory, with precious stones, with enamels, and with decorations of every kind, could only be suitable for the missals, and the antiphoners placed in churches. On seeing at the Exhibition, enclosed in the beautiful articles of furniture from Austria, the superb bindings in ivory, carved with so much art, or in gold and silver inlaid with gems, and enamels still more precious, it might be supposed that these were shrines enclosing sacred relics, or even the casket of Darius, in which Alexander deposited the poems of Homer.

"Between simple bindings, and those in which costliness is carried to extreme, a medium may be found which lovers of books delight in, combining elegance with solidity and simplicity, qualities preferable to richness of gilding. At the period of the *Renaissance*, artists of great taste executed admirable bindings for kings, princes, and a few rich and learned amateurs, whose names are preserved in the recollection of bibliopoles, who maintained in their houses, binders, whose taste they directed. Some chose the Byzantine style; but the greater portion adopted the style called the *Renaissance*. After them the binders confined themselves to imitation, applying this style of ornament indiscriminately to every species of book. Some attempts have been made to submit bookbinding to general principles, and to adopt the binding either to the period in which the books were written, or according to the subjects of which they treat; and a variety of ornaments have been devised in consequence. The idea, though a happy one, is not new, but has not generally been adopted. We have seen the cap of liberty, the owl, and the wand of Æsculapius applied to bindings with respect to the contents of the works. The Egyptian, Grecian, and Roman ornamental emblems have been resorted to, as well as the Gothic, borrowed from monuments. Others have thought it desirable that bookbinders, departing from the beaten track, should endeavour to give a more peculiar character which should mark our era; and that thus the choice of colours, more or less sombre, or more or less bright—might always be in accordance with the nature of the subject treated of in the books. They contend that this system would at once afford, in a large library, the advantage of facilitating the search for books, by immediately striking the eye: that it is also to be desired that certain styles of ornament should indicate whether such a work, on Egypt for example, belonged to the Pharaonic, the Arabic, the French, or the Turkish era; and that it should be the same with ancient Greece, Byzantine Greece, or modern Greece, the Rome of the Cæsars, or the Rome of the Popes."

These suggestions are not altogether to be disregarded. Whatever facilitates the ready attainment of the intellectual wealth that our libraries contain, is worth consideration. In concluding these observations, we may perhaps be allowed to remark, that books are made to be handled and to be read; in providing them, therefore, with decent and respectable binding, if we avoid on the one hand the homely parsimony observed with respect to those neglected shelves, where, as the author of the *Dunciad* has recorded,—

> "—— Caxton sleeps, with Wynkyn by his side,
> One clasped in wood, and one in strong cow-hide."

So it is equally desirable that we should not clothe our books, our intellectual companions, in such gay and costly liveries, as to render them too fine for every-day use; too splendid and pretentious for the philosopher and the student.

STATIONERY.

From bookbinding to stationery is a very natural transition. We shall, accordingly, before we conclude our chapter, present our readers with a few observations upon the subject, which we extract from the pages of an able contemporary.

On the north side of the western nave, near the Fine Arts Court, was the modest space occupied by this important group of manufactures, which, but for the attractive folding-machine of Messrs. De la Rue and Co., placed at its portal, might have escaped the scrutiny of all but the systematic visitor. Bookbinding occupied the lion's share of the allotted ground, and paper but a very small portion. It is to be regretted that our paper manufacturers did not contribute more generally, for, undoubtedly, in many descriptions of paper we stand unrivalled. The number of contributors was in reality so small, that, had it not been for the energy of Messrs. Venables in collecting papers of many varieties, and from all sources, Great Britain would have made but little show in comparison with the productions of our continental neighbours. Whilst on this subject, we must advert to the advantage which would have resulted from the display of a paper machine in operation, with all the modern improvements, instead of the model exhibited by the Messrs. Donkin—a name, however, which must always be mentioned in honourable connexion with the paper-making automaton. Here our French brethren had the start of us, for, instead of a model, they exhibited the paper-making machine of Varrall, Middleton, and Elwell—a small one, it is true, and not at work. Had the Messrs. Donkin availed themselves of the opportunity of showing one of their paper machines in full work, the public would have better appreciated the importance of that art, which transforms rags and refuse into a tablet on which all the results of human knowledge are stored, and but for which the dependent art of printing would be useless.

In Great Britain alone, about one hundred and thirty million pounds weight of paper are annually manufactured—estimated as worth upwards of three million pounds sterling, and yielding to the revenue £870,000. Nine-tenths of this quantity are consumed in this country, the exports not amounting to more than £300,000; yet this noble art was represented by only some half dozen British exhibitors. Mr. Joynson, of St. Mary Cray, and the Messrs. Spicer, exhibited a roll of paper 2,500 yards in length; thus proving the perfection of the machinery which converts the water-suspended pulp, flowing continuously at one end of the machine, into an unbroken sheet of well-sized writing paper, which comes out dried and ready for use at the other end. They also displayed a sheet of brown paper, 93 inches in width, and 420 feet in length, besides mill-boards of a new kind, and specimen reams of writing paper. Mr. Fourdrinier exhibited a sheet of pottery paper, two miles and-a-half in length. This paper is employed in the potteries as a vehicle to receive the impressions from the engraved plates, to be transferred therefrom by the burnishers to the unglazed ware. This class of paper is of great strength, and, in illustration of this, we may mention an anecdote which occurs to us. With this paper, twisted into a rope, the proprietor of one of our potteries repaired, rapidly and efficiently, the broken traces of a carriage, which had conveyed a party of friends over the rough road leading to his works. Mr. Fourdrinier's name must not be passed without paying a tribute to the memory of his spirited and energetic relatives, to whom is mainly due the perfecting of the first crude thought of the continuous paper-making machine. There were likewise specimens of pottery paper exhibited by Mr. Lamb, in connexion with the rope used in its manufacture, and the pottery ware with the transferred designs; and some were also contributed by Mr. Saunders, of Dartford, who illustrated the strength before alluded to, by suspending four half-hundred weights to a sheet only twenty inches in width. We here found Dewdney's well-known blue paper, which is used by the starch maker to wrap up his goods, and which must sustain the ordeal of a good baking in contact with the moist starch without losing its colour. Glazed boards, used in pressing cloths, were exhibited by Mr. Hamer, of Horseforth; also by Messrs. Hastings and Miller, who likewise displayed gun-wadding and brown papers. There were also brown papers from E. Smith, of Fellingshore. We have now enumerated the principal objects in the plain paper section, with the exception of those sent by Messrs. Cowan, of Edinburgh, and the excellent and well-arranged selection of Messrs. Venables—which comprised, besides papers of their own make, most of the varieties manufactured in Great Britain, with the name of each maker prominently stated. Amongst them we noticed the universally-celebrated drawing papers of Mr. J. Whatman and those of Mr. George Wilmot. There were also brown papers, in which the most highly polished steel goods may be safely packed without fear of rust; together with the unrivalled plate papers of Mr. Charles Venables, and the hand papers by his relative, George Venables.

Of highly-glazed and tastefully packeted writing papers, Messrs. De La Rue and Co. were the principal exhibitors. Some of the novel papers with water-marks, invented by Mr. Oldham, and manufactured by Mr. Saunders, were placed against the glass partition which divides off the machinery, and they produced effects very similar to the celebrated porcelain pictures, and received ample patronage from the public. Among the water-marks shown in the paper were some illustrations of sculpture from Nineveh, some Roman heads, the Madonna and Child, rural scenery, a medallion of her Majesty, the Exhibition building, with portraits of her Majesty and Prince Albert, a view of York Minster, and various others. The invention appears to be admirably adapted for paper for bank-notes, and other descriptions in which security from fraud or forgery is desired.

Switzerland contributed well-made music-papers, writing papers of tolerable quality, and white and tinted tissues, which are very inferior to those made in England. Rome sent remarkably good drawing papers, made by M. Millani; and Tuscany, good machine writing papers, pelure of good quality, and laid papers, in which there is still room for improvement. France came out well in plain papers. The well-known Mongolfier sent excellent tinted drawing papers, tinted and white printed papers, and a very remarkable description called "*parchemin animal*," possessing surprising tenacity—so much so, that it is difficult to believe in its being only ordinary paper. Some of the specimens of this artificial skin are prepared with a kind of oil varnish, which adapts it for the preservation of artillery cartridges, especially during the long period of peace which it is our happiness to live in.   The Société Anonyme du Marais (Seine et Marne) sent specimens oι writing and printing papers, coarse papers used for the manufacture of pasteboard, and likewise a fine sort of millboard employed as a substitute for pasted cardboard, but not possessing its strength and firmness.   The Société Anonyme Soucle (Vosges) sent tinted writing papers, and tinted tissues, which would bear comparison with the best of our English manufactures—especially the pink, which surpassed in beauty of colour any other that we have seen.   The French have always been famous for their tracing papers, especially those made transparent without the use of varnishes, and the examples here exhibited maintained their reputation.   We now pause to examine more closely the splendid writing papers of Lacroix, whose thin post surpassed every thing which we had seen.   The influence which local circumstances, especially the postal arrangements oι different countries, have on this branch of art, cannot be more forcibly exemplified than in the paper productions of France, as compared with our own.   In England the aim is generally to produce a stout paper, that the writing may not show through on the opposite side.   We certainly surpass all other countries in the beautiful laid or ribbed papers, which the French are only now attempting; whilst, on the contrary, we are far behind them in their writing papers, as exemplified in M. Lacroix's beautiful and almost spotless pelure adapted to the postal laws of France.

Belgium sustained her reputation in this manufacture by a single, yet excellent, contribution from Godin and Son.   It was most extensive, containing rolls of packing and printing papers, machine-made drawing papers, and pelure writing papers, which are very excellent, but which do not equal the specimens of M. Lacroix.   In the northern gallery, Russia exhibited some packing, printing, and writing papers, which show that that country is advancing, although their manufacture is still behind the western states of Europe.   Holland sent laid papers for account books, and likewise writing papers by Honig and Son, all good of their various kinds; and Van Gelder and Sons exhibited paper, blue on one side and white on the other, for the use of sugar refiners.   There were several exhibitors from the different states of the Zollverein.   We particularly noticed the productions of the mill of Dilligen, in Prussia.   They contained, among other matters, specimens of the papers produced at these works from 1760 to 1850, showing at a glance the various improvements which have taken place; likewise a group of raw materials, and the papers produced from them.   We also noticed straw papers of excellent quality.   A short time back a mill was started in England for manufacturing paper from straw, but the speculation does not appear to have answered commercially.   In the section of Sweden and Norway we searched in vain for the filtering paper so valuable to the experimental chemist, which is made with the water resulting from the melting of the mountain snows, and is said to be the purest of all papers.   Denmark sent some vellum post of good quality, and likewise machine drawing papers. India exhibited some curious specimens of native manufacture; that contributed from Nepaul being remarkable for its extreme thinness and lightness.

SPANDRIL FROM HEREFORD CATHEDRAL,

DESIGNED BY N J COTTINGHAM.

Engraved by W Lacey, from a Daguerreotype by Beard

MONUMENTAL CROSS

EXECUTED IN CAEN STONE BY THE HONBLE MRS ROSS

Engraved by W Lacey from a Daguerreotype by Beard

CHAPTER XXXVI.

THE MEDIÆVAL COURT.

STOVE—OAK NICHE—GREAT ROOD—STONE CARVING—THE NICHE—THE TABERNACLE—TOMB OF DR. WALSH—HIGH ALTAR—CHIMNEY-PIECE—THE FONT—PAINTED GLASS—FURNITURE—CHURCH ORNAMENTS—METAL WORK, ETC. ETC.

AMONG all the numerous attractions of the Great Exhibition, perhaps, on the whole, the Mediæval Court, as a department, excited the most general interest. Its contents were of great variety, consisting of furniture, and church decorations after the fashion of the mediæval period, presenting a rich combination of stained glass, hardware, wood-carving, hangings, encaustic tiles, &c., perhaps a little too theatric in effect, but still harmonious and suggestive. In making these remarks, and in proceeding to enter into a detailed account of this remarkable apartment, we by no means would wish to imply that we are among the votaries of mediæval models : far from it. We entirely agree with an acute and learned contemporary, who says, " we consider that they have served their time, and in their time satisfied the general purposes of feeling and convenience then existing ; the attempt to revive them now, however, is a mistake ; the sentiments which dictated many a pious, but often mistaken act of laborious decoration, exist no longer. Truer principles of art and rules of taste have begun to influence society ; and the decorative fancies which in real mediæval works become curious to us as matters of comparative history, are lifeless, tame—not to say absurd—when copied in a more enlightened age. We object to all backward movements when once we have arrived at a safe ground to stand upon ; and considering that the classic models, which reached us at the period of the revival, are to all intents and purposes preferable to the barbarism and clumsy contrivances of the middle ages, we object to abandon them until something better is offered to us in their stead. At any rate, we must strenuously resist retracing our steps from the revival to the mediæval ; which, to speak plainly, we look upon as the culminating point of barbarism. Nevertheless, as we said before, the Mediæval Court, tricked out in gaudy-coloured draperies, in coloured glass, and glittering brass, and cold monumental stone effigies, presented a striking *coup-d'œil*, and deserves analytical description. The credit of the general arrangements, we understand, was due to the late Mr. Pugin, well known as a devotee to this style of art and contrivance. The principal objects may be described as follows,—in the language, as will be perceived, of a veritable enthusiastic mediævalism :—

Stove.—On the north side of the court was a large square stove of remarkable character : it was composed of glazed tiles in relief, of various colours, of which a considerable number were pierced to permit the exit of the hot air. These were fixed in an iron frame, with angle shafts terminating in coronals, and small vanes of gilt metal painted with heraldic bearings. The whole was enclosed with a wrought-iron grille of ingenious construction, all the enrichments being produced by hand, after the manner of the ancient Flemish smiths, and not cast. The crockets and finials were all bent up and twisted out of thin metal, and the general effect was most striking, reminding the spectator of the ancient stoves in the castle of Nuremberg, and converting what is generally an unsightly object into a highly decorative adjunct to an entrance hall or gallery.

Oak Niche.—Immediately over the south-east door was a wooden niche, containing a finely carved image of St. John the Baptist ; the great peculiarity of this niche consisted in its being designed after the old principle, to suit the material in which it was executed. All the enrichments were sunk out of the thickness of the stuff ; there was neither mitering nor lateral projection: the cross pieces were terminated and keyed with wedges, which effectually held the work together without glue; the canopy was also carved out of three pieces, with sunk enrichments, and crocketed with continuous foliage.

Great Rood.—In the south-east angle stood the Great Rood, intended for the loft of St. Edmund's College, near Ware. The whole was richly crocketed and foliated. At the four extremities were emblems of the Evangelists, surrounded by rich foliage-work, and on the reverse the Four Doctors. Attached to the lower portion of the framing were two pedestals for the images of the Blessed Virgin and St. John. The intermediate panels were filled with rich perforated tracing; and metal branches for lights were affixed to the stanchions.

Stone-Carving—Altar and Reredos—East Side.—This altar was intended for the lady chapel of a country church. The subject was that of the Annunciation. The whole reredos was divided into five compartments. The two outer ones contained images of the Virgin and the angel Gabriel; and in the centre the pot of lilies, most delicately relieved in the carving, and interwoven with a label inscribed with the angelic salutation. The whole was surmounted by a very rich bratishing of quatrefoils and crocketed work.

The Niche.—Adjoining the reredos was a niche, surmounted by a rich and lofty stone canopy, for the same chapel. This niche contained an image of the Virgin holding our Lord in her arms. The dignity of the Divinity was expressed in the countenance of the infant, and in his hand he bore the orb and cross. The Virgin was attired in a long tunic, and a mantle, with an enriched border, gathered gracefully into long folds; a silver parcel gilt crown, enriched with stones, was placed on the head. The image rested on a high pedestal, with highly relieved foliage, and the angle pinnacles of the canopy rested on two angle corbels issuing from the sides.

Tabernacle.—Immediately opposite the high altar was a stone tabernacle intended for the reservation of the holy sacrament. It was quadrangular at bottom, with four crocketed gablets, three of which were filled with rich tracery, and the fourth was the door, of perforated brass. From the four angles rose buttresses and pinnacles, terminated by angels with musical instruments. From this point the canopy became octagonal, and was connected to the square base by crocketed flying buttresses. It was terminated by a cluster of pinnacles, and niches filled with angels of most elaborate design and exquisite workmanship. Its entire height was upwards of twenty feet.

Stone-Carving.—West Side.—Tomb of the late Rev. Dr. Walsh.—This monument, intended to be erected in St. Chad's Cathedral, Birmingham, in memory of the late Dr. Walsh, was designed in the third printed or decorated style, and executed in a very perfect manner. The effigy was recumbent, the head supported by two angels; it was attired in full episcopal vestments of the ancient graceful form, and the pastoral staff was borne in the right hand. The minutest details of the embroidery were most carefully carved in the stone, and the whole was a *fac simile* of the actual vestments used by the deceased prelate. The effigy had a striking resemblance to those venerable and dignified effigies still remaining in our ancient churches. A richly crocketed canopy surmounted the recess, flanked by two buttresses and pinnacles; the back of the recess was diapered, and the centre, within a quatrefoil, was a bas-relief, representing the Doctor, attired as a Bishop, kneeling, and offering the church of which he was the founder. The base of the tomb contained five quatrefoils, floriated and studded with wallflowers, with enamelled shields of family and ecclesiastical bearings; and along the upper edge was the following inscription, engraved in brass :—

Orate pro anima illustrissimi Reverendissimi Dom. Thomae Walsh, Ep. Cambysop., in dist. centralis per annos 25 Vic. Ap., et hujus ecclesiæ Cathedralis fundatoris. Obit. Vic. ap. Londinen. xviii. Feb. MDCCCXLIX.

High Altar.—The centre of the east side was occupied by a stone altar, intended for the chancel of a parish church; the front was supported by four marble pillars, with sculptured caps. These stood some distance in advance of the block part of the altar, which contained three deeply-mounted quatrefoils, surrounded by wallflowers, with three subjects in bas-relief—the "Agony in the Garden," "Our Lord bearing the Cross," and the "Crucifixion:" these groups were sculptured with great severity and truth, and possessed a most devotional character. The space between the marble pillars and these sculptures will eventually contain reliquaries like small shrines.

Chimney-piece.—On the west side of the court was a richly-carved fire-place, worked in Caen stone; it was intended for the mansion of F. Barchard, Esq. The whole of the ornaments were heraldic, and the crockets were formed by birds encircled with foliage. The centre panel contained the Barchard arms, and the initials of the family filled the lateral quatrefoils. The recess for the grate was lined with tiles, charged with the crest and initials F. B. alternately. The grate was solidly formed of wrought iron, standing on two dogs of the same material, surmounted by brass birds, and enriched with metal badges of beaten work; a stone fender enclosed the hearth, which was composed of red and yellow tiles. The whole of the stone-work in this court was executed by Mr. Myers, of Belvidere-road, Lambeth, London, inventor of the machine for cutting Gothic tracery and mouldings: specimens of the work executed by it were deposited in the court, close to the bishop's tomb. There was a smaller fire-place at the north-east angle, also executed in Caen stone: it was square-headed; the hollows of the mouldings were filled with running foliage; the upper part was divided by beads into three panels, filled with Minton's tiles, chastely and elaborately painted with floral and geometrical patterns. The sides of the fire-place were lined by high tiles of a rich and original pattern, and the hearth was encircled by a stone fender. The whole fire place had a rich and pleasing effect, produced by the combination of carved stone and the enamel painting of the tile-work. There was a small but appropriate grate, supported on dogs, in the fire-place.

The Font.—In the centre of the court was a font and cover raised on octagonal steps, the risers of which were enriched with tracery. The bow was also octagonal, four sides being carved with the following subjects from sacred history:—"The Fall of Man," "St. John Preaching in the Wilderness," "The Baptism of our Lord," and the "Crucifixion." From the four other sides were projecting images of angels, which acted as corbels to support the four principal shafts of the canopy. Round the pedestal were images of the Evangelists, the "Blessed Virgin," "St. John the Baptist," "St. Peter," and "St. Paul."

The canopy, which was entirely of oak, and supported by the angle-shafts, was raised up to a considerable height by a succession of pinnacles and tabernacle-work, and was sufficiently lofty to receive the cover of the font, consisting of an octagonal top, surmounted by open tray panels, the whole of which rose up into the canopy by the action of counterweight when the font was used; and when lifted to its proper elevation, formed a ceiling, with the Holy Dove in the centre. This principle of uncovering the font was a considerable improvement on the old method of opening a compartment of the high covers, and was at once more elegant and convenient.

Painted Glass.—The north side of the court was filled with painted glass. Over the entrance-door was a portion of the south window of the new dining-hall at Alton Towers. The centre light contained an effigy of the Grand Talbot, faithfully delineated from his tomb at Whitchurch. On either side were shields with his various quarterings, supported by Talbots, and intersected with foliage and branch-work on a quarry guard, surrounded by a neat border of T's and coronals.

There were two long lights of the Decorated period, with compound niches and pinnacles, each containing an image; one of St. Thomas the Apostle, the other St.

3 N

Thomas the Martyr, in rich costume, on diapered grounds. These were intended for the court windows of the chantry chapel of the late Dr. Griffiths, in the Collegiate Church of St. Edmunds, near Ware. Over the lower doorway were placed three lights, representing two groups, from the life of St. Andrew, and an effigy of the saint, all under very elaborate canopies. This glass was designed in the style of the fifteenth century, as it is to be fixed in a parochial church of that period. Adjoining the centre pillar were two lights, forming the centre light for the great court window of the same church : the subjects represented were the Transfiguration and Crucifixion of our Lord. At the east end were four lights of grisaille work, each containing two quatrefoils, filled with subjects from the life of the Blessed Virgin. These groups were relieved on rich blue glass, diapered, and the grisaille was intersected with ruby and yellow bands, &c., upon floriated centres of varied colours, and each light was surrounded by a varied border. These windows were to be placed on the south side of the Lady Chapel of St. Augustine's Church, at Ramsgate. At the opposite end was another window of two lights, containing niches and canopies, with images of St. Ethelbert of Kent and his Queen, the blessed Bertha. The richness of the habits of the two principal figures was well relieved by a white ground ; and this style of glass, treated on the old principles, has all the advantages of producing a rich effect, without impeding the sufficiency of light from entering the edifice. This window was also for St. Augustine's, Ramsgate, and was presented to that church by J. Herbert, Esq., the celebrated painter and Academician.

There was a very translucent image of the Virgin, in a blue mantle, of a rich, but subdued colour, precisely similar to that so frequently seen in the old windows, and which is most difficult to attain. A decorated canopy surmounted the light, and the groundwork was a white diaper. The whole of the glass was painted in the old manner, and without any attempt at antiquity, but left precisely in the same state as that of the old glass, when originally executed. In all the designs a due proportion of white was introduced, without which it is impossible to attain a brilliant effect.

Furniture.—The centre of the south side was occupied by a carved oak sideboard, of massive construction : the back was raised in panel-work to the height of several feet, and supported an overhanging canopy, richly carved, and divided into arched panels by moulded ribs ; these panels were diapered in colour, on gold ground. The centre compartment of the back was hung with scarlet cloth, and served as a background to several large ornamental dishes, parcel gilt, beat up and raised into heraldic devices and bearings, with rich and varied borders, containing crests and mottos, all referring to the house of Talbot, as they are intended for the new dining-hall at Alton Towers. The constructive framing of this sideboard was richly ornamented by carving of vine and hop foliage, boldly executed. The two extreme stanchions were carried up in an octagonal form, and terminated by two clusters of foliated brass branches, supporting lights. The doors of the side recesses were elaborately carved, and fitted with pierced ornamental hinges and lock plates, in the style of those so skilfully made in the fifteenth century. The sideboard was the production of Mr. Crace, of Wigmore-street. The dishes were executed by Mr. Hardman, of Birmingham. Immediately in front of the sideboard was a large octagonal table, executed in walnut-tree. The frame and stand was designed on the strongest constructional principles, and its enrichments were only adjuncts to the necessary framing. The top was elaborately inlaid with woods of various colours, and fully proved the applicability of mediæval designs and decorations to every want of the present age. The general effect had all the richness of marqueterie, with purer forms, and a more pleasing combination of colours.

The next most striking piece of furniture was a long book-case or cabinet. The centre doors were filled with open-wrought brass-work, of intricate foliated design, and were intended to admit a view of costly objects preserved in this compartment; the two side-doors were panelled with rich flamboyant tracery. The spaces were divided by carved and moulted muntons, and the whole was surmounted by an elaborate foliated bratishing in oak, interspersed with shields, charged with various devices. The locks, fastenings, and hinges, were of brass, and perfectly carved out in character with piercing and chasing.

Adjoining the cabinet was a praying-desk, surrounded by a triptych, intended for a bedchamber or private oratory. On either side of the desk were carved corbels, supporting a pair of gilt candlesticks, ornamented with fleurs-de-lis, and the monogram M.R. The panels of the triptych, when open, displayed two miniature paintings of St. Katherine and St. Margaret, and the centre recess was richly dispersed in gold and colours. This piece of furniture was executed by Mr. Crace, for C. R. Scott Murray, Esq., of Danesfield. On this side of the court were several pieces of furniture, such as tables, some inlaid at top, chairs, with gilt supporters and velvet coverings; others, more simple in form, of oak, and covered with leather, but as commodious in shape as those of ordinary modern use. In the centre was a cheval screen, consisting of a richly-carved frame, decorated with the rose, shamrock, and thistle, supported by the lion and unicorn at either end, with the royal arms,—a combination, however, involving a glaring anachronism. The whole was filled with elaborate needlework, executed by a number of ladies, whose names were inscribed in scroll-work on the reverse. At either end of this side was placed a piano, the cases of which were designed in the same style as the rest of the furniture. A piano is so modern an invention, that it has hitherto been considered almost hopeless to combine its construction with old details suitable for the rooms of an ancient mansion; but the present examples fully show that mediæval detail and design are perfectly applicable to all the requirements and inventions of the day. One of these instruments was executed in oak, and was of simple character; the other was most elaborately carved and gilt, the fall painted with flowing borders, and the keys inlaid. The pianos were made by Messrs. Burns and Lambert, of Portman-street. Interspersed with this furniture was a variety of brass candlesticks, sconces, and branches for lights, either standing or projecting from the wall. They were light in design, and well adapted for their purposes, yet most original in form and effect. In stuffs for hangings there were a great variety of elaborate and most effective old patterns, executed by Mr. Crace, some in tapestry, others in silk and woollen stuffs, which, by their design, perfectly recalled those gorgeous bandekins so often mentioned in the pages of the old historians, and depicted in the works of the ancient painters. There were also several carpets of the same character, full of rich colour and design, and without any attempt at false relief and shadow. Over the stone fire-place a large carpet was suspended, all the details of which, without a single architectural feature, or anything that would be commonly denominated Gothic, by the arrangements of its foliated enrichments and the combination of colours, possessed a most distinct and mediæval character.

Church Ornaments, Metal-work, &c.—A very large portion of the contents of the Mediæval Court came under this head. Immediately in front of the great sideboard hung a chandelier of striking appearance and considerable dimensions. It was constructed on the octagonal principle, and was composed of a number of shafts terminating in pinnacles passing through frames of pierced-work, fixed to a central shaft of tinted brass. From each pinnacle sprung a succession of light foliage in the form of branches, the stems of which terminated in coronals and sockets supporting the candles. Shields charged with the Talbot lion were interspersed among the branches, and by the colour heightened the general richness of effect. The first idea of this chandelier was taken from the celebrated one at Nuremberg; but it was larger in dimensions, and much lighter and stronger in construction. It was intended to be suspended in the centre of the new dining-hall at Alton Towers. Immediately opposite was a large brass cornice of an early style, executed for a church of Byzantine character. It was composed of segments of circles filled in by rich intersecting open-work, and supporting a deep rim and bratishing. To these were attached the standards which carry the tapers, and were composed of chased stems, with crystal nobs and small coronals. The weight of the lower crown was partly carried by chains of a very ornamental character fastened to an upper crown; and the effect of the whole was extremely rich and striking. Round the high altar on the east side, a set of six brass pillars, about twelve feet in height, was erected. These pillars were highly ornamented in their shafts, with moulded caps and bases, and sustained six angels, also in brass, with outspread wings, bearing standards with tapers: between every pillar was a brass rod with open-work bratishing, and rings from which silk curtains, wove with sacred emblems, were suspended. This kind of inclosure was formerly to be found in the majority of the foreign cathedrals, and occasionally in our own; but a more correct taste and revolutionary changes have completely stripped the ancient churches of these unnecessary arrangements, and they have been now revived for the first time for the chancel of St. Thomas's church at Erdington, for which the whole of this work was designed and executed. In front of the high altar hung a carved beam, similar to those described as having been suspended in Canterbury Cathedral and other churches. It was intended for chapels dedicated to the reservation of the holy sacrament. At the centre and extremities were quatrefoils filled with foliage, and to these the iron-work, by which the whole was suspended, was attached. Along the upper edge was an open cresting of brass-work, supporting bowls and prickets for tapers. To the lower side of the beam were suspended seven silver lamps of the ancient form, several of which were enriched with enamels. The wick burns in a ruby glass dropped into a silver collar hung from the small chains attached to the larger ones, which sustain the chased basins hanging beneath to receive any drippings of oil. These were designed on the real principles of church lamps, and according to the most ancient customs, and they are perfectly consistent in form, and convenient for their purposes; while modern church lamps are usually made like huge bowls full of emptiness, with a glass stuck in the top of them. The beam and its appurtenances are a most satisfactory revival of one of the most beautiful ornaments that formerly decorated the ancient churches. Round the high altar were placed several high-standing candlesticks, terminating in branches and coronals for lights, intended for the elevation or benediction. There were also six silver candlesticks on the altar, of twisted and chased-work rising from octagonal bases, ornamented with crystals and knops. The flowing of this design is particularly well adapted to the metal, as they produce an infinite variety of bright and reflected lights.

The candles themselves are remarkable amongst the revivals of the present age. The large candle, which is called a "Paschal Candle," was intended as symbolical of the glory of Christ's resurrection. It is lighted during the offices of the Romish Church from Easter to the Ascension. It was elaborately painted round the base with various inscriptions and devices. The triple candle, which is composed of three equal parts twisted together, is used on Holy Saturday for the "Lumen Christi," in the procession from the church porch. The twisted torch is a revival of those borne on various occasions in the middle ages, especially at funeral processions and entertainments. The custom of enriching candles for sacred purposes, by painting and gilding, is very ancient; and the same principle was formerly carried out with regard to candles for domestic use in great feasts, these being painted with heraldic devices. On the eastern side of the court were two glass cases filled with silver work and jewellery: that on the north side was devoted to ecclesiastical ornaments, and the opposite one was filled with secular plate, jewels, &c.

In the former there were several richly enamelled chalices of the ancient form, with chased perforated knops of intricate design and hexagonal feet most richly chased and decorated with enamel and precious stones. There were two monstrances of elegant design, but of very different character. The first was a circlet of rich tracery, like a crown supported by a high stem, and surrounded with enamelled quatrefoils representing cherubim in adoration. The second was like an open spire or canopy of octagonal form, springing from four pinnacled shafts, supporting images of angels with scrolls. The execution of this, even to the minutest details of the crockets and pinnacles, would bear comparison with some of the best works of the old silversmiths, and may be considered a great advance in the revival of this art. On one side of the same case was a pastoral staff for a bishop, enamelled, crocketed, and containing several images in the crook under canopied-work. This case also contained some richly enamelled pyxes, candlesticks, crosses, bindings of missals, and a variety of church ornaments most elaborate in detail. The opposite case, devoted to secular plate, contained a variety of specimens of candlesticks, salt-cellars, dessert services, flagons, &c., of simple form, but designed in the metallic feeling which may be discerned in the productions of the ancient silversmiths. The effect is produced by beating-up and engraving. There were no cast ornamaments of heavy foliage, but the nature of the material is well-considered in the designs, and has a great effect in production at a comparatively small cost There were several trays of jewels, the setting of which was according to the old Venetian manner, the stones being almost detached, and held by points, by which a transparent effect is obtained. The specimens consisted of crosses, bracelets, necklaces, brooches, rings, and a girdle. The casket made to contain them was exceedingly elaborate, and of elegant design, with enamelled lock and heraldic devices. On the opposite side of the court were two other cases, containing church vestments, made after the ancient form, which has been recently revived, and presenting a pleasing contrast to the modern stiff and buckram *chasuble* of France. The laces which form the orphreys were adapted from ancient examples, and a great variety of these were exhibited on the sides of the cases. There was also an albe with the ancient apparel as seen in the habits of ecclesiastics on tombs and sepulchral brasses, and two copes, one of which was of white cloth of gold. There was also a variety of stoles, maniples, and chalice-veils, in the same case. Adjoining were three lecterns. The first was designed with two branches, separating from a solid stem (the base), and supporting two kneeling angels, who carry a perforated tracery panel to receive the book. The second was a large eagle, with outspread wings, resting on an orb supported by an hexagonal pedestal of open tracery-work, from whence sprung three flying buttresses, resting on pinnacled shafts, surmounted by half images of angels bearing scrolls. The base was very massive, and rested on three lions couchant. Two large foliated branches were attached to the shafts, and carried tapers, to afford light to the *lector;* these branches were moveable, and might be adjusted at pleasure. This noble lantern was presented to St. George's Church, Southwark, by the Rev. D. Haigh, of Erdington. The third lectern was designed from an ancient example at the Cathedral at Courtrais. The desk was perforated with a device of the holy name spread out into flamboyant tracery; the shaft was terminated by an image of St. John the Evangelist. Opposite these, and in front of the niche, was placed an iron candlestick, of wrought-work, which turned on a centre, and was intended to receive offerings of tapers for the Lady Chapel of St. Augustin's Church. This was a most elaborate piece of iron-work, worthy of the ancient smiths, and was a striking proof that our operations, when under proper directions, are quite capable of representing the most beautiful works of mediæval skill. Near this was a credence-table of wrought brass, with a marble inlaid top, and many other objects all from the workshops of Mr. J. Hardman, of Birmingham.

3 o

CHAPTER XXXVII.

LETTERS FROM M. BLANQUI—*continued.*

LETTER III.

THE more we examine in the Crystal Palace the portion devoted to English industry, the more we perceive that the English have neglected nothing to appear to the utmost advantage at this memorable tournament. They are completely equipped, armed at all points. They only, perhaps, amongst all the competitors, are in a position to be judged without appeal, for they have unreservedly put forth all their strength. When the Exhibition had once been determined upon, the fiercest protectionists, who had most strongly opposed it, made every effort to appear to the greatest advantage. They yielded with good grace, and not a manufacturer of any importance failed to respond to the summons : they were all ready on the opening day. They occupy, as we have already stated, one-half of the entire space devoted to the Exhibition, and they have established themselves methodically and in admirable order. All their machines are in operation in a series of bays, to which the steam required to put them in motion is conveyed under-ground in tubes. Whether from motives of economy, or for the purpose of avoiding the terrible din caused by so much machinery, each machine is only worked at intervals, so that a portion of the machinery is at rest while the other is at work. The overlookers everywhere explain the processes to the public; there is spinning, weaving, embroider-ing, stocking-weaving, lace, riband, and cloth manufacturing. It is a veritable acting industrial encyclopædia. The steam is conveyed to machines of 20-horse power, and to small models the size of a card-table. Have a care how you pass unheeded these innumerable instruments of production : not one of them but which presents some novel amelioration or some improvement in the details.

There is not an European nation, even among those which excel in the construction of machinery, which offers so brilliant and complete a collection as England. The Eng-lish are here in truth upon their natural ground : their hydraulic presses, their locomo-tives, their maritime steam engines, exceed all known proportions. They exhibit rails of 20 metres long in one piece, cranks of forged iron for machines of 800-horse power, spinning frames with 1,200 spindles; that is to say, instruments of gigantic motion and production. Their cranes, their exhausting pumps, their waggons, their models of bridges, are of remarkable daring. The perfection of their agricultural implements, so varied and so different from our own, does not excite less admiration. Were there no other subjects for study, that of these instruments would suffice to prove how much their agriculture is advanced and worthy of their industry. Their superiority is still more strikingly manifested in all their iron works or cutlery. Iron and coal are the principal elements of the wealth of the British people. Enter the smallest village, wherever we use wood the English use iron or brass. The enlightened observer who examines the Exhibition, is particularly struck with the admirable perfection and the variety of their tools—from the axe to the plane, from the boring machines to the most delicately made files. Their lock-smiths' work, of excellent workmanship, adapts itself with precision to all description of fastening. Their knives, their scissors, their razors, their pen-knives, these indispensable instruments of everyday life, the imperfection of which in France causes us so many daily annoyances, are here of a solidity above all proof, and of exceedingly moderate price. Their hardware and edge-tools likewise exhibit the effects of the price of the raw material and of mechanical execution. Our superiority commences the moment when taste and objects of art are concerned, and this superiority, entirely French, shines pre-eminent, not only in our struggle with the English, but with all other nations. The form, the elegance, the grace, that indescribable something which gives life and soul to matter, perfume to flowers, colour to objects, this is the incontestable attribute of French genius. In this respect, I dare to say it without national vanity, our exhibition, though incomplete, is absolutely overwhelming. The question of prices, the question of labour, of political economy, will have to be considered hereafter, and we shall discuss it against all men; but the question of art and taste, that great trial which might have been lost, is won without appeal by the avowal of all our rivals. Behold the Austrians, the Belgians, the Spaniards even, and the English, as regards the artistic working in wood in a great and beautiful branch of industry—that of furniture. Assuredly, they have exhibited serious works—tables, sofas, arm-chairs, bookcases; but what absence of taste, what sheer waste of talent and ability, for want of design, of art, and of sentiment. It is the same in respect to bronzes and works in precious metals; although MM. Denière and Thomire —doubtless content with their laurels—have let judgment go by default. They are wrong. Englishmen, Prussians, Saxons, Austrians, all are rapt with admiration before the works of our founders. There is in these works such an extraordinary vigour and spirit, that every one is struck. These are the great artists, the men of taste, the inventors, the men who are imbued with the sacred spark of art. I have visited repeatedly the entire Exhibition with several able foreign manufacturers, who expressed their sincerest admiration for so many *chefs-d'œuvre*.

Everywhere we find this immortal fire of French genius, which is to us what the iron and coal mines are to the English, and more than that, an inexhaustible capital. No sooner have the manufacturers of Mulhouse displayed their printed jacconets, their printed calicoes, their chintzes, their mousselines-de-laine, than the victory is already assured to them. Look at the same articles in the English, Austrian, Belgian, Saxon, Swiss, or Russian compartments; everywhere you will be compelled to admit, with the progress which has been made, the decisive superiority of the French goods. And this time the question of prices excites no doubts—nobody manufactures better and cheaper. Here we have for less than a shilling per yard fabrics for curtains, or rather real masses of roses, lilacs, camelias, which float in the air, on calico grounds, and which M. Jean Dolfus still considers too dear. Jean Dolfus is right. Jean Dolfus is an upright and able manufacturer, who has perfectly understood that cheapness is the great question of the day, and who has thrown himself into the conflict for the triumph of true principles. What says he? A very simple thing. He says this:—"Since we are the first calico printers (and he has a right to say it, for he is one of the ablest), we have only one thing to wish for: it is, that the manufacturers of calico shall furnish us the raw material for our prints at the lowest possible price. Our superiority as printers is only weakened by our inferiority as weavers. Our weavers only sell us the calicoes at such high prices because the spinners are protected by prohibition below certain numbers. Let us abolish prohibition, which is absurd and impertinent in every respect, and the branch of industry of calico-printing will probably be trebled or increased tenfold. We shall purchase grey calico cheaper, and we shall resell it embellished with a thousand colours." Upon this there is a great outcry at Mulhouse, where there are, as elsewhere, many manufacturers ignorant on political economy, less peremptory and intolerable, however, than M.M. Lebeuf, Mimerel, those great proficients in closing the ports and building China walls, and for whom the whole of France is Creil and Roubaix. These illustrious "representatives of the people" exhibit nothing in London. They have dreaded the comparison of their products. Those who think as they do at Mulhouse, do not desire that our printers, who print so well, should print cheaper, that consequently they should employ more workpeople and create more national labour. This is the trial, be assured, which will be judged at the Exhibition in London from the most irrefutable evidence. Oh! Sir, how I lament to think that for more than twenty-five years my masters and myself have written and taught to demonstrate to this people, that it is better to have a good knife of thirty sous than a bad blade of three francs, and that to make steel, Swedish iron is better than ours. This is very unpatriotic, we are told, and you are the enemies of national labour; as though national labour were not interested in the cheapness of raw materials, and as though there were not in France millions of men who use iron compared with a few thousands who produce it! At this great gathering of the industry of all nations, it is easy to judge of the influence of low prices of the raw materials. The ascendant prosperity of the English is entirely owing to this. Every day they free their raw materials and articles of consumption. Bread, coffee, sugar, meat, tea, articles of food and of clothing, are all brought within reach of the greatest number, and increase at once the revenue of the state and the welfare of the people. When we consider, in this vast bazaar of the Universal Exhibition, what every nation wants, it is easy to see that it is principally the liberty to procure it to itself by the aid of that which it does not want. The United States exhibit varied raw materials in large numbers, and few and very mediocre manufactured articles. It is to their interest to sell us their raw materials and to purchase our products.

Before concluding this rapid sketch of the general facts of the Exhibition, I may allude to the interest which is attached to the countries now behindhand, in times of yore prosperous, of the old civilised world. The products of India and of China represent with sufficient accuracy the state of industry as it was two thousand years ago, when France and England were covered with forests. The Great Exhibition, therefore, does not only present the different industries of nations, but that of centuries; nor is it a spectacle devoid of interest to behold the spoils of animals from all parts of the globe—such as Bengal tigers, African lions, Russian bears, American beavers, and even hides of hippopotami perfectly tanned and bullet-proof.

LETTER IV.

At length France has hoisted her flag amidst the applause of all Europe, and in a few days hence her arts and manufactures may be appreciated at their true value. The city of Lyons has been somewhat behindhand, as this will sometimes happen to ill-tempered potentates; but nobody has lost anything in consequence. The Exhibition could scarcely be said to be opened as long as the marvels produced by that city were wanting. Now that Lyons and Mulhouse have completed their elegant, simple, and synoptical display, myriads of lookers-on crowd the brilliant galleries; it is a perpetual stream of visitors, who come to greet the queen city of our industry. On all hands nothing is heard but the exclamations—"Beautiful! handsome! very nice!"

This is the fitting opportunity, Sir, to reassure our countrymen upon the subject of the reports which have been circulated in Paris relative to our inferiority at the Exhibition. There can only have been some foundation for these reports during the first days, when, in fact, we had scarcely anything unpacked, and when the public, very much astonished, passed by our empty glass cases and our packing cases filled with straw. It was a lamentable spectacle, and the much more to be regretted since first impressions are enduring, and often outlive the reality which ought to modify them. But it was the fault of the exhibitors, who nearly all waited until the last moment, some to complete, others to send off their goods. Everything now has been set to rights; and previous to entering upon the comparative examination between our various arts and manufactures and those of our rivals, I can confirm, without an overweening patriotism, everything that I had led you to foresee in my first letters, that our triumph is certain in nearly everything, brilliant above all in the department of Lyons. Not that I do not see appearing in the horizon threatening powers : until further information, I shall merely name them to you. Switzerland has ribands, Italy velvets, and Spain silk goods, worthy or the greatest attention. China, of which I will speak presently, has very remarkable crapes and shawls, even as regards the taste of the embroidery. But rest assured that we shall remain the incontestable masters of the initiative and of art. An Englishman, who understands these matters, said to me yesterday : "We have quantity, you have quality." The Englishman was right. It will be easy to prove that we might have both. To achieve this it will suffice to admit the raw materials of labour at the lowest prices in whatever part of the world they are found. That which most usually interferes with the sale of our articles, is their relative dearness; and this dearness arises principally in consequence of the high price of the raw materials. As soon as it will be understood that the national genius gives to our works a greater value than other nations impart to theirs, the only means of not losing our superiority will be not to let the other nations be able to procure the elements of labour cheaper than ourselves. It is a question of customs; for as far as arts and taste are concerned, this is a sacred fire which cannot be purloined; the Universal Exposition sufficiently proves this, and, to me, beyond my most sanguine hopes. It will be as easy to deprive us of this privilege as of the mildness of our climate or the grace of our women. I would ask you whether grace can be taught or purchased?

Thus, Sir, until we reconsider this grave subject, naturally reserved until the end of our studies, I may recapitulate in a few words the position which we occupy at the Universal Exhibition. We are evidently without rivals as regards form, design, and colour in everything : precious metal-work, cabinet-work, bronzes, paper-hangings, printed calicoes, fancy articles, philosophical instruments, guns, &c. We have made no show of pottery or glass. Saint Louis and Baccaret have deserted in the face of England and Bohemia. We have few machines, and it would be a great error to judge of the power of France from what we have exhibited in this department, although what we have shown is very beautiful. Our former royal manufactures—Sèvres, Beauvais, and Gobelins—occupy a room by themselves, which is the admiration of all visitors. Our organs, our pianos, resound pre-eminently all over the Exhibition. Everywhere you behold a multitude of useful articles; you return at all times to the French department to find the real type of the beautiful. Even this morning I had the honour to accompany the duchess of Orleans over the Exhibition, who said to us, with visible satisfaction : "Decidedly, gentlemen, France is ever France; and her greatness shines here anew by the light of comparison !" I shall now conduct your readers over the ground most favourable to comparisons between our European industry and that of the old world. I allude to British India and China, which have displayed at the Universal Exhibition products which are really marvellous in point of make and variety. Manufacturers of every description, and of all countries, will do well to study the articles sent by China and India, for in them they will find precious indications to renew or modify their designs, their forms, and even the arrangement of certain weaving-looms. The collection of products of British India is peculiarly interesting in this respect, inasmuch as it is more novel and less known than the Chinese articles. It is also more complete, and it is easy to see that the orders of the English government have not contributed a little to the

care with which it has been got together. Those who only know India through the
medium of books—and there is not a better one on the subject than that of our unfortunate countryman, Jacquemont—may here see that country alive and stirring, without
trouble or fatigue; here it is entirely, the climate only is wanting; and I venture to say
that this collection of itself presents sufficient interest to attract thousands of visitors in
England.

The first thing which strikes the eye is a military and naval collection—that of all the
weapons of the country, and of all the ships, large or small, which navigate these
distant seas. What means of destruction, what curious shapes of guns, of heavy cannons, of pistols, of arrows, of sabres, of daggers ornamented in every fashion, daggers
with straight blades, with bent blades, gilt and enamelled poniards, yataghans—frightful
and beautiful instruments of death, and very few of production. You would think
that life is too long in that country, and that it is an evil of which you cannot get rid too
soon. The ships, likewise, seem rather constructed for the purpose of piracy than for
commerce. Behold those of Mindanao, with two rows of oars and square sails; the
sampans of Singapore, with lateen sails; the ship serpent of Cochin-China, with small
shovels in the shape of oars; and this whole fleet of sea-rovers, which the steam-frigates
of England gradually sweep away from this archipelago of thieves;—are not these the
image of the old East, which yields every day before the ascendancy of the genius of
Europe. The study of this collection is more easy, inasmuch as the English have omitted
nothing. There is probably not a single profession which has not been represented by
a statuette in the costume proper to it. These costumes are often somewhat light,
giving an idea of the climate, and particularly of the condition of the people of that
country. When you see these heavy palankins, carried by half-naked men with the
gait of beasts of burden, and contrast these with the brilliancy of the trappings, embroidered with gold, that of the golden fabrics inlaid with precious stones—all this
Oriental magnificence created by so much indigence—you learn only too much of the lot
of humanity in these old starting-points of civilisation. Here you may easily see that if
socialism is a chimera, misery is a reality. The works of their industry are nevertheless worthy of the liveliest interest. If our prohibitionists had condescended to appear
at the Universal Exhibition, we would have taken the liberty to show them the collection of Indian pottery, the forms of which are contemporaneous with the conquest of
Alexander, and which, for their variety and originality, are deserving the attention of all
those engaged in the ceramic art. This pottery, fine as well as coarse, forms a veritable
museum, of a striking local colouring, and which must be of great value, as I noticed
with regret that it was forbidden to take drawings of them *without permission;* but it is
not forbidden to carry away the idea. This exhibition is a mine of ideas. The two or
three charming little compartments devoted to the woven fabrics of India, from shawls
down to the slightest fancy neckerchiefs, appear to me capable of themselves of revolu-
tionising the fashions. Let me entreat of you to send the largest possible number of
workmen. Would they could all be sent here! What creations, what riches, would be
the fruits of this journey! What new fabrics might we not produce with the aid of
these patterns, three thousand years old! Besides, it appears to me that, since the
republic of Plato is fashionable in Paris, we ought also to study the contemporaneous
industry of Aristotle, whose pupil in days of yore conquered India. There was a great
industry in the East in the time of Alexander, just as there was one in Europe in the
time of Napoleon. If these two great men could now meet in London, they would both
find again the furniture of their closets and the swords of their soldiers; they would only
find the heroes wanting. The men of the present day are more ingenious, but they
are matter-of-fact. Let us therefore leave them alone, and let us return to our Indians.

The great value of this portion of the English Exhibition is, that it is impossible to find it elsewhere, either on a large or small scale. The greater portions of the Indian articles, not being in conformity with European taste, very few are generally imported into Europe, and we cannot adapt to our use all which would be applicable to it by means of some unimportant modifications. Yesterday, for instance, I was admiring several oriental fabrics brocaded with gold and silver, which the slightest change would suffice to transform in the most original fashion, and render them appropriate to the refined and elegant taste of our ladies. A thread of white silk substituted for the silver, a thread of yellow silk for the gold, and all would be accomplished. Once more, send us workmen by hundreds. Preach this crusade. I dare to assert that not a single good workman can spend a fortnight here without trebling what we political economists call his *moral capital*—the capital that belongs to him, his intrinsic value, that is to say, without becoming richer. The Indian exposition has likewise its philosophical and political point of view for me. I may inform you of a discovery which is connected, through Calcutta, with the Indian exhibition, although the discovery is carried out in Scotland. It is the introduction of a new textile product, which is called here *jute*, which holds a medium between flax and hemp. *Jute* is a species of hemp, which grows abundantly in the plains of Bengal, and which, strange to say, possesses along with the properties of flax, those of cotton, that is to say, of being combed in parallel staple, and of being carded. A distinguished manufacturer, the Chevalier Clausen, has succeeded in bleaching it so perfectly, that there is no silk more glossy than *jute*, after being bleached by a new process, which constitutes the most curious application of chemistry which has ever been made to manufacture—a process, which might be called bleaching by means of distension. The *jute* can be made into parallel threads, like silk, or in wool, like cotton. It mixes equally well with silk, wool, yarn, and cotton. Its mixtures are as curious as its use is isolated. The English exhibit flannels, hosiery, and cloth of various kinds in which it has been introduced. I have found all competent persons much impressed with these important experiments upon a new textile fabric.

LETTER V.

I cannot refrain from bringing your readers back to the exhibition of the products of British India. This is an entire industrial world, new to us even from its antiquity, carrying us back to the heroic ages, and which, from its perfectly original character, resembles no other. The East India Company has expended upwards of £80,000 to appear worthily at this great federation of nations. It desired that its empire of fifty millions of subjects should be fittingly represented, and it has admirably succeeded in so doing. Since the commencement of the Exhibition new products have been added almost daily. Some of these are even more beautiful than those which have gone before, and attract in the highest degree the attention of visitors. Indian art, in truth, is deserving of this preference—it resembles no other. It has not the whimsicalness of Chinese taste, nor Grecian or Roman regularity, nor modern vulgarity: it is a special art, more simple than is generally believed, even in its digressions, and which never appears to have varied nor borrowed anything elsewhere. Applied to ceramic manufacture, it is full of grace and simplicity. The curves are of an undulated kind, supple and flexible, like the forms of the serpent; and as rich and varied in the coarser as in the finer descriptions of earthenware. There are thousands of specimens in the Exhibition which cannot fail to be imitated in France, for the eyes of all manufacturers are upon India. The art of weaving cloth has evidently attained a high degree of perfection in that country. Without mentioning the Cashmere shawls, which have become the beau-ideals of their kind, everything exhibited by the East India Company

appears a collection of *chefs-d'œuvre*. Muslins embroidered with gold, kerchiefs variegated with a thousand colours, gorgeous scarfs of the most exquisite taste, tablecloths
enamelled with flowers woven fabrics of every description *inlaid* with emerald green,
saddles, cloaks, stuffs for hangings, handkerchiefs for Odalisks, with small plaids of a
delicate red embroidered with silver—every tint which nature has lavished on the wing
of the butterfly is found in this Indian collection, which a company as powerful as
that of the East Indies only could bring together by its sovereign commands. The
entire East has hastened to obey its summons.

Nothing is wanting. Every calling of the land is here represented under the guise of
those who follow it. Poor people! unclad, fed with a little rice, habitually dwelling
beneath the canopy of heaven or of trees, paid none know how! We see them in their
attitudes of work, their implements in their hands, their miniature looms before them—
they really live before us. The East India Company has not even forgotten the musical
instruments which charm them, and which frighten me. Come and see these, my
friends; you will probably find some new acoustic resources in this kind of cymbal with
twenty dirks strung together in the middle around a large circle a yard in diameter, in
these small shrill tom-toms which pass so rapidly from lively to severe, and in these
primitive mandolins with gilt copper cords. Behold these elephant saddles—the teams
for men—the palanquins to carry you! All this strange civilisation is admirably illustrated by its works: luxury and indigence sum it up in two words. It is here that the
ancient and modern history of India may be studied. It is completed by the picture of
all the useful arts in which the Oriental mind seems to live its usual strange, heavy,
and monotonous round. I do not talk to you of those diamonds before which the crowd
of visitors are in rapt admiration. I leave you to guess what value is to be attached to
the statements of the appraisers of the famous Koh-i-Noor who reason thus: the diamond
cost £40,000 so many years ago; if this sum had been accumulated with interest it would
now represent £2,000,000—*ergo*, the diamond is worth £2,000,000. We neither admit
this arithmetic nor this political economy. Diamonds have always to me been the most
foolish and useless things, although women are said to covet them as the superlative
ornament; as far as I am concerned, I prefer the Spanish aphorism: "To youth, love;
to age, respect." It is less costly.

I insist greatly upon the particular merit of the Indio-Britannic collection. It has
produced a great sensation amongst all connected with art and manufacture; and in
the period of transition in which we live it is deserving of the most serious attention.
The interest which it excites increases every day at the sight of those marvels which
are like a veritable revelation of this ancient and original art. It is, however, to be
feared that our industry will not benefit by the samples which the East India Company
has got together, for they are nowhere else to be procured. I will not say as much of
China. China is more known and less worthy of being imitated. Its whimsical and
fantastical taste does not merit so much esteem and attention as the industrial genius of
the Indians, though perhaps it has never appeared to greater advantage than at this
Exhibition. I have been particularly struck with the abundance of her raw materials,
and, above all, with the beauty of her silks. They shine in quantities, and with a
brilliancy only equalled by that of her embroidered crape shawls, her classical pottery,
and her marvellous works in ivory, horn, and marqueterie. After all, the Chinese are
a people very much advanced in industry, although stubborn and almost immovable.
All that they have is of ancient date, and they had what we have long before we had
conquered it. They invented gunpowder before us; they knew the compass before we
had discovered it; and we have seen in London products the manufacture of which
dates back 1,753 years before Christ—that is to say, more than 3,500 years ago—and

which are remarkable for their excellent workmanship. The Chinese, however, with all their antiquity, are a stationary people.

The English could scarcely fail to present us with several valuable collections of tea, and there are very fine ones at the Exhibition. But this article presents to the English, only, any serious object of interest.

On taking a temporary leave of these agreeable effusions, we may remark that lively and original as they are, they are by no means deficient in that tone of self-complacency and self-esteem which is rarely wanting in our Gallic neighbour. To use his own phrase, "La France est toujours La France," and we have no doubt she will remain so while she exists as a nation. In the midst of their most reprehensible deeds they boast of their noble qualities. "La France genereuse comme elle est toujours" was the expression we heard from the lips of a young French officer, at the very time the soldiers under his command were bombarding the walls of unfortunate Rome. Proh pudor!

CHAPTER XXXVIII.

COUNCIL MEDALS: KISS, MAROCHETTI, PRADIER, WYATT, GIBSON—PRIZE MEDALS: BAILEY, BELL, BENZONI, DEBAY, DRAKE, ETEX, FOLEY, FRACCAROLI, FRAIKIN, GALLI, GEEFS, HOGAN, JENNINGS, JERICHAU, LAWLOR, LESCHESNE, MACDOWELL, MARSHALL, MONTI, RAMUS, RIETSCHEL, SHARP, SIMONIS, STRAZZA, THRUPP, TUERLINCKX, WATSON, WOLFF—ACCOUNT OF HIS STUDIO AT ROME—SCULPTURE IN BRONZE: JEAN DEBAY, FRATIN, LEQUESNE.

In resuming our notices upon the Sculpture in the Great Exhibition, we must not neglect to draw the attention of our readers to such of the numerous candidates for fame in that department as received honorary distinction from the jury appointed to examine into their respective merits. At a meeting held on the 5th of June, long before the question of individual rewards came under consideration, the jury agreed upon the following resolution :—

"That it is not desirable to assign the council medal to every object of art preeminently beautiful or excellent in its kind, whether it be executed in an inferior section of the class or not, but that it should be rather limited to the highest works of the highest class." This resolution, consistent with the view of the Fine Arts taken throughout by this jury, precluded them from awarding the highest honours to any but works of art of the highest class. Their awards, therefore, must not be compared with those of other juries guided by different principles, but must be tested only by the rules which the jurors of Class XXX. have laid down for their own guidance. The holders of the several marks of approbation by which this jury have distinguished merit, ought to appreciate them according to the high value set upon these several marks of approbation by those who conferred them. In forming their judgment upon works in the highest branch of art coming within their jurisdiction, the jury have principally looked for the embodiment of ideas, thought, feeling, and passion; not for the mere imitation of nature, however true in detail, or admirable in execution. They have looked for originality of invention, less or more happily expressed in that style which has for twenty-three centuries been the wonder of every civilised people, and the standard of excellence to which artists of the highest order have endeavoured to attain. Wherever indications of originality, chastened by a successful adaptation of this style, have been met with, the jury have acknowledged a corresponding amount of merit; and it is this originality of conception, improved by such style, which the jury have recognised by the honours placed at their disposal. They have endeavoured to record, in the most emphatic manner, their anxious wish that artists should study to give their ideas that form and life which spiritualizes every-day nature, and elevates a work of art to the place of a type of nature itself. The jury of Class XXX. would point to the remains of the Parthenon as embodying the result of the great principles which they have been anxious to inculcate, and which they desire to see universally adopted. The limited number of council medals awarded must not, therefore, be regarded as a proof of deficiency of talent in the bulk of the works exhibited, but as evidence of the severity with which the principles adopted by the jury have been applied. It was agreed to recommend that council medals should be awarded to the following works:—

To Professor A. Kiss, of Berlin, for his group cast in zinc, and bronzed by M. Geiss, representing an Amazon on horseback attacked by a Tiger. This work we have already noticed at some length, and shall not therefore offer any further remarks upon it.

To Baron Marochetti, of Turin, now of London, for his colossal equestrian statue, in plaster, of Richard Cœur de Lion. Our readers will recollect this statue, which was placed at some distance from the building at the western end, and looking towards Kensington-gardens. The grace and vigour it displayed were universally admired. The warrior-king bestrode his steed in true chivalric guise, and filled the mind with recollections of many a tough encounter with Paynim knights and ruthless Saracens in the Holy Land, in days of romance and fanaticism long since passed away.

To M. J. Pradier, of Paris, member of the Institute, for his marble statue of Phryne. In this youthful female figure the beauty of feature, the subtle refinement of form, and the sprightly elegance of the attitude, alike corresponded with the name of the celebrated *Hetaira*, which M. Pradier gave to his work. The premature death of this gentleman, which took place a few months ago, has deprived France of one of her ablest sculptors.

The late Mr. Richard Wyatt, also, had he lived, would have received a council medal for his inimitable marble statue of Glycera, exhibited by Captain Leyland, and which we have already eulogised; his representatives, however, have been presented by the jury with this mark of their approbation and distinction of the deceased artist.

It was the unanimous impulse of the jury, on the awards being taken into consideration, to recommend that the same high distinction should be conferred on Mr. Gibson, for his marble group of a Hunter and Dog, exhibited by the Earl of Yarborough. Their intention was defeated by Mr. Gibson himself, who, well knowing that should he accept the office of a juror of Class XXX., he could no longer receive a prize from that jury, preferred serving his brother artists, to his own individual gratification, and thus disqualified himself for receiving the honour which he so well deserved.

The prize medals were more numerous, and were distributed to the following artists, whom we shall proceed to notice alphabetically.

To Mr. E. H. Bailey, for his two plaster statues of a Nymph preparing for bathing, and a Youth resting after the Chase.

To M. J. Bell, for his statue of the Eagle-Slayer, cast in bronze, and also in iron. This figure represented a powerful man in very strong action, at the moment after shooting an arrow into the air. The violence of the exertion had brought the muscles into full play. The artist admirably succeeded in expressing the momentary and transient character of the action, and the form was modelled with a knowledge and truth of detail which are seldom found in the English School. In his statue of Falkland, executed for the new Houses of Parliament, was displayed a mastery rarely attained in

A YOUTH RESTING AFTER THE CHASE

Engraved by C.Holl, from a Daguerreotype by Beard

FROM THE ORIGINAL BY E.H.BAILY, R.A. F.R.S

A NYMPH PREPARING FOR THE BATH

Engraved by C.Holl, from a Daguerreotype by Beard.

FROM THE ORIGINAL BY E.H.BAILY, R.A. F.R.S

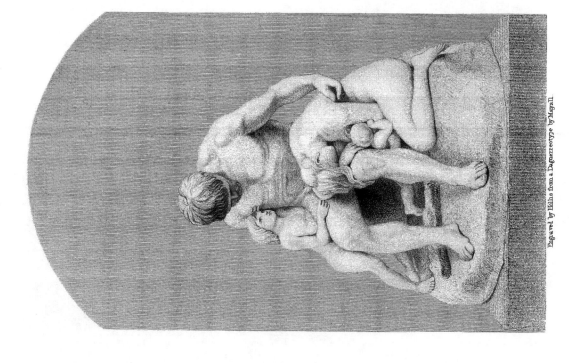

A GROUP IN PLASTER BY ETEX

Engraved by Hollis from a Daguerreotype by Mayall

SEE OFFICIAL CATALOGUE Nº 1216

A GROUP IN PLASTER BY ETEX

Engraved by Hollis. from a Daguerreotype by Mayall.

SEE OFFICIAL CATALOGUE Nº 1216

Engraved by Hollis from an Original Drawing by Tomlinson.

G R A T I T U D E

M. BENZONI, ROME.

Engraved by Hollis from an Original Drawing by Tomlinson.

F I D E L I T Y

M. BENZONI ROME.

portraiture; the conception was spirited, the treatment throughout strictly plastic, the figure was remarkable for its noble presence, and its attitude of calm and dignified repose.

To Signor Gio Mario Benzoni, of Rome, for two groups of a Little Girl with a Dog. In one of these the child was represented drawing a thorn out of the dog's foot; in the other the dog, after having killed a snake which was threatening an attack, sought to awaken the child thus rescued. The motive of these works was attractive, and they were carefully executed in marble, but they were by no means of sufficient importance to be considered adequate representations of the modern school of sculpture in such a city as Rome. It is to be regretted that the most distinguished artists of that city, and especially Tenerani, the greatest living sculptor of Italy, sent no specimens of their works to the Exhibition.

To M. Auguste Debay, of Paris, for his group in marble representing Eve, with Cain and Abel asleep in her arms, and designated as "Le Premier Berceau." In the form and attitude of Eve there was great beauty, truth, and refinement of feeling, and the countenance admirably expressed the tenderness of a mother. The treatment of the figure, however, was rather too picturesque in character, and the general motive somewhat strained and violent; the forms of the children were not happily composed, and there was a want of style in the hair of Eve, which was gathered together behind in a somewhat clumsy mass.

To Professor F. Drake, of Berlin, for a reduced cast of part of the marble pedestal to the monument of Frederic William III. of Prussia. The statue which this pedestal supports was erected by the inhabitants of Berlin, as a token of their gratitude for the embellishments which this monarch has bestowed on their Thiergarten (Zoological Gardens.) The work exhibited was in plaster, half the size of the original pedestal. In the reliefs with which it was ornamented, the sculptor selected subjects which contained allusions to the local destination of his work. Thus he represented a number of figures, of every age and sex, enjoying themselves in the open air. We observed groups of children looking into a bird's nest or feeding the swans, young maidens weaving garlands, old people leading children to the scene of the sports, or contemplating their youthful gambols with an air of calm enjoyment. There was much beautiful feeling in the treatment of this subject: the heads were full of expression, the movement of the figures very spirited, and the different groups were skilfully connected. The composition was executed in a very good style of alto-relievo, the details finished with the greatest care. On the whole, this work was deserving of the very great and general admiration that was bestowed upon it. It may, however, be noted as a defect, that the artist did not throughout preserve the relative proportions of the figures.

To M.A. Etex, of Paris, for his various works of sculpture in plaster and marble. Of the three groups exhibited by this artist, the most agreeable is that in marble of Hero and Leander, standing mournfully beside each other. In the group of Cain and his Family, the characteristics of a base, abandoned nature, were admirably expressed in the countenance and coarse clumsy limbs of Cain, which were very carefully studied from the life. The allegorical group of the City of Paris imploring Heaven to take away the Plague of the Cholera, was a less agreeable work, on account of the manner in which the subject was treated. The city was represented as a seated female figure, with an old man and a youth expiring of the pestilence, one on each side. In these figures the moment of death was expressed with wonderful truth. This work was a specimen of that class of art which, seeking to act on the feelings through the representation of mere physical suffering, may be called the revolting; a style which appears to be little cultivated or admired except in France, notwithstanding her supreme excellence in point of refinement and taste, which M. Blanqui, in his letters on the Exhibition, so confidently asserts.

To Mr. J. H. FOLEY, of London, for his statue of a Youth at a Stream; also for his group representing Ino and Bacchus. The former of these works we have already sufficiently noticed, as well as the statue of Hampden by the same artist. The group of Ino and the infant Bacchus exhibited much grace and refinement of form, but altogether was not so generally attractive as the Youth at the Stream.

To Signor M. J. FRACCAROLI, of Verona, for his two statues in marble, representing Achilles wounded in the heel, and David in the act of slinging the stone at Goliath. The design of this last-mentioned figure was very spirited, but a little strained; the features had a noble expression. The youthful character of the head, however, did not altogether accord with the rest of the body, in which the muscles were too strongly marked.

To M. C. A. FRAIKIN, of Schærbeck, near Brussels, for a plaster group of Psyche carrying off Cupid. The motion of this figure was spirited, and the forms were expressed with great tenderness, and from several points of view the group was very attractive. The movement of the head of Psyche, however, struck us as rather affected, and in the style of Canova.

To Signor A. GALLI, of Milan, for his statue of Susanna. The forms in this figure were youthful and pleasing, the attitude agreeable, and the execution extremely careful; but without the introduction of the two Elders, the subject would be difficult to recognise.

To M. G. GEEFS, of Schærbeck, near Brussels, we have already paid honour due, for his admirable group of the Lion in Love, and we shall therefore direct the attention of our readers to another work by this skilful artist—a bust of his Majesty the King of the Belgians, which was full of spirit, and very carefully executed.

To Mr. J. HOGAN, of London, for his reclining figure in plaster, representing a Drunken Fawn. This personification of the sylvan deity, "ripe with the purple grape," and reeling from excess, appeared to be making a last effort to save himself from falling. The work indicated careful study, but the attitude was rather violent and ungraceful.

To Mr. JENNINGS, of London, for his marble statue of Cupid. Among the few poems of Sappho that have come down to us is her charming lyric of "The Rose," wherein Cupid asserts her right to be made the queen of the flowers. This subject has been treated by the late celebrated Thorwaldsen, with his usual felicity, in a basso-relievo, where Cupid is represented bringing the rose to Jupiter and Juno, who are seated side by side, with the attendant eagle and peacock at their feet. Mr. Jennings presented us with an abridgment, as we may term it, of the story, in the person of Cupid alone. His attitude, as he extended the rose in one hand, and pointed exultingly to it with the other, as if claiming admiration of its beauty, showed to great advantage his finely formed limbs: an air of gaiety and enjoyment befitting the brightness of youth, pervaded the whole figure, which seemed to breathe of spring and blossoms. At his side the trunk of a tree, round which the rejected lily twined her delicate tendrils, along with the rose, showed that her modest charms had been cast into the shade by the glowing attractions of her more brilliant sister.

To M. J. A. JERICHAU, of Copenhagen, for a group in plaster, representing a Hunter carrying off the Cub of a Panther. It was for Denmark that the great Thorwaldsen, unquestionably the finest sculptor that has appeared since the time of Phidias and Praxiteles, embodied his spiritual conceptions in such a number of masterpieces of sculpture; and there are not wanting in Denmark at the present day, distinguished sculptors, who follow in his footsteps with greater or less success. Among these, M. Jerichau takes no inferior position. In this able group of a Hunter and Panther, he has exhibited great spirit and fine conception. The execution also is skilful, and the details well attended to.

To Mr. J. Lawlor, of London, for his statue in marble of a Nymph Bathing, a work of considerable merit.

To M. A. Leschesne, of Paris, for his admirable groups in plaster of Dogs and Children. As we have already noticed the productions of this artist in a former chapter, we shall pass on to Mr. Lawrence Macdonald, of Rome, whose studio is crowded with busts and portraits in marble and plaster, of most of the celebrated personages who have passed a season within the walls of the Eternal City. The Iconic figure by this sculptor, for which he received his prize medal, executed in the manner and costume of classical antiquity, showed that the artist has a just perception of style, and sound knowledge.

To Mr. P. Macdowell, of London, for his plaster statue of Eve; also for his statues of Cupid, and of a Girl at Prayer, in marble. The most remarkable work of this sculptor was his Eve, which was modelled with great knowledge, the attitude also was graceful, and the expression of longing curiosity well rendered. His Girl at Prayer was treated with simplicity and depth of feeling, and very carefully executed. His figure of Cupid had also great merit.

To Mr. William Marshall, of London, for his plaster figure of Sabrina. Sabrina is familiar to us from the beautiful invocation of Milton :—

> "Sabrina fair,
> Listen where thou art sitting
> Under the glassie cool translucent wave,
> In twisted braids of lilies knitting
> The loose train of thy amber-drooping hair,
> Listen for dear honour's sake
> Goddess of the silver lake,
> Listen and save."—*Comus.*

The Sabrina of this artist was remarkable for its feminine grace; the head had a fine character of individuality, and there was great beauty in the form, and in the general expression.

Signor Raffaelle Monti, of Milan, and Mr. Hiram Powers, of the United States, both of whom received a prize medal, have already had their respective performances sufficiently commented on by us in a former part of this work: we shall therefore pass on to M. J. M. Ramus, of Paris, who received the same mark of distinction for his marble group of Cephalus and Procris. Cephalus was represented tenderly supporting in his arms the dying Procris. This group was, in its leading lines, very happily composed, and showed in the forms much knowledge of nature; but the modelling was not in a sufficiently large style, and was not sustained throughout.

To Professor Ernst Rietschel, of Dresden, for his plaster group, designated as *La Pietá*, representing Mary kneeling at the dead body of our Saviour; and for his bas-reliefs in marble. This distinguished artist, one of the ablest pupils of Rauch, exhibited three works, the varied character of which showed the versatility of his talents. 1.—A group of the Virgin weeping over the body of our Saviour, cast in plaster, from a model executed for his Majesty the King of Prussia. In the figure of our Saviour, anatomical truth was combined with nobleness of form; the countenance wore a fine dignified character; its mild transfigured expression proclaimed the triumph over the agonies of death. In the Mary, the countenance and the clasped hands revealed the deepest, but most resigned sorrow of the soul. The drapery was fully worthy of the invention shown in the group. 2.—Angel of Christ, a very noble relief in marble. The Angel was represented in the form of a graceful youth, floating in the air, with the infant Saviour in his arms; two infant angels attended his course. This group had a peculiar charm, from the beauty of the heads and figures, the grace of the action, the suddenness of the movement impressed on the flying drapery, and the masterly, yet tender handling of the marble.　3.—Love riding on a Panther, whose course he tries to arrest, eagerly grasping his neck with both his hands.　This beautiful conception was quite in the spirit of ancient art, and was expressed with great vigour of hand.

To Mr. T. SHARP, of London, for his marble figure, representing a Boy frightened by a Lizard.　This was a remarkable work—quite unlike in choice and treatment of subject any we have as yet noticed.　The artist did not hesitate to express that dryness and meagreness of form which characterizes the particular stage of boyhood selected for representation; but these details were executed with the utmost accuracy, and with an admirable feeling for nature.　The eye of the ordinary observer, habitually accustomed to the specious effect of mere smoothness of surface, may, in some degree, be repelled by this truthfulness of representation; but, like all other truth, it will not the less be ultimately appreciated, and we may regard this figure as in itself a proof how great an effort the English school of sculpture is making in the right direction.

To M. E. SIMONIS, of Brussels, for his equestrian statue of Godfrey of Bouillon, and other works.　A colossal figure of Godfrey of Bouillon on horseback, raising the banner with which he led the crusaders to the Holy Land.　Cast in plaster from the original in bronze, which is placed in the Place Royale, at Brussels.　In this work the expression of the head is full of life and animation, the action very emphatic, the execution very careful.　To compensate for the optical diminution which causes statues placed in the open air to appear meagre and deficient in mass, the artist in this group exaggerated the forms both of the warrior and the horse.　This departure from nature was perhaps carried too far.　In his group representing Truth trampling on Falsehood, the same artist showed power in the representation of delicate female forms, and the work was carefully executed.　Two figures of boys, one of whom is crying over his broken drum, prove that M. Simonis has been successful in that class of subjects called "genre," and which are altogether treated in a realistic manner.

To Signor G. STRAZZA, of Milan, for his reclining figure in marble, representing Ishmael.　We have already noticed this striking and admirable performance with due praise.　Perhaps the truthfulness with which the dying youth is represented, renders the subject too painful a one for general approbation.　In the treatment of this subject by painters, an angel bringing help to Ishmael is always introduced, and from the absence of this figure, the impression produced by the work of Signor Strazzi is unrelieved by any mitigating circumstance.

To Mr. E. THRUPP, of London, for his statue of Arethusa, a recumbent figure, gracefully enough designed, but rather deficient in life and individuality.　A Boy catching a Butterfly, was a very carefully executed and attractive work.

To M. J. TUERLINCKX, of Malines, for a figure in marble, representing the celebrated Giotto when a boy, looking at his first attempt at drawing, with an expression of joyful surprise.　The conception of this work was very spirited, and it was carefully executed.

A prize medal was also conferred upon the representatives of the late Mr. L. WATSON, of London, for his admirable portrait statue of the celebrated Flaxman, a noble performance, which we have already sufficiently described.　As also for the colossal figures of Lord Eldon and Lord Stowell, which showed how greatly this artist excelled in Iconic sculpture.

We next turn our attention to M. ALBERT WOLFF, a native of Berlin, who also received a prize medal for his group of a Young Maiden holding a Lamb in her arms.　This figure was entitled by the sculptor, Innocence, and its purity and simplicity of character fully expressed such an idea.　The drapery was throughout treated in a plastic style, and the execution was exceedingly careful. M. Wolff, though a Prussian by birth, has long fixed his residence in the Eternal City, and his studio there, in the Via Quattro Fontane, is altogether, perhaps, one of the most interesting in that grand emporium of the Fine Arts; not only from the surpassing elegance, but also from the extraordinary variety of its contents. Let us attempt a brief description. Believing that mythology is the basis of sculpture, and being an enthusiastic admirer of classic story, M. Wolff devotes much of his talent to representations from Greek and Latin fable; as we see in his "Prometheus," in the act of coming stealthily away with the divine fire, which he has stolen and secreted in a reed; "Thetis, seated on a Dolphin," conveying arms to Achilles, the tender anxiety of the mother being happily conjoined with the dignity of the goddess; "Diana, resting from the Chase," in which we see, by her trophies of game, she has been successful; "Cupid clad in the spoils of Hercules"— one of the many delightful ideas which have come down to us from the gems of the ancients; another Cupid sleeping upon his quiver, his bow at his side, and at his feet a dog that seems intent on preventing his repose from being broken in upon; and pity that it should be, for never was repose, profound, innocent, and sweet, more charmingly expressed. Then there is the ever-lovely and poetical character, Psyche, with the vase which tempts her to her second act of disobedience; and another personification of her, extremely beautiful, seated on the ground, her lamp at her side, her dagger in her hand, her lovely features betraying, though without disturbing their symmetry, the vague uneasiness and jealous doubts infused into her bosom by the artful suggestions of her sisters. This production now graces the collection of Lord Yarborough, whose taste is fully commensurate with his liberality in the fine arts.

In smaller compositions M. Wolff is not less happy. "The Seasons as Children," strike us as the very prettiest miniature representations of them that we have ever seen. Spring, a lovely little girl, is crowned with flowers, and scattering them around her. Summer has his sickle in one hand, some ears of wheat in the other, whilst on the ground at his feet a rustic flask, formed out of a gourd, reminds us of the sultry skies under which he is performing his harvest task. Autumn displays her grapes, her vase, and drinking cup. But Winter is still more characteristic. The sly little fellow has wrapped himself up in the skin of a wolf, and so snug and comfortable does he look in it, that we can scarcely feel any concern for his having to face the biting blast, which we almost fancy we hear whistling round his well-defended ears. How well would these pretty figures grace the corners of the entrance-hall in some of those abodes of which so many are to be found in England; particularly in the vicinity of its capital, where every elegance and refinement are frequently introduced on a lesser scale, which more than makes up by the harmony and completeness of its arrangements for all that it may fall short of in magnitude. To us, moreover, they appear to afford happy vehicles for the portraiture of children under such playful disguises, for those parents who may be able to perpetuate them in marble. "Jephthah and his Daughter" belongs to a different style of art, in which M. Wolff has shown himself not less happy. The dignified despair of the father, the touching submission of the daughter, as she clings to him, with an obedient love in which we see, we feel, there is not even the shadow of reproach, are finely expressed. The devoted girl is very graceful, in her bending figure, and drooping head, whilst her father exhibits a regal majesty shrouded under the bitterness of his grief. But of all the productions from M. Wolff's chisel, we see none more to our individual taste than his "Nereid," which he has, indeed, been called upon to repeat more than once, so much has it been admired. She is leaning on her left hand, and raises her right, armed with a spear, in the act of transfixing one of the finny tribe, which her animated countenance shows she beholds in the clear stream, on which we fancy her looks are eagerly bent. The grace, the vivacity, the loveliness of this figure, are incomparable. How admirably would it adorn some of our suburban villas on the banks of the Thames, or some noble sheet of water in the grounds of our patrician seats, not to be rivalled in the world for their combination of exterior splendours and internal comforts. M. Wolff has also enjoyed the patronage of Her Majesty the Queen, having executed the bust of the Princess Royal during his late visit to this country. He has also had the honour of sculpturing Prince Albert in the costume of a Greek warrior, which well becomes the figure of His Royal Highness, of whom the likeness, individually considered, is true in point of fidelity, and pleasing in that of expression. We take our leave of M. Wolff's studio, asking pardon of our readers for the short digression our visit to it has occasioned, by observing that, besides the highest degree of excellence in the range of classic subjects, he is peculiarly happy in the representation of that individuality of character and expression so necessary for the formation of a good bust; and an opportunity of appreciating his merit, in this most desirable walk of art, is agreeably afforded, to those who may have the opportunity, by the contemplation of many resemblances of eminent and well-known personages who owe the perpetuation of their features to his talent.

To sculptors in bronze the following prize medals were awarded; with a brief account of which we shall conclude our present chapter, reserving for future notice such works as were distinguished by "honorary mention" on the part of the Jury.

To M. Jean Debay, of Paris, for his group of a young Hunter, rushing forward to despatch a Stag, pulled down by a Hound. The Hunter was naked, and the whole subject was conceived in the spirit of ancient art. This group, from the natural manner of the action, formed a very pleasing composition. The hunter and the animals were modelled with great knowledge, and a good style was shewn in the execution.

To M. Fratin, of Paris. This artist, the most celebrated sculptor of animals in France at the present day, contributed to the Exhibition Two Eagles with a wild Goat, which they have slain; a greyhound, another hound, life size, and several animals on a smaller scale, all in bronze. These works were fully worthy of the artist's reputation. The general conception was most spirited, the details of nature were most faithfully rendered; and the treatment throughout, particularly of the plumage and the skins, was most careful, and in very good style.

To M. E. L. Lequesne, of Paris, for a Satyr, cast in bronze, represented after the manner of the ancients, dancing on a wine-skin, in a state of joyous drunkenness. In this figure, the character of the head, and of the strong, hard muscles, quite corresponded with the general satyr type created by the imagination of the ancient artist. The motion was easy and natural, and the carefulness of the execution was maintaine throughout.

CHAPTER XXXIX.

DESCRIPTION OF TECHNICAL TERMS — BRYSON — ROSKELL — KRALIK — THE ALPHA CLOCK — BLAYLOCK — DENT — GOURDIN — BAILLY COMPTE — WAGNER — LOWRY — LEVER AND CHRONO METER WATCHES, ETC. ETC.

"We take no note of Time but from its loss,
To give it then a tongue was wise in man."

Such is the observation of the philosophic author of the *Night Thoughts*; and often, indeed, has the world had occasion to be thankful that the skill and ingenuity of

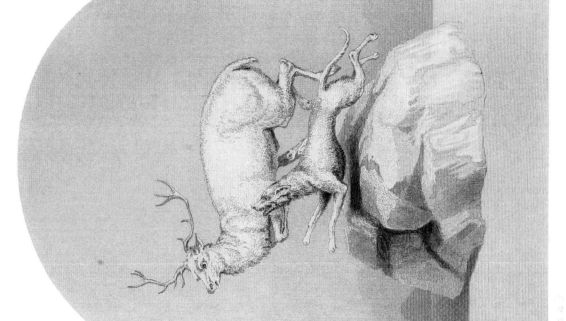

Engraved by H. Bibby, from a Drawing by T. H. Wilson.

STAG AND HOUND

STATUETTE IN GUTTA PERCHA

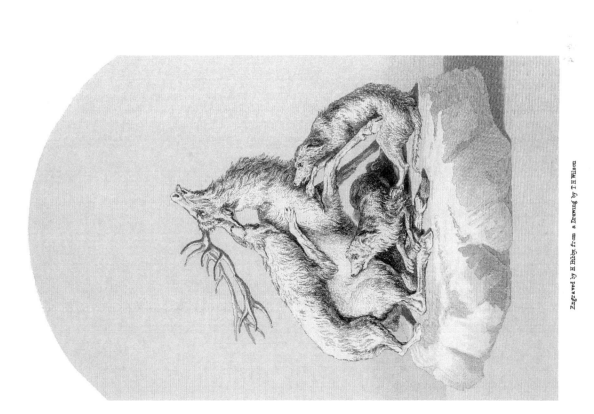

Engraved by H. Bibby, from a Drawing by T. H. Wilson

STAG HUNTED BY DOGS

GROUP IN TERRA-COTTA BY SANGIOVANNI

man have endued with a warning voice the otherwise silent progress of Time, reminding us of its continuous and rapid flight, and awakening us to the necessity of employing to advantage that portion of it which is yet before us, and which, once suffered to pass unimproved, can never be recalled. "Tempus fugit nosque fugimus in illo," was a wise remark of the poet, and however trite it may appear, it is one which we cannot too frequently bear in mind. These and similar reflections irresistibly presented themselves to our imagination as we contemplated the profusion of ingenious machinery to mark the revolving hours, with all their minute divisions and subdivisions, that was exhibited to the curious public in the Crystal Palace.

In all ages, in all countries, however barbarous or uncivilised, some division of time, some mode of marking its progress, has been attempted; and science, in lending her aid to the more perfect accomplishment of this endeavour, has also herself derived benefit from the success she has obtained—the determination of the longitude, and the safety of our hardy seamen, in their long and perilous wayfare, greatly depend on the accuracy with which our horological instruments are constructed. As our present article is not designed solely for the information of those who are already well acquainted with the leading features of the construction of horological instruments, we shall probably render the subsequent details more generally intelligible to our readers, if we briefly explain some of the technical terms which must of necessity constantly recur in our descriptions, such as *escapement, compensation, remontoire,* &c.

By the term *escapement* is meant that portion of the mechanism of a clock or watch, by which the teeth of the last revolving wheel of the train of wheels, commonly called the "scape-wheel," communicate an alternating motion to the balance or pendulum, as the case may be—and by which also the teeth are successively permitted to escape, after giving an impulse to the balance or pendulum. An escapement is called a *detached escapement* when the piece or part that permits the escape of the teeth of the scape-wheel is not attached to the balance or pendulum, but is moved or acted upon by either of these, at some particular point of their swing or *oscillation.* The ordinary clock escapements are the dead beat, and the common or recoil escapements, neither of which is detached. The effect of the recoil escapement will be most easily recognised, in any common clock that has a seconds hand, by a backward jerking motion of that hand; and this is also visible in the minute hand, previous to each advance. It is owing to the form of the pallets and teeth of the scape-wheel, which is necessary for rough work. In the dead beat escapement no such recoil is observed, but the hand remains stationary between its successive forward movements. This, therefore, is a more delicate escapement, and much more easily deranged than the recoil. Another, which is frequently met with in the clocks exhibited, is known as the "pin escapement."

The principal kinds of timepieces which have a balance, and not a pendulum, are watches, carriage timepieces, marine and pocket chronometers. All these are required to keep time under sudden and various changes of position—disturbing causes which are incompatible with the free motion of a pendulum. The more usual escapements applied to this class of timepieces are—(we arrange them in the order of merit)—the chronometer, the duplex, the cylinder, the lever, and the verge, or common vertical escapement; of these the chronometer and the lever are the only detached ones.

A very neatly-finished series of models of watch escapements was exhibited by Bryson, of Edinburgh, and a series of skeleton timepieces, exhibiting the various escapements, by Roskell, of Liverpool. There was another well-executed series of models by S. Kralik, of Pesth, in the Austrian department. This series comprised the chronometer escapement; the duplex—in this the points of the teeth of a second and smaller scape-wheel perform the office of the usual pins; the lever—in this the teeth are terminated by oblique

3 s

surfaces, instead of being pointed as usual, an arrangement which probably wears better, but the friction must be greater; the cylinder, and a modification of this—in which a curved tooth on the balance axis performs the office of the cylinder. There was also a model of the pin escapement applied to a balance, and of two unusual vertical escapements. In one, the scape-wheel is like that of a common recoil escapement. There are two circular plates on the balance axis, with a notch in each. A tooth of the scape-wheel, in passing the notch in the first plate, gave an impulse in one direction to the balance, and fell on the second; on the recoil of the balance the tooth is released from the notch in the second plate, and in passing gives an impulse to the balance in a direction opposite to the former. In the other there are two scape-wheels, at a small distance from each other, on the same axis, the teeth of which are placed intermediately to each other. There is a cross bar on the balance axis which releases a tooth of the two scape-wheels alternately, and in passing receives an impulse from each.

By the term *compensation* is meant the action of some mechanism by means of which the balance or pendulum of a timepiece is made to oscillate in very nearly the same time, notwithstanding considerable changes of temperature. As the physical causes which influence the time of oscillation of a balance are in part essentially different from those that affect the pendulum, we shall leave the question of compensation in balances until, in a subsequent article, we give an account of the construction of the various marine and pocket chronometers which were presented to our notice in the Exhibition; and for the present we shall confine our attention to the compensation of pendulums. The time of oscillation of a pendulum depends, not on its entire length, but on the distance between the point of suspension and a point called the centre of oscillation— the point at which, if the whole weight of the pendulum were concentrated, it would still oscillate in exactly the same time. The mathematical consideration of this point need not here be entertained, as it may be found in any standard work on dynamics; we need only further remark, that the *greater* the distance between these points, the centres of suspension and oscillation, the *slower* will be the oscillation of the pendulum, and *vice versa*.

If a pedulum be not compensated, the least variable material of which it can be made is a rod of some tolerably light and porous wood, as deal or Honduras mahogany, the length of which is very slightly affected by changes of temperature and moisture; but the small changes produced by these agents cannot very readily be distinguished from each other. If, however, as is more frequently the case, the rod of a pendulum is of metal (usually iron or steel), it is evident that the weight at the end of the pendulum will be carried further from the centre of suspension by expansion of the rod when the temperature rises, and again brought nearer when the temperature falls, as all metals expand by heat and contract by cold, though in very different degrees.

If, then, to the lower end of the pendulum is attached a certain portion of some metal that expands by heat much more rapidly than steel, the centre of gravity of the added or *compensating* metal may be carried upwards by its own expansion, sufficiently to counteract the descent of the centre of gravity of the remaining portion of the pendulum by the expansion of the steel rod; and thus an invariable distance may be maintained between the centres of suspension and oscillation under all ordinary variations of temperature. One of the oldest forms of compensation consists of a series of brass and steel rods placed alternately, and the adjacent rods connected alternately at the top and bottom, the weight being attached to the outer pair of steel rods. In this arrangement, to which, on account of its shape, the name of "gridiron pendulum" was given, the excess of expansion of the brass rods is sufficient to compensate the expansion of the whole length of the pendulum. In clocks of the best description, such as astronomical clocks and "regulators," the compensation is usually effected by means of a glass or iron cistern of mercury, attached to the bottom of a steel rod, which supplies the place of the ordinary weight. Owing to the very large expansion of mercury, which is much greater than that of any other metal, a column of about eight or nine inches high is sufficient to compensate by its expansion for the whole length of an ordinary seconds pendulum.

In the turret clock exhibited by Dent, the compensation is effected by a hollow cylinder of zinc, which surrounds the rod of the pendulum; and in several of the French clocks, by a brass rod placed between two steel ones. The brass rod, by its expansion, raises the steel ones and the weight, or the weight only, through a space sufficient to compensate for the expansion of the steel rods; this is effected by means of two levers, which are placed either at the top or bottom of the rod, but more frequently the latter. Some other special modes of compensation must be mentioned hereafter, in speaking of the clocks to which they are applied.

But there is yet another important source of error in the rates of clocks, more particularly affecting those of large clocks. To obviate this, a mechanical arrangement has been devised, which is known by the term *remontoire*. In clocks of large size, the irregular action of the coarse teeth of large wheels, and the ever-varying weight of the portion of the rope by which the clock-weight is suspended, that is brought into action, as it is uncoiled from the barrel, are perpetual sources of irregularity in the impulse given by the scape-wheel to the pendulum. In the best description of turret-clocks these sources of error are now obviated by disconnecting the scape-wheel from the train, which, when released at short intervals (usually of half a minute) raises a small weight or lever, which in its descent communicates to the pendulum, through the medium of the scape-wheel, either uniform impulses, or a series of impulses varying very slightly, but recurring uniformly at each descent of the weight or lever. This, from its being periodically raised up, has been termed *remontoire*. The various mechanical arrangements applied to the clocks exhibited will be more appropriately described when we speak of them individually.

Having thus briefly described the leading features that characterize the construction of first-class clocks, we will now proceed to notice the large or turret clocks that were presented to us in the Exhibition. The English department contained, it must be confessed, but a small amount of variety. On the right of the great organ was a large turret clock, called the Alpha Clock, by Mr. R. Roberts, of Manchester, which unquestionably presents a stronger evidence of original genius than any other clock in the Exhibition; there is, in fact, nothing about it at all that is common-place. The frame was of a quadrangular pyramidal form, which is admirably adapted for solidity; the large wheels being placed near the base of the pyramid, and the smaller parts above them. The teeth of the wheels and pinions were all cast, except those of the scape-wheel; this must, of course, influence considerably the cheapness of construction. The escapement is detached, and of a novel construction; there is a detent with two arms, on an axis which has also a pinion in gear with a wheel on the same axis with the scape-wheel, so that the detent axis makes half a turn to release each tooth of the scape-wheel. The detent is held by a tooth at the end of an arm that hangs from the point of suspension of the pendulum; this arm is moved by a pin projecting from the pendulum near the end of its oscillation, and releases the detent, when the pendulum receives an impulse from an oblique surface of a tooth of the scape-wheel. The scape-wheel is impelled by a remontoire of perfectly uniform action; this consists of a weight attached to an endless chain, which is wound up every half-minute, on the release of the train, by the arm of another two-armed detent. The clock weights themselves also form part of an endless chain; but this seems to be an unnecessary refinement. The construction of the hammer by which the bell is struck is also quite new. The head of the hammer is a ball of gutta percha, by which the tone of the bell is at once brought out, unimpeded by the secondary vibrations that result from the blow of an ordinary metallic hammer. Again, the fly is superseded, and the hammer is made to perform the office of a fly. It revolves at right angles to an axis, and, in making one revolution, acquires sufficient centrifugal force to throw the head outwards, and enable it to reach the bell; after striking, the hammer remains quiescent. Near the end of the south-west gallery, was exhibited an accessory to turret clocks that deserves notice. This was a simple and ingenious mode of self-regulating the supply of gas to illuminated dials, by J. Blaylock, the length of time being daily increased or decreased by the mechanism, as required. The action requires to be reversed on the longest and shortest days. In the western avenue was a turret clock by Mr. Dent. In this the train is released by a detent every half-minute, and winds up a spring contained in a box, through which the scape-wheel axis passes. The end of the spring is attached to the axis, and consequently the spring acts as a remontoire. As the object of a remontoire is to obtain uniformity of impulse on the pendulum, this, of all the contrivances exhibited, appears the least calculated to attain the desired object, owing to the variation in the strength of the spring from change of temperature; especially when we remember that turret clocks are, from their situation, exposed to great vicissitudes of temperature.

In the French department, M. Gourdin exhibited a beautifully finished piece of workmanship, but greatly wanting in solidity. Two ornamented open-work girders, on which the whole weight of the clock rests, were evidently bent by the weight that they were unduly called on to sustain. The remontoire consists of a weight hanging by a thread from an arc at the end of a lever; this renders the action of the weight constant, but the action is not entirely constant, as the short arm of the lever carries an axis on which are two wheels—one in gear with the train, the other with the scape-wheel pinion; the escapement is a dead beat, the teeth of the scape-wheel being obliquely truncated. M. Bailly Compte showed a well-finished clock, with a pin escapement. The remontoire gear is one of which there were several examples amongst the French clocks. The last axis in the train, and the scape-wheel axis, are in a line with each other, and have two bevelled wheels of equal size at their adjacent ends, which are separated by an interval equal to the diameter of the wheels. The remontoire, which consists of a lever with a weight near the end of it, has a bevelled wheel attached to it at right angles to, and in gear with, the two former bevelled wheels. Thus the train, which is periodically released, raises the weight that in its descent impels the scape-wheel. This appears to us, on the whole, the best arrangement of the remontoire. Some little irregularity would of course arise from the variation of the length of the lever by temperature, but we doubt whether this would be sensible in the rate of the clock, and if sensible, it might be very easily compensated. The series of clocks by M. Wagner of Paris, were entitled collectively to more study than the works of any other exhibitor. No. 3, a striking clock, with pin escapement. No. 7, exhibited a novel detached escapement; two jewelled pallets at the ends of short-balanced levers are attached to the pendulum, one above and another below the circumference of the scape-wheel, the axis of which passes through a space cut out of the pendulum. We should suppose the action to be very light, and to have little friction. The next article was a clock with pin escapement, and pallets attached to the pendulum. The remontoire is a weighted lever, which when down, releases a fly, that prevents the weight being raised by a jerk. This, no doubt, would interfere with the sudden jumps of the minute hand, as in Dent's clock; but this advantage we think may very well be sacrificed to the steadiness and uniformity of the movement. An endless screw on the axis of the fly, and a pinion with oblique leaves, are both in gear with a wheel having oblique teeth on the barrel axis. This clock had few wheels, and its construction appeared very simple. There was also deserving of notice a clock with pin escapement and bevelled wheel remontoire, kept wound up by the continuous motion of the train regulated by a fly, to which a cap, suspended to the short arm of the remontoire lever, acts as a governor. This is a very ingenious contrivance, by which the continuous motion of the train is rendered isochronous with the alternate motion of the pendulum, and may therefore be used to carry an equatorial movement, or a heliostat, or for any other purpose for which a perfectly uniform continuous motion is required. A highly finished clock, with detached pin escapement, compensated pendulum, and bevelled wheel remontoire, also deserved notice. The impulse here was given to the pendulum by a detached bar, the ends of which were alternately raised by two arms fixed on the axis which carried the pallets. Any sudden motion of the remontoire is prevented by a fly. The pendulum is compensated by the brass bar between two of steel, and levers as previously described. There was lastly a clock with a pin escapement—the remontoire and the pendulum the same as the preceding. The pallets were attached to the pendulum, but the friction of the pins on the horizontal surfaces of the pallets was very ingeniously prevented by their being received on pieces projecting from two arms, moving on the same centre as the pendulum, and on which they rested, until they were delivered on to the inclined surfaces of the pallets. This appears to be a great improvement on the ordinary pin escapement, and well worthy the attention of our clock-makers.

Among the watches exhibited, were several novel inventions, displaying considerable ingenuity, and very perfect workmanship: among them was a lever watch by Mr. Samuel Lowry, of Spencer-street, Clerkenwell, which we think deserves especial notice; it was arranged to show dead and complete seconds on the one train only. This watch is so constructed that the seconds hand is made to drop, without recoil, sixty times in the minute, or once in every second of time, thus the seconds are as accurately shown as by an astronomical clock or regulator. The train, or vibration of the balance, is not altered in any way from those of ordinary watch movements, and the price is very little additional to that of an ordinary watch, from one train only being requisite. This principle of the seconds is also applicable to marine chronometers, &c. The importance of this invention in cases where accurate notation of minute portions of time is required, is at once obvious.

CHAPTER XL.

VARIETIES.

ROYAL VISITS — PETTY LARCENIES—GEORGE CRUIKSHANK'S GREAT ETCHING—VISIT OF THE SUSSEX PEASANTRY—ANECDOTE OF THE DUKE OF WELLINGTON—FUTURE DESTINY OF THE CRYSTAL PALACE—THE ATHENÆUM—LORD CAMPBELL—EARLY MORNING VISIT OF M. HECTOR BERLIOZ—THE SOLITARY CHINESE, AND THE SOLITARY SPARROW.

DURING the "high and palmy state" of the Great Exhibition, while the World's Wonder was new, and its praises in everybody's mouth, all the leading and popular journals of the day delighted to expatiate on the inexhaustible subject, and the events of each passing hour in connection with it, were the constant theme of their eloquent admiration. No topic, however, was more eagerly brought forward, and none was more agreeable to the public consideration, than the frequent visits that were paid by Royalty to the Crystal

Palace. At one time the public were informed that " Her Majesty arrived for her almost daily visit to the Crystal Palace, at a quarter past nine yesterday morning. The royal party consisted of the Queen, Prince Albert, the King of the Belgians, and the Princess Charlotte, attended by the usual suite. Mr. Wentworth Dilke, Colonel Reid, and Mr. Cole, accompanied the illustrious visitors through the building. The Austrian sculpture-room was first inspected, after which her Majesty and friends proceeded to the collection of English marbles, which were subjected to a lengthened examination; Bell's 'Babes in the Wood,' and Gibson's 'Hunter,' receiving warm commendation. The party then promenaded through the fine arts room, and after a glance at the Mexican figures, went on to the foreign nave, where the beautiful Mosaic, newly placed there by Lord Foley, was eagerly examined and much admired. This picture, which is a very large specimen of the art, representing the ruins of Pæstum, has all the variety of light and shade which one would expect in a finished oil painting, with the brilliancy of colour which is peculiar to the material employed. It was surrounded by crowds of visitors during the day, and much admired. Her Majesty's next visit was to the English glass and china, after which the royal party descended to the nave, where the company were drawn up as on her Majesty's previous visit, in double file, and greeted their Sovereign with loyal respect and courtesy as she passed out of the building. All cheering was suppressed from feelings of respect, but her Majesty's gracious acknowledgments of the loyalty of her reception were universally and deeply appreciated. The number of visitors was not much greater than on the previous day, and consequently there was free circulation throughout the building. The various fountains were in active requisition, and, towards the close of the day, exhibited a peculiarity which would be well worthy of investigation by the commissioners of water supply. Any one mingling at that hour with the crowds by which they are surrounded, could not fail to detect a strong odour of brandy, and seeing that spirits are so strictly prohibited in the Crystal Palace, there must be some extraordinary quality in the sources of supply to give rise to so curious a delusion. The number of petty thefts in the Crystal Palace seem rather on the increase, and demand increased vigilance on the part of the police. Another amateur collector was detected yesterday pocketing cigars in the Zollverein section. On his apprehension he stated himself to be a gentleman's servant in Bedfordshire, and urged a curious taste in his smoking as his excuse. He was immediately despatched to reason the matter over with the magistrate. Besides watching the thieves, the police have also a good deal of trouble with lost articles. Upwards of a hundred articles have already accumulated at the station, for which no owners can be found, and people are constantly coming in with parasols, bracelets, and other articles (chiefly female property), which they have found in the course of their perambulations. It is noticed that very little is lost or found on Friday or Saturday."

Then again, after the interval of a few days, the grateful intelligence was made known that " Her Majesty, Prince Albert, the King of the Belgians, the royal children, and the usual suite, visited the Crystal Palace yesterday morning, and inspected the goods in the North Germany, Russian, and Zollverein compartments. The royal party were conducted through the sections by Mr. Cole, Mr. Belshaw, and Mr. Edgar Bowring. The weather was oppressively hot in the course of the day, and had a perceptible effect in keeping away the ticket-holders."

Several attempts have been made to pourtray the first great day of the Great Exhibition, when the Queen of England, surrounded by some thirty or forty thousand of her most distinguished subjects, inaugurated perhaps the grandest show that was ever presented for the wondering admiration of a civilised nation. The scene in Hyde-park on that day was full of those effects which a painter delights to find. People of all ages and all nations, habited in the richest and most varied fabrics which the ingenuity of the world's looms and workshops could supply—youth and age—beauty and dignity—assembled under a lofty roof of glass, in which were piled the masterpieces of the workman's skill. Beauty of form, and richness and variety of colour, were mingled in gorgeous profusion, whilst rank, wealth, talent, and dignity thronged a scene in which all were alike charmed to take part. But though these mingled and varied points and excellencies, when assembled, might gladden the eye of an artist, to realize them on canvass, or on paper, was no easy task. The very size of the place and the spreading of its interest over a multitude of actors, presented a source of difficulty to those who desired to delineate it. The group on the royal dais did not include the sentiment and action of the great scene. The story could not be told by a few figures. It was necessary to include the great army of spectators, before a satisfactory idea could be given of the opening of the Crystal Palace, and hence the danger of losing, in a fritter of detail, the sentiment and real grandeur of the occasion. We shall, doubtless, hereafter have many pictures on so attractive a subject more or less successful; but whilst they are in embryo, George Cruikshank has prepared and given us in his views of the affair, "taken on the spot," as he describes it, etched and printed upon a handsome sheet, at a moderate price. This veteran artist's version of the thing is just what might have been anticipated. He gives us the multitude of figures, each made out with curious nicety, and many of them bearing traces of the humour for which he has so long been celebrated, the whole, meanwhile, presenting no semblance of caricature, but, on the contrary, displaying a large amount of the genuine character of the scene. The raised dais for the Queen, her husband, and her two eldest children, the crystal fountain, the acres of human heads and shoulders that thronged the nave, the old elms overhead budding in an early and unexpected summer, the strange tropical plants beneath them, the galleries radiant with colour, and thronged like the ground-floor of the building, with a very host of waiting, wondering, and admiring spectators, are all seen in Cruikshank's etching. Statues, pictures, and draperies, are cleverly managed to make up a picture, without injury to the vraisemblance of the whole; and, indeed, it may be said, that up to this time no representation has been offered to the public at once so artistic and so truthful as this print of the opening of the Great Exhibition of 1851. Those who saw, and those who regret they did not see it, will alike be glad to possess so satisfactory a representation of so remarkable a scene.

Inclemency of weather was no obstacle to the regularity or frequency of these royal visits, and the public likewise were not behindhand in due attendance and respectful demeanour. "Yesterday," says our journalist, "there was a full average attendance at the Crystal Palace, although the weather during the greater part of the day was pertinaciously wet. The first visitors, as usual, were her Majesty and friends. The royal visitors proceeded at once to the Russian section, and curiously examined the various costly products. Her Majesty was particularly struck with the richness and designs of the silks from Moscow, and also spent some time in examining the curiously embroidered leather, and other articles which come from the more Asiatic portion of the great Russian empire. The furs attracted a good deal of notice, the imperial pelisse, in particular, being taken out of its case and minutely inspected by her Majesty. A very interesting episode in the day's proceedings was the arrival of the whole adult population of three parishes in Sussex, headed by their clergyman, who had come up by excursion train early in the morning from Godstone. They had a previously prepared plan of the campaign, according to which they were first mustered in heavy marching order, each having a well-filled basket of provisions slung round his neck, under the transept The word was then given for every one to go where he or she liked, but all with strict injunctions to meet at the trysting-place at four o'clock. It was quite amusing to see the punctuality with which they kept the appointment at that hour, and allowed themselves to be regularly marshalled two and two, to the number of 800, by their worthy pastor. They seemed to be mightily pleased with everything they had seen, except the agricultural implements, which they thought might do very well for the Crystal Palace, but would hardly do for the stiff clays of Sussex. The men were all dressed in new smock frocks, and the women most tidily and neatly attired, and did infinite credit to their district, and to the generalship of their worthy leader."

The late illustrious Duke of Wellington was also a not unfrequent visitor to these all-attractive precincts. Indeed his mind appeared to be singularly disposed, considering his great age, to investigate whatever was making progress in science, manufactures, or art. On one occasion, however, an incident occurred which, for a moment, occasioned some little anxiety, not to say alarm, yet from a cause which no effort of prudence could have prevented. When the crowd assembled within the building was at its culminating point, it was suddenly discovered that the Duke of Wellington was present. Instantly the manifestations of public admiration arose. Hats were taken off, and loud cheers burst forth, which were prolonged with immense energy. Those who were at a distance, surprised by an unwonted agitation which they could not understand, fancied that there was something wrong, and rushed towards the doors. The duke also felt the awkwardness of his position, and beat a retreat. His great age did not then permit him to execute such movements with the precision and firmness which in former days were his characteristics, but he made his way, nevertheless, to the south entrance of the transept with surprising alacrity, followed as he went by the most vigorous demonstrations of popular regard. Superintendent Pearce, with great tact, stopped the rush towards the places of exit, and, by his judicious management, the fears of the most timid spectators were in a few minutes effectually quieted.

While all classes of the people were thus passing their time in daily gratification, mingling enjoyment with instruction, a natural anxiety began to pervade the public mind respecting the future destiny of the glorious show that was so liberally spread out before them; of the transcendent edifice itself that, as if by magic, had suddenly arisen upon their astonished sight in full beauty and perfection; was it doomed as suddenly to disappear from their enraptured gaze—

> " And like the baseless fabric of a vision
> Leave not a wreck behind ?"

The question "to be or not to be," was agitated on every side, and various opposite and conflicting opinions were advanced and argued. We may, however, assuredly now congratulate ourselves that it was finally determined not to preserve it, beyond the period originally fixed upon, since to that wise measure we shall be indebted for a still more glorious Exhibition, upon a still more advantageous site, where, phœnix-like, it will arise from the destruction of the former one, and to which, if universal report is to be credited, we shall be able to apply the encomium of the prince of Roman poets,—

> "O mater pulcher
> Filia pulchrior."

The *Athenæum* in particular advocated the the preservation of the Palace of Glass. "From the moment," they observed, "when the Crystal Palace rose from the ground in its grace and beauty, for ourselves we never doubted, as our readers well know, about its fate ; but even on that auspicious May-day we heard persons, anxious as ourselves for the success of the Exhibition, declare that in less than two years the grass would be again growing greenly over the area now inclosed within the crystal walls. Day by day, however, these misgivings have been abating, and at the end of three weeks we may assert that the financial success, too, of the great undertaking is assured. To pay the entire expenses of the Exhibition, and to buy the building as a perpetual palace for the people, will require about £300,000. Towards this sum £65,000 have been raised by subscription—£65,486 have been received for the sale of season tickets; and up to Thursday night the amount received at the doors for admission was £37,702; making altogether, at the end of only three weeks, a total of £168,188. As the masses have yet to come in at the reduced rates, the receipts at the doors will probably not fall much below the average of £1,500 a day for the next hundred days :—and if so, we may add to the present total a prospect of £150,000. This, it will be seen, leaves a margin of surplus—though not a large one. Some of our sanguine contemporaries, astonished at a success so far beyond their pre-calculations, indulge in magnificent projects for the investment of a fund which seems to them boundless. There have been divers hints of buying up, not only the Crystal Palace, but all that it contains. Nothing seems impossible in face of the huge facts before them—and even figures would seem to have acquired a new power as applicable to the Great Exhibition. We are sorry to interfere with this calenture of the imagination—but Cocker must have his rights even in the Palace of Glass. The value of its contents has been variously estimated ; but we have heard no one appraise them at less than twelve millions, and some calculations go up as high as thirty. Let us assume the lowest figure to be correct, for the sake of a sum to be worked after the venerable shade whom we have invoked. How soon could the Royal Commission raise twelve millions of money, even were they certain to receive from the public at the doors £2,000 daily over and above all the expenses of management? In just six thousand days, after deducting Sundays and other religious days, when the palace must of course be closed,—in exactly twenty years! Look at the question n another point of view. At £5 per cent. per annum, the interest on twelve millions is £600,000 a-year ; or, leaving out Sundays and a few other as non-productive days, just £2,000 a day! If the contents of the Exhibition be really worth twenty millions, a daily income of £3,300 would not discharge the mere interest on the capital lying dead in the Crystal Palace. The suggestion, therefore, of purchasing the Exhibition, in order to keep its contents together, is one which merely shows to what wild poetic heights the imagination may climb up to the wonderful shafts of the Palace of Glass.

Yet it is extremely desirable, if any means can be thought of to that end, that the collection should not be again dispersed. Probably no one has ever walked across that marvellous transept, or gazed down that extraordinary nave, without thinking with a pang on the probability of a coming day when the glorious vision is to dissolve—when this prodigious manifestation of the result of thought, genius, industry, and science, is to be resolved into its separate elements, never to be again united in the same mighty and marvellous whole. The world once possessed of an encyclopedia of knowledge like this, who can bear to think that the volume shall ever be closed, and its pages scattered to the distant corners of the earth? We never have, from the first, regarded this collection merely as a bazaar of all nations. We repeat, it is the first University in the large and full meaning of the word that the world has had : of which, Universities like Oxford and Cambridge look merely like affiliated colleges. But what is to be done? Why not this? We will take for granted, at the moment, that the royal commissioners, before laying down the temporary offices which they were appointed by the Queen to discharge, will purchase the Crystal Palace in the name of the English people. Should it then be announced to all the present exhibitors in the first instance, that such of them as have fitted up stalls or obtained spaces, may retain them for, say a year, on the condition of

3 U

keeping them filled with their present or other contributions of the same high class of excellence—we think it probable that a great majority of the most useful and beautiful articles would be left on such terms. The workers in silk, wool, worsted, gold, silver, iron, and copper, mahogany and other woods—the makers of musical and scientific instruments, watches, chronometers, carriages, agricultural machines and fountains; the producers of flowers and plants, decorators and stained-glass makers, sculptors and carvers in wood and ivory, printers and hand-workers of most kinds, would in all probability be glad to have such a universal and permanent exhibition-room for their wares, works, and discoveries. Many things of mere curiosity and rarity would no doubt be removed; but the absence of the Koh-i-Noor, the Spanish jewels, the Indian diamonds, and similar articles, if it should be proved to lessen the mere splendour of the Exhibition, would not materially detract either from its moral interest or its practical usefulness. The earnest seeker after knowledge is more attracted by a collection of minerals and metallic ores than by the Russian or the Portuguese diamond valued at millions.

Specimens of the jewellery which borrow their highest value from the genius of the artist would probably be left as examples and advertisements. We do not doubt that it would be worth the while of our most eminent goldsmiths to maintain a show-room in the Great Exhibition, to be from time to time supplied with whatever is new and excellent in their current manufactures. The same may be surmised of our great drapery and silk mercers. What artist would not be glad to have a certain space assigned to him on the walls of the National Gallery on the easy condition of always having a picture hung there? In the Crystal Palace the artist and the artisan in silk, cotton, wool, metal, and so forth, might, under some such arrangement as we are proposing, obtain their National Gallery and Academy. Even in the series of costly and complicated machines in motion, we imagine that not a few of the most beautiful and interesting would be willingly allowed to remain. Most of these machines, we believe, are made in model. They cannot be sold or used in actual factories. If taken away, they will either be broken up or buried in local museums. Their proprietors would naturally prefer that they should remain as their advertisements and representatives in the great centre of observation. There is plenty of room, besides, for a winter garden. Indeed, the place is a garden now; and its beauties in that respect would increase with every year. The contributions of industry leave plenty of space for trees, and shrubs, and flowers. The elm and the palm tree here grow side by side; and there will be room abundant for exotic plant and indigenous parterre. The works of mind and the works of nature already blend here with a harmony of tints and tones beyond the power of imagination to have conceived. There never was an epic thought or an epic poem at once so vast and so full of beauty. The infinite multiplication of the varieties have produced a great unity. The place is even now all that the heart, the senses, and the imagination can desire.

On the other side of the question, Lord Campbell, with all the authority of fur and ermine, speaking of the Palace of Crystal in the House of Lords, observed, that "from Penzance to Inverness and Aberdeen, the people were all called upon to join in sending up petitions, of which the common burden was to be the expediency of having a public promenade in a summer climate at all seasons of the year. He wished to bring under the notice of the house an authority against this project, which was to be found in the *Quarterly Review* just published. He knew not by whom the article was written, but it was evidently written by a gentleman skilful in literature and profound in science. He would only read two sentences from that article, but they should be the following :— "Were the Crystal Palace to be kept up in spite of rather strong pledges, and, as some prophesy, to present us by and by with a wilderness of walks meandering through bowers of exotic bloom, it would be the most insalubrious promenade in London. If ever our admirable Palace of Glass becomes a showy, steamy, suffocating *jardin d'hiver*, it will be a capital thing for the apothecaries; such a vigorous crop of colds, coughs, and consumptions will be raised that it will be the walk, if not the dance, of death, to frequent it." The writer gave this testimony against the visionary prophecies of Mr. Paxton, who talked of transferring to this country the sunny climate of Southern Italy. He (Lord Campbell) thought that the most useful object to which this building could be converted was that of an enormous shower-bath; for, even now, it was found that, when a heavy shower, or thunder-storm came on, it was necessary for the visitors within it to raise their umbrellas. The present was the last time that their lordships would be troubled with his voice on this subject, for he was about to leave town to administer justice in the country to her majesty's subjects. He left town, however, without anxiety, for he could not suppose that their lordships would assume the prerogative of his holiness the pope, and absolve the government and the royal commissioners from the promises which they had made solemnly and deliberately."

We shall conclude our present chapter with a few extracts from an admirable letter from the able pen of M. Hector Berlioz, on the occasion of an early morning visit to the Crystal Palace.

"You will not, I hope," observes our lively correspondent, "be under the apprehension of receiving from me a hundred-thousandth description of the Crystal Palace and its wonders, an ode to English industry, or an elegy on French indolence, with sundry digressions, in which would be found, more or less literally reproduced, the observations of the host of people who crowd the colossal glass edifice, the murmurs of the fountains which pour their freshness around, and the solemn peal of the organ, concealed amidst the foliage of druidical trees, rising heavenward, as in one incessant prayer, and consecrating human industry. You know my opinion of *impertinent* music; you need not then fear that I will add my impertinent prose to that with which so many pens, eloquent or frivolous, ignorant or 'savantes,' artistical or venal—pens of gold, of silver, of ivory, of goose-quill—have inundated the two hemispheres on this subject.

"No, no. I said '*Hug!*' like a Mohican, the first time I entered the edifice. I uttered an English exclamation that I need not repeat on entering a second time; and I so far forgot myself as to suffer a French 'sacrebleu!' to escape me on my third visit: but to define to you precisely these three celebrated exclamations, I will not venture; besides, I should not succeed in the attempt—the 'hug!' especially is indefinable."

After a lengthy disquisition on instrumental and vocal music, and the description of a visit to the cathedral of St. Paul's, on occasion of the anniversary meeting of the charity children, our worthy critic finds his way to the Crystal Palace, having been appointed one of the Jury. We will give his account of this visit in his own words.

"On leaving St. Paul's, in a state of semi-stupefaction, as you may readily conceive, I took boat on the Thames; and, after almost unconsciously having been drenched to the skin in a transit of some twenty minutes, I landed, half-drowned, at Chelsea, where I had nothing to do, and I had the right to expect to sleep. I heard incessantly re-echoed in my ear that harmonious swell, 'All people that on earth do dwell,' and I saw whirling before my eyes the cathedral of St. Paul. I was in its interior; it was by visionary transformation changed to Pandemonium. I had before me the celebrated picture of Martin; instead of the Archbishop in his pulpit, I saw Satan on his throne; in lieu of thousands of the faithful and children grouped around him, it was peopled with demons and the damned, who darted from the depths of visible darkness their looks of fire; and the amphitheatre of iron, on which these millions were seated, vibrated in a frightful manner, giving out harrowing and discordant sounds.

"At length, weary of the continuance of these hallucinations, I leapt from my bed, though scarcely light, went out, and wandered to the Exhibition, where, a few hours later, I had to attend as one of the Jury. London was still slumbering; neither Sarah, nor Molly, nor Kate, were yet to be seen, mop in hand, washing the doorways. An old Irish crone, somewhat 'aginée,'* smoked her pipe, crouched under the entrance to one of the houses in Manchester-square.

"The listless cows were ruminating, stretched on the turf in Hyde Park. The little ship, this plaything of a maritime people, lay at anchor on the Serpentine; already some luminous 'gerbes' detached themselves from the elevated panes of glass of the palace open to 'all people that on earth do dwell.'

"The guard who kept the door of this Louvre, accustomed to see me at all kinds of unreasonable hours, allowed me to pass, and I entered. It is certainly a spectacle of singular grandeur, the Palace of the Exhibition at seven in the morning; the vast solitude, the silence, the softened light, the *jets-d'eau* motionless, the organs mute, the trees, and the surprising show of rich products brought from all nations of the earth by hundreds of rival peoples, ingenious works, the sons of peace, instruments of destruction which remind one of war,—all these causes of motion and noise seemed at such time to be conversing mysteriously among themselves, in the absence of man, in some unknown language, understood by 'l'oreille de l'esprit.' I felt disposed to listen to their secret dialogue, believing myself alone in the palace; but there were three of us,—a Chinese, a sparrow, and I. The eyes 'bridés' of the Asiatic were open before their time, as it would appear; or, perhaps, like mine, had been but imperfectly closed. With a little feather brush he was dusting his beautiful porcelain vases, his hideous grotesque figures, his varnished goods, and his silks. He then took, in a watering pot, some water from the fountain, and watered tenderly a poor Chinese flower, emaciated, doubtless, from being in an ignoble European vase; after which he went to sit down a few paces from his stall, looked at the tamtams hung there, made a movement as if to strike them, but remembering that he had neither relations nor friends to awaken, he let his hand, in which he held the gong-stick, drop, and sighed. 'Dulces reminiscitur Argos,' I mentally repeated. Assuming, then, my most winning manner, I approached him, and, supposing that he understood English, I addressed him with, 'Good morning, sir.' The only notice I received, however, was his rising, and turning his back on me; he then went to a cupboard, took out some sandwiches, which he began to eat without even honouring me with a look, and with an air of some disgust for this food of 'barbarians.' Then he sighed again. He was, no doubt, thinking of those savoury dishes of shark-fins, fried in castor oil, in which he delighted in his own country, of the soup of swallow nests, and of that famous jelly of caterpillars which they make so exquisitely at Canton. Bah! the cogitations of this rude 'gastronome' disgusted me, and I went away.

"Passing near the large piece of ordnance, the forty-eight, cast in copper in Seville, and which always seems, being placed opposite the stall of Sax, to defy him to make a gun of its calibre, I perceived a sparrow hidden in the mouth of the brutal Spaniard. Poor tiny one! do not be alarmed, I will not denounce thee. On the contrary—here— and drawing from my pocket a bit of biscuit that the steward at St. Paul's had obliged me to accept the evening previous, I crumbled it on the floor.

"When the Palace of the Exhibition was built, a tribe of sparrows had taken up their domicile in one of the great trees which now ornament the transept. They determined to remain there, notwithstanding the menacing progress of the work of the operatives. The poor birds could not imagine that they would have been enclosed in a large glass

* A word cleverly coined by the writer,—*Anglice*, under the influence of gin.

and iron cage. When they found how matters stood, they were a little astoinshed. They sought an exit right and left. Fearing that they would injure the articles exhibited, it was decided to kill them all, and this was effected with cross-bows, nets, and the perfidious 'nux vomica.' My sparrow, whose hiding place I now know, and whom I will not betray, is the sole survivor.

"As I ruminated on these matters, a noise resembling heavy rain was heard in the vast galleries; it was the *jets-d'eau* and fountains which were set playing. The crystal 'chateaux,' the artificial rocks, vibrated under the fall of their liquid pearls,—the policemen, these 'bons gens-d'armes,' unarmed, which every one respects with so much reason, assumed their posts,—the young apprentice of M. Ducroquet took his seat at the organ of his master, thinking of the new polka with which he would treat us,—the ingenious manufacturers of Lyons were finishing their admirable display,—the diamonds, prudently hidden during the night, reappeared sparkling in their cases,—the great Irish clock, in D flat minor, which surmounts the eastern gallery, struck one, two, three, four, five, six, seven, eight, proud of giving the lie to its sister of the church in Albany-street, which strikes in a major key. Silence had kept me waking, these notes made me drowsy, and the want of sleep became irresistible. I sat down before the grand piano of Erard, that wonder of the Exhibition. I leaned on its rich cover, and was about to take a nap, when Thalberg, tapping me on the shoulder, exclaimed, 'Holloa! *confrere!* the Jury is assembled. Come, wake! we have to-day thirty-two musical boxes, twenty-four accordions, and thirteen 'bombardons' to inspect!'"

CHAPTER XLI.

PERFUMERY.

GREAT ANTIQUITY OF — KNOWN AMONG THE EGYPTIANS—RECORDED IN HOLY WRIT — EMPLOYED IN ANCIENT GREECE AND ROME—VARIOUS PERFUMES, AND ARTIFICIAL ESSENCES. PERFUMERY FROM AMERICA, AUSTRIA, EGYPT, FRANCE, GERMANY, TUNIS, TURKEY, UNITED KINGDOM—A SONNET.

> " Now gentle gales,
> Fanning their odoriferous wings, dispense
> Native perfumes, and whisper whence they stole
> Those balmy spoils."—*Milton.*

As the all-bountiful hand of our beneficent Creator has decorated the surface of the earth with flowers innumerable, displaying on every side the richest and most variegated hues to attract and delight the sense of vision, so has He also gifted their graceful and elegant forms with sweet and refreshing odours, to sooth and gratify the sense of smell. We do not, therefore, consider it to be beneath the dignity of our pen to devote a few pages to the subject of perfumery. "From the earliest times of which we have any record," observes an able writer in the Reports of the Juries, upon whose observations we shall draw largely in our present article, "the sense of smell has been gratified with perfumes; the Egyptians applied them as conservative of the bodies of their deceased friends, and as incense before their venerated deities. On the wall of every temple in Egypt, from Meroe to Memphis, the censer is depicted smoking before the presiding deity of the place; on the walls of the tombs glows in bright colours the preparation of the spices and perfumes for the embalming of the mummy; and these very

3 x

mummies and the vases of oriental alabaster transported to our museums, tell with eloquence the same tale. From the time of the *Exodus*, throughout the long period of Jewish history, Holy Writ records the use of perfumes. Moses speaks of being directed by the Lord to prepare two perfumes, according to the art of the apothecary or perfumer, one of which was to be offered from the Golden Altar, and the other to be used on the person of the officiating priest. The 'Spouse,' in the Canticles, is enraptured with the spikenard, the cinnamon, the aloe, and the myrrh; and Ezekiel accuses the Jews of diverting the use of perfumes from the holy things to their own persons. In the New Testament, also, are contained frequent references to the use of perfumes, many of which will be in the memory of our readers. Especially, however, they will remember, in chap. xiv. of the Gospel of St. Mark, that when Jesus sat at meat in the house of Simon the Leper, 'There came a woman having an alabaster box of ointment of spikenard, very precious, and she brake the box and poured it on his head.'"

Of the use of these luxuries by the Greeks, and afterwards by the Romans, the detail is more copious. Anacreon makes frequent mention of ointments and odours in his charming lyrics; and we are all, from our school-days, conversant with the celebrated ode of Horace—

> " Quis multa gracilis te puer in rosa
> Perfusus liquidis urget odoribus,
> Grato, Pyrrha, sub antro ?"

Pliny also gives much information respecting perfume-drugs, the method of collecting them, and the prices at which they were sold. Oils and powder-perfumes, according to Seneca, were most lavishly used; for even three times a-day did some of these luxurious people whom he describes anoint and scent themselves, carrying their precious perfumes with them to the baths in costly and elegant boxes called *Narthecia*. Hence the elegant reproof of Horace—

> " Persicos odi, puer, apparatus."

The trade from the East in these perfume-drugs caused many a vessel to spread its sails to the Red Sea, and many a camel to plod over that track which gave to Greece and Syria their importance as markets, and vitality to the Rock City of Petra. Milton, in the following beautiful lines in his *Paradise Lost*, refers to this trade,—

> "As when to them who sail
> Beyond the Cape of Hope, and now are past
> Mozambic, off at sea north-east winds blow
> Sabean odours from the spicy shores
> Of Araby the blest; with such delay
> Well pleased they slack their course, and many a league
> Cheer'd with the grateful smell old Ocean smiles."

And Southern Italy was not long ere it occupied itself in ministering to the luxury of the wealthy by manufacturing unguents or perfumes. So numerous were the "*unguentarii*," that they are said to have filled the great street of ancient Capua, the Seplasia. In short, whether to regale the nostrils of their deities while sacrificing, or their own while feasting, or to prevent those nostrils from being offended by defunct humanity, or the exhalations from crowded masses of people, the consumption of perfumes by the ancients was enormous. Happily, in modern times, the use of soap has superseded the necessity for their lavish employment. When we consider that there are some persons who appreciate the strong-smelling musk—and we confess ourselves to be among the number—more highly than any other, and another who would

> " Die of a rose in aromatic pain,"

the definition of perfume becomes a matter of some difficulty. Notwithstanding, however, the various impressions that volatile substances make upon different constitutions, a few general principles may be determined by which perfumery may be judged. In the first place, it is necessary to distinguish whether the substance is a chemical compound, or whether it is a mechanical combination of various chemicals. In the former case, if carefully prepared, it is independent of the perfume, and its odour, whether agreeable or repulsive, has a determined character of its own. In the latter case, that is, if the scent depends upon a mixture of substances, an opportunity is offered to the manufacturer of exhibiting his skill. Perfumes, on evaporation, should yield no resinous residue, and the various essential oils of which they are made ought to be combined so harmoniously that none of the components is perceptible, not only at first, but even during the progress of evaporation. The less the ingredients differ from one another in odour and volatility, the less difficult it becomes to achieve this desideratum. Hence, well-prepared Eau-de-Cologne is generally considered to be the perfection of perfumery. The constituents of this scent are, so far as is known, the essential oils of the lemon, the citron, and orange, prepared from the fruit in different stages of maturity, and they approximate so closely to one another, as to produce a single aromatic impression. Other oils are added to Eau-de-Cologne, but in so minute a proportion that they scarcely demand any notice in comparison with those mentioned. Eau-de-Cologne that leaves a residuary odour, either of otto of roses, oil of cloves, or oil of cinnamon, after volatilization, however agreeable these oils may be to individuals, must be designated as of inferior quality.

Still much practice is necessary to ascertain differences in the quality of the perfumes, and the task is rendered more difficult if numerous specimens have to be compared; for this reason the Chemical Committee returned repeatedly to the examination of the various specimens before reporting to the Jury, by whom the awards were only fixed after a further investigation. Several of the perfumes, or rather essences, exhibited are of peculiar interest, and deserve an especial notice. We allude to a series of artificial organic compounds possessing qualities which permit of their substitution for natural volatile oils and essences. Most of them are substances belonging to the group of compound-ethers. The fruity odour of these bodies has been long known, but they do not appear to have been used in flavouring until the chemist had shown that many of the oils of vegetable origin resemble in their composition the above-mentioned products of the laboratory. For some years past a scent called winter-green oil has been extensively used in perfumery; it is obtained from an ericaceous plant, the *Gualtheria procumbens*, and is imported from New Jersey, in America, where it is obtained in considerable quantities. Chemical analysis of this oil has yielded the interesting result that it is a true compound-ether, consisting of salicylic acid and pyroxylic spirit, which may be formed by a combination of its proximate constituents, so as to possess all the characters of the natural substance. This observation was not lost upon commercial enterprise, and several of the numerous ethers prepared by the chemist were soon discovered to present the odour of certain fruits in so marked a degree, that it was difficult not to conclude that the fruits in question owed their smell to these ethers. Several artificial essences of this kind were exhibited. Neither the time nor the quantity of material at the command of the reporters permitted them to examine all these products, they were, therefore, obliged to confine themselves to a notice of the following :—

Pear Oil is a spirituous solution of acetite of oxide of amyl. The latter may be obtained with facility and in any amount by distilling equal parts of concentrated sulphuric acid and fusel oil (the oily residue obtained by the rectification of potato or grain spirit) with two parts of acetate of potash. It is remarkable that the ether itself does not possess a very pleasant odour, and that its striking resemblance to that of pears does not become apparent until properly diluted with spirit. Artificial pear-oil is now prepared in large quantities in England. It is chiefly employed in the manufacture of the lozenges called peardrops, of which the Exhibition presented some specimens, so that the flavour in its applied state may be tested side by side with the perfume.

Apple Oil consists mainly of valerianate of oxide of amyl. It is obtained as a secondary product in the preparation of valerianic acid, by the distillation of fusel oil with bichromate of potash and sulphuric acid. The distillate has to be shaken up with a dilute potash solution, in order to remove the valerianic acid, when the ether floats on the top, and may be removed with a pipette.

Pine-apple Oil was contributed by most of the exhibitors of artificial essences. The specimen analysed was found to consist almost exclusively of butyrate of oxide of ethyl, or common butyric ether. It is easily obtained by boiling butyric acid (obtained from sugar by fermentation with putrid cheese) with strong spirit and a small quantity of concentrated sulphuric acid. It resembles the acetate of oxyde of amyl, in not presenting the characteristic agreeable fruity flavour, in a pure state; it requires to be considerably diluted before the odour appears. This oil is largely manufactured in England, and is employed in the preparation of a beverage called pine-apple ale. The process commonly used for its preparation does not yield perfectly pure butyric ether. It consists in saponifying fresh butter with potash; the soap that forms is separated from the liquor, dissolved in strong alcohol, and distilled with concentrated sulphuric acid. This yields a mixture of butyric ether, and various other ethers, but the liquid obtained is perfectly adapted for the purpose of flavouring.

Cognac Oil and Grape Oil.—Specimens of these oils, especially of the former, were contributed by English, French, and German manufacturers. They seem to be often employed with the view of giving ordinary varieties of brandy the prized flavour of genuine cognac. Unfortunately, the samples exhibited were too small to admit of a careful analysis. A few superficial examinations proved undoubtedly that they are compounds of fusel oil dissolved in a large quantity of alcohol; and it is curious that a substance which is most carefully eliminated from brandy, on account of its offensive flavour, should be introduced in another form, and in minute quantities, in order to render the same beverage aromatic.

Artificial Oil of Bitter-Almonds.—As early as 1834, Professor Mitscherlick, of Berlin, pointed out a peculiar liquid formed by the action of fuming nitric acid upon benzole, and possessing the odour of natural oil of bitter-almonds in a high degree. It was called nitro-benzide, or nitro-benzole. The preparation of this compound was, however, too expensive to admit of its substitution for natural oil of bitter-almonds, as the sole sources of benzole, at that period, were the compression of oil-gas, and the distillation of benzoic acid. In 1844, one of the reporters, Dr. Hoffman, succeeded in demonstrating the presence of this substance in common light coal-tar-oil; and in 1849, C. B. Mansfield showed, by a careful investigation, that benzole may be easily obtained in large quantities from tar oil. In the French department, under the fanciful title of "*Essence de mirbane,*" the reporters met with several specimens of oils, which, on examination, proved to be nitro-benzole, of more or less purity; they were, however, unable to obtain any positive information as to the extent of this manufacture; but it does not appear to be very considerable. The method employed in England for its preparation was devised by Mr. Mansfield, and is very simple; his apparatus consists of a large glass tube, in the form of a coil, which at the upper end divides into two tubes, each of which is provided with a funnel. A stream of concentrated nitric acid flows slowly into one of the funnels, and benzole, which for this purpose need not be perfectly pure, into the other. The two substances meet at the point of union of the two tubes, and chemical combination ensues with the evolution of much heat; but as the newly-formed compound flows down through the coil, it becomes cool, and is collected at the lower extremity. It then merely requires to be washed with water, and lastly, with a dilute solution of carbonate of soda, to render it fit for use. Nitro-benzole is closely allied to oil of bitter-almonds in its physical characters, yet it presents a slight difference of odour, which may be easily detected by an experienced person. It is very useful for perfuming soap, and is probably capable of application in confectionary and cookery, as its flavour resembles that of bitter-almonds, without containing any hydrocyanic (prussic) acid.

We will now proceed to notice the various specimens of perfumery which were sent for exhibition from different parts of the world. We shall proceed alphabetically, and accordingly commence with—

America, whose display in this article was not very imposing, consisting chiefly of spirituous essences, and which were found to be inferior to those exhibited by other countries.

Austria had only one exhibitor, John Maria Farina, whose contribution, however, of Eau-de-Cologne, was upon a very magnificent scale, which nevertheless was so liberally distributed to the public by means of a small fountain, that the supply in charge of the attendant was exhausted before the Jury made the awards, so that only the residue left in the fountain was submitted to them. As the specimen had evidently lost much of its perfume from exposure to the air, the reporters, at the request of the Austrian Commissioner, M. C. Buschek, and with the sanction of the executive, examined, subsequently, a fresh sample, which was taken from a cask of Eau-de-Cologne, which had remained under the care of the customs, and which had been overlooked by the attendant. This sample was found to be equal in quality to the Eau-de-Cologne rewarded with honourable mention.

Egypt furnished a few interesting and excellent specimens of perfumery, comprising rose-water of Fayoum, orange-flower-water, and mint-water of Rosetta.

France.—The Parisian perfumers produced excellent toilet-soap, remarkable for the fragancy of the perfume. Many French people, however, never use soap to their faces, employing as a substitute aromatic vinegar, a few drops of which are added to the water used in washing. Hence the "vinaigre-de-toilette," is an important manufacture, which is chiefly monopolized by Paris, whence it is sent to all parts of France. There were three exhibitors of this aromatic vinegar. Spirituous perfumery is prepared in great perfection by the manufacturers of Paris, some of whom distil their own essential oils; they generally, also, combine with it the manufacture of toilet-soaps, and hence, with a few exceptions, toilet-soaps and perfumery were exhibited together, and were conjointly rewarded. In the preparation of essential oils, the flowers are placed in a still, with water, and distilled. The vapour of the water carries over with it that of the essential oil, and both condense together, the essential oil swimming on the surface of the water, which, however, always retains a minute portion in solution. To recover this, the water is usually returned to the still, and again passed over; M. Piver, one of the French exhibitors, however, instead of so doing, employs the water for the perfuming of pomatum and hair oil, which from their attraction for essential oils, withdraw them from the water. In 1847 there were, it appears, 110 perfumers in Paris, employing 721 workpeople in the manufacture of toilet-soaps, cosmetics, essential oils, and spirituous and aqueous perfumery, the value of whose productions was £389,681. The workmen earned, on the average, 2s. 7d. per day, the workwomen 1s. 4d. According to M. Natalis Rondot, 12,042,970 lbs. of soap, valued at £142,012, were exported in 1850 from France, a quantity which, as will be hereafter seen, nearly equals that exported from Great Britain in the same year: besides which, 3,398,930 lbs. of perfumery, in value, £431,638, were also exported from France. There were two exhibitors of artificial essences in France. One sent simply a series of compound flavourings, intended to imitate the savour of various fruits; the second exhibited two specimens of chemical compounds, namely, artificial essence of bitter-almonds, and artificial essence of pine-apple.

Germany.—The perfumers in Germany were in great force, being eight in number, and reckoning two John Maria Farinas in their ranks, making no less than four Farinas in the Exhibition, all claiming to be the original. It appears that speculation is carried to so high a pitch in Cologne, that any child entitled to the surname of Farina, is bargained for as soon as born, and christened Jean Maria; at times this event is even anticipated. The perfumery of Germany is generally very good.

Tunis.—The Tunisian collection of perfumery consisted of scented waters, without any admixture of alcohol; they are prepared by distilling the flowers with water in a copper still. The ottos of Tunis, which are obtained by repeated distillations, are prized as being more fragrant, and are consequently more costly than those made in Eastern countries, the usual price being from £3 : 15s. to £5 per ounce, according to the description of flower from which they are obtained. Perfumery constitutes a most important branch of commerce in Tunis, a great quantity of scented waters being annually exported to France, Genoa, and Malta. There were also specimens of swak, which is used by the Moorish women for whitening their teeth; and perfumed necklaces, noticed in the list of awards.

Turkey sent a great variety of soaps, many of which were perfumed with musk, and ornamented with inscriptions; one kind, from Adrianople, was made up into hollow balls, containing a small bell, similar to those sometimes attached to the collars of horses; the purpose of these, however, could not be ascertained. The perfumery exhibited by this country, consisted of orange-flower-water and rose-water, both very fragrant. Tensouh, or musk-paste; Kouderma, or pastiles, for burning in the Seraglio; Tensough, or musk-paste medallions, purses, and necklaces; and amber Tesbihs or chaplets, made of a paste composed of various perfumes. As the names of the exhibitors of these various articles were not given, and as it appeared that the specimens were bought at the bazaars, they were included in one general award to the Sultan.

United Kingdom.—In no country in the world is the manufacture of soap carried on to so large an extent as in the United Kingdom, in which there are 329 makers, besides 68 soap-remelters (perfumers). Ireland not being subject to a duty on soap, there are no ready means of ascertaining the quantity which is there manufactured; but in Great Britain alone the production amounted in the year 1850 to 204,410,826 lbs., and yielded an excise duty of £1,299,232 : 10s. : 6d. Of this quantity, 12,555,493 lbs. were exported to foreign parts, the drawback on it being £82,308 : 18s. : 9d. The total quantity consumed in Great Britain, therefore, amounted to 191,855,333 lbs. In order to obtain toilet-soap, the ordinary soap has to undergo a second process of clarification, and after having been perfumed, has to be made up in some presentable form; it is this which has given rise to the business of the soap-remelter, who buys his soap of the maker, remelts, perfumes, and then makes it into tablets. Two exhibitors of toilet-soap, however, carry on all the operations in their works. In Ireland the perfumer generally makes his own soap by the " cold process," and one exhibitor sent toilet-soap made in this way.

The English toilet-soaps are in no respect inferior to those of other countries, and are generally far superior in their detergent qualities, on account of their being made from soap manufactured exclusively by the "large-boiler-process." The high reputation of the so-called Windsor-soap in all civilised states is an ample testimony of the estimation in which English toilet-soap is held by the makers of other countries, who adopt its name for any sort they wish particularly to recommend. The preparation of toilet-soaps is generally confined to the remelter, who perfumes and ornaments them in various ways.

The marbling is effected by rubbing up the colours, such as vermillion or ultramarine, with a little olive-oil or soap, and taking a small portion on a palette-knife, which is pushed through the melted mass, and moved about according to the fancy of the operator. Many soaps are coloured throughout their mass with mineral colours. Vermillion is used to produce the pink colour of rose-soap, artificial ultramarine to produce blue, and various ochres to produce browns. Tablets are made by placing a soft mass of soap into a mould, fixed in a lever-press, and composed of a top and bottom die, which fit into a loose ring; by a rapid pressure the shapeless mass takes the form of the ring, and is at the same time embossed on the top and bottom of the cake. The ornamenting by means of coloured cameos is effected in a similar manner, but requires two presses, one of which forms the cake, and makes depressions for the reception of a different coloured soap, which is filled in by hand, and the cake is then placed in the second press, which embosses the coloured portion.

No less than 12 out of the 68 soap-remelters of Great Britain exhibited. Most of them sent also perfumery; and eight manufacturers, besides the 12 above-named, exhibited perfumery only. The English perfumery was found in many cases to be very fragrant and agreeable; but in others, the employment of an excess of some strong-smelling essential oil, rendered the compound anything but a desirable article for the toilet. The imports of perfumery into the United Kingdom, in the year 1850, were valued at £1,907, and a duty was paid of £191, but in all probability some spirituous perfumes were included under the head of "oils, chemical, essential, and perfumed," of which 172,139 lbs. were imported, and which yielded a duty of £12,772. Two exhibitors contributed specimens, to which allusion has been made in the preceding pages, and to which a degree of interest attaches, as being among the first attempts at the application of harmless chemical compounds, for the imitation of the flavour of fruits and liqueurs, namely, oil of pears, oil of grapes, oil of apples, oil of pine-apples, oil of cognac, and onion sauce. Prize medals and honourable mention were not wanting to reward various exhibitors of the several articles described above. We had just concluded our dissertations on this subject, so important to the toilet, when we were broken in upon by a literary lady, whose advice we are always glad to take on matters of taste and *virtù*. The foregoing pages were accordingly submitted to her inspection, and her opinion requested. After due perusal of them, and a few minutes' deliberation, my fair monitress, assuming an air of poetic inspiration, expressed herself in the following lines, which struck us as so elegant and appropriate a termination to our chapter on perfumery, that we make no apology for presenting them to our readers.

Take back your " Essence of a thousand flowers,"
The scents compounded by the chemist's art
Suit only crowded rooms and midnight hours;
Give me the native perfumes that impart
Their fragrance to the breath of early morn:
I love " the firstlings of the infant year,"
The pale primrose, the violet steeped in dew,
The " dancing daffodils," to poet dear,
The yellow cowslip, and the hare-bell blue,
The milk-white blossoms of the rugged thorn,
The wild-rose, and the slender eglantine,
The clustering honey-suckles that entwine
Around my lowly cot, and rustic bowers;
Keep then your " Essence of a thousand flowers."

Thus far, gentle reader, have we threaded the mazes of the Crystal Palace, well pleased to examine and comment upon a portion of the various wonders that on every side solicited attention, and excited admiration. The field, however, is not yet by any means exhausted; new subjects start up for examination, and fresh objects of interest demand our notice and our praise. Like the waves upon the pebbly shore,

" Another, and another still succeeds."

In the mean while, our lucubrations have been most favourably received; public approbation has been liberally bestowed, and we are on every side invited to extend our researches and continue our graphic delineations among the treasures that the rival nations have so abundantly contributed to furnish forth the World's Great Wonder. Our materials crowd upon us,—so much so indeed, that the dimensions of our book would enlarge into undue proportions, were we not to divide it into reasonable sections. We, therefore, here conclude our first volume, and shall proceed to usher in a succeeding one, we hope, under equally favourable auspices.

END OF VOL. I.

Printed in the United States
By Bookmasters